THE BIG BOOK OF
JOB-HUNTING HACKS

THE BIG BOOK OF
JOB-HUNTING HACKS

HOW TO BUILD A RÉSUMÉ, CONQUER THE INTERVIEW, AND LAND YOUR DREAM JOB

BY THE EDITORS OF THE AMERICAN LIBRARY ASSOCIATION, BRENDA BERNSTEIN, AND JOHN HENRY WEISS

Skyhorse Publishing

Skyhorse Publishing books may be purchased in bulk at special discounts for sales promotion, corporate gifts, fund-raising, or educational purposes. Special editions can also be created to specifications. For details, contact the Special Sales Department, Skyhorse Publishing, 307 West 36th Street, 11th Floor, New York, NY 10018 or info@skyhorsepublishing.com.

Skyhorse® and Skyhorse Publishing® are registered trademarks of Skyhorse Publishing, Inc.®, a Delaware corporation.

Visit our website at www.skyhorsepublishing.com.

10 9 8 7 6 5 4 3 2 1

Library of Congress Cataloging-in-Publication Data is available on file.

Cover design by Daniel Brount

Print ISBN: 978-1-5107-6348-7
Ebook ISBN: 978-1-5107-6349-4

Printed in the United States of America

CONTENTS

PART 3: MOVING FORWARD IN MID-CAREER　209

Introduction　211

INTRODUCTION
BY JOHN HENRY WEISS

The purpose of this book is twofold—to help laid-off workers deal with the trauma of having their paychecks and benefits suddenly disappear, and to guide them through the job-hunting process. The tips in this book provide job seekers with practical advice for finding a new job no matter the state of the economy.

The Big Book of Job-Hunting Hacks is a compilation of three books written by authors with expertise in the job-hunting process. Their philosophy is that proven methods for job hunting transcend good times and bad, which includes challenges caused by the worldwide coronavirus pandemic that began in December 2019.

The first two books in this compilation deal with job hunting as a comprehensive multi-step process. The third book focuses on a critical step in the process—writing a dynamite résumé that will move the candidate forward to an online or in-person interview with a hiring authority or human resources director. The books in this compilation are:

1. *How to Get a Great Job: A Library How-to Handbook*, edited by the American Library Association
2. *Moving Forward in Mid-Career: A Guide to Rebuilding Your Career after Being Fired or Laid Off*, by John Henry Weiss
3. *How to Write a Stellar Executive Resume: 50 Tips to Reaching Your Job Target*, by Brenda Bernstein, JD, CMRW, CERM

The reader can study these books in sequence, or focus on topics of immediate interest. Following is a review of each book in this compilation.

1. HOW TO GET A GREAT JOB: A LIBRARY HOW-TO HANDBOOK

The first title reflects the accumulated wisdom of librarians and their associates who serve the job-hunting needs of workers throughout America. It emphasizes that job hunting is a process with a number of steps that need to be implemented in order to accomplish the mission—hearing the hiring authority say, "You're hired!"

Do not mistake this book as something written for librarians seeking employment. It was written for all workers in job-hunting mode at any time in the economic cycle and offers helpful tips for workers seeking employment during a pandemic. There are more than 100 tips in this book, five of which all job hunters should consider indispensable.

Tip #1. Begin by making sure that your online profile and résumé profile are the same. The reason? The first thing a hiring authority reviewing your candidacy will do is go to LinkedIn to examine your profile. If your résumé and LinkedIn profiles are in conflict, you are history. Read more in the first chapter of this book.

Tip #2. A successful job search begins with crafting a plan to implement the process. This tip is particularly important for workers who were laid off because of an unforeseen event, like the COVID-19 pandemic. Such a jarring event often leaves the laid-off worker in a state of panic because of its many negative ramifications, like loss of income and insurance benefits. While in panic mode, the worker begins job hunting by hastily crafting a résumé and sending it to multiple job boards and company career pages with meager results. This tip recommends making a rational plan that begins with determining skills and career interests

and concluding with how to negotiate a job offer.

Tip #3. A job search is a job in itself. Reserve a space in your home to conduct "business." You will need a quiet space equipped with a desk or work table, technology tools, and storage space. Trying to wing it from the kitchen table after your third cup of coffee at 10:30 a.m. will impede your success.

Tip #4. The rubrics for conducting a job search are the same no matter what the reason was for your being let go. Going forward, you will need to research the job market for industries and companies within that are hiring. Even when the economy was in lockdown mode, there were companies still hiring. For example, at the height of the COVID-19 crises, companies like Albertsons, Amazon, Costco, CVS, Dollar General, Domino's, Johnson & Johnson, PepsiCo, Walmart, and Zoom were aggressively hiring.

Tip #5. Access the many online, print, and media resources to keep updated on the state of the economy. Two helpful TV sources are the many CNBC financial programs, which begin at 6 a.m. Eastern, and *Mad Money* with Jim Cramer at 6 p.m. Eastern. Among the print and media resources recommended in this book are *Forbes* magazine, the *Wall Street Journal*, and the *Occupational Outlook Handbook* published by the U.S. Department of Labor. All are available in print and eBook formats.

Libraries often go unnoticed and unused by job hunters. Be sure to visit their brick-and-mortar locations or visit them online for current information to facilitate your job search.

2. MOVING FORWARD IN MID-CAREER: A GUIDE TO REBUILDING YOUR CAREER AFTER BEING FIRED OR LAID OFF

The second book in this compilation is the go-to resource for job hunters looking for a paycheck in order to survive. Author John Henry Weiss, an executive recruiter and former corporate executive, wrote this book because so many workers are let go every day of every year. According to the Bureau of Labor Statistics (www.bls.gov), 52,500 workers are let go every day during a normal economy and many more during a recession caused by something unexpected like COVID-19. Workers are laid off in good times because employers are always in a state of reorganizing, downsizing, rightsizing, expanding, or entering bankruptcy.

This book emphasizes job hunting as a process, not as a one-step deal like how to make it through an interview. It contains 250 practical tips for job hunters focusing on managing finances, working from a home office, writing résumés and cover letters, managing interviews, negotiating employment offers, networking, where and how to find employers, consulting career coaches and counselors, and seeking support from spiritual sources.

Moving Forward points out that being let go is something that most workers will experience during their time in the workplace, even when the economy is robust and the unemployment rate is below 6 percent, a number that most economists consider full employment. This book has four major parts to help laid-off workers through the job-hunting and rebuilding processes.

Part 1, Coping with the Ramifications of Job Loss. Weiss tells us that laid-off workers encounter many family challenges when job hunting from home. Some of them relate to childcare, aging parents, trauma, divorce, and separation. He provides solutions that will result from using your intelligence, psychic and physical energy, and passion. Also covered in Part 1 are solutions for handling financial matters relating to savings, investments, and insurance.

Part 2, The Process of Moving Forward in Your Career. Here workers will learn how to define or redefine career objectives, how to craft a résumé and corresponding online profile, how and where to find employers and decision makers, how to prepare and carry out personal and online interviews, how to handle objections to your candidacy, and how to negotiate a job offer.

Most job seekers submit their résumés and cover letters online, along with millions of other candidates. For example, Southwest Airlines receives over 100,000 résumés each year. Google and Microsoft receive over one million each year, most of which end up in the trash because the hiring authority and human resources director never see it. How do you distinguish yourself from the rest of the pack? Consider implementing a tip in this book. Send your résumé and formal cover letter by FedEx overnight shipping with next-day delivery. This method guarantees that the FedEx envelope will be placed on the recipient's desk. Nobody disregards a personally addressed FedEx envelope!

Part 3, Finding Your Spot in the Workplace. Workers laid off with little warning, as many were in the COVID-19 crisis, frequently ask, *Am I in the right job? Am I in the right industry? Should I start my own business? Should I pursue a government job?* All are valid questions, and *Moving Forward* has the answers. Thought-provoking items in this part include a listing of profitable major US industries and the names of top-ranked large companies in industries such as food, clothing, insurance, retailing, finance, and technology.

Part 4, Reaching Out to Career Care Providers. Here, job hunters will learn that emotional support is available to laid-off workers from online and personal sources such as secular career coaches and counselors, and from faith-based organizations found at churches, colleges, and universities. Job hunters can find spiritual guidance as well in the book's final chapter, Moving Beyond the Temporal.

At the end of each chapter in *Moving Forward*, you will find a series of important takeaways and a listing of print and digital resources to extend the chapter content.

3. HOW TO WRITE A STELLAR EXECUTIVE RESUME: 50 TIPS TO REACHING YOUR JOB TARGET

The third book in this compilation was written by award-winning author Brenda Bernstein. She is a certified executive résumé master (CERM), a certified master résumé writer (CMRW), an editor, and a LinkedIn trainer. She holds a law degree (JD) from NYU School of Law. Brenda has coached a multitude of workers in the résumé-writing process along with establishing their profiles for LinkedIn. Her book provides fifty numbered tips for getting the job done in a complete and professional manner. Here are five of her most important tips for crafting a professional résumé:

Tip #1. Write for the Future. When hiring authorities or human resources directors read your résumé, they are concerned not only about what you have done in the past, but also about what you can do for the company going forward.

Tip #2. How Long Should My Résumé Be? This is a nagging problem for most candidates. Some sources advise limiting your résumé to two or three pages, but is this correct? Read this important tip to learn more before you make a serious mistake.

Tip #3. Focus on Accomplishments. One of the most serious mistakes one can make on a résumé is listing only job functions and responsibilities, which the reader can find online. The prospective employer wants to know what you *accomplished* in your previous jobs.

Tip #4. Yes, You Need a Cover Letter. Submitting a résumé without a cover letter will have a definite result: rejection. A cover letter must accompany a résumé, and it must be addressed to a named person with a job title and company name. For example: Ms. Mary Jones, Vice President, Marketing, ABC Technology Inc. This is such an important item that Bernstein offers six separate cover letter tips.

Tip #5. Proofread, and Proofread Again! One of the most common errors in the résumé-writing process is to assume that your grammar and spell checker will correct all mistakes. Think again. Proofread your completed résumé at least three times, twice aloud. Executive recruiters can tell you many stories about candidates who were rejected because of one spelling error. In the world of job hunting, you get only one chance. Don't blow it with a spelling or grammar mistake.

MOVING FORWARD IN THE JOB-HUNTING PROCESS

There are times when the unexpected happens in the workplace, something like an economic recession caused by our recent health pandemic, which saw the unemployment rate zoom upward from 3.5 percent to 15 percent in less than three months. This unprecedented economic disaster resulted in the termination of more than 40 million jobs in less than four months. Powerhouse companies like Disney found it necessary to lay off 100,000 workers in just two weeks in order to remain solvent. American icons like J.C. Penny, J. Crew, Nordstrom, and Nieman Marcus filed for bankruptcy in an effort to restructure their finances. The result of this economic chaos? Millions of workers laid off permanently or furloughed indefinitely.

It's important to remember that rules for job hunting do not change during a recession or during a full-employment economy. All three books in this compilation emphasize that point. However, there are trade-offs that workers might need to make to remain solvent during a recession. For example, a vice president of sales who loses her job might need to take a job as a territory sales representative until the economy improves.

The Big Book of Job-Hunting Hacks will provide you with a framework for finding new employment, but the next step is up to the job seeker. Translate what you have read in this book into actionable items while remembering that the American economy is the most robust in the world and that it will recover to pre-COVID-19 status. Companies in most industries are hiring. They are looking for job candidates with intelligence, energy, and passion to accomplish the mission.

PART 1

How to Get a Great Job

INTRODUCTION

"BEYOND THE BOOKS" IN TODAY'S PUBLIC LIBRARIES

Are you aware of all the resources that your public library offers "beyond the books"? Today's community libraries offer a lot more than books, audiobooks, and movies to check out. You can attend a free workshop or lecture, browse online resources that aren't available anywhere else, and use your library's computers and software programs to prepare for a test or master a new skill—all for free.

CHECK IT OUT!

You probably used public library resources as a grade-schooler and are familiar with the basics of locating a specific book or magazine. (If you're not, ask a librarian for help—you'll relearn this very quickly!) But you should also be aware of these basics offered by any public library today:

INTERLIBRARY LOAN:

If your library doesn't have the book or resource you want, you may be able to borrow it from another branch or library system through interlibrary loan. It's easy to use, and you can pick up your requested materials at your local library.

REFERENCE SECTION:

Generally, reference materials are not available for checkout, but you can browse, read, and photocopy them in the library. The *Occupational Outlook Handbook* is a good example.

COMPUTER STATIONS:

Your library may require that you reserve a computer, that you limit your time to a half hour or hour at a time, or that you use certain computers for certain tasks. (Some libraries have computers dedicated to homework or to job searches.) Check the rules before you sit down.

INTERNET ACCESS:

Your library is likely to offer wireless Internet access in addition to computer stations. In this case, you can bring your laptop computer (or see if library laptops are available for checkout), find a comfortable seat, and surf the job sites for free.

SUBSCRIPTION DATABASES:

You'll read about specific databases in this book that can give your search a boost. Public and school libraries have paid subscriptions to various comprehensive online databases of job-search information that simply aren't available anywhere else.

SPECIALTY LIBRARIANS:

Depending on the size of your library system, librarians specializing in jobs and careers may be available in your local branch or elsewhere within the library system.

CLASSES, WORKSHOPS, PROGRAMS:

Public libraries routinely offer free classes, tutorials, workshops, and other educational programs. Job-search topics may include résumé writing, basic computer skills, interviewing, and more.

LIBRARIES AND JOB SEEKERS

Part of the mission of any public library is to meet the needs of its community. So, beyond stocking resources to help students with schoolwork; providing books, magazines, and newspapers for entertainment and information; and offering Internet access to the public, your library should be doing *something* to help local job seekers find work. How much it offers will depend on the library's budget, available resources, and innovation. Many libraries are relying on volunteers and partnerships with local employment groups to offer workshops or one-on-one help, or providing a meeting space for a job support group. Others may simply be adding books, software programs, and subscription databases that can help with job research.

Find out what your local library is doing—no matter how scant the available resources there, the research expertise of librarians, the information and lists already compiled, and the print and online materials available are sure to save you time and money while you look for a great job.

ASK AND YE SHALL RECEIVE

What if your library is small, understaffed, or simply doesn't offer much for job seekers? You can request that resources be added. If the library has a suggestion box or the online equivalent, use it. If not, ask for the name of the head of the reference section and write that person a letter or e-mail. However you request additional materials, be specific about what you want. You don't need to know the exact resource; you can state your need:

"I would like to be able to practice interviewing for a job with someone who can give me objective, concrete advice and feedback."

"I am studying to take the GED and understand there are software programs to help with this. If the library could provide a program for community use, that would really help me."

"I know that some libraries around the

country are offering résumé workshops. Our library should add this type of workshop."

SIX SIMPLE STEPS

For people who haven't used a public library much lately, these should be the first steps you take:

1. If you don't already have a library card, get one. All it takes is a photo ID and proof of address—check with your library to find out exactly what's required. A library card is free, but it acts as the "membership card" that's needed to access materials, including online databases you can search from home, interlibrary loans, and, of course, books, DVDs, and other materials for checkout.

2. Visit your library's website to explore the resources it offers. Browse the entire site to get an overview and then see if there is a special webpage or section devoted to job search, career help, etc.

3. Go to your library in person to talk to a librarian. Explain that you are looking for help with a job search and ask if there is a jobs and career specialist, a general business librarian, or a reference librarian who would be the best person to talk to about your search.

4. Some libraries let you schedule an appointment to talk one-on-one with a specific librarian for a set amount of time. If your library does this, by all means make an appointment! If not, find out when your chosen librarian has some time to talk to you.

5. Ask which resources are available to help you, including compilations of job websites, databases, workshops or classes, résumé review, etc. Your library may also offer lists of community resources that can help you.

6. Finally, learn how to physically find the resources—books, periodicals, reference materials, etc.—that you'll be using in your search. Explore your library and note where job-search information can be found.

THE LAST WORD

Libraries are continually changing and adding to the resources they offer. Even in times of tight budgets and reduced staff, they will find ways to share information, even if it is simply a photocopied list of local resources or websites on a specific topic. So if you think you know what your library has to offer for your job search based on what you found last year— don't be too sure. Head straight back to the reference desk and check out what's new.

CHAPTER 1
BEFORE YOU BEGIN

Think of this chapter as laying the groundwork for a successful job search. Before you update your résumé, click on your first "apply now" link on an online posting or pick up the phone to call a former coworker for a job lead. Take the time to make sure you're prepared.

Following all the advice in this chapter should take some people as little as an hour, and others no more than a day—not a bad investment for something as important as finding a great job!

BEST IN SHOW—GENERAL WEBSITES

Job-hunt, www.job-hunt.org.

The Riley Guide, www.rileyguide.com.

Toronto Public Library, "Career and Job Search Help Blog," http://torontopubliclibrary .typepad.com/jobhelp.

The Wall Street Journal, "Careers," www .careerjournal.com.

Weddle's, www.weddles.com. Sign up for the free e-newsletter *WEDDLE's Newsletter for Job Seekers & Career Activists* at www.weddles .com/seekernews/index.cfm.

WetFeet, www.wetfeet.com.

Quintessential Careers, www.quintcareers .com.

LIBRARY RESOURCES
Check Out Your Library

We may be biased, but your public library has valuable resources you can use to start your search that will help out for its duration. You're likely to find the job-search information you're looking for already neatly compiled, along with knowledgeable help and guidance, free computer and Internet use, and perhaps even valuable workshops and meetings.

"I think people want individual attention," says librarian Bonnie Easton of the people who come to her Career Center at the Cuyahoga

County (Ohio) Public Library. "They want some sense that they're going in the right direction. This is hard to figure out when you're on your own."

Jerome L. Myers, MLS, the main library manager at the Tacoma (Washington) Public Library's Education and Job Center, adds, "The first thing job seekers have to do is look into what they want to do and figure out the career they want. This is a great place to start."

INVENTORY YOUR CONTACT INFORMATION

As soon as you get the word out that you're looking for work, you should be ready for potential employers and your extended network to contact you. So before you contact anyone, take an inventory of the ways *they* can contact *you*:

1. YOUR E-MAIL ADDRESS

You'll need an address to sign in to many websites, to include in online job applications, and so that employers can communicate with you. Make sure you use the same e-mail address for all your job-search activities. Consider setting up a separate account just for job-search-related communications; this will make it easier to track your search. Just remember to check that in-box frequently!

TIP: NEVER USE YOUR WORK E-MAIL ADDRESS TO LOOK FOR A NEW JOB. NOT ONLY IS IT AN ABUSE OF YOUR EMPLOYER'S RESOURCES THAT CAN GET YOU IN TROUBLE, IT SENDS A TERRIBLE MESSAGE TO ANY POTENTIAL HIRERS.

Whichever e-mail address you decide to create or use, make sure it sounds professional. If you're currently found at tequilalover@freeemail.com or adasmommy@hotmail.com, take a few minutes to create a second address for job-search communications.

FOUR FREE E-MAIL OPTIONS

You can set up and use an e-mail account without spending a dime. Consider any of the following easy-to-use options for your job-search e-mail:

Gmail—http://mail.google.com
Offered through Google, with the side benefit of automatic access to Google Docs.

Mail.com—www.mail.com
Choose from 250 different addresses, including @techie.com or @ accountant.com.

Yahoo! Mail—http://mail.yahoo .com
While Yahoo! doesn't seem as professional as Gmail or mail.com, it's easy to use and perfectly acceptable.

Windows Live Mail—http://mail .live.com
Formerly Hotmail, and still found at hotmail.com with @hotmail addresses.

Because they are web-based, these accounts can be accessed from any computer, anywhere, including the stations in your library.

2. YOUR TELEPHONE

Before you draft a résumé or input contact information into a search site, decide which telephone number you're going to use throughout your search. (Again, don't even consider using your current work number.) Your cell phone is the most logical choice, because it is your personal number and completely in your control.

Listen to the voice-mail recording on the phone you've chosen to make sure it sounds appropriate to potential employers who may hear it. Ditch any jokes or silliness, background music, and rambling. Rerecord it if necessary, to include your name ("You've reached the voice mail of . . .") and the promise to call back as soon as possible.

During your search, focus on professionalism every time your phone rings. Be careful to check the caller ID readout and, unless you are absolutely sure that you know the friend or family member who's calling, answer the call in a professional way, the way you might if you were already working at your great job: "Good morning, this is Jim."

3. YOUR MAILING ADDRESS

It's always been standard practice to include street address on every résumé and cover letter—but consider whether you want to do this. If you think that sharing this information may be unnecessary or even harmful to your search—revealing an extralong commute may bring up doubts that you will stick with the job long term, for example—you may want to avoid including a "snail mail" address.

Of course, another option if you don't want to publicize your address, either to specific hirers or the entire Internet world, is investing in a PO box and using that as your job-search address.

4. YOUR WEB PRESENCE

Prepare to be Googled. One last "before you . . ." step in your prejob search process: browse the Internet to see what kind of presence you have. Search on your full name with and without your town (and town of employment) to see what comes up.

GOOD things include projects you've been involved with in your current and past jobs, your LinkedIn profile, and community activities.

BAD things include inappropriate remarks and photos posted by yourself or "friends" on Facebook. If your search turns up drunken poses, sexually suggestive comments, etc., try your best to have them removed. If a friend refuses to delete something from Facebook, ask that they change privacy settings so that only friends can see it.

FACTOID

Microsoft commissioned an online reputation survey in 2009, in which 79 percent of U.S. hiring managers and job recruiters said they conducted online searches on job applicants. And 70 percent of those potential hirers stated that they had rejected a candidate based on what they found online!

ARM YOURSELF WITH BASIC SKILLS, SOFTWARE

The absolute basic skills needed for any job search now include the ability to use a computer well enough to find and fill out an online job application—which in turn will require an e-mail address. This is true even for positions that will never require you to use these skills on the job—including retail store workers and fast-food restaurant employees.

If you're not comfortable using the Internet, your public library may be able to help. "You can learn basic computer skills here, and then learn every stage of the job search," says Jerome Myers, the main library manager at the Tacoma (Washington) Public Library's Education and Job Center.

WEB USE 101

If you're not familiar with using the Internet, you will be—your job search will teach you browsing skills fast! But here are some basics to keep in mind as you get started:

Logging In: Many job-search sites will require you to set up an account and then log in every time you want to check listings. Put some consideration into creating a user name and password for these sites.

Secure passwords use a combination of letters, numbers, and symbols. You can use the same user name and password for every job-search site to ensure you'll remember them.

TIP: Your user name may be seen by the public, so choose something professional, just like your e-mail address.

CAPTCHA: Completely Automated Public Turing Test to Tell Computers and Humans Apart is the program that asks you to type in one or more words displayed as distorted images. This is becoming standard for many sites that require users to input personal information; it proves that the person entering the site is a real human being and not a web-crawling robot used to hack sites.

Protect Your Privacy: Check each job-search site (and résumé-writing service or other site that requires you to enter personal information) for a privacy policy. This is a legal document that outlines how your personal information may be used. Consider that you're typing in all sorts of information that can be used for unwanted solicitations and even identity theft.

Keep in mind that any information you post on sites, including your résumé, can be found and read by anyone—so be stingy with how much you share! This includes posting any contact information for your references.

RÉSUMÉ AND LETTER WRITING

In addition to an Internet connection, you'll need software to create and revise your résumé and cover letters. Microsoft Word is the most common, but there are specific programs for this. If you don't own Word and want a standard-format résumé, you can use Google Docs, a free online service that includes a résumé template. You simply type over the sample résumé to create your own, without purchasing or using any word-processing software (https://docs.google.com/Doc?id=dghd5rk7_0hzd4bzfx).

You will also need to create PDFs. If you don't have Adobe Acrobat and you are using a Windows operating system, you can download free software called PDFCreator from http://sourceforge.net/projects/pdfcreator.

Again, if you don't have any of these programs, your public library can probably help.

> TIP: If you are creating or revising documents at a computer outside your home, buy a usb flash drive (also called a thumb drive or memory stick) and save all your documents on it so you'll always have them handy. Never save your personal documents to the hard drive of a computer you don't own!

And if you're creating your résumé while away from your home, make sure you bring (or have memorized) all the necessary information to be included, including dates of past employment.

Any additional software you might need would be for keeping your search organized, which is covered in the next section.

WORK YOUR PLAN

Aside from some basic computer knowledge, an Internet connection, and a couple of software programs, you need one more thing to begin your job search: a plan. Your plan should include:

1. A clear strategy on what you want in your next job and what you don't
2. A schedule to hold yourself accountable
3. Goals to keep your job search moving ahead
4. A system for tracking what you've done
5. A plan for improving your salability on the job market

> TIP: Your job search is like a job in itself, so make it seem like one. Choose an area in your home as your "job-search office" and keep all information, files, and supplies there, including your calendar and to-do list.

1. WHAT DO YOU WANT?

Take some time to think through what you are looking for. You should have a clear idea of what type(s) of positions you want and which you can realistically apply for. You should also calculate how much money you need to pay your bills and meet financial obligations (including savings) and how much you *want* to make. Other general "wants" might include:

- Location: How far are you willing to commute? Are you willing to relocate?
- Does your family or personal life put any constraints on your work, such as

inability to travel or need for flexible hours?

- Are there any "must-haves" to include in your search? These may include certain benefits, an option for working from home, or a certain level of management responsibilities.

2. STICK TO A SCHEDULE

Most full-time employees today have a forty-hour workweek. If you're out of work, that's how much time you should dedicate to your job search. If you're employed while you're job hunting, you'll have to find as much personal time as you can for your job search.

No matter what your employment situation, your first step is to figure out a realistic schedule for each day and each week that devotes plenty of time to researching, networking, and reading and answering ads for open positions. Then stick to that schedule. This can be the toughest part of any job search, but you can do it! Write your daily schedule in your calendar if necessary, or create a daily to-do list that includes your job-search steps. Or do both!

For example, in addition to a preset number of hours spent browsing job boards online, you might block out every Wednesday morning from 9 to 11 a.m. for research at your public library, and then dedicate Wednesday afternoon from 2 to 4 p.m. to commenting on online industry and job-search forums and blogs.

TIP: If you are having trouble sticking to your job search, enlist a colleague or friend who will hold you accountable. Perhaps you can team up with someone in your job support network, or just a supportive friend. Simply telling someone what you plan to accomplish today (or this week) will give you a nudge to do it. If not, having that person ask you if you completed what you planned should help you stay on schedule.

DAILY JOB-SEARCH TO-DO LIST

- Check your e-mail (at least twice a day)
- Respond to any employer, recruiter, or networking contact who e-mails that same day
- Check voice mail throughout the day if you're away from your phone
- Log all jobs applied to, contacts talked to (or e-mailed), and events attended

---

3. SET SMALL GOALS

Putting in the time is not the goal; getting results is. With this in mind, set specific goals for each day, week, and month. Rather than aiming for a certain number of jobs applied for—this will lead you to send applications or résumés for unsuitable fits—set goals for new research sources found, the number of in-person networking events you'll attend, the number of telephone cold calls you'll make, etc.

At the end of each day and each week, note your progress. Did you meet your goals? What were the results you gleaned? If you find that your goals were set too high (or too low), adjust them accordingly for the days and weeks ahead.

4. GET ORGANIZED

Your job-search plan must include an organizational system. This includes the schedule (with daily and weekly to-do lists) and goals you've set up, along with ways to keep track of what you've done. This is much easier if you "log in" each activity as soon as you've completed it.

KEEP RECORDS

Later in this book you'll get specific information on what types of records to keep, but you should be prepared from the start to record every position you apply for, every promising contact you make through networking, and every step that follows either of these.

You can keep your records electronically or on paper, but you'll need a system that alerts you about when (and how) to follow up and helps you remember which résumé went to which company.

If you've already started your job search, go through every application or résumé you've turned in and try to reconstruct what you've done.

ORGANIZE YOUR FILES

As you'll find out in Chapters 4 and 5, you're going to end up with multiple versions of your résumé and cover letter. You'll want to save these so that you can retrieve them in the event that you get a call-back about an opening you

applied for, or simply because you want to re-revise a certain version of your résumé.

All these documents should be saved electronically; there is no reason to print out every version. Devise a naming system for your files that is easily scannable and understandable and keep everything in a folder such as "Résumés." This should be placed in another folder with any other job-search documentation you may acquire.

If you prefer, you can store your résumés and letters online, using Google Documents (http://docs.google.com). This free system lets you upload documents and then access them from any computer with an Internet connection anywhere.

If you find it difficult to work with a completely computer-based system, you can keep notes of which résumé went to which job ad by either printing out a spreadsheet (covered in Chapter 3) or writing it out in longhand.

TRACK YOUR EXPENSES

As part of your general organizational system, keep track of any expenses related to your job search. The costs of getting business cards printed, mileage and parking fees for interviews, phone calls, and much more may all be tax deductible. The IRS states, "You can deduct certain expenses you have in looking for a new job in your present occupation, even if you do not get a new job." Note that expenses related to looking for a job in a new field are not deductible.

5. GET SKILLED

Are there skills you need to acquire in order to apply for your dream job? What about skills that may boost your income level? If you know of something that will give you an edge in your job hunt—like learning a new software program or understanding the key concepts in an emerging trend—devote some of your time to learning it. You may be able to do this by reading, by taking a class or practice exam at your local library, or through volunteer work.

FINAL STEP: GET CONNECTED

Looking for a job can be lonely work—especially if you're unemployed and cut off from the busy work environment you're used to. To stay connected to the professional world, get the support and advice you need, get out of the house and find a job-search club or a networking support group. (See Chapter 6.) A group like this will provide emotional support, and you'll be able to share advice and even your contacts with other members.

If you can't find a group you like, consider starting your own—or you can go the online route with a group on Meetup.com, Yahoo! Groups, or Google Groups. But don't let your online relationships be your only support— you should also regularly ask friends, former coworkers, and new networking contacts to meet you for a cup of coffee or a walk around the park. Discuss your job search, ask for ideas, or simply catch up on news from the "outside world."

THE LAST WORD

You will almost certainly revise your job-search plan as you go. Once you have spent some time in the trenches looking for a job, you'll have a better understanding of the commitments, activities, and results involved. This should lead you to add and revise goals, shift your schedule around, and tweak your organizational system. This is fine—just be sure that you are working as hard as you need to in order to find a great job!

CHAPTER 2
RESEARCHING THE JOB MARKET

Before you start your job search (or get any further with the one you're in the midst of), take some time to put your search in a larger context. Every job seeker should know the "lay of the land" for his targeted industry or profession. Start by asking yourself these questions:

- Do you know the titles or descriptions of positions you should be applying for?
- What is the current outlook for the jobs you're seeking in your geographic region?
- Do you have the appropriate qualifications for the level and type of job(s) you're searching for?
- Are there other industries or positions you might be qualified for that you should include in your search?
- And finally, if the outlook for your targeted industry/positions is not good, can you find a different profession that might be easier to be hired into? If so, what will it take?

You can improve your odds of finding great jobs that match your qualifications by starting out with a broader search. As you research the job market and review job postings, look at *all* types of jobs within your targeted industry or industries and see what is available. If this becomes too overwhelming, you can begin to narrow your search by eliminating certain positions or other criteria from your search.

FOR INSTANCE . . .

"Lateral" moves like the examples below don't involve a complete career change; they simply stretch the options for using the skills and experience a professional has already acquired:

- daycare worker to teacher's assistant
- telemarketer to receptionist
- office manager to computer tech support
- ad agency graphic designer to account representative (or vice versa)

- high-speed Internet installer to high-speed Internet customer-service rep

You may need to sell yourself a little more strongly in your résumé and interviews to convince an employer that your experience will translate.

"If you read the odds of your résumé getting you an interview, it's depressing. Statistics are always against you—but just keep at it. Your qualifications will be a perfect match for a job somewhere, and they'll find you, if you just do the homework."

—Bernice Kao, job/career specialist and job service outreach librarian at Fresno County (California) Public Library

BEST IN SHOW—OCCUPATION/ CAREER LISTINGS ONLINE

The **Riley Guide's Career Research Center** at http://rileyguide.com/careers/index .shtml. "This library includes job descriptions, salary data and employment statistics, and education information for over 160 occupations!"

The **Vocational Information Center's** www.khake.com/page5.html offers lots of valuable links to sites with employment trends, state-by-state labor market information, economic statistics, and more.

Job-posting aggregator **Indeed.com** adds statistics for a dozen industries each month, providing at-a-glance information on where the jobs are. Click on "trends" from the home page to get started.

GET AN INDUSTRY SNAPSHOT

So what do you need to learn about your industry in order to shape your search? Your industry or profession snapshot should include answers to questions such as:

How is the industry's overall economic health? What is the forecast for job growth in the field? What is the unemployment rate within the industry? Are the companies that are major players doing well in the stock market?

What's happening in your neighborhood? Which organizations are located in your city or county? Are they hiring? Is growth in your area increasing or decreasing?

What's on the horizon in D.C.? Is there any pending legislation that will affect your industry's trends or economic health? (For example, the Homebuyer Tax Credit in 2008 and 2009 gave real estate a short-term boost.)

What are the trends? What does the business press have to say about your industry? Are there new technologies, new organizations, or changes in the business world that will affect your career?

YOUR FIRST STOP: THE LIBRARY'S INFORMATION COUNTER

Public libraries serve their communities—and if your community's needs include help with job searching, your library should be able to provide information and resources to help with your research. Check your library's website for job or career pages and stop by the reference desk to see what type of help is available. You may find that a librarian has already created a ready-to-use list of Internet resources you can get started with, or you may be able to access the library's information databases to gather information.

"Right now, we're seeing more interest in career planning. As jobs are disappearing, people are seeking new industries with better demand."

—Bonnie Easton, librarian at the Career Center of the Cuyahoga County (Ohio) Public Library

HIT THE BOOKS (ONLINE)

The federal government compiles industry information every year in volumes that are now available online for free. These are absolute "musts" to include in your research:

1. **Occupational Outlook Handbook (OOH)** Published by the U.S. Bureau of Labor Statistics (BLS), this guide should be available at your library in print and can be found online at www.bls.gov/oco. Revised and updated every two years, it includes detailed career information for all types of occupations, including a description of what workers do on the job, training and education needed, expected job prospects, salaries or wages, and working conditions. You'll also find links to information on state-by-state job markets, job-search tips, and more.

2. **Career Guide to Industries (CGI)** A companion to the Occupational Outlook Handbook, this BLS publication is only available online, at www.bls.gov/oco/cg. It is similar to the OOH and provides information on careers by industry, including occupations in the industry, expected job prospects, training and advancement, earnings, and more.

3. **Occupational Outlook Quarterly** An online quarterly magazine published by the BLS that covers a variety of career topics, such as new and emerging occupations, training opportunities, salary trends, and results of new studies from the BLS. The "magazine" is available at www.bls.gov/opub/ooq/ooqhome.htm.

4. **O*NET Online** Visit http://online.onetcenter.org to browse the O*NET OnLine database of occupational information. The Occupational Information Network (O*NET) is

sponsored by the U.S. Department of Labor/Employment and Training Administration, and the database is a user-friendly resource with information on nearly 1,000 occupations. Browse by occupation or by skills (e.g., How can I use my teaching skills and desire to help people?). There is a lot of information and a lot of ways to search or find it—so take some time to click around O*NET.

FIVE MORE RESOURCES

There are other outstanding sources for up-to-date information. Check these additional online and print sources for details on your industry and/or career:

1. **Wetfeet.com** offers its own insights and information on trends, major players, and job descriptions in major industries, as well as career information, at www.wetfeet.com /careers—industries.aspx.

2. **The Career Project** (thecareerproject .org) is a site that provides a brief description of thousands of jobs— from the workers themselves. Select an industry and see comments from actual people working in it. Better yet, you can ask any of these "mentors" a question via e-mail if you want more information on the kind of work they do (or money they make).

3. Another place to check is the listing of "**Best Jobs in America 2009**" at http://money.cnn.com /magazines/moneymag/bestjobs/2009 /snapshots/1.html. You won't exactly find the "best" jobs, but you can see those with the most growth, highest pay, and highest-rated quality of life.

4. The websites or member publications of any professional associations related to your chosen work. Associations will report—either directly or indirectly—on trends, pending and current legislation, and other factors that influence jobs in the field.

5. For general business information that may affect your chosen industry, browse these well-known publications online or in print at your public library:

Wall Street Journal (http://online.wsj.com /home-page)

Fortune (http://money.cnn.com/magazines /fortune/)

Fast Company (www.fastcompany.com)

Forbes (www.forbes.com)

ENTRY-LEVEL WORKERS AND CAREER CHANGERS

If you are planning to change careers—or are just starting out in your first career—you'll face your own unique challenges. Job seekers in these two categories are similar, because a complete change in careers can put an experienced professional back at the starting gate, looking for entry-level jobs. An employer is unlikely to give you credit—or a salary increase—because of past experience that will not translate to your new job.

> ## CHANGE RULE
>
> To be clear, changing careers refers to a complete shift to a new industry, requiring different skills or knowledge from your previous positions. A legal secretary who wants to become a teacher is changing careers; a legal secretary who wants to become a paralegal is not.

Whether you're a new graduate, a mom reentering the workplace after a multiyear hiatus, or simply want to change careers, you're in for a lot of research. You need to figure out three things:

1. Where the jobs are
2. What you *really* want to do
3. How to make it happen

You know about the first item—just follow the advice for all job seekers at the beginning of this chapter: head to the library, hit the web, and research the job markets. Don't choose a profession simply because the employment outlook is good! Training to become a nurse just for the guaranteed job security is sure to lead to unhappiness, stress, and possibly bad patient care if you're not suited for the work. So head back to the library, because the second item may take some additional research.

TAKING APTITUDE AND ASSESSMENT TESTS

An assessment test or career aptitude test can reveal what specific jobs might best suit your abilities, interests, and personality. Ask a librarian what the library—and the Internet—has to offer in this area.

The most widely known assessment tests are the Myers-Briggs Type Indicator, the Strong Interest Inventory, and the Campbell Interest & Skill Survey, but there are dozens of them. Some library subscription databases include assessment tests. For example, "Gale's Testing and Educational Database includes many employment and aptitude tests that are very useful," says Jim DeArmey, coordinator of information services at Baltimore County (Maryland) Public Library.

The results of your aptitude or assessment test(s) should give you some specific ideas on careers to pursue. If the results simply outline your skills and aptitudes, match those up with the skills listed in the O*NET OnLine database to find careers. (That website again is http://online.onetcenter.org.)

GAINING SKILLS AND QUALIFICATIONS

Finally, you need to determine what qualifications you need to begin working in your chosen career. If you need some experience, look for an internship or volunteer position or project that might apply. (A librarian can help with this!) Perhaps you need to take a class—or earn an entire degree. Maybe you need to learn new skills or specific business expertise, or will have to pass an industry-specific exam. Again, the library may be able to help. Many libraries own software that teaches or tests specific skills—from an extensive program on studying for the GED, to learning Spanish, to a practice exam for master carpentry.

Jerome L. Myers, MLS, main library manager at the Tacoma (Washington) Public Library Education and Job Center, says, "There are certain careers that require applicants to pass a test, whether it's for air traffic control or typing skills. The civil service job exams are our most popular—for employment as a postal worker or police officer, for example. You can come to the library—or log in from home if you have a library card—and take a practice exam. You can work at your own pace; it's very beneficial."

BEST IN SHOW—CHANGING CAREERS

Jansen, Julie. *I Don't Know What I Want, But I Know It's Not This: A Step-by-Step Guide to Finding Gratifying Work*. (New York: Penguin, 2003).

Tieger, Paul, and Barbara Barron. *Do What You Are: Discover the Perfect Career for You through the Secrets of Personality Type*. (New York: Little, Brown, 2007).

Lore, Nicholas. *The Pathfinder: How to Choose or Change Your Career for a Lifetime of Satisfaction and Success*. (New York: Simon and Schuster, Fireside, 1998).

STUDY YOUR SUBJECT

You'll see this same advice at various points within this book: research your target industry. Make it part of your job-search research to stay abreast of what's happening. Don't wait until you have an interview lined up—do it now so that while you're networking, or leaving a comment on an industry insider's blog, or meeting your new neighbor who happens to be a headhunter, you're knowledgeable, up to date, and prepared with facts.

"Do your own research. It's in the newspaper every single day."

—Bernice Kao, job/career specialist and job service outreach librarian at Fresno County (California) Public Library

YOU SHOULD KNOW

- Major players in your industry and/or region—the organizations and perhaps the people who run them.
- Any recent changes to those major players. Mergers, moves, new

products introduced, or headline-making news.

- The latest trends. By monitoring professional associations' websites and publications, relevant news sources, blogs, and LinkedIn groups, you'll see patterns emerge—those are the trends.
- Industry lingo, acronyms, and jargon. Want to write websites? It's easy enough to find out what SEO stands for—and you'll need to know!

NEWS DELIVERED TO YOUR IN-BOX

You can stay up to date on industry news with daily or weekly e-mail alerts by setting up a Google News Alert. From Google.com, click on "About Google" and select "Google Services and Tools" to find "Alerts." Type in specific phrases and words on what you'd like to see. For example, you may choose to see news items (and blog entries, discussions, and videos) on "property management." If you then find that you're seeing too many items that aren't relevant, you can refine your search criteria to "property management," "condominiums," and "Florida."

GET THE INSIDE SCOOP

If you feel you need some specific insights into the state of your chosen industry, try for one or more information interviews. These are one-on-one meetings that you set up with established professionals in your field. For more on information interviews, see Chapter 8.

THE LAST WORD

The time you spend researching your chosen industry will pay off. It will help you set parameters for your job search now, and you can draw on the information you find when you're in an interview—to demonstrate your knowledge and insights in your field—as well as once you get a job. In fact, staying abreast of what's happening in your industry, including hiring trends, is always a good idea, even when you are employed. So make this type of research a habit!

CHAPTER 3

GETTING DOWN TO BRASS TACKS: THE ONGOING JOB SEARCH

If you're unemployed and looking for a new job, your job search *is* your daily work. If you've got a job but are looking for another, you need to set time and energy aside each week for your job search, or you'll find you don't get very far. Here are some basic tips to help keep your search on track:

- **Be patient.** The length of time you look for a job before you get the perfect offer—or even the first phone interview—may be longer than you might expect. Depending on the state of the overall economy, the health of your industry, and just plain luck, you may have to spend many months on your search. That can be discouraging—especially when you don't hear back from many employers, or when you get multiple rejections— so steel yourself for the long haul.
- **Put in the hours.** Remember how you set a schedule at the beginning of your job search (Chapter 1)? As your job

search winds on, it's important to stick to that schedule. Do what it takes to put in the time you promised yourself, even if you have to break the time spent into two- or three-hour blocks.

- **Keep meeting your goals.** Your daily and weekly goals go hand in hand with your schedule. Keep striving for them, but if you find that the targets you originally set for yourself are unrealistic or too repetitive, it's OK to set new ones. Try to broaden your search without easing up on the amount of effort you put in.
- **Step away from the computer.** Remember—while the Internet is an amazing source for browsing job openings, career advice, and company research, there's more to a job search than Google. Make a point to get out of the house to volunteer and network formally and informally. You can start by heading over to your public library . . .

"Take advantage of the Internet. You have multiple ways of reaching companies. Of course, you certainly have to follow the directions for applying for an open position. But you can also follow up [through different channels] to differentiate yourself."

—Dionna Keels, a member of the SHRM (Society for Human Resource Management) staffing management expertise panel

BEST IN SHOW—ONLINE JOB SEARCH

Bolles, Mark Emery, and Richard N. Bolles. *Job-Hunting Online: A Guide to Job Listings, Message Boards, Research Sites, the UnderWeb, Counseling, Networking, Self-Assessment Tools, Niche Sites.* (Berkeley, CA: Ten Speed Press, 2008).

Dikel, Margaret Riley, and Frances E. Roehm. *Guide to Internet Job Searching, 2008–2009 ed.* (New York: McGraw-Hill, 2008).

Doyle, Alison. *Internet Your Way To a New Job: How to Really Find a Job Online.* (Cupertino, CA: Happy About, 2009).

Levinson, Jay Conrad, and David E. Perry. *Guerrilla Marketing for Job Hunters 2.0: 1,001 Unconventional Tips, Tricks, and Tactics for Landing Your Dream Job.* (Hoboken, NJ: John Wiley & Sons, 2009).

Job-hunt, www.job-hunt.org.

The Riley Guide, "Sites with Job Listings," www.rileyguide.com/jobs.html.

Weddle's, www.weddles.com.

WetFeet, www.wetfeet.com.

FACTOID
Where Recruiters and HR Professionals Plan to Post

WEDDLE's consulting firm surveyed 3,900 recruiters and HR professionals in 2005. Of those,

11 percent said they plan to use "general recruitment" websites.

84 percent said they preferred niche job boards.

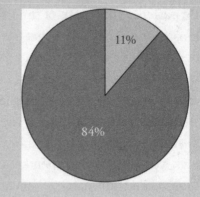

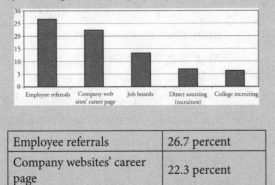
WHERE TO LOOK ONLINE

CareerBuilder.com and Monster.com . . . industry-specific online forums and discussion groups . . . LinkedIn . . . about.com and career information sites . . . the Internet offers countless sites and pages that include job postings (such as local newspapers' online classified sections), career advice, and how-to descriptions for every aspect of job seeking. The trick is to "search smart" and make your time online count.

HOW TO SEARCH

In order to find the best sites and the best individual listings, you have to choose your search words and phrases wisely. You can use the database resources listed in the "Sources for Keywords" section of Chapter 4 to make a list of words to use in your Internet search.

"You have to find all the key terms that are going to deliver good search results," says Damone Virgilio, staff development manager at Memphis (Tennessee) Public Library. "Online searches are about sitting and combing through results. It can be tedious—but if you've been looking for a long time with no results, maybe a broader selection of results is better for you."

The library staff reviews the sites listed on their webpage regularly and adds anything they find useful, such as résumé how-tos and the library's Testing and Educational database.

Visit Baltimore County Public Library's Jobs and Info page at www.bcpl.info/info/jobs—then see what your own library system might offer online.

CHOOSE THE BEST JOB BOARDS

Your online job search should include regular visits to job boards—sites that display job postings. There are so many . . . how do you choose which sites to bookmark? Your list of regular boards might include:

- **The big national sites,** which all allow you to post one or more versions of your résumé, so when you're ready to apply for a job you can do so quickly and easily.
- **Your local newspaper's job listings**. Yes, some employers still advertise job openings in the newspaper—and those ads are typically found online.
- **Industry-specific job boards,** which are a must for just about every job search. More efficient than wading through mismatches on the general national sites, and providing an at-a-glance overview of all opportunities within your profession. Simply plug

appropriate words into your search engine to turn up sites for your career or industry, or try the Job Spider at www.thejobspider.com/job/directory/employment-resources.asp.

- **Sites of professional associations.** Websites for most large associations now include job postings, and these can be even more targeted than industry job boards.
- **Craigslist,** for the city or region where you want to work. Yes, there are "real" jobs posted on Craigslist all the time—many younger professionals consider Craigslist the go-to site for everything from selling furniture to buying event tickets, and that includes seeking job candidates. Plus, many employers love Craigslist because the ads are free!
- **Aggregators.** These sites can save you time and unearth more job postings than you might. They automatically draw job postings from numerous online sources large and small, including the major job boards and search firms, smaller niche sites, and corporate career sites. Damone Virgilio, staff development manager at Memphis (Tennessee) Public Library, prefers the aggregator Indeed.com. "It pulls job openings from different sites so it casts a wide net," he says. "It's also extremely easy to use; just enter your ZIP code and the job title."

JOB BOARD EXAMPLES
BIG NATIONAL SITES
www.CareerBuilder.com
www.monster.com
INDUSTRY-SPECIFIC JOB BOARDS
www.accounting.com
www.hrcareersusa.com (jobs in HR)
www.dice.com (careers in technology)
PROFESSIONAL ASSOCIATIONS
Automotive Service Association: www.asashop.org
Marketing Research Association: www.mra-net.org
National Association of Veterinary Technicians: www.navta.net
AGGREGATORS
www.indeed.com
www.simplyhired.com
www.topusajobs.com
www.linkup.com (aggregates only from company websites)

JOB BOARDS RANKED
If you'd like some help from expert opinions and job-seeker statistics to help you determine the best (or most popular) job boards, check out these sources:

WEDDLE's User's Choice Awards (www.weddles.com/awards/index.htm), published each year, lists the winning general and specialty sites nominated by job seekers and career activists.

The Classifieds News Blog posts an annual ranking of the top fifteen U.S. job-search websites at http://blog.daype.com/tips/top-us-job-search-websites.html.

ONLINE EMPLOYMENT TESTING
When applying for jobs online, you may come across an employer that requires you to take an online test as part of the application process. Preemployment tests or assessments are used as a first step to narrow the field of candidates. These tests may contain questions about your personality and work style, or they could check your hands-on skills at clerical tasks or work-related knowledge.

If you come across an opening that requires a test, make sure you are ready. Check that you are using a reliable Internet connection, have ample time, and—most important—understand what the open position entails and have some knowledge of the employing organization.

Be aware that some Internet applications enable employers to check how long it took you to complete the test and see how you may have corrected or changed answers as you went.

LOG IN TO SEARCH EVERY DAY
Do your research: investigate all likely job boards, decide which are the best fit for you, check their privacy policies and security, and

eliminate any aggregators that provide too many duplicates. (Note, too, that aggregators don't pull job listings from Craigslist.)

Bookmark all the boards you're interested in following and visit each one often to check for new listings—if possible, do this every day. It doesn't take long to review only the latest listings, and you want to be able to respond to a job ad as soon as possible after it's posted: "I generally go through applicants chronologically, so it's good to be among the first to apply," says Dionna Keels, a member of the SHRM (Society for Human Resource Management) staffing management expertise panel. "That means you need to search for openings every day."

Many sites will send you regular updates with new listings via e-mail, but don't rely on these—you'll find many of the job mentions are off-target, because they are compiled by a software program.

COMPANY WEBSITES

You'd think that if an organization has a job opening, it would be posted on one or more of the job boards mentioned here. That is not always the case—so an organization's own website may be a gold mine of information. Part of your job-search time online should be spent researching likely employers, and when you find one, visit their website and look for "careers," "employment," "career opportunities," or a similar link to view open positions. You'll find a lot more detail here than in a paid ad—possibly the full job description, salary information, and more.

LINKEDIN JOB LISTINGS

LinkedIn has job listings, but the pickings are relatively slim compared to the types of sites listed above. However, time browsing on LinkedIn can definitely be well spent: if you find a LinkedIn job posting you're interested in, you can apply using copy-and-paste sections from your plain-text résumé, as explained in Chapter 4.

Each job posting will reveal whether you are "linked" to the posting company. On the right side of the page with the job description, you'll see any once-, twice- or three-times-removed connections. Click on one to see who you know that is connected. You'll also see whether you share any LinkedIn groups with the company's employees. Note that you have to view the actual job posting to see how you're connected to the hiring company.

If you see any connections to the company you're interested in working for, you can use LinkedIn to ask your connections for a referral (by clicking on the "Request Referral" button), which can greatly enhance your odds of standing out from other candidates for that job. You can also request an introduction to someone. If you want to contact a LinkedIn user who is two or three degrees away from you, you can request an introduction through one of your connections. Your connection will, in turn, decide whether to forward it on to the desired recipient (if in your "second-degree" connections) or to a shared connection (if in your "third-degree" connections). You'll learn more about the networking power of LinkedIn in Chapter 6.

BEWARE OF SCAMS

As you browse job listings, keep in mind that there are job scams out there. Don't answer any "employer" inquiries for personal information such as your Social Security number or bank account number—that goes for contact by phone, e-mail, on a website, or even in person. Sharing this information is never part of the interviewing process.

And don't believe the job description that's too good to be true; if you could make $100,000 working from home, we'd all be doing it already!

WHERE TO LOOK OFF-LINE

Step away from the computer to find more opportunities to research, find, and apply for jobs. Remember that face-to-face networking is an important component to any job search (covered in Chapter 6). Here is a look at other "off-line" resources and events to include in your search:

JOB FAIRS

Job fairs are hosted by colleges and universities, communities and profession-specific groups, or consortiums. Many job fairs are extremely general, with a wide range of employers and positions. Others are targeted to specific industries or professions, such as a Technology Job Fair.

FINDING A FAIR

If you're plugged into the job-seekers' network, you'll automatically learn about upcoming job fairs through online forums and groups; they'll be advertised on career sites, and fellow members of your job support group or networking circle will tell you. You may also find out through local newspapers, bulletin boards, and your local unemployment office.

PREPARING FOR A FAIR

It's important to do your legwork in advance of showing up at a job fair. This includes more than just preregistering and ironing your best shirt:

1. Find out which prospective employers will be participating and select which you want to be sure to meet. Take time to do some online research to check out each one before the fair.
2. If a map of the fair is available, literally plan your route.
3. Know what you want from this particular fair and have an appropriate elevator speech prepared. (For an explanation of elevator speeches, see Chapter 6.)
4. Have plenty of copies of appropriate résumés and business cards ready.
5. If you have a portfolio, prepare that, as well.
6. Rehearse your elevator speech and practice answering interview questions.

7. Select the business attire you plan to wear, clean and prepare it, and try it on to make sure everything is ready.
8. Have a professional-looking briefcase ready to hold résumés and portfolio and use it to carry the materials you gather at the fair.

WORKING THE FAIR

If possible, get to the job fair early, get through registration, and start working your map route by visiting your list of "top picks" first. (Don't forget to check at registration to see if there are any last-minute additions of hiring companies.) At each table or booth you visit, try these strategies:

- Pick up the handouts they provide and review them if possible before engaging in conversation.
- When you're ready to talk—or when the recruiter makes eye contact—greet them and give a firm handshake along with your elevator speech. Keep in mind that the employees working the job fair are probably not the hiring managers; they are HR professionals who are screeners for the company.
- Take notes during each conversation or interview so you'll be able to keep them straight when you get home.
- Make sure you get business cards or contact information for everyone you might want to follow up with—and give them yours.

- Take advantage of the pool of job seekers and network with them, as well. Find out what's working best for them.

AFTER THE FAIR

When you get home from the job fair, organize the business cards and information you collected. Input all relevant details into your job-search organization system. And be sure to write thank-you e-mails or notes to each recruiter you talked to—and send those thank-yous within a day or two.

> ### BEST IN SHOW—JOB FAIRS
> CollegeGrad.com, "Job Fair Success," www .collegegrad.com/jobsearch/Job-Fair-Success.
> Quintessential Careers, "Career Fair Tutorial," www.quintcareers.com /career_fair_tutorial.

PUBLICATIONS

The printed page still plays a role in your job search. Browse these sources—at least some of which may be found for free at your local library—to look for job openings, keep up with industry and business news, and find key players you might contact for an information interview or even a job interview:

- Your local newspapers
- Industry trade journals (*Midwest Engineer, Journal of Hospitality Financial Management*)
- Association newsletters and magazines (*Professional Photographer* magazine, *Interior Design in Practice*)
- Your college's alumni newsletter or magazine

GOVERNMENT AND NONPROFIT AGENCIES

Every community has public and private agencies that serve job seekers. Ask the reference librarian at your public library about resources (and job listings) offered by your local unemployment office, state and local government agencies, and nonprofit offices. You might get advice from these groups on interviewing, résumés, and much more. And each will have compiled sources of job listings that may be new to you. Look for agencies such as:

Maryland's Office of Workforce Development
Cincinnati's SuperJobs, a nonprofit center for job seekers
The Nashville Career Advancement Center
Michigan Works

RECRUITMENT AND TEMP AGENCIES

Signing up for temporary work is a great way to look for a job. Many companies will hire a temporary worker who has proven herself on the job, despite an often-hefty fee they must pay to the temp agency. Even if a temp assignment doesn't lead to a permanent job, you'll find it has other benefits:

1. Working at a company for a day, week, or many months will help you clarify your employment goals. Which type of corporate culture do you prefer? Which type of boss do you work well with?

2. You'll pick up new skills with every assignment, whether it's mastering a telephone system or getting training in specialty software.

3. You can broaden your network with every assignment. Connect with your coworkers and let them know you'd like to find work in their industry.

4. Temp agencies often do general recruiting, as well. You can prove yourself with an agency—especially if you didn't sign on with a strong background—and increase your chances of landing an interview for a permanent job.

5. At the end of a long-term temp assignment, ask your direct manager for a letter of recommendation. This can help fill a large unemployment gap if you've been job seeking for many months.

WHAT RECRUITERS SAY

Two professional recruiters reveal how they search for the best candidates ...

Jill Silman, SPHR, vice president at Meador Staffing Services and a spokesperson for the Society of Human Resources Management (SHRM):

"Our number one method has always been referrals. But we're finding that social media is becoming more effective and efficient. That's quickly becoming number two: as individual recruiters and as an organization, we'll use Facebook, LinkedIn, and Twitter to look for candidates."

Dionna Keels, a member of the SHRM (Society for Human Resource Management) staffing management expertise panel:

"I've been in recruiting for about ten years. Over the past four to five years, online resources have been huge for me. The big online boards are a really good tool. I'll search the online résumé banks by skills, job titles, and even by company.

"I use the big job boards—Careerbuilder and Monster—but I definitely use more specific ones also. Dice is a good one for IT positions. I also look at association job boards. Being involved in an [industry-related] association is a great way to look for a job.

"How do you stand out in a group of 500 résumés? Well, if you're applying for a position that looks like a perfect match for your skills and experience, you can also do some research on, say, LinkedIn, and maybe shoot a separate e-mail to HR or the hiring manager to highlight yourself. In one case where I had 500 résumés to look at, I got separate e-mails from ten or fifteen people. I was more likely to look harder at those résumés."

STAY ORGANIZED FROM THE START

As you begin your job search, keep track of everything. You'll be glad you did—especially when you get a call from a company you don't remember applying to or meet someone for the second time at a networking event.

You'll need to devise a system that keeps track of details on all jobs you apply for—at every stage, your networking contacts, and your prospects for hiring companies. You'll want to note *at least* the following information:

JOBS APPLIED FOR

- Where you found the job posting—list the specific job board or publication
- The job title and any identifier code

- The company name and address if available
- Contact names and titles, with phone number or e-mails
- The date and time you applied or responded
- Which version of your résumé and cover letter were sent or used to complete the application

IF YOU INTERVIEWED, ADD:

- The names and titles of everyone you spoke with
- The date and time of your interview
- Notes you might need to refer to for a follow-up interview
- What follow-up you took and when—thank-you notes sent, phone calls, etc.

Here is an example of what your "jobs applied for" tracking might look like:

Date	Ad source	Position	Company	Contact	Address/phone	Website	Résumé/application	Result	Follow-up
11/3/10	Omaha job board	Sales associate	unknown	unknown	unknown	unknown	Sales11.1.doc		
11/5/10	Career-builder	Regional sales representative	Meteor Marketing	Sally Cottering, HR	*cotterling@ meteormar -keting.com*	*www. meteormar -keting.com*	Sales.11.5.txt		
11/5/10	Career-builder	Assistant manager, sales	Premium Coffee Co.	unknown	unknown	*www good -coffeesales. com*	Salesmgmt. 10.15.doc		
11/7/10	Omaha sales meet-up	Sales associate	Greens-Jeans Co.	Bertram Green	1444 W. Grand Ave., Omaha Ste. 322	*www.greens -jeans.com*	Sales11.1.doc	phone interview scheduled 11/20/10	

IN A DIFFERENT AREA, RECORD YOUR NETWORKING CONTACTS. FOR THESE, INCLUDE:

- Which event—or where or when you met the person
- The name, business title, and company of each individual, along with contact information
- Notes to help you remember them

What follow-up you took and when e-mail sent, information interview requested, etc.

If a networking contact becomes a "job applied for," simply copy the information to your other tracking sheet.

You can record your entries on paper if you prefer—dedicate a notebook or file to your job hunt—but using computer software like Microsoft Excel will be better. That's because you will be able to search on a company name, sort your search chronologically or alphabetically by any field, and easily add or revise information.

Here is an example of what your "networking" tracking might look like:

Date	Event/network	Name	Company	Address/phone	Website	Follow-up	Result
11/7/10	Omaha sales meet-up	Bertram Green	GreensJeans Co.	1444 W. Grand Ave., Omaha Ste. 322	www.greens-jeans.com	sent e-mail 11/9/10	phone interview scheduled 11/20/10
11/7/10	Omaha sales meet-up	Joe Carlson	Carlson Recruiting	4422 W. Grand Ave., Omaha	www.carl-son-places.com	sent résumé 11/9/10	interview 11/15/10
11/7/10	Omaha sales meet-up	Wendy Maris	GBV Partners	3321 Yarrow St., Omaha	www.gbvpinc.com	sent résumé 11/9/10	
11/15/10	Library job group	Sandra Anders, Regional sales	ABC Corporation	832 SW 124th Place, Omaha	**unknown**	Send article on Google marketing	
11/15/10	Library job group	Sarah Jones, Director of Sales	Meteor Marketing	9324 Great Neck Drive, Omaha	www.mete-or-marketing.com	none	
11/15/10	NSWA Nov. Meeting	Fred Fred-ericks, Sales manager	Premium Coffee Co.	693 W. Grand Ave., Omaha	www.good-cof-feesales.com	requested info interview 11/16/10	Call back after holiday

WHY STAY ORGANIZED?

Primarily, your tracking system will help you remember when and where you applied for jobs and possibly connect some very important dots: when you realize that the person you met at a fund-raiser last week works at a company that just posted a promising job, for example. But it can also help you in other ways:

- You can use your tracking system(s) to set and check your job-hunting goals. For example, you may decide that you must attend at least one networking event every week and collect at least five relevant business cards at each. Your tracking sheet will hold you accountable!
- By logging where you're finding job openings and which ones have netted you results (a phone interview, for example), you can see at a glance which resources are the best. When you take a little time to look at all the data you've collected over a month, you may see that while the majority of jobs you applied to all came from one major online job board, the two interviews you had were for openings you found through a professional networking group.
- Your list of networking contacts may come in handy throughout your

career. Save it, update it, and keep adding to it even after you land your perfect job. These people may be resources for future projects or future employers—or future employees, when you're ready to hire someone in your own department!

FREE ONLINE RESOURCE

Before you set up your perfect tracking system, check out Jibber-Jobber. This is a free online service that provides all sorts of tracking functions, including tracking expenses for your job hunt, interview prep, a calendar, and a contact management function. Basic membership is free, but the premium package will cost you. It's definitely worth a look: http://jobhunt.jib-berjobber.com/index.php.

THE LAST WORD

Be prepared to remain ignorant. That's because many hiring companies simply don't contact job applicants who don't make the cut. Some don't even contact those who make it to the interview stage to let them know "Thanks, but no thanks." You'll send out many résumés, fill out many applications, and shake many hands with absolutely no idea what happened . . . The only thing you can do is follow up if possible and bide your time. Keep your records of jobs applied for, in case the Silent Company does indeed contact you down the road.

CHAPTER 4
WRITING RÉSUMÉS RIGHT

Your résumé holds the most prominent place in your job search. It acts as your foot in the door and your handshake; it summarizes your experience and unique qualifications and is pretty much the single most common step (if not hurdle) in gaining any interview.

While opinions vary on how résumés are used by employers, what they should look like, and the information they should contain, you have to have one—and it should be the best résumé you can manage to create!

> "Your résumé is your opportunity to make a first impression."
>
> **—Jill Silman, SPHR, vice president at Meador Staffing Services and a spokesperson for the Society of Human Resources Management (SHRM)**

7 WAYS YOU'LL USE YOUR RÉSUMÉ

1. As part of networking. In a one-on-one follow-up meeting or at an information interview, ask your new contact to critique your résumé and your experience. This is an acceptable, discreet way to see if your experience and qualifications are in line with the type of position you're looking for.
2. In response to an advertised job opening. Most employers request a copy of your résumé as the very first step in choosing a candidate.
3. As an introduction when no job opening has been advertised. E-mail or hand your résumé to a hiring manager.
4. As the basis for your profile on LinkedIn or for online job applications.
5. Keep a copy handy to refer to for phone interviews and conversation points during networking events.
6. Bring multiple copies to job fairs that you attend.
7. Have at least one copy with you for all in-person interviews.

BEST IN SHOW—RÉSUMÉS

Dikel, Margaret, and Frances Roehm. *The Guide to Internet Job Searching*. (New York: McGraw-Hill, 2008).

McGraw-Hill's Big Red Book of Résumés. (New York: McGraw-Hill, 2002).

Ireland, Susan. *The Complete Idiot's Guide to the Perfect Résumé*. (New York: Alpha Books, 2010).

Whitcomb, Susan Britton. *Résumé Magic*. (Indianapolis, IN: JIST Works, Inc., 1999).

Whitcomb, Susan Britton, and Pat Kendall. *e-Résumés: Everything You Need to Know about Using Electronic Résumés to Tap into Today's Job Market*. (New York: McGraw-Hill, 2002).

The Riley Guide, http://rileyguide.com /resprep.html.

The Damn Good Résumé website, www .damngood.com.

Dummies.com, "Résumés," www.dummies .com/how-to/business-careers/careers/Résumés .html.

RÉSUMÉ WRITING 101
CHRONOLOGICAL VS. FUNCTIONAL RÉSUMÉS

There are two main formats for résumés. The chronological résumé is the most common, listing your work history in order with your most recent job first. The other format is the functional résumé, which contains the same general information and categories as the chronological résumé, only reorganized to highlight your strengths—typically in order to downplay your work history (or lack thereof).

The functional résumé is best used when:

- You are changing careers and your work history doesn't apply very well to your desired position.
- You are a recent graduate or have limited work experience.
- You have long gaps in employment, a widely varied work history, or other work-history issues that may be glaringly obvious in a chronological résumé.

You can begin your functional résumé with a section on "Accomplishments" or "Achievements," where you list three to five skill areas. If possible, use career skills (such as bookkeeping, computer repair, or project management) instead of personal ones (attention to detail, technically savvy, organized). Each accomplishment or skill can be described succinctly. Note that you still need to include a work history section within your functional résumé, but it can be a basic listing of job title, employer, and length of employment.

FOR INSTANCE . . .

The job seeker who just lost his job as regional sales manager of a well-known company is going to highlight his work history—particularly that last job. The newly minted college grad is going to highlight her new information technology degree, her student activities and honors in college, etc.—before listing her history of part-time retail jobs.

REGARDLESS OF FORMAT, ALL RÉSUMÉS SHOULD INCLUDE:

- A letterhead-like heading that includes your name, one phone number and one e-mail address where you can be reached, and possibly your mailing address
- Some work history, no matter how brief or relevant
- Education history (at minimum, schools attended and degrees or certifications earned—or classwork completed)

YOUR RÉSUMÉ MAY INCLUDE:

- A career objective or similar statement about what type of position you're seeking
- Keywords section (see top of p. 38)
- Educational honors, extracurricular activities
- Volunteer work and experience
- Professional honors
- List of professional memberships
- Special skills, software or computer systems mastered, typing speed, etc.

"I don't think everyone has to follow 'hard and fast' résumé rules—it's all relative to the person and their situation."

—Damone Virgilio, staff development manager at Memphis (Tennessee) Public Library

LIBRARY RESOURCES

When you're ready to write or revise your résumé, head straight to your public library to find out what resources they can offer. Ask a reference or business librarian what the library has. In addition to books and possibly Internet-based resources, you may find in-library workshops or classes on résumé writing, or one-on-one résumé review from a librarian or volunteer.

RÉSUMÉ Q&A
Q: I HAVE A LOT OF WORK HISTORY. HOW LONG CAN MY RÉSUMÉ BE?

A: "It depends on the person, the experience, and the job," says Damone Virgilio, staff development manager at Memphis (Tennessee) Public Library. "If there is a lot of experience, you may get into two pages. But my theory is that if you're going to two pages, use *all* of those pages. If you end up with a page and quarter, you need to edit back to a single page." If your résumé is two pages long, keep the most important information on the first page and make sure the second page includes your name.

Q: IS THAT TRUE FOR MY ELECTRONIC RÉSUMÉ?
A: When sending your résumé in the body of an e-mail or copying its content into an online form, the rule is to "write tight." Shorten all sections of text to keep everything as brief as possible. You can bring a printout of the full version of your résumé along to your first interview!

Q: DO I HAVE TO LIST EVERY SINGLE JOB?
A: Not necessarily. If experience is not relevant to the job(s) you're applying for, you can leave it out—unless that will leave a suspicious gap in your work history. Space on your résumé is valuable, so don't waste it on a job that doesn't translate to what you're looking for now.

Q: HOW SHOULD I HANDLE GAPS IN MY EMPLOYMENT?
A: "If a person lacks education, has gaps in their work history or a number of jobs of very short duration, that doesn't look good," says Virgilio. "In these cases, you may focus on the skills you've acquired throughout your career. You still have to list past jobs with dates, but if you pack the front of the résumé with your core competencies and with measurable evidence of achievement, you switch the focus to what you can do."

Q: I'VE NEVER WORKED BEFORE. WHAT SHOULD I PUT IN MY RÉSUMÉ?
A: This is a perfect situation to use a functional résumé format rather than a chronological one. Put the focus on your strengths, knowledge, and intelligence. Start with a statement of what you can offer the hiring company and include the following, if applicable:

- Volunteer work. Don't have any? Get some immediately—preferably something related to your field.
- Work experience. Briefly mention any work experience at all, to show you know how to be responsible and earn a paycheck.
- Internships. New graduates should definitely highlight any they have worked.
- Extracurricular activities, including sports.

THE SKINNY ON CVs

What if a job posting requires a CV? Typically used for academic or research positions, educational administration jobs, or admission to graduate school, a curriculum vitae—CV for short—is Latin for "the course of (one's) life." A CV includes much more detail than a résumé and outlines your academic and professional accomplishments.

For more on CVs, visit www.career.vt.edu /JOBSEARC/Résumés/vitae.htm.

KEYWORDS
THE KEY TO EMPLOYERS FINDING YOU

Later in this chapter you'll learn about creating multiple versions of your résumé—but all versions should include the most crucial component of any job search: keywords.

When your résumé is received by a potential employer, it will be scanned—either by a human or a software program—for keywords. If your résumé doesn't include enough keywords, or the right keywords, it won't even make the first cut.

FOR INSTANCE . . .

You're applying for a position as a payroll clerk. Your résumé might be scanned for the following words and phrases:

- Payroll
- Timekeeping
- Payroll discrepancies
- Verify
- Exemptions
- Earnings and deductions
- Compile
- Analyze
- Names of software programs or degrees specified in the job posting

---

One way to ensure the appropriate keywords end up in every version of your résumé is to include a specific section just for this purpose. In *Job-Hunting Online*, 5th ed., Mark Emery Bolles and Richard Nelson Bolles state, " . . . it has become standard practice to place a line or two at the end of a résumé intended for online submission, headed by the term 'Keywords:' and followed by a series of words, separated by commas, that are designed solely to trigger the search engine when an employer enters his search terms."

Part of Virgilio's job is to help Memphis Public Library patrons create and revise their résumés. He says, "I'll generally insert a table at the top of the résumé and put bullet points of core competencies. This is similar to a keyword section."

If you're changing careers, or looking for your first job in your chosen profession, load keywords into a section on "career goals" or "career objective" so that your résumé will survive the scan.

"Keywords are vital if job seekers are to be found in an online database. . . . Without a doubt, a résumé posted at a career site such as Monster.com will be warehoused in a searchable database. Here, paid subscribers search résumés using keywords . . . the right keywords will determine whether your résumé is 'lost' or 'found.'"

—Susan Britton Whitcomb and Pat Kendall in *e-Résumés: Everything You Need to Know about Using Electronic Résumés to Tap into Today's Job Market*

SOURCES FOR KEYWORDS

How do you find keywords? Virgilio states, "You definitely want to look at the job posting, and get a hold of the job description if you can—that's fantastic. Look at the words used and focus on including those words. Also, look at the industry and use the jargon and terms that employers will look for and recognize."

Another great keywords source is databases available online for free or through your public library's website: "Databases are very good for finding keywords," says Barb Vlk, business librarian at Arlington Heights (Illinois) Public Library. "The best is the *Occupational Outlook Handbook*, published as a free website and in print by the Bureau of Labor Statistics. It's got lots of information under each occupation. Everything there will give you keywords you can use in your résumé."

Vlk's advice is "Start making a list of keywords from all these resources. Then beef up your résumé every time you apply for a job."

BEST IN SHOW—DATABASES

"A lot of people come in looking for help with their résumé-writing skills. Our databases offer great templates and tools that they can use," says Jerome L. Myers, MLS, main library manager at the Tacoma (Washington) Public Library's Education and Job Center.

1. Myers's current favorite database for job-seekers is **JobNow**, which offers services that are free to library patrons. (The library pays a hefty subscription fee.) "JobNow lets you submit your résumé for review by a résumé specialist—you get their suggestions back within twenty-four hours," says Myers. "You can also chat live with someone through JobNow to practice your interview skills. Log in between one and five in the afternoon, and you can have a trial interview. They'll type in an interview question and you respond with your answer, then they critique it and tell you what you should and shouldn't have said."

2. "The **Testing and Education Center** database from Gale has a feature where you can store your résumé as a PDF. Most people bring a flash drive" so they can carry their résumés home or use them on different computers, says Myers.

3. "**The Job and Career Accelerator** has a component where you can research careers. It also includes job listings for a real job search."

Myers explains, "Some databases are more user-friendly than others. Some are easier to use and might seem too basic to some users."

READY TO WRITE?

For many people, getting started on writing or revising their résumé is the toughest part. Follow these steps to get past "résumé-writer's block":

1. Look at sample résumés to get ideas. Check out books on résumé writing from your library or look at samples online. One site to visit is http://wetfeet.com/Experienced-Hire/Résumé—Cover-letter.aspx.

2. Dump all information for your work history and education into a word-processing document. Double-check the dates, titles, and details of each job position; make sure your education, grade point average, or other information is included; then save that document.

3. Write to your audience. How can your experience, skills, and degrees benefit *them?* How will your work history translate to learning a new job?

4. Next, outline the information and add sections as preferred: keywords, summary statement, etc.

5. Go back and edit. Tighten up the writing to keep it concise and action-oriented (lots of verbs) and include focus on specific accomplishments or responsibilities. You don't have to use complete sentences; bulleted lists of statements are best.

6. Once you feel you have a complete draft, format the document so that it's visually appealing.

7. Proofread the final document twice, then once reading it backward.

8. Ask at least one other person to review it and proofread it again.

9. Save your final document and prepare to rewrite a version for each job you apply for.

> "People will hire you for one of two reasons: because they want to make money or they want to save money. So anything you can say in your résumé to show you've done that in the past is guaranteed to get you noticed. Use specific numbers, percentages, budget responsibility, etc., to demonstrate what you've done."
>
> **—Jill Silman, SPHR, vice president at Meador Staffing Services and a spokesperson for the Society of Human Resources Management (SHRM)**

FORMATTED AND PLAIN-TEXT RÉSUMÉS

Today's job seeker will most likely be submitting résumés via e-mail or websites. So you'll need your beautifully formatted word-processing document to use for a hard-copy résumé, but you'll also need to be ready to have an electronic and plain-text version as well, so you can quickly submit your résumé according to the job posting's requirements. Here's an overview of these résumé formats:

YOUR FORMATTED RÉSUMÉ

So you've written a solid draft of your résumé in a word-processing program such as Microsoft Word. What should it look like?

RÉSUMÉ-FORMATTING DOs AND DON'Ts

DO start with your biggest selling point. "I like to recommend a section at the beginning of the résumé that stands out, something that brings out the best that the person can bring to the table," says Virgilio. "It could be a list of skills, certifications, or software mastered. You have to emphasize what separates you from the pack."

DON'T cram in as many words as possible to fill up the page. This makes it uninviting to read or even skim. "Someone who's looking through 150 résumés is looking for a reason to eliminate as many as possible," Virgilio points out. "If a résumé is not easy to read, they're going to throw it out." He recommends using a 12-point font with at least the standard space between lines.

DO edit every job description down to the most salient points. "One of the biggest problems I see with résumés that people bring in is formatting," says Virgilio. "I see lots of text on a page with way too much description of duties, so nothing jumps out."

DON'T forget to proofread! A résumé with a typo will end up in the trash can. "My advice is as basic as please, please, please proofread anything before you send it," says Jill Silman, SPHR, vice president at Meador Staffing Services and a spokesperson for the Society of Human Resources Management (SHRM). "Use the old trick of reading something backward to make sure your mind doesn't jump ahead."

DO print out the résumé on good-quality white (or off-white) paper. Always have a crisp, clean copy or two ready at an in-person interview.

Once you have your résumé final and looking good, you can print it out and use as hard copies, or send it as an e-mail attachment—either as a Microsoft Word or PDF document. If you use a word-processing program other than Word, you should save it as a file type that anyone can open—and these days, that includes Word files. Other options are PDFs or Rich Text Files.

A CASE FOR SENDING PDFs

"We always have people do a Word document, then tell the person they can save it as a PDF and e-mail it," reports Virgilio. "A PDF can't be inadvertently changed by someone else, and any computer can read it—you don't have to worry about software versions. It also shows a bit of tech savvy on the sender's part—you know how to make a PDF."

If you don't have Adobe PDF Writer, you can download free software that allows you to easily convert a document into a PDF. PDFCreator is available at http://sourceforge.net/projects /pdfcreator. (For Windows systems only.)

YOUR PLAIN-TEXT RÉSUMÉ

In addition to your carefully formatted résumé, you'll want a plain-text version as well—one that has all formatting and special characters stripped out. You will use this to copy and paste into the body of an e-mail (see "send two in one" below) or to copy and paste sections into an online application form. Some employers may even request that you send in this version, if they are using certain software to scan all submitted résumés.

TURN YOUR RÉSUMÉ INTO A JOB APPLICATION

Many of the general job boards (including CareerBuilder.com and Monster.com) include an online application for any position; this is where you'll copy and paste your plain-text résumé into appropriate fields. The employer will never see your actual résumé—until you hand it over at your first in-person interview.

Here are five tips for turning your résumé into a plain-text document:

1. Strip out all formatting, including bold, italics, centering. Use one typeface and size—preferably something commonly used like Times or Arial.
2. Change formatting to remove columns or tabbed sections.
3. Remove bullet points.
4. Remove hard returns at the end of lines.
5. Save your document as a text file with the extension .txt to ensure all invisible coding is stripped out.
6. Review the plain-text document using a text editor program such as Notepad or SimpleText to ensure you're seeing it accurately.

ASC WHAT?

A plain-text document may also be called an ASCII file—pronounced ASK-ee. ASCII is short for American Standard Code of Information Interchange. Saving a document as a text file and stripping out all coding and special characters (characters that use keyboard commands such as accented e's or em dashes) is basically the same thing as creating an ASCII file.

SENDING RÉSUMÉS BY E-MAIL

When you respond to a job posting—especially an online posting—you will more than likely be submitting your résumé electronically. But what exactly does that mean? Here is a handy checklist of points to consider.

1. Meet their requirements. Double-check any details on *what* the employer requires from applicants and *how* they wish to receive it. If possible, check the employer's company website for information on preferred method.

NOTE: If a job posting simply says "e-mail your résumé . . .," then it's safest to send your résumé as plain text (see below) within the body of your e-mail—with no attachment.

If the employer requests an attached file for the résumé, do they specify what file type? They may want résumés only submitted as Microsoft Word documents, or PDFs, or plain-text files, depending on their screening procedures.

2. Don't get blocked! With today's sophisticated spam filters, many company e-mail servers will block all attachments from certain types of e-mail addresses—or they may block only certain types of attachments such as Zip files or PDFs.

3. Send two in one. If an employer requests your résumé as a Word document, PDF, or other attachment, your best bet is to attach your résumé as requested, but also copy and paste the plain-text version of your résumé into the body of the e-mail. That way, if your attachment is not received, your résumé will still be in their hands.

4. Choose your subject line carefully. The subject line—the text that appears in the receiver's in-box—should make it clear what your e-mail is in response to and perhaps sell you a little, too. If responding to a specific job opening, use the job title or code used in the posting. If you're sending your résumé unsolicited, make the subject line a descriptor of you: "Database manager with 12 years experience" or "Physical therapist seeks challenging opportunity."

5. Be savvy about attachment names. If you're sending your résumé as an attachment, make sure you name it so that it's easily identifiable. Yourlastname_résumé.doc is your best bet—and be sure to include the extension .doc or .pdf so that it can be opened easily!

CUSTOMIZE YOUR RÉSUMÉ

"These days, you create a master résumé, and then every time you apply for a job you have to save it and tweak it for that specific job."
—Barb Vlk, business librarian at Arlington Heights (Illinois) Public Library

You'll never finish writing your résumé.

That's because every time you apply for a posted job opening, you should review your original résumé, save it as a new document, and then revise to best match the advertised opening. This might include changing or adding keywords, shifting emphasis within your work history, tweaking your summary statement, or all of the above.

Keep all versions of your résumé so that you can refer to which document you sent to which employer—and so that you have multiple versions to fine-tune for future applications. This is true for both your formatted résumés and your plain-text résumés.

Why do you need to keep all those résumés? Let's say you e-mailed a résumé to apply for a job two weeks ago, and now you need a print copy for your first interview. Which version did you send? You'd better find out, so that all copies of your résumé match exactly!

That's why you need to include your résumé version in your job-search tracking system.

If you do your job searching and résumé writing from more than one computer—or if you want to take information to your public library to revise or apply—consider keeping all your résumés on a flash drive, so you can update, revise, and send from another computer if necessary.

One last word on creating multiple versions of your résumé: Be sure to thoroughly proofread all new versions before you send them out!

POSTING YOUR RÉSUMÉ ONLINE

Many job boards and career-oriented sites allow you to post a version (or more) of your résumé so that hiring companies and recruiters can find you. This is typically done by filling out an online form (copying and pasting from your best plain-text version).

KEEP IT CONTAINED

While it may seem like a great idea to post your résumé everywhere you possibly can in order to get the most exposure, consider this: it's a better idea to maintain control of your own information. Don't allow a site to "blast" your résumé to various places and don't fill out a profile that contains all your personal contact information. This will protect you from e-mail spam, unwanted contacts, and even identity theft!

Consider this strategy instead: definitely post one or more versions of your résumé on CareerBuilder.com and/or monster.com, as well as a couple of more specialized job sites for your industry or region. But before you choose those smaller sites, read their privacy policies to see if they can sell or share your information.

KEEP IT PRIVATE

If you're discreetly looking for a new job while still employed, keep in mind that your posted résumés may be found by coworkers and supervisors at your current employer. If you want to keep your job search on the down low, you can remove employer company names and replace with descriptors. If your current employer is Advanced Computer Systems and you don't want to be found by a search on that name, replace with "midsize technology consulting company."

Position applied for	Company	Résumé used	Date sent
Sales associate	GoodJeans Co.	Sales11.1.doc	11/3/10
Regional sales representative	Meteor Marketing	Sales.11.5.txt	11/5/10
Assistant manager, sales	Premium Coffee Co.	Salesmgmt.10.15.doc	11/5/10

KEEP IT FRESH

It's true for the large job sites and may be for some smaller sites, as well: when you revise and update your résumé, it moves back to the top of the list in associated databases. So try to add or change something every month or so to "refresh" your standings.

CREATING YOUR OWN RÉSUMÉ SITE

Another way to share your résumé with potential employers is to post it on your own website, or simply create a one-page site that is your résumé.

An added bonus for those job seekers who show portfolios of their work, such as graphic designers or architects: you can post samples on the same site.

Pros and Cons

Pros

1. A web-based résumé is easy to share during networking, telephone interviews, and other meetings—just tell the other person the URL where it can be found.
2. Employers and recruiters may find you first, if they are searching the web for candidates with keywords.
3. An online résumé can include live links to your work samples, previous employers' websites, etc.

Cons

1. You'll need to purchase or find space on a web server to host your résumé—and hire someone to create an HTML page from your current résumé, or learn how to do it yourself.
2. If you're currently employed and your employer doesn't know you're looking for a new job, your résumé may pop up during a Google search.
3. Forget about the various versions of your résumé—you should post only one, which might end up being too limiting.

If you're a university student or recent grad, check with your school to see if provides web space for graduates.

One last word: **Don't** use your personal or family website to hold your résumé. Pictures of your grandchildren—or of you cavorting at a wedding—are not to be associated with your search. If you decide to post your résumé online, keep it separate!

WHAT HIRERS SAY

As you're sending out dozens of résumés, answering online job ads every day, and cold-calling local companies, do you ever wonder what the people at the other end of your job search are thinking? Here are a few "inside tips" from professionals who read résumés like yours every day:

Jill Silman, SPHR, vice president at Meador Staffing Services and a spokesperson for the Society of Human Resources Management (SHRM), says that her recruiting company receives résumés by e-mail (as attachments) or uploaded to their website. Therefore, "The more plainly they're formatted, the better. We prefer [Word documents] so that if we need to reformat it for a client, we can." She encourages job seekers to also check the format of their résumé for consistency: "If you put one employer name in boldface, use boldface for all of them."

Her company keeps résumés in a database and searches on keywords for each specific opening: "We get some résumés that have a keywords section, and that's fine—I don't have a problem with that. We do see some where the person has been counseled to put keywords in small, white type at the bottom of the résumé so they're invisible; the problem with that is that if the words aren't used in the body of the résumé, when the recruiter goes to look at the résumé, they can't see the words."

Dionna Keels, a member of the SHRM (Society for Human Resource Management) staffing management expertise panel, says,

"I definitely prefer a Word document that's nicely formatted. Your formatting is really important. A résumé that's formatted well is more appealing to the eye and it's easier to read."

She adds, "What's important now is that people are able to point out specific things they've accomplished rather than a laundry list of job duties. Include measurable accomplishments, such as 'I saved x amount of dollars by improving a process.'"

And if your work history includes gaps or multiple short stays at jobs, Keels recommends, "Consider including a footnote about why you left. That way you're not leaving it up to the recruiter's imagination." Another option is to address the issue in your cover letter.

THE LAST WORD

The job seeker who has been on the market for a while will end up with many, many different versions of her résumé. Be precise in naming each document, use electronic folders for different categories, and periodically refresh your memory as to which jobs you've applied for. That way, when you come across an open position you want to apply for, you can quickly decide which résumé version to work with, find that document and revise to fit the opening, and you're good to go. Just remember to save and file the new résumé, as well!

CHAPTER 5
CRAFTING EFFECTIVE COVER LETTERS

As with résumés, just about every job-search expert seems to have a different opinion on the worth of cover letters. But we're here to tell you: cover letters matter. A good one can enhance your résumé. A great one can move it to the top of the stack. A lousy one ... well, you get the picture.

> "We don't see many cover letters anymore, but they are very important. The letter is your opportunity to really sell yourself."
>
> **—Jill Silman, SPHR, vice president at Meador Staffing Services and a spokesperson for the Society of Human Resources Management (SHRM)**

COVER ALL BASES

A cover letter serves multiple purposes. Traditionally, it has served as a formal introduction, but a savvy job seeker can use it to do so much more. For example:

- You can show off your knowledge of the company or industry that you learned thorough research.
- You can highlight a specific skill or experience you have that's a great match for this opening.
- You can explain—briefly and with a positive spin—any possible red flags in your résumé, such as a long gap in employment or multiple short-term jobs.
- You can demonstrate your sharp communication skills and business writing abilities with a well-crafted letter.
- You can let your personality peek through a little. Show some enthusiasm and verve in describing how much you want the position!

CUSTOMIZE EACH COVER

Always write a fresh cover letter to match the job you're applying for. It's even more important to customize the cover letter than the résumé. That's because you use the letter to pinpoint why you are perfect for this particular job. Study the job description or posted ad carefully and make sure you address every point mentioned.

And be sure to save all your cover letter versions just as you do your résumés; you'll want to pull phrases and sentences from previous letters to build current ones. It's not as important to keep track of cover letters after you send them, but your letter may come in handy as a reminder of the key skills or accomplishments you spelled out for a particular job.

Finally, remember to proofread every single version of your cover letter before you send it. A single typo or misspelled word spells R-E-J-E-C-T-I-O-N.

BEST IN SHOW—COVER LETTERS

Betrus, Michael. *202 Great Cover Letters*. (New York: McGraw-Hill, 2008).

Enelow, Wendy, and Louise Kursmark. *Cover Letter Magic*. (Indianapolis, IN: JIST Works, 2010).

Yate, Martin. *Knock 'em Dead Cover Letters: Great Letter Techniques and Samples for Every Step of Your Search*. (Avon, MA: Adams Media, 2008).

Wall Street Journal Careers site, "How to Write a Cover Letter," http://guides.wsj .com/careers/how-to-start-a-job-search /how-to-writea-cover-letter/.

Dummies.com, "Cover Letters," www .dummies.com/how-to/business-careers/careers /Cover-Letters.html.

Purdue Online Writing Lab, "Cover Letters," http://owl.english.purdue.edu/engagement/index .php?category_id=34&sub_category_id=42.

WRITING THE PERFECT LETTER, TOP TO BOTTOM

Once you get the hang of it, writing a cover letter is easy. You can follow this simple outline—just take it from the top and work your way down the steps.

START AT THE TOP

Always use a formal business letter style and format. (See example, p. 50.)

YOUR INFORMATION:

As with any business letter, your name and contact information should appear at the top. If you're formatting a document, it's a good idea to use the same layout and font you use on your résumé. Otherwise, simply type it in below the date. Include the contact information the employer will need, especially phone number and e-mail address.

DATE:

Unless your cover letter appears in the body of an e-mail message, date it. If you're writing your draft over the weekend, for example, use the date you plan to drop the letter in the mail so the letter looks as recent as possible.

SALUTATION:

Ideally, you will use the recipient's name, as in "Dear Mr. Brown:"; because few job postings include a person's name, try browsing the company website LinkedIn and other Internet sources to see if you can find the name of the current department head, hiring manager, or HR professional. If you can't find a name that you're certain will be the end reader, use something like "Dear Human Resources Professional:" or "Dear IT Manager:" as an opener.

Anything but the frigid "Dear Sir or Madam:" or "To Whom It May Concern:"!

OPEN WITH YOUR STRONG SUIT

Start the body of your letter by identifying the position you're applying for. Don't assume the reader will know this; their organization may have multiple positions open. Other things to include in your first paragraph:

- If you've been referred by, or know, someone whom the reader knows, mention their name right off the bat: "Your director of operations, Samantha Samuels, suggested I contact you. . . ."
- If you don't have an "in" or introduction, find a strong start. For example, showcase your knowledge of the hiring company or department, or of the industry. This is where the research that you'll learn to do in Chapter 7 will really pay off!

THE MIDDLE MATTERS

Now that your first paragraph has caught the reader's attention, hit 'em with your sales pitch. The second paragraph should highlight your qualification, skill, or experience that makes you the best candidate for this particular job. Don't simply restate your résumé, but pull out one or two points and expand on them, with a focus on how they can be applied to the open position and that employer.

If you want to touch on multiple points, one way to stay concise is to use bullet points. This makes your letter shorter and easier to read.

MAKE YOUR CLOSING ARGUMENTS

Use your final paragraph for what direct marketers call a "call to action." Encourage the reader to contact you and let her know you're interested in the job. But if you have—or can get—the telephone number of the hiring manger or HR professional you are addressing, say that *you* will call *her* next week and do it! If you can keep control of the contact rather than passively waiting by the phone, take advantage—just don't become a pest.

Include a "thank you" to the reader—for her consideration, for her interest, or for her prompt attention.

When signing off of a cover letter, use "Sincerely" or "Yours Truly" above your signature. These are the most businesslike options.

Add a P.S. below your signature. Direct marketers know that a postscript stands out and that letter readers will skip down to read that first. So use that "last word" for something important.

ESSENTIAL WRITING TIPS

While you're drafting each cover letter, keep these tips in mind:

- Keep it short. Each letter should be just one page with plenty of white space.

- Whether you're e-mailing or mailing the letter, it's a good idea to refer to your attached or enclosed résumé— this directs the reader to look at that important document.

- Try to avoid starting every line or every paragraph with the word "I." You don't have to twist your words too much to change "I can do this" and "I can do that" to "ABC Corporation's data entry department provides the perfect opportunity for me to. . . ."

- Keep using those keywords! Recruiter Jill Silman says her firm scans each cover letter with its résumé—and is included in a keyword search. "The cover letter and résumé are really treated as one document," she says.

FORMATTING YOUR COVER LETTER

Your cover letter should match your résumé. Use the same typeface and type size in both. If you have a graphical or fancy heading for your contact information at the top of your résumé, repeat it in your cover letter. Use the same margin widths.

And as with all business letters, your cover letter should be single-spaced.

EXAMPLE OF FORMATTED LETTER (Condensed for space)

October 12, 2011

Eva M. Thornton
1234 S. Bly Ave., Apt. 23
Baton Rouge, LA 49302

evamthornton@122.com

123/345/5678

Dear Human Resources Professional:

Your job posting on Batonrougejobs.com for a sales support associate sounds like a good fit for my skills and experience—especially given your company's recent acquisition of ABC Technology. As you can see by my enclosed résumé,

- I have experience supporting a sales team at TRG Industries, where we sold customized computer components for the restaurant industry. There I quickly learned the ins and outs of a new market, technical components, and sales service.
- I am proficient in Microsoft Office software as well as Access and have completed extensive coursework in Word and Access.
- My previous jobs working in retail sales gave me invaluable experience in customer relations, handling complaints, and working as a member of a team.

Please feel free to contact me by phone or e-mail. I'd be happy to come in to meet with you in person. Thank you for your consideration.

Sincerely,

Eva M. Thornton

P.S. Your posting requested that I state my salary requirements. At my last job I was earning $36,000 per year and shared my team's annual bonus. I am looking for a position that would offer a salary comparable to that.

SALARY REQUIREMENTS: GIVE THEM WHAT THEY WANT

If the job posting calls for applicants to give their salary history or salary requirements, you'd better include it! Countless hirers and recruiters said that if they ask for this and don't see it, that résumé doesn't make the cut.

Your cover letter is the ideal place for this. (Consider using your valuable P.S. slot to convey the information.) To give yourself the most flexibility, give the most general information.

Your salary history might consist of:

"I started my last position with an annual salary of $43,000, and when I left I was earning $46,500."

Your salary requirements might state:

"I am looking for a position that offers a salary in the range of $43,000 to $50,000."

You will, of course, do your salary research before you state any requirements so that you're sure your expectations are realistic! (See Chapter 9.)

E-MAILING YOUR COVER LETTER

When answering a job posting by e-mail, the body of your e-mail message serves as your cover letter. It's a good idea to draft the letter in a word-processing document so that you can easily edit, proofread, spell-check, and save it—and when you have a final version, then copy and paste that into your e-mail. Proofread one more time before sending to check line breaks and remove bullet points and other formatting that might not appear properly.

Other tips for using your e-mail as a cover letter:

- E-mails often tend to be rushed, informal, and terse. Do not allow this with your "cover e-mail." You should still use formal language.
- If your e-mail program allows, create an automatic e-mail signature that includes your contact information. This way you don't have to type it in every time.
- If you don't use an e-mail signature, be sure to include your phone number *and* e-mail address in the body of the letter. Your call to action close is the perfect place for this.
- Obviously, you won't sign your e-mail, but still use the business close "Sincerely" or "Yours Truly," followed by your full name.

HOW TO HANDLE HARD COPIES

It's rare that you will end up mailing or giving a prospective employer a hard copy of your cover letter and résumé. But if you do, be sure to print both documents out on the same good-quality paper and remember to sign the cover letter!

If you're mailing your résumé and cover letter, fold both documents together and use a #10 envelope.

THE LAST WORD

When you come across a job opening that sounds like a great fit, it's natural to want to hurry up and get your application or résumé in fast. But slow down—take the time to do some research so that you write specific information or ideas related to that position into your letter. Make sure you understand current salary and benefits ranges for the position, too, so you can base any salary information on that research.

Then sit down and write a carefully crafted, pinpoint-specific, killer cover letter. Proofread it, proofread it again, and then, before you hit that send button or lick that envelope flap, remember to proofread it.

CHAPTER 6

MASTERING TWENTY-FIRST-CENTURY NETWORKING

"A very important tip that people forget about: you have to work your network. People hire based on relationships, so if you know anyone who works for a company with an opening, that can greatly increase your chances."

—Damone Virgilio, staff development manager at Memphis (Tennessee) Public Library

"Networking is *huge* now. The more people you meet, the more likely they will search for you. And of course you can do a lot of networking online."

—Dionna Keels, member of Society for Human Resource Management (SHRM) staffing management expertise panel

Y ou may be able to find a great job all on your own. But it is much, much, *much* more likely that someone else—maybe a lot of some-ones—is going to personally connect you to that perfect job. So start working the power of network-ing, both face-to-face and online. Make connections with people you know and the people *they* know, and with people in the industry and the organizations you want to work in—and it's likely you'll connect to some major help in your job search.

What can networking do for you?

- Lead to information on job openings not yet posted
- Lead to an inside connection at a company who may put in a good word for you
- Provide you with insights and ideas into an industry or profession that's new to you
- Give you guidance in your job-search methods, including résumé review

> "When people come to us and I sit down with them, I tell them the top ways people find jobs these days are networking and through company websites."
> —**Barb Vlk, business librarian at Arlington Heights (Illinois) Public Library**

BEST IN SHOW—NETWORKING

Benjamin, Susan. *Perfect Phrases for Professional Networking: Hundreds of Ready-to-Use Phrases for Meeting and Keeping Helpful Contacts Everywhere You Go.* (New York: McGraw-Hill, 2009).

Hansen, Katharine. *A Foot in the Door: Networking Your Way into the Hidden Job Market.* (Berkeley, CA: Ten Speed Press, 2008).

Levinson, Jay Conrad. *Guerrilla Networking: A Proven Battle Plan to Attract the Very People You Want to Meet.* (Bloomington, IN: AuthorHouse, 2009).

McKay, Harvey. *Dig Your Well Before You're Thirsty: The Only Networking Book You'll Ever Need.* (New York: Currency Books, 1999).

Pierson, Orville. *Highly Effective Networking: Meet the Right People and Get a Great Job.* (Pompton Plains, NJ: Career Press, 2009).

YOUR NETWORKING TOOLKIT
TOOL #1: A FINE-TUNED ELEVATOR PITCH

You've heard of an elevator pitch, right? It's a brief—no more than two-minute—explanation that you can state in the time it takes to share an elevator ride. Practice your own pitch, telling who you are and what you want, so you can be ready to introduce yourself clearly, succinctly and without rambling into why you lost your last job or how long you've been unemployed.

TOOL #2: A BOX OF BUSINESS CARDS

Have brand-new business cards printed for your job search. (It is a definite DON'T to use business cards from a previous or current position to look for a job!) It's cheap, easy, and fast to get hundreds of cards printed that you can use to network during your job search. These cards should include:

- Your name and the contact information you want potential employers to use. (Do not use your work phone or e-mail address, or your partyanimal@yahoo.com address!)
- The job title you want—or, if more practical, a general industry or profession. You want the card recipient to quickly understand what you're looking for when they come across your card days later.
- Three to six bullet points on the back that list your strengths
- If you have a website with additional information or an online portfolio, include your URL.
- Space for writing a personalized note

TOOL #3: A WELL-HONED STRATEGY

The better you plan your networking, the better it will work for you. Take time to determine what types of people may best help you in your search, and where you might find them. For example, if you're looking for people who can help you get your foot in the door with an IT career, what groups or associations might they belong to? What meetings might healthcare administrators attend? When is the next national conference related to your industry coming to town? Do your research before you choose a local networking venue!

NETWORKING WITH THOSE YOU KNOW

Before you attend your first formal networking event, work your own network. Contact the following people in your life to let them know you're looking for a job, what type of job you want, and how they might help you:

- Extended family members
- Friends
- Neighbors
- Former work colleagues
- Former classmates
- Fellow members of your church, clubs, civic organizations, etc.
- Everyone else you know

You might feel uncomfortable approaching people you haven't spoken to in a long time, or who may not seem appropriate to contact. But once you get over your initial apprehension, you'll find that businesspeople find networking a perfectly natural thing.

FOR INSTANCE . . .

"When I first decided to go freelance, I had only a few clients lined up. So I fearlessly listed all the people I knew who might hire me—then proceeded to call only the 'easy' ones. Within a year, I got phone calls from two of the people on my list who I had not had the nerve to call for work. Each one had heard through the grapevine that I was a freelancer and had a project to offer! If I had only called those managers right away, I might have gotten even more work."

—Jane Jerrard, freelance writer, Chicago, Illinois

USE THE STRENGTH OF WEAK TIES

Ask your social network to spread the word of your job search to *their* networks. According to sociologist Mark Granovetter, author of "The Strength of Weak Ties," the people who are most helpful to us are those we don't know well. Granovetter's theory posits that in marketing or politics, the weak ties enable reaching audiences that are not accessible via strong ties. Granovetter told *Forbes* magazine that "informal contacts" account for almost 75 percent of all successful job searches.

In other words, if your brother can't help you get a job, it's more likely that his buddy—or his buddy's buddy—might be able to.

NETWORKING GROUPS, EVENTS, AND MEETINGS

How do you find local networking opportunities? Ask a librarian, check a directory, or surf the web—or ideally, do all three. Your best bet is to find associations or networking groups affiliated with the career you're looking for. Join local chapters or groups, or just attend their meetings. There may be a fee for joining and/or one for attending, but if you choose the groups carefully, these are wise investments.

"You start with your local library or any type of local organization. Call them up or check their websites and find out if there are any networking groups or job clubs."
—**Barb Vlk, business librarian at Arlington Heights Public Library (Illinois)**

Example: The Career Center of the Cuyahoga County (Ohio) Public Library has four permanent job clubs, serving forty or fifty people.

If you join an association, make your membership pay off by getting involved. Volunteer to work on the newsletter, meeting programs, board of directors, or other areas. This will increase your visibility and expand your network within the group.

ONLINE RESOURCES FOR FINDING F2F NETWORKING

Browse the many groups included in the websites Meetup.com and LinkedIn to find local groups of like-minded professionals who meet in person:

- At www.meetup.com, you can enter your town and area of interest to find groups that meet regularly in-person. Whether your interest is "web development" or "skiing," the groups you find exist solely to help you meet and network with like-minded people in your area!
- www.linkedin.com also offers a multitude of groups, only some of which meet in person. Click on "groups" at the top of any LinkedIn page, then "Groups Directory." When you search the groups, select "Networking Groups" and type in the category and keywords that fit your job search.

"Associations geared toward your industry give you an opportunity to meet people, maybe volunteer, and make personal connections."
—**Dionna Keels, member of Society for Human Resource Management (SHRM) staffing management expertise panel**

JOB SUPPORT GROUPS

"As far as resources, I've collected a list of networking groups in our area. And I start every [library] program and class by saying coming to this event is networking too."

—Barb Vlk, business librarian at Arlington Heights Public Library (Illinois)

What librarian Vlk calls "the infamous networking support group" offers terrific networking opportunities as well as an ego boost. "That word *support* is key," says Vlk. "You need someone to talk to about your job search, and you need reinforcement that you're not alone and it's not your fault."

How does a job support group work? Here is an example of the groups run by Bob Podgorski, coordinator of the St. Hubert Job and Networking Ministry, which offers nondenominational job groups throughout the northwest suburbs of Chicago. Podgorski says, "Group networking typically involves being in a group of anywhere from six or seven people to thirty or forty people. Each individual provides an elevator speech—a two-minute overview of her skills, abilities, achievements and job desires—followed by a request for assistance from the group. Typically, contacts are sought, or help with identifying companies in key industries, or even suggestions of alternate industries where the person might apply their skills and background.

A résumé or handbill is passed around to the group so that everyone has your basic information and contact information. A handbill is preferred—this is a concise, to-the-point, one-page document that provides a section that lists target companies.

The real benefit of the group is the strength of weak ties theory: "People know people who know people," Podgorski points out. "A support group broadens your visibility to the point where you get the broadest distribution possible."

Job support groups work best when you target industries, occupations, and key company contacts that you'd like. You need to ask for help as precisely as possible in order to get the best help. Including a job title helps. It's a concise way for people to quickly understand what you want.

"Association meetings and industry networking events aren't necessarily (or likely to be) focused on job search," says Podgorski. "Job-search support groups are. Their entire goal is to get individuals to find jobs."

NETWORK THROUGH VOLUNTEERING

Another great way to target your networking is through volunteer work. While any community or civic volunteering will increase the number of people you meet, consider zeroing in on either gaining valuable professional experience, or demonstrating your skills:

- Looking for a marketing position? Offer to write news releases, promote fundraising events, and create a marketing plan for the local charity you're interested in.
- Aiming for a career transition to retail sales? Offer to man the counter at your local food pantry.
- Not sure of your career path? Volunteer for a community or national charity and meet professionals from all walks of life. Find out what they do for a living, what it's like, and whether it would be a good fit for you.

You can add new skills or strengthen others through the right volunteer position:

- Want to learn to sell? Offer to fundraise!
- Want to master public speaking? Volunteer to give one or more presentations to the local chapter!
- Want to gain some leadership experience? Sign up to lead a committee, or serve on the board!

Volunteering is also a great way to plug gaps in your work history. If you can point to some professional work you've done in the year you've been unemployed, it looks good!

STEPS FOR IN-PERSON NETWORKING EVENTS BEFORE YOU GO:

1. Craft—and practice—a one- or two-minute introduction of yourself and what you do or would like to do

(your elevator pitch). This might be different for different networking opportunities.

2. Have a couple of conversation points ready—perhaps on the latest news within the industry. When in doubt, ask the other person about herself.

3. Set one specific goal before each event. Examples:

- Are you looking for a job lead?
- An information interview?
- Someone to review your résumé and job-search plan?
- Tips on breaking into the industry?

WHILE YOU'RE THERE:

1. Keep plenty of your business cards on hand (literally—you can put your hand on one without fumbling in your purse or briefcase), along with a pen.

2. Work the room. No matter how shy or uncomfortable you may feel, approach people and introduce yourself.

3. Find the "movers and shakers." Use your powers of observation, the goodwill of the meeting's organizer or greeter, and ask questions of others you approach to find the people at the event who are most likely to help you—whether you think they are the officers of the association, employees of certain companies you

are prospecting, or "big names" in the industry.

4. Be efficient with your time and with others'. This includes coming prepared to politely disengage yourself from unproductive conversations.

5. Don't ask anyone to hire you. Instead, ask for their help and advice with your search.

6. Hand out your business card to everyone you meet and ask for theirs. If you discuss anything you'd like to follow up on, jot down a note to yourself on their card.

WHEN YOU GET HOME:

1. Whom did you meet? Look through the business cards you collected and add any notes you might have missed while the event is still fresh in your mind.

2. Go to your LinkedIn profile and invite the most promising contacts you made to join your network. (See "online networking", p. 61.)

3. Organize your contacts. Ideally, you should do this electronically so that your growing database of job-search contacts is searchable. You can use Microsoft Outlook or create an Excel spreadsheet. Include the person's contact information, title and company, where and when you

met him (every time if ongoing), and any notes about his background or expertise that might aid your search.

4. Follow up if you said you would—or even if you didn't, in the case of the most valuable contacts you made.

5. Review the networking that you did, and what you'd like to do differently the next time you go out.

FOR INSTANCE . . .

Say you land an interview at the Promising Company. The name sounds familiar, so you search your electronic database of networking contacts to find the Promising manager you met a couple of months ago. You can leverage this connection a number of ways: contact her before your interview to reconnect, ask for her overview of the workplace; consider asking her to put in a good word for you—she may reap a finder's fee for doing so; and bring up her name during your interview to demonstrate your connection to the Promising Company.

FOLLOWING UP:

1. If you agreed to follow up with someone you met, call or e-mail the person within a day or two, while your encounter is still fresh in her mind.

2. Suggest a prescheduled phone call or an in-person meeting as an opportunity to discuss your goals. If she is amenable to a one-on-one meeting, suggest having coffee near her office or home, and pick up the tab.

3. Again, don't ask for a job—ask for advice, industry information, leads, etc. Sample questions:

• How do you/your company generally seek job candidates these days? Online job boards, or through recruiters?
• Can you recommend professional associations or industry networking organizations that I should join?
• What is your opinion of the state of our industry today?

4. Be sure to open that follow-up conversation with a big THANK-YOU and end it with an offer or question about how you can help them. Don't be a user! Networking is a two-way street.

Here is what your networking contact tracking system might look like:

Name	Company	Title	Where met	Follow-up
Sandra Anders	ABC Corporation	Regional sales	5/12/10 library meeting	Send article on Google marketing
Sarah Jones	Meteor Marketing	Director of Sales	5/12/10 library meeting	None
Fred Fredericks	Premium Coffee Co.	Sales manager	May meeting—NSWA	Call for information int.

ONLINE NETWORKING

While face-to-face networking is crucial, you can turbo-boost the number of professionals you meet and connect with by using social media websites, online discussion groups, and other web-based tools.

Remember—the Internet provides many respected and relevant sites you can use to "see and be seen."

SIGN UP NOW!

Here are the basic sites to visit, check out, and sign up for in order to network online:

- LinkedIn: The undisputed champion of online networking for professionals
- Facebook: This highly personal site can be used to your advantage
- Meetup.com: This networking site can help you organize or join groups in your community.
- Online discussion forums on sites for appropriate professional associations, including "affinity groups" such as the American Assembly for Men in Nursing and the California Association of Black Lawyers

- The website for your alumni association
- Twitter

Most, if not all, sites will require you to sign up with some personal information and create a user name and password for future use. Remember to keep track of these names and passwords so that you can get back into a site once you've registered!

BEST IN SHOW—ONLINE NETWORKING

Crompton, Diane, and Ellen Sautter. *Find a Job Through Social Networking: Use LinkedIn, Twitter, Facebook, Blogs and More to Advance Your Career.* (Indianapolis, IN: JIST Works, 2010).

Jacoway, Kristen. *I'm in a Job Search—Now What???: Using LinkedIn, Facebook, and Twitter as Part of Your Job Search Strategy.* (Cupertino, CA: Happy About, 2010).

Vermeiren, Jan. *How to Really Use LinkedIn.* (Charleston, SC: Book-Surge Publishing, 2009).

websites/online articles:

"LinkedIn Tricks for Networkers,

Job Hunters and Hirers" by Lisa Cullen for Time.com. http://workin -progress.blogs.time.com/2007/06/07 /linkedin_tricks_for_networkers/.

"Top 10 Social Media Dos and Don'ts: How (and How Not) to Use Social Media to Job Search" by Alison Doyle for About.com. http: //jobsearch.about.com/od/onlinecareernetwork -ing/tp/socialmediajobsearch.htm.

"Ten ways to use LinkedIn" by Guy Kawasaki (blog post). http://blog.guyka -wasaki.com/2007/01/ten_ways_to_use .html#axzz0nAh7w5bx.

"Blog Basics: How a Blog Can Boost Your Career" by Cara Scharf for Wetfeet.com. www .wetfeet.com/Experienced-Hire/Getting-hired /Articles/Blog-Basics—How-a-Blog-Can-Boost -Your-Career.aspx.

CONNECT TO THE POWER OF LINKEDIN

LinkedIn is a job seeker's dream. It exists solely for business professionals to network with one another and provides a wealth of information (sometimes available only for actual wealth) for those researching hiring managers and organizations.

With LinkedIn, you create a personal profile, then link to other people on the site to create your own network. You can only view complete profiles of (or send a message or "InMail" to) those you are personally connected to—but you can see basic identifying information for anyone on the site.

If you're not "linked" already, follow these steps:

1. Visit www.linkedin.com.
2. Take plenty of time to carefully craft your profile. This will serve as an online résumé, an introduction, and an identifier.
3. Use as many keywords as you can in your profile—it is searchable by other LinkedIn users, including recruiters and hiring managers!
4. Next, invite everyone you know to join your network: former and current work colleagues, bosses, friends, classmates, family, neighbors, etc. But focus on those who might be in a position to help you search: well-connected people, or anyone who has anything to do with your industry.
5. To find contacts you know, search through provided lists of company employees and university graduates. Also try browsing the connections of those you connect to, to see if you can find mutual acquaintances. Note that ethically, you can only connect to people you already know, even if you only met that person once.
6. When you invite someone to join your LinkedIn network, always include a personal note, no matter how brief.
7. Once your profile is complete and your personal network is up and growing, seek recommendations from

some of your connections. Consider which of your acquaintances are most beneficial to your job hunt, then send each a brief but polite message through LinkedIn requesting a personal recommendation about specific skills, knowledge, and/or strengths. All recommendations will show up on your profile for visitors to see. An added benefit: if your former manager writes you a recommendation, all of *his* connections will be notified, drawing their attention to you!

8. Update your profile regularly or post your latest accomplishment, activity, or thought. Those you are connected with will be notified of your new status, keeping you front-of-mind.

> "LinkedIn is not the easiest thing to learn, but it includes a page that offers free tutorials on how to use it."
>
> **Barb Vlk, business librarian at Arlington Heights Public Library (Illinois)**
>
> Check with *your* local library to see if it offers workshops or tutorials on using LinkedIn or other social media for job hunting.

As you build your LinkedIn connections, you will be able to see second- and third-level connections. That is, the people to whom your connections are connected and the people to whom *those* connections are connected. You can see at a glance the strength of weak ties when you see that your former work colleague is connected to a hiring manager at the company you want to work for.

JOB SEARCHES ON LINKEDIN

LinkedIn does include a job-search area (see Chapter 3), but the true value of this site for a job seeker lies in the wealth of organizational and employee information available, and the possibility of reaching out to connections of connections. In fact, each job posting includes an option to "find people in your network at [company]." You can ask your common connection for an introduction to that inside connection, or you can "upgrade" your LinkedIn account, meaning you'll pay a monthly fee for the ability to send a specific number of InMails to secondary connections. Such upgrades start at $24.95 a month for three InMail messages to "strangers" and a certain number of peeks at profiles.

> ### FOR INSTANCE . . .
>
> Congratulations! Your online job search landed you a coveted interview with Premium Corporation, a large company based in your city. Here are three ways to use the power of LinkedIn to prep for your interview:
>
> 1. Do you have any connections there? LinkedIn's search capability allows you to search by company. Type in "Premium

Corporation" to find a list of all employees (past and present) on LinkedIn. The search results page will tell you right up front (literally) if you have any connections there, and if your connections have any connections there.

2. **Get the basic dope.** If you're searching for details on a larger company, that company page will reveal some basic information, including an overview statement, number of employees, revenue, and "recent activity" showing employee promotions, departures, and more.

3. **Scope out the person or people you'll be meeting.** If you have a name and/or job title of your interviewee, search them out. You won't be able to see complete profiles (unless you pay to upgrade your account), but you may be able to figure out chain of command and verify the job title and spelling of their names.

FACEBOOK: FOR FUN ONLY?

Facebook (www.facebook.com) is used primarily for personal, not professional, information sharing and networking. However, you can—and should—incorporate it in your online networking plan to a certain extent. Here's how:

Posting on your Facebook "wall" is an efficient way to let everyone you've connected with know that you're looking for work. You can do this frankly, which gets the message across:

"Amy Anderson is . . . looking for an entry-level job as a receptionist. If you know of anything, please call or e-mail me!"

Or you can be more subtle—a good tactic if you plan to post gentle reminders throughout your job search:

"Amy Anderson is . . . prepping for a phone interview for a part-time receptionist gig. Keep your fingers crossed for me."

Use Facebook's search function to find specific organizations. Many businesses and associations now have their own pages, which can include a gold mine of information including insights into corporate culture, the very most recent happenings, and even specific job postings!

"We just had a corporate recruiter do a program on Facebook. Now, they're not looking at people's Facebook pages, but they are posting jobs on their own page. LinkedIn has job listings too—and employers *will* go to LinkedIn to look at your information."
—**Barb Vlk, business librarian at Arlington Heights Public Library (Illinois)**

A WEALTH OF NETWORKING VIA MEETUP

Meetup.com describes itself as "the world's largest network of local groups." Members in more than two thousand different groups meet face-to-face every single day, all over the world. Some groups are based on hobbies, interests, even finding dates—and many are based on professional networking. Sign up for one or more appropriate Meetup groups and go to a meeting—it's a perfectly natural way to meet new people in your profession.

You can also use a specific group's Meetup.com page as a discussion forum, to connect with other group members, ask questions, etc.

SAMPLE MEETUP GROUPS

Transitioning Professionals of Albuquerque
North Pittsburgh Professional Women's Network
Marketing Methods for Business Owners
Chicago Health Care Professionals Social Group

ONLINE DISCUSSION FORUMS

The number of online discussion forums devoted to specific topics is limitless—more are being formed every day, as people seek out new ways to connect and share information. To find specific forums best suited to help you network for a job, consider finding forums about job searches in general, the business world, and your target industry or profession.

Job-Search Forums

- Monster.com
- About.com Job Search Discussion Forum
- Simply Hired (www.forums.simplyhired.com)

General Business Forums

- Fast Company's Company of Friends (Fastcompany.com/cof)
- Yahoo! Groups
- Vault.com discussions

Industry-Specific Forums

Search on your industry (or profession) and "discussion forum" or "chat room."

IT'S NOT NETWORKING IF YOU DON'T COMMENT!

Simply joining a Meetup group or your alumni association is *not* networking. Your real networking occurs when you add a comment or start a discussion in a forum, reach out to selected individuals and ask questions or offer advice, and generally showcase your professional know-how and experience.

Use these forums to post questions, share your own knowledge, or start an insightful discussion. This is a good way to introduce yourself as a member of the industry or profession and can even serve as a real introduction to an in-person meeting.

TWEETING AND BLOGGING

If you want to cover all your bases with networking online, try using Twitter (twitter.com) and/or creating your own blog. The catch with both is that they can be time-consuming while the payoff is uncertain; the effectiveness of your communication depends on who is reading your posts.

Twitter is ideal for broadcasting short calls for help with your job search, giving updates, and more. It's free, you have to sign up (of course), and each tweet is limited to 140 characters, ensuring brevity. As with LinkedIn, you should look for business contacts to connect with (or "follow," in Twitter-speak). The more people you sign up to follow, the more followers you are likely to attract.

In addition to tweeting your job search, you can search Twitter for posts on "job search," "résumé," "interviewing," etc., to find links to articles, advice, or just general news. There are even some random job postings on Twitter: to find them, search for "#job."

You can also create a blog and write regular posts that demonstrate your expertise, skills, and insight in your chosen career field. It's unlikely that hiring managers or recruiters will find you through your blog, but it could serve as a valuable supplement to your résumé and cover letter in getting your foot in the door.

TWITTER DOs AND DON'Ts

DO start tweeting about business topics—load your tweets with keywords that might be searched on. You can post about the state of the industry, the latest business news, how you just mastered a new skill, etc.

DON'T post about your job search incessantly. No one wants to read that.

DO tweet when you need an immediate answer to a question: "Does anyone have a contact at Major Marketing?" "How do I dress for an interview with a graphic design firm?"

DON'T ask for a job.

DO offer your own tips, links, and entertainment—no one will follow you if all you do is ask for help!

"People don't know how to network—or they're shy. But you have to do it. No matter where you go, you could be talking one-on-one to the person who may give you that job lead. They may know of a job that's just opened up."

—Barb Vlk, business librarian at Arlington Heights Public Library (Illinois)

THE LAST WORD

Keep in mind as you're searching the web for networking opportunities, posting comments on discussion forums, and entering today's post for your LinkedIn profile, Facebook page, and Twitter that you should limit the amount of time you spend in online networking. It's easy to devote hours of every day to your job search, but you'll do best if you set a time limit for yourself to avoid getting sucked into an afternoon of browsing. If necessary, set the alarm on your cell phone—or your kitchen timer—to allot a specific, reasonable amount of time to networking in one sitting.

CHAPTER 7
EXAMINING POTENTIAL EMPLOYERS

All successful job seekers must become expert researchers. How else will you figure out where to find the most relevant job openings, the employers most likely to hire you, and the details you need to arm yourself with before you walk into your first interview?

This chapter focuses on one area of research: uncovering information about the specific organizations you want to work for. Whether you've already got an interview scheduled or want to ID a company to cold call, the more you know about the organization in advance, the better off you'll be.

"I advise people to do a lot of research. Read anything and everything you can find about that company—and *then mention it* in your interview. Even if it's not local news, you can share general information or reviews you've read. Ideally, you can follow up the interview by sending the person a copy of what you mentioned. This makes you stand out from the other candidates."

—Bernice Kao, job/career specialist and job service outreach librarian at Fresno County (California) Public Library

LIBRARY RESOURCES
You may think you know how to research ... but you've got a lot to learn. And who better to guide you than a librarian? Stop by your public library's reference desk and ask if a librarian-specialist can walk you through using available resources to investigate your potential employers.

IDENTIFYING POTENTIAL EMPLOYERS
Simply checking job listings every day is the most passive form of job hunting. One way to be more proactive in your search is to carefully consider which organizations you'd like to pursue as your next employer and then contact

those companies. Researching employers by location, industry, corporate stability, and other factors can help you focus your search—and possibly pursue an opportunity that has not been advertised yet.

There are three sets of tools you can use for this research:

1. LIBRARY DATABASES

Barb Vlk, business librarian at Arlington Heights (Illinois) Public Library, asks, "How do you know what companies to go to?" Check with your local library to see which databases it subscribes to that might contain company information. "You can call up your library and ask which databases are good for this type of research," urges Vlk. "There are a number of databases where you can find company information, often with live links so you can just click through to their website. Some libraries restrict their databases to their cardholders; others let anyone access them."

BARB'S BEST DATABASES

Vlk's top three databases for researching potential employers:

1. **Reference USA**—"probably the best because it's the most comprehensive. It's really a phone book online. If I search for all the businesses here in Arlington Heights, I'm going to get around five thousand. That's because it will list every Panera Bread and McDonald's in town, along with home

businesses. You can search by type of business and by number of employees. It's the best place to start."

2. **Million Dollar Directory**—"is good too, although it only includes larger companies."

3. **Lexus Nexus Library Express Edition**—"is a good place for getting news items on companies. Check this before you go to the interview, or to find something you can tie into your experience in your cover letter. Just let the hiring manager know that you've done your research and you know who that company is."

Vlk adds, "All of these can be downloaded to Microsoft Excel, so if you're familiar with Excel, then you've got a really nice working list for a job searcher."

> ### FACTOID
> Small businesses (those with 500 or fewer employees) have generated nearly two-thirds of all new jobs over the past fifteen years, according to the U.S. Small Business Administration in 2007.

2. WEBSITES

Of course, the Internet provides plenty of information on companies by industry, location, etc. Try these sites to start:

Hoover's (www.hoovers.com) is the granddaddy of company information, now online with free, up-to-date, and detailed information on more than 50,000 companies. Includes privately owned companies, which is rare on other sites. You can access some information for free, but much of it is fee-based.

Jigsaw (www.jigsaw.com) is primarily a source for employee directories within companies, but you can browse their site by industry, company name, state, or city to find an extensive list of companies. While individuals' contact information may prove invaluable, you can also use Jigsaw as a starting point to develop a list of potential employers in your area, then check out each company's own website.

Top 100 Inc. 5,000 Companies by Industry (www.inc.com/inc5000/2007/lists /top100-industries.html) provides basic information on what they have found to be the "fastest growing" organizations within each industry.

Guidestar (www2.guidestar.org) includes a searchable directory of nonprofit organizations.

Fortune's list of best companies to work for (http://money.cnn.com/magazines /fortune/bestcompanies/2010/) is updated annually.

Price's List of Lists (www.specialissues .com/lol) is a database of ranked listings of companies, people, and resources.

3. PERSONAL CONTACTS

Work your network. As you attend meetings and events, or introduce (and reintroduce) yourself to others during your job search, ask about which companies you should include in your search. If you're talking to someone in your targeted industry, ask where they work, where they've worked in the past, and which are the "local leader" companies in that industry.

And if you're talking to someone who is not in your targeted industry, it's still worth finding out if they have any contacts or knowledge about that field—you never know!

BEST IN SHOW—RESEARCHING COMPANIES

The Riley Guide: "How to Research Employers." www.rileyguide.com/employer.html#tutor

Quint Careers' Guide to Researching Companies, Industries, and Countries. www .quintcareers.com/researching_companies.html

LIST YOUR CONTACTS, THEN CONTACT YOUR LIST

This research aspect of your job search should be an ongoing task; don't wait to compile a complete list of potential employers before you act. If you put in some time browsing a library database, or Hoover's.com, and come up with an organization you think is a good fit for your talents, act right away! Follow these steps:

1. Study the company's website before you do anything. (See "How to Use a Company's website", p. 72.)
2. Check their website (and a few job listing sites, too) to see if there are any open positions in your area. If there are, apply for the position(s).
3. Find the most likely hiring manager using Internet research and consider how you might best contact that person. Options include e-mailing your résumé (or request for an information interview) or sending a snail-mail letter. Phone calls are rarely welcome interruptions, as are unscheduled in-person visits. But you might consider sending an e-mail that states you will follow up by phone, and then calling a few days later. This will turn your "cold call" into a warmer one.

LEARNING MORE ABOUT A COMPANY

The second aspect of researching an organization is when you've decided to contact a company about a job opening, or after you are invited to an interview. The timing on this type of research is crucial, because the more you know about the organization, the industry, the geographic region, and even the individuals you may interview with, the more likely you are to impress the hirers, stand out from your competition, and get the job!

WHEN TO RESEARCH A POTENTIAL EMPLOYER:

*   **Before** you write your cover letter and customize your résumé
*   **Before** you visit a company at a job fair
*   **Before** you contact a hiring manager for an information interview
*   **Before** your initial job interview—including telephone interviews!

"Do your research *before* you send out your résumé. That way your résumé will be custom-made to that job. Match your qualities listed in the résumé to the job ad—and come up with three stories for when you interview. I have my [job-seekers'] class write their résumé to a specific job opening for practice."

—Bernice Kao, job/career specialist and job service outreach librarian at Fresno County (California) Public Library

WHAT YOU SHOULD LEARN—AND WHERE

OK—you've found a promising job opening, registered for a job fair, or earned an appointment for an interview, and you're ready to start your research on a specific organization. What information should you gather on the company you're targeting?

Start with the basics:

*   The history, size, and scope of the organization

- Its financial health and stability
- Any recent news involving the organization
- The organizational chart for the department or location you'll be working in
- The corporate culture

And don't forget to educate yourself on . . .
- Current state of industry, area
- Latest news in industry
- Most recent changes in the organization (executives hired, layoffs, awards, etc.)

For a company's history, size, and scope, look . . . in the "about us" section of the **organization's own website.** If the organization you're targeting is owned by a larger corporation, has changed its name, or has a second identity, try a Google search on additional names to see what information you might unearth.

For financial health, look . . . at a number of financial sites. If the organization is publicly traded (that is, it is owned by stockholders), you can easily check its financial performance. Start with the **Edgar database** of the U.S. Securities & Exchange Commission (www.sec .gov). **Yahoo! Finance** (http://finance.yahoo .com) compiles financial news on specific publicly traded companies—just type the company name into the search field. Also check the **organization's own website** for an annual report, which will include the year's financial performance. Nonprofit organizations as well

as publicly traded ones may post their reports online.

For recent news, look . . . on sites for **industry trade journals, local newspapers,** and perhaps **professional associations.** A carefully worded general search may yield recent news articles and announcements, as well.

For org charts and corporate culture information, look . . . on the **company website.**

HOW TO USE A COMPANY'S WEBSITE
Of course, you should take time to thoroughly review the website of the company you're targeting. Pay attention to these areas of information:

About Us/History/Mission: In addition to a broad overview of the company, you may be able to figure out values, corporate culture, and even key words to use in writing or conversation.

Products/Services: A great way to introduce yourself to what exactly the company does and imagine how you might fit in. Memorize product names, or at least categories, before you interview.

What's New/Press Releases: Glean the latest news about the company for excellent points to bring up in an interview or cover letter. Past news provides an instant time line for developments, product releases, even new hires—and demonstrates what the company thinks is newsworthy.

Leadership/Staff Directory/Structure:

Find out who the major players are as well as who you may be working with and/or for in the open position. Note the names and titles of all of the above before heading in for an interview.

HOW TO KEEP UP ON INDUSTRY NEWS

It's a good idea to read up on general news about your profession, industry, and area throughout your job search. That way you'll be knowledgeable and insightful on cue when you unexpectedly meet a potential contact, while you're networking and especially while you're applying for and interviewing for positions.

> "You just have to pay attention to your own industry. Read all media and talk to people at [networking events]—and expand your interests to the bigger picture."
> —**Bernice Kao, job/career specialist and job service outreach librarian at Fresno County (California) Public Library**

Here is the bare minimum of industry research and news reading you should do throughout your job search:

1. Select one to three sources of industry-specific news (most likely trade journals) and at least skim every issue or update. If a publication is not available online for free, see if you can sign up for a trial subscription,

borrow hard copies from a subscriber you know, or consider sharing the cost of a subscription with one or more fellow job seekers.
2. Bookmark the website of a trade association. Check for recent updates to discussion forums or press releases. If you're a member, you may be able to get automatic news e-mails.
3. Join a profession- or industry-specific group on LinkedIn and monitor the discussion forums.
4. Scan the headlines in your local or national newspaper every day. (Do this online for free.) This will prepare you for "small talk" at networking events or targeted comments in an interview situation. Job hunters can sometimes be isolated—demonstrate that you know what's happening in the world!

HOW TO USE LINKEDIN

More and more companies are adding a corporate profile on LinkedIn, with basic (but valuable!) information. Perhaps most important, you can see which employees are on LinkedIn and whether you have any first-, second- or third-level connections.

Find companies through people's profiles or search LinkedIn for a company profile by name or keyword.

You can also choose to "follow companies" on LinkedIn, which enables you to receive automatic updates on changes to the profile, new developments, and job openings.

HOW TO LEARN FROM EMPLOYEES

Several websites offer information and insights into companies from current or past employees. All organizations are not included, of course, and remember to take comments with a grain of salt—a disgruntled employee may be settling a score. Try these:

Glassdoor.com lets employees post reviews of the companies they work for.

Vault.com's "Employer Reviews" (www .vault.com/wps/portal/usa/companies) gives you a peek at insiders' comments on current and former employers. You need to create an account and log in to view many of these.

"Use your research to connect. When you read a news article where someone is quoted, write to that person to let them know you agree or disagree with what they said. Be a little aggressive, be alert, and connect to your own interest.

"Build your own network so people will know you."

—Bernice Kao, job/career specialist and job service outreach librarian at Fresno County (California) Public Library

OFF-LINE RESEARCH

Bernice Kao recommends doing some in-person research using what she calls "guerilla networking" techniques:

"See if you can find an inside source within the company. Maybe you're in a coffee shop or a [restaurant] near the company and you see someone wearing the corporate nametag. Ask them for a couple of minutes of their time—and buy them coffee. Tell them you're interested in the company and ask questions. Get their name and give them your business card. It may just work out that when there's a job opening, they can deliver your résumé to the personnel office."

If this is too aggressive for you, at least ask the professionals in your network if anyone has information on the specific organization you're targeting. You may find out important information on corporate culture, history of layoffs, etc.

RESEARCHING INDIVIDUALS

Once you've got a specific organization in your sights, remember to include the hiring managers and other potential interviewers in your research. Why?

- So that, when you are contacting a company for an unadvertised or "blind" job opening, you can address (and customize) your cover letter and résumé to a specific hiring manager. Use this tactic carefully, as some people may not appreciate your circumventing the HR department.

- To make networking easier. If you want an information interview from a specific company, you can find out the most appropriate person to talk to.
- For interview prep. When you haven't been told with whom you'll be meeting, you can make a best guess.

The two main places to look up titles, names, and contact information for employees within a company are that company's website and LinkedIn. You might also try a Google search on the person's name (if you know it) and company to see if any news items come up.

USE YOUR INFORMATION WISELY

If you find out details about your interviewers beyond their title and name, be tactful in how you use it. It's not a good idea to blurt out, "I

Googled you!" But if you know the HR professional you're talking to went to your alma mater, find a way to bring up the name of your school.

And keep in mind, if you're going in for an in-person interview (or even a telephone interview), it is likely that the interviewer has also checked *you* out on LinkedIn and through a general Google search.

THE LAST WORD

As you gather your research on organizations you apply to or are considering applying to, keep those notes handy. Consider creating a folder (paper or electronic) for each company you research and keep it even if you stop pursuing that particular organization (or vice versa). Here's why: the company you're targeting today may be one of the main competitors of a business you interview with tomorrow, and it might come in handy to walk in armed with some information about that!

CHAPTER 8
HONING YOUR INTERVIEW SKILLS

Those who have been job hunting for a while know that just getting a call for a first interview feels like you've met your goal. But that phone call is just the beginning of a new phase of the search. Interviewing for a job entails a lot of work: research, careful consideration, practice, and preparation. Because when you've put in the hours and effort to reach that first goal of an interview, you don't want to blow your chances!

> "The only purpose of your résumé and of interviewing is to *be memorable*. So go in and tell your story, and connect yourself to the job and their company."
> **—Bernice Kao, job/career specialist and job service outreach librarian at Fresno County (California) Public Library**

BEST IN SHOW—INTERVIEWING

Beshara, Tony. *Acing the Interview: How to Ask and Answer the Questions That Will Get You the Job.* (New York: AMACOM, 2008).

Oliver, Vicky. *301 Smart Answers to Tough Interview Questions.* (Naperville, IL: Sourcebooks, 2005).

Burns, Dan. *The First 60 Seconds: Win the Job Interview before It Begins.* (Naperville, IL: Sourcebooks, 2009).

Schuman, Nancy. *The Job Interview Phrase Book: The Things to Say to Get You the Job You Want.* (Avon, MA: Adams Media, 2009).

LIBRARY RESOURCES

Does your public library offer classes or workshops in interviewing skills? What about one-on-one practice sessions or consultations? You may think such services aren't part of a library's mission, but many public libraries are partnering with local job service organizations, finding skilled volunteers, or training librarians to help with steps like interviewing so that they can help out the job hunters in their communities.

So call your library, visit its website, or stop in to see what help it might offer with interview prep, planning, and practice.

TYPES OF INTERVIEWS

It's true: there may be more than one type of interview involved in your job search. Whether you've requested an information interview, been asked to a participate in what is clearly a prescreening telephone call with a recruiter, or are going for the whole enchilada—the one-on-one, suit-and-tie, formal first interview—prepare thoroughly for each interview and always act in a businesslike manner. For more particulars on each type, read on.

INFORMATION INTERVIEWS

An information interview is different from a standard job interview. You should try to set up your own information interviews when you're trying to break into a field (as a new graduate or as a career-changer). You want to pinpoint someone who is established in that field—with the purpose of learning his insights into the state of the industry in your area, typical duties and responsibilities, skill set and education needed, and just about anything else that might help you target your search.

Not only can you learn a lot from an information interview, it is a powerful way to build your network. You might even get a job offer! An added benefit: information interviews allow you to practice for interviews and get comfortable with the format, without the pressure of trying for a specific job.

WHO?

Whom should you ask for an information interview? If possible, try to set up several. Start with people you know from your personal network, then consider professionals you've met while networking for a job. Then browse listings of professional associations: board members and committee chairs are good bets for industry insiders who are willing to give up their time to help others. Consider only people who have worked in your target industry for at least several years; managers or executives are best.

HOW LONG?

Because this interview is a favor to you, keep it short—half an hour at the very most. Use every minute of that time to get the information you want: that means taking time well in advance to plan what you want to cover. Consider what would benefit you most and focus on one or two areas such as those listed under "What to Discuss?" below. For best results, let your interviewee know in advance what area you'd like to learn about.

WHAT FIRST?

Treat an information interview as you would a "real" job interview. That means:

- Doing your research on the company in advance
- Having questions and statements ready and rehearsed for a smooth conversation
- Preparing and bringing at least two copies of your résumé (and your portfolio)
- Dressing appropriately
- Starting the meeting by exchanging business cards: now the professional has your contact info at hand (and you have hers)

WHAT TO DISCUSS?

What do you want to know the most about? Possibilities include:

- What is it like to be a typical fill-in-the-blank worker? What are the job responsibilities and duties, and skills and knowledge required?
- How's my job-search strategy? Have the professional review what you're doing, where you're looking, and your résumé and experience.
- What is the state of the industry? Cover job outlook, salaries, changes coming up, major players in the area.

INFORMATION INTERVIEW DOs AND DON'Ts

DON'T ask for a job in an information interview. People are willing to give you their time because you expect you to *not* do this. (But if someone offers you a job interview, an internship, or a position at the company, that's fine!)

DO ask for suggestions (or recommendations) of whom to contact for a job, or ask her to do some light networking on your behalf.

DON'T let the established professional take control of the conversation. To ensure you cover what you want to discuss, begin the meeting with a brief introduction and explanation of what you'd like to learn during the meeting.

DO ask your interviewee if you can contact her again within a couple of weeks to see if she has any ideas for your job search.

DON'T ask for a job. (We can't stress this enough!)

DO take notes. Jot down names of individuals and companies that might be job leads, write down their advice, and mark up a copy of your résumé if the person reviews it.

TELEPHONE INTERVIEWS

A hiring company or recruiter may conduct the first interview over the telephone, as this is more time-efficient for the interviewer (and you, too!). Here is what a professional recruiter has to say about phone interviews:

"The trend right now is to do a phone screen first," says Dionna Keels, a member of the SHRM (Society for Human Resource Management) staffing management expertise panel. "The goal is for the recruiter to be sure they're comfortable bringing a person in to meet with the hiring manager, without wasting anyone's time. Phone screens are almost a weeding-out process.

"A phone interview really is a first interview—so don't make the mistake of thinking it's not important," Keels stresses. "Do your preparation before the call. Do some research on the company you're interviewing with."

She encourages job interviewees to make it easier on the other person by holding a two-way conversation—which demonstrates your intelligence and personality. "Ask questions and find out more about the [job opening]," she recommends. "Your personal skills are very important over the phone. Talk openly about your experience and skills; have a real conversation."

Keels explains that what the telephone interviewer is after is proof that your work experience is a good match for the opening. "But they may also be doing a culture screen. They want to find out what you're looking for and see if it's a match," she says. How do you "ace" a culture screen? Make it part of your preinterview research. Keels says, "If you go to the company's career page on their website, they may have videos and information that describe their culture. You may also find an HR professional through LinkedIn or the website, and call them up to explain that you're interviewing for a position there and have a couple of questions about the corporate culture. Also, ask anyone you know who has ever worked there. Look for employee blogs . . ."

In a way, telephone interviews are easier than in-person interviews because you can refer to notes or an outline when answering (or asking) questions. Have a copy of the résumé you sent in and highlight the areas you'd like to talk about.

TIP: Bernice Kao has two recommendations for speaking well on the phone: smile when you speak and place a mirror where you can see it. Check your expression in the mirror when you answer the phone and throughout the interview to ensure you are speaking clearly and naturally—and putting that smile in your voice.

"PHONE-PLUS-VIDEO" INTERVIEWS

According to an article in *Time* magazine, job interviews via computerized video chats are growing in popularity—especially for interviewing out-of-state job candidates. In "How Skype Is Changing the Job Interview," Barbara Kiviat offers pointers for preparing yourself and your "set" to appear on-screen at www.time .com/time/business/article/0,8599,1930838,00 .html#ixzz0ffanZJBc.

TIP: Whether you're scheduling a telephone interview, a first interview, or a follow-up interview, make sure you get the details. If your contact doesn't offer you the information, ask how many people you'll be meeting with and write down everyone's name and title. Ask for an estimated time frame (will you be there one hour or all afternoon?), if you will be expected to take any tests (assessment, skills, or software tests). Finally, make sure you understand where to show up, including the floor number and whom to ask for when you arrive.

IN-PERSON INTERVIEWS

The key to a successful in-person interview is preparation. That includes doing your research on the company and industry (Chapter 7), and thoroughly practicing interviews. Part of your practice should include:

- Researching, brainstorming, and asking professional friends to come up with likely topics that will be covered, such as your strengths and weaknesses, your ideal day at the job, etc.—and then decide how you want to answer those. "But don't try to guess interview questions and then memorize answers," warns Kao. "It's not going to sound like you."

- Coming up with real anecdotes, examples, results, and challenges from your previous work that you would like to mention. Then write them down and/or say them out loud a few times. Memorize any percentages, years, etc., you'd like to include. "Practice telling your stories beforehand," urges Kao. "Make sure each one illustrates a skill. You can practice short speeches very casually, by telling a friend."

- In order to conquer nervousness, asking a friend to hold a practice

interview with you. "Practice each interview as if your life depends on it. Then treat the real interview as if it's another practice," advises Kao. "It's fine to be nervous when you're interviewing—but practicing will help with this. You have to practice over and over in order to gain confidence."

- Rehearsing your stories, anecdotes, etc., in front of a mirror, or even videotaping yourself. Check your body language: do you look engaged, interested, and vital? Try leaning forward, keeping an open expression on your face, and uncrossing your arms.

WHAT TO WEAR

These days, company dress codes range from business suits to blue jeans, making it difficult to know what to wear to a job interview. Jill Silman, SPHR, vice president at Meador Staffing Services and a spokesperson for the Society of Human Resources Management (SHRM), offers a good guide:

"Dress for the job. The whole interview is to prove you fit in; you want your clothes to help send this subconscious message to your interviewer. If you have to, stalk the company and see how people are dressed as they come out for lunch. If they all look like an ad for the Gap, you don't want to wear a suit, hose, and heels to your interview."

Silman says its OK to call the company's human resources before the interview to ask about the dress code for employees. "And if you're in doubt, you should dress up, not down."

Kao adds some good advice: No matter what you plan to wear, "Get used to your interview outfit," she says. "Practice wearing the whole outfit while standing, walking, and sitting. Never wear the outfit for the first time to an interview unless you want to look like a robot."

FOLLOW-UP INTERVIEWS

If your first interview goes well, you may be asked back for a second—and possibly a third—meeting. These follow-up interviews are likely to include more or different interviewers, as you are scoped out by all the key players.

Every company has its own procedure, but you may be offered the job as early as the end of the second interview—so be prepared beforehand to negotiate your salary and other terms. (Chapter 9 will help you plan for this.) Or you may be invited back for a third or even fourth time.

Treat all follow-up interviews much like your first interview; don't slack on review of your previous research and repeat your preparation. You should have noted the anecdotes and accomplishments you mentioned during all subsequent interviews, so review that information, as well. You don't want to repeat a long anecdote to the same person a second time!

Instead, consider what you didn't get a chance to say, or a point you didn't get a chance to sell, and try to work that into your conversation.

Keep in mind that if you passed the first interview, subsequent meetings may be to see if you are a good fit for the personality or culture of the company, so the questioning may be more personal: What would you do in this situation? How do you handle conflict? What types of activities do you enjoy in your off-hours?

TIP: Be sure to ask more questions in follow-up interviews; you want to have all the information you need to make a decision and start negotiating!

PANEL INTERVIEWS

Don't be too surprised if your first or second interview for a job is conducted by a panel of managers or employees. "Many companies are using panel interviews to save managers' time," says Keels. "Also, a lot of companies feel that in a panel interview, the interviewers can feed off one another's questions, and this makes them better interviewers and keeps them more comfortable."

Make sure you ask with whom you'll be interviewing when you set up the appointment, so that you can be prepared to face a panel or group if necessary. Kao recommends that at a panel interview, you should address and thank the person who asks the first question, then go around the panel while you talk until you come back to the first panelist.

Continue to "rotate" your attention as you answer each question.

WHAT TO ASK, ANSWER, AND SAY

A lot of people have trouble talking about themselves and their accomplishments. Some have trouble simply talking when under pressure. That's why it's important to practice interviewing: what you'd like to say, how you'll respond to questions on the fly, and what you want to ask.

Kao coaches job hunters at her library every day, and based on her extensive experience, she says, "Don't mumble. Take your time while talking, and pause. . . . Pauses are a way to turn an interview into a relaxed conversation. They encourage dialogue instead of a lecture." Another tip: "Talk for two minutes at a time—no more. Let them ask for more information if they want it."

TIP: Part of your preparation for an interview should be self-introspection. That means considering and knowing your greatest strengths and how they match up to the open position, your personality, your style of work, and your work values.

TAKE CONTROL OF THE INTERVIEW

Try to get the interviewer to talk first—even if it's just a brief overview of the open position. The more she tells you about the position, department, and organization, the better you can tailor your own comments to demonstrate what a great fit you are.

If the interviewer jumps right in by asking you to talk about yourself, lob the ball back into his court with a request like "If you don't mind, can you first tell me a little about the position, so that I can better describe how my experience might fit here?" Then you can launch into your concise description of your experience, skills, and qualifications. This question offers a golden opportunity to highlight what you had planned to say to sell yourself—so do some planning and practicing, and be ready for it!

TELL A STORY

Kao is a proponent of job hunters being proactive while interviewing. This entails planning and practicing specific "stories" to tell while you're being interviewed. Formulate these stories based on the research you've done on the organization and the open position, to highlight areas that fit well with what you've learned. Your stories might include:

- A specific accomplishment from your most recent job: how you cut your department's budget by 23 percent last year, how you upgraded the customer-service software system, or how you wooed a new corporation into becoming the company's largest customer.
- An enthusiastic description of recent learning: the workshop you attended on a new industry-specific software package, the book you just finished on teamwork.
- An event that demonstrates a personal skill: how you handled an unexpected challenge, how you successfully managed a team of colleagues, how you juggled two jobs while your manager was on maternity leave.
- An anecdote that showcases your work values: how you mentored a new employee, how you volunteer in your professional association.

"Think of ways to communicate your value, how you can help your future employer," says Kao.

SHOW OFF YOUR RESEARCH

You did the hard work of researching the hiring organization and industry—don't forget to let your interviewers know!

Find a way to work your knowledge of the company and of the latest industry news into the conversation. Better yet, share your personal insights and opinions on that news. "They want to find out what you know that *they* don't even know yet," says Kao. "So talk about news items, industry trends, new technology as it relates to their business. You want to be the person who can tell them something that none of the other candidates can."

"Never say 'I don't know.' Instead, say something like 'I'm not too familiar with this subject, but let me tell you about . . .' and go on to relate a story about how you mastered a new skill, or how your experience fits with the overall subject."
—Bernice Kao, job/career specialist and job service outreach librarian at Fresno County (California) Public Library

ASK QUESTIONS

Any job interview should be a two-way conversation. That means not only should you reply to questions, but ask some of your own. This demonstrates that you're curious about the open position and the company, that you understand the industry, work, structure, etc., and that you have a unique mind!

- Ask questions to clarify details you find unclear.
- Ask questions that demonstrate your own values and work culture: Does teamwork play a big part in the work style here? Do you value independence in your staff?
- Interview the interviewer: Why does he like working there, or why has he been there so long? What does he see as the department's strengths or weaknesses?

- Don't pretend to understand something you don't! Ask for definitions or explanations.

TESTING, TESTING, 1–2

Many organizations use some type of test to help qualify job candidates. At some point in the interviewing process, you may be asked to take:

- An assessment test: Typically multiple-choice in format, these tests are designed to reveal your personal characteristics, values, etc., which lets the hirer know whether you are ethical and honest or whether you are a good match for their corporate culture.
- A skills test: depending on the job you're applying for, you may be tested on knowledge of a specific software program, your writing skills, or your math abilities.
- A typing test: how many words per minute can you type?
- A drug test: if the company requires drug screening, you may need to pass a drug test as a last step in the employment process.

Do your best to find out about any tests beforehand, so that you know what you'll be expected to do during the interview.

AFTER EACH INTERVIEW

Whew—the interview's over! That hurdle has been crossed, but you're not finished yet—you have a few follow-up tasks:

1. Take notes. As soon as possible, write down your impressions of the company, the job, and the interviewers for your own future reference. And make sure you have the names and titles of everyone you spoke to.

2. If the organization asked for references, contact those people immediately to notify them that they may soon be hearing from your prospective employer. If appropriate, remind them or coach them on what to emphasize about you.
3. Send a thank-you to anyone who might have referred you for the interview, letting him know how it went.
4. More important, send thank-you notes to your interviewers.

GIVE THANKS

Sending a prompt, succinct, and well-written thank-you note or letter to each person you interviewed with is a crucial step in your job-search process. Why? Because it is one more opportunity for you to make an impression and stand out from your competition, to sell your best qualifications, to prove you are an excellent match, and to ask for the job.

Here are the rules of writing thank-yous:

- Write a separate (and unique) note to every person you interviewed with.
- Send your notes within twenty-four hours of the interview.
- It's acceptable to e-mail a thank-you note, but writing or typing one and mailing it is better. A handwritten note is best used for a very brief communication, such as when you are thanking each of the four staff members you met with in addition

to the department manager. (The manager may warrant a longer, typed letter.)

- Send a thank-you even if the interview did not go well or if you know you are no longer in the running for the position. Thank the interviewers for their time and consideration.
- Keep it brief—state your thanks, give one highlight of your accomplishments or one reference to a point that came up during the interview, and state your interest in the job.

TIP: Kao recommends, "Follow up any way you can think of. Try to be a memorable candidate. Mention something unique in each thank-you note that you have discussed during the interview. It is OK to enclose articles you talked about, or some extra writings you have done. But not photocopies of your award or trophies!"

TIP: If you're good at writing on demand, here's some great advice from Susan Strayer of susanstrayer.com: "Bring blank thank-you notes [with you to the interview]. Write them immediately afterward and ask receptionist to hand-deliver—a huge WOW."

CHECKING IN

It's OK to check in on the status of your candidacy if you don't hear back from the interviewer. If you asked—and were told—that the hiring decision should be made within two weeks, contact the company a couple of days before that estimated deadline. If you don't know the time frame, wait about a week before making contact.

Call or e-mail the person you interviewed with to say thank you again and restate your interest in the job. You can leave this information in a voice-mail message—but only call once to leave your message. If you keep hanging up on the person's answering message, they may see your number come up on Caller ID multiple times, which makes you look like a stalker.

If you still don't hear back after your first follow-up e-mail or voice mail, try again a week later. If you don't get a reply to your second message, you're not likely to hear back about the job. It's time to stop trying to contact them and move on with your job search.

THE LAST WORD

Interviewing for a job can be a nerve-racking experience—especially for a job hunter who is eager to be employed and put all the hard work of the search behind him. But try to relax and enjoy the interview portion of your search. It will help make you a better interviewee, and it will allow you to take a close and objective look at your potential employer while you're on the premises and get a good feel for what it would be like to work there.

CHAPTER 9

NEGOTIATING THE BEST PAY AND BENEFITS FOR YOUR NEW JOB

Wise job hunters will be ready and willing to negotiate salary and benefits when the appropriate time comes. Those who aren't prepared with solid research, industry knowledge, and confidence in their position are likely to lose out. And as negotiation expert Cheryl Palmer points out, once the opportunity for negotiating the terms of your new job is over, you'll never be able to make up the difference between what you get and what you could have had.

> "It's critical to practice negotiating. You may read books on the topic and understand the concept of negotiating, but it's a different story when your living is on the line."
>
> **—Cheryl Palmer, CECC, negotiation expert and president of Call to Career**

BEST IN SHOW—NEGOTIATING

Fisher, Roger, and William L. Ury. *Getting to Yes: Negotiating Agreement Without Giving In.* (New York: Penguin, 1991).

Miller, Lee E. *Get More Money on Your Next Job ... in Any Economy.* (New York: McGraw-Hill, 2009).

Wegerbauer, Maryanne. *Next-Day Salary Negotiation: Prepare Tonight to Get Your Best Pay Tomorrow* by (Indianapolis, IN: JIST Works, 2007).

Pinkley, Robin L., and Gregory B. Northcraft. *Get Paid What You're Worth: The Expert Negotiators' Guide to Salary and Compensation.* (New York: St. Martin's, Griffin, 2003).

Garlieb, Stacie. *My Job Offer Negotiation Skills Are Solid (I Think) ... So Why Didn't I Get Anything I Asked For?* (Charleston, SC: CreateSpace, 2010).

QuintCareers, "Salary Negotiation and Job Offer Tools and Resources for Job-Seekers," www.quintcareers.com/salary_negotiation.html.

Salary.com, "Negotiation Clinic," www.salary.com/Articles/ArticleDetail.asp?part=par186.

Susan Ireland's Résumé Site, "Salary Negotiation Skills," http://susanireland.com/interview/salary-pay.

WHY NEGOTIATE?

If you're uncomfortable talking about money or asking for what you want, don't worry—go ahead and do it. Employers and HR professionals *expect* you to negotiate your starting salary. It's very rare that the first package offered—pay and benefits, that is—is fixed. So think of it as a starting point and reach higher. Basic tips for successful negotiation include:

- Have a solid grasp of what is realistic in terms of pay, benefits, and perks for the type of job you've been offered.
- Also understand where you fit in the range of experience, skills, and value.
- Let the other person begin. This ensures it's the right time to negotiate—and you hold the advantage if the employer names their figure first.
- If negotiations reach a point where the final salary offer is still low, move on to negotiate for more or better benefits.

If you don't negotiate for what you want at this stage of accepting employment, Palmer warns, "You're likely to leave several thousand dollars on the table. And you'll never make that money up."

TIMING FOR MONEY TALK

The appropriate time to talk money (and benefits) is one of the firm rules in job interviewing. While the topic of pay may come up early—in a request for your salary history or requirements along with your résumé, for instance—the rock-solid rule is, don't bring up the subject until the employer makes you a job offer.

It's important to understand that that initial question is not part of salary negotiation or discussion, but simply to see if you fall in the general range of what they're paying.

TIP: If asked to supply your current or previous salary, don't lie! If you're hired and the lie is found out, this is legal grounds for termination.

DOs AND DON'Ts FOR TALKING MONEY

DO be prepared to start negotiations as soon as your second interview—though the topic may not come up until the third or fourth interview. (See Chapter 8.)

DON'T ask about salary during your interviews. "It's not considered appropriate," says Palmer. "It's expected that when you get the job offer, you'll have done your research and be prepared to negotiate."

DO have any notes on your salary research ready to reference during discussions.

DON'T accept a job, salary, or benefits that you don't want.

DO ask for time to consider the final offer once you've reached an agreement on salary and benefits. It's acceptable to request a day or two to consider the final offer.

HOW JOB NEGOTIATION WORKS

Every organization has its own time line and process for hiring new employees, depending on its size and agility, procedures and protocols, and the difficulty of finding the best candidate for a particular position. Here is a general guide for how job negotiations might take place:

"Typically, after all the interviews are over and the company has decided whom they want for the position, an HR professional will make a phone call to extend the offer. That's when the negotiation takes place. You want to be prepared for that call. You don't want that HR person to have to go back to the hiring manager with your questions, so when you're interviewing you need to have the mindset that you're going to be hired. That's when you should have asked all your questions. You want to come away from that phone call with the company's best offer. Once you feel you have that, say, 'I'd like a couple of days to think about it. Can I call you on Wednesday?'"

—Cheryl Palmer, CECC, negotiation expert and president of Call to Career

NEGOTIATION PREPARATION

You can't successfully negotiate unless you know the realities of the marketplace. What is the typical salary range for the position you applied for? Does that range apply in your geographic region? And when and how do you bring this up during negotiations?

DO YOUR RESEARCH

Study up on salaries in your industry. You can start this research way in advance of a first interview, but by the time you've sent out your thank-yous for that interview, it's time to start getting serious about money matters. This includes:

Know what you need. How much do you pay in total monthly bills, including housing, various insurance, utilities, and groceries? What benefits do you absolutely need—such as health insurance?

Know what you can command. Your own experience, education, and other qualifications will dictate where you are on the salary scale. Be realistic in assessing what you bring to the table.

Know how your geographic area stacks up. Is the cost of living the same in your small town as it is in Manhattan? You can compare cost of living in various locations with the online calculators at Move.com (www .homefair.com/real-estate/salarycalculator .asp?cc=1) and the Cost-of-Living Wizard at

MySalary.com (http://swz.salary.com/costof
-livingwizard/layoutscripts/coll_start.asp).

Know the salary range for the position.
This is the key element to negotiating. You
need to research salaries and typical benefits
by industry, position, area, and for the current
economic climate. Don't worry, we're about to
tell you how to do this!

USE THREE SALARY SOURCES

For good general salary information, Cheryl
Palmer recommends salary.com and payscale
.com.

"I also tell my clients to look for salary sur-
veys from professional associations. Just be sure
to look at more than one source, because there
will be slight variations in information; consider
your local geographic area. If you check three
sources, you'll be pretty well armed for salary
negotiation."

Find good salary info online at:

- Salary.com: Type in the position title and
  city/state you're interested in and get
  base salary range for free. More detailed
  information is available for a fee.
- Payscale.com: Identify yourself as a job
  candidate, job seeker, current employee,
  or a business to get a free salary report
  based on your education/experience
  level, etc. The report is e-mailed to you.
- The Salary Info section on www.job
  -smart.org.

- SalariesReview.com (but most information will cost a fee).
- Glassdoor.com has information from
  real-life employees, including salaries by
  industry, by occupation, and by company.
  Even if the company you're interviewing
  with is not included, this gives you some
  valuable comparisons.

TIP: Before negotiations start, try simply asking
the hiring company what the salary range is for
the position. You can call the human resources
department and explain that you're interviewing for the position. See if they'll give you the
information.

PRACTICE MAKES PERFECT

As with interviewing skills, practicing negotiation sessions can polish your skills and prepare you like nothing else.

Palmer agrees that you should "absolutely"
practice negotiating. "There's a lot of stress and
a lot of pressure—mainly, pressure to just cave
and accept what they offer," she warns. "You
play the part of the job candidate, and have a
friend or family member play the employer—
or better yet, a career coach. You need someone
who's going to be tough on you. It's likely the
person who's offering you the job is trained in
negotiation."

LIBRARY RESOURCES

If you want a tough practice partner, look for a career counselor or job coach. Some public libraries have partnerships with nonprofit career services to help job seekers in the library; perhaps a volunteer can schedule a practice negotiation session with you.

NEGOTIATION CHECKLIST

Your preparations will be complete when you:

1. Have salaries or salary ranges for a comparable position from three different sources, giving you a clear picture of the package you should be offered for the job.
2. Believe those salary ranges are in line with what you need or want to earn. (If they aren't, you may be applying for the wrong jobs—or you need to rethink either your career or your budget!)
3. Have statements prepared for arguing in favor of your specific qualifications—an advanced degree, a particular skill, excellent experience.
4. Have practiced different scenarios for tough negotiations and are comfortable pressing the interviewer for what you want and deserve.

READY TO NEGOTIATE!

So: you're armed with some hard figures on what the salary range should be for the position you're being offered, you know what you need and what you want, and you've practiced some negotiation scenarios. Sounds like you're ready!

BEGINNING TACTICS

Much like when you started interviewing for the position, you want your interviewer to give you some information before you jump in.

"The basic rule of thumb is that whoever brings up salary first loses. The company very often doesn't want to reveal what they can pay, and the job seeker shouldn't want to reveal what she wants."

—Cheryl Palmer, CECC, negotiation expert and president of Call to Career

Some interviewers will simply come out and say, "This position has a salary range of $34,000 to $38,000." Most companies are likely to have salary ranges set for each position; but that doesn't mean those ranges are set in stone. "Usually HR sets the parameters for [salary and benefits], but it's driven by the budget of the department or company that's hiring," says Jill Silman, SPHR, vice president at Meador Staffing Services and a spokesperson for the Society of Human Resources Management (SHRM). So if the stated salary range isn't as high as you had expected or hoped, keep up the negotiations!

Other interviewers will ask you what you'd like to earn. It's OK to dodge the question by asking if there is a set salary range. "However, you can't continue to hedge indefinitely," says Palmer. "After you go back and forth a few times, you'll have to answer the salary inquiry. At that point, give a range, based on the research you've done. This is a good time to mention your research and the sources."

IF THE SALARY RANGE STATED IS TOO LOW AND DOES NOT MATCH YOUR RESEARCH:

- State, "I understand that your organization has a set salary range for this position, but I'd like to make a case for increasing that range in this case."
- Point out your salary sources and the industry averages. (Don't use your own previous or current salary as an example!)
- Remind your interviewer of several of your top selling points, illustrating why you are a valuable candidate.
- Don't turn down the job right away, but make it clear that you are concerned about the money offered.
- If at this point it seems the top end of the range stated is as high as the organization will go, consider whether it's worth negotiating on other points. (See below.) If you can't get a package

that suits your needs or wants, end the interview politely but try to leave the door open in case the organization's decision makers change their minds.

IF THE SALARY RANGE IS IN LINE WITH WHAT YOUR RESEARCH REVEALS:

- Negotiate for the highest end of the range. Reiterate your selling points to show your value to the company.
- Try for a higher salary rather than a middle-range amount with the promise of a bonus or future raise; your agreed-upon starting salary will be set in stone, unlike promises of extra cash in the future.
- Even if you get the salary you wanted, continue to negotiate benefits and perks.

IF THE SALARY RANGE IS HIGHER THAN YOU EXPECTED:

- Don't express excitement or delight. You still want to negotiate the best salary and benefits you can get, so push for the higher end of the range.
- Consider that there may be a reason the pay is higher than usual. You may be expected to work longer hours or travel extensively—so make sure you continue negotiations!
- Wait to see if the benefits package is decent. Is the higher salary range compensation for lack of health insurance or a retirement plan? If

so, use your "thinking time" before accepting the offer to research how much of the high salary you'll spend making up those benefits. Is it still a good salary?

Be reasonable in your requests when you make a counteroffer to the initial offer or statement. Bernice Kao, job/career specialist and job service outreach librarian at Fresno County (California) Public Library, recommends, "Lay out your counteroffer two steps above the original offer. Reassure [your interviewer] of the experience and benefits you will bring." Ideally, your negotiating partner will meet you in the middle, which is what you wanted in the first place. Here's an example:

HR professional:	"The Sales Associate job is what we call a 'grade 2' position and has a salary range of $28,000 to $32,000. We think that is generous for an entry-level position."
You:	"That range seems in line with my research. I know this is an entry-level job, but I worked an internship this summer at a company like yours, so I bring some recent experience as well as my Bachelor's of Marketing, so I think I would warrant $32,000 a year."
HR professional:	"That wouldn't give you any room for a raise or cost of living increase. Why don't we say $30,000 to start."
You:	"That makes sense. But I'm confident that I can prove I'm worth more. Can we agree to schedule my first performance review for six months from my start date, with a potential raise based on my performance?"

Once you agree on salary, go on to review the benefits and perks that come with employment. These, too, are negotiable—so if the final salary offered is not what you had hoped, consider ways to make up the difference in either benefits or quality-of-life factors. "They've already made the offer, so see what you can get," advises Kao. "You might give them five options and they'll take three. Give them a choice, but base it in reality."

WHAT'S NEGOTIABLE?

The answer, in short, is "everything." Most job candidates focus on the size of the paycheck offered—but that's not all you can (or should) negotiate.

"It's easy to be dazzled by what appears to be a higher salary—but the total compensation package includes benefits like a retirement plan and health insurance," Palmer points out. "You have to look at that whole package."

Look at the entire package. "These things will affect your pocketbook and your life," Palmer stresses. You can negotiate:

- Flextime/telecommuting from home
- Health insurance: if you are already covered by your spouse, or by the military, can you negotiate a higher salary instead of health coverage?
- Vacation time
- When you get your first salary review (negotiate it earlier, in hopes of getting your first raise sooner)
- Retirement plans
- Bonus plans
- Tuition reimbursement
- Stock options
- Signing bonus
- Relocation allowance
- Start date

These days, more people are negotiating based on time. Parents of young children and Generation X in general value time off, so workers are bargaining for flextime, shorter days, or more days off. "Time is the new currency," says Silman.

THE FINAL STEP: ENDING NEGOTIATIONS

Once you and the employer have reached an agreement on all the factors of your salary and benefits package, conclude with these steps. If the negotiations occurred in person, you can state them; otherwise, it's a good idea to send in an e-mail immediately to:

- Acknowledge the offer.
- Make sure the terms of the offer are clear. If not, ask for clarification.
- Thank the employer for the offer.
- Ask for time to consider. You want to think about the job, the salary, and everything that goes with it— anywhere from overnight to two days should be acceptable.
- Find out whom you should contact with your final decision. It may be the HR person or the hiring manager.

MAKING THE DECISION

No matter how perfect the job seems, or how generous the package offered, always ask for some time to consider the offer before making a decision. This is an important step that will affect your career, your life, and your bank account, so sleep on it. Use the time you've requested to review everything you learned about the position, the organization, the salary and benefits. Be honest in assessing whether the job and the employer are good fits for you. Once you've made your decision, it's time to act:

ACCEPTING THE OFFER

When you accept a job offer, even verbally, it's like signing a contract. So don't say "yes" if you are not 100 percent certain you want that job and are willing and able to take it. If you accept a job in the excitement of the offer—say, you're swayed by a sizable salary but have second thoughts later—it will be embarrassing to back out, and can damage your personal and professional reputation.

Here's how you should formally accept the job:

1. Telephone the hiring manager or HR professional to let them know the decision—before the deadline you promised. (You should have asked whom to contact at the end of your negotiation meeting.)
2. Follow up with an e-mail message stating that you've accepted the offer and requesting a letter of agreement or contract stating the terms agreed to.
3. Play it safe—wait until you get that letter, review it, and finalize the offer before you give notice at your current job, bow out of any other positions you may be interviewing for, or move across the country to start your new position.

Most employers have a hiring process they'll follow, which includes drafting a letter of agreement for new employees. This letter—or formal contract, in some cases—should include at least the salary and benefits you agreed to in negotiations, and perhaps other details including your start date and to whom you will report.

You should carefully review the letter, compare the terms to those in your notes, and—if all details look accurate—sign it and send it back promptly. If you find a discrepancy between what you agreed to in negotiations and what the letter states, follow these steps:

1. Make a photocopy of the letter (or print out a second copy).
2. Use a pen to note the discrepancy. You can draw a single line through any text that you want deleted and make notes in the margins for what you'd like added.
3. Don't sign the letter. In fact, you may want to write Xs or draw a line through the signature line.
4. Draft a brief cover note explaining the changes.
5. Send the marked-up copy and the cover back to the original sender, by fax or mail, and ask about next steps.
6. If the employer does not agree with you on the final terms, it's time to either reconsider the "new" offer or request another meeting for further negotiations.

If your new employer does not provide a letter of agreement—perhaps it is a very small company, or a start-up business—you should take it upon yourself to draft one and ask your new manager to review it and sign it. It's important for both parties to understand and agree to clear terms and conditions of employment up front.

GIVING NOTICE

Once you've officially accepted the job offer and have a signed letter of agreement from your new employer, you can safely give notice at your current job. For decades, the rule of thumb is to give two weeks' notice before leaving. This is not a law; it is an ethical practice to give your employer time to cover your responsibilities.

Give your notice in person to your immediate supervisor and let her know your last day. You don't have to go into specifics, just that you've accepted a position with another company. And DON'T accept a counteroffer from your employer if you've already accepted a new job!

TIP: Be prepared for the possibility that the day you give your notice may be your last day of work there. Some companies and departments are concerned about security or confidentiality and may decide not to let a departing employee stick around. This is legal, but know your rights:

- You're entitled to be paid for all the days you've worked and, depending on your employer's policies, any vacation or personal time you've accrued.
- You don't have to sign anything or do anything in order to collect the pay that is owed you.

DECLINING THE OFFER

If, after you take some time to consider the final offer, you opt not to take the position, do the right thing: "Call them back. Be polite and thank them for considering you," says Palmer. Let the employer know as soon as possible. After all, that organization has a position to fill, and other candidates are eager to get the call.

To decline a job offer:

1. Call the hiring manager or HR professional to let them know your decision.
2. Follow up right away with an e-mail to that person, thanking everyone involved for their time and consideration, and restating that you are declining the offer.
3. If appropriate, give your reasons for declining—you are taking another position, or you could not reach agreement on salary or benefits. Keep this message positive, and if you can't state the real reason (you hated the hiring manager), then simply state you are declining and leave it at that.

Keep your tone professional and courteous. "Even if you decide not to take the job, leave on good terms," says Palmer. "Don't burn any bridges."

THE LAST WORD

Once you've learned how to prepare and practice for negotiating, keep those skills fresh! They will come in handy throughout your career—whether you are negotiating your first raise at your new job a year after you're hired or angling for more responsibilities. You'll find that the more you practice negotiating, and the more you actually engage in negotiations, the better you are!

BIBLIOGRAPHY/ WEBLIOGRAPHY

GENERAL JOB-SEARCH BOOKS

Bolles, Mark Emery, and Richard N. Bolles. *Job-Hunting Online: A Guide to Job Listings, Message Boards, Research Sites, the UnderWeb, Counseling, Networking, Self-Assessment Tools, Niche Sites.* Berkeley, CA: Ten Speed Press, 2008.

Dikel, Margaret Riley, and Frances E. Roehm. *Guide to Internet Job Searching, 2008–2009 ed.* New York: McGraw-Hill, 2008.

Doyle, Alison. *Internet Your Way To a New Job: How to Really Find a Job Online.* Cupertino, CA: Happy About, 2009.

Levinson, Jay Conrad, and David E. Perry. *Guerrilla Marketing for Job Hunters 2.0: 1,001 Unconventional Tips, Tricks and Tactics for Landing Your Dream Job.* Hoboken, NJ: John Wiley and Sons, 2009.

Shapiro, Cynthia. *What Does Somebody Have to Do to Get a Job Around Here? 44 Insider Secrets and Tips that Will Get You Hired.* New York: St. Martin's, Griffin, 2008.

Whitcomb, Susan Britton. *Job Search Magic: Insider Secrets from America's Career and Life Coach.* Indianapolis, IN: JIST Works, 2006.

Yate, Martin. *Knock 'em Dead 2010: The Ultimate Job Search Guide.* Avon, MA: Adams Media, 2009.

GENERAL JOB-SEARCH WEBSITES

Job-Hunt, www.job-hunt.org.

The Riley Guide, www.rileyguide.com.

Toronto Public Library, "Career and Job Search Help Blog," http://torontopubliclibrary.typepad.com/jobhelp.

Quintessential Careers, www.quintcareers.com.

Wall Street Journal, "Careers," www.careerjournal.com.

Weddle's, www.weddles.com.

WetFeet, www.wetfeet.com.

BOOKS ON JOB FAIRS

CollegeGrad.com, "Job Fair Success," www.collegegrad.com/jobsearch/Job-Fair-Success.

Quintessential Careers, "Career Fair Tutorial," www.quintcareers.com/career_fair_tutorial.

ORGANIZATIONAL TOOLS FOR JOB HUNTS

JibberJobber, http://jobhunt.jibberjobber.com/index.php.

OCCUPATION/INDUSTRY RESEARCH WEBSITES

Bureau of Labor Statistics, "Career Guide to Industries," www.bls.gov/oco/cg.

Bureau of Labor Statistics, "Occupational Outlook Handbook," www.bls.gov/oco.

Bureau of Labor Statistics, "Occupational Outlook Quarterly," www.bls.gov/opub/ooq/ooqhome.htm.

Fast Company, www.fastcompany.com.

Forbes, www.forbes.com.

Fortune, http://money.cnn.com/magazines/fortune/.

Indeed. www.indeed.com.

Money, "Best Jobs in America," http://money.cnn.com/magazines/moneymag/bestjobs/2009/snapshots/1.html.

O*NET OnLine, http://online.onetcenter.org.

The Career Project, www.thecareerproject.org.

The Riley Guide, "Career Research Center" http://rileyguide.com/careers/index.shtml.

Vocational Information Center, www.khake.com/page5.html.

Wall Street Journal, http://online.wsj.com/home-page.

WetFeet, "Industry Profiles" and "Careers," www.wetfeet.com/careers—industries.aspx.

BOOKS ON CHANGING CAREERS

Jansen, Julie. *I Don't Know What I Want, But I Know It's Not This: A Step-by-Step Guide to Finding Gratifying Work.* New York: Penguin, 2003.

Lore, Nicholas. *The Pathfinder: How to Choose or Change Your Career for a Lifetime of Satisfaction and Success.* New York: Simon and Schuster, Fireside, 1998.

Tieger, Paul, and Barbara Barron. *Do What You Are: Discover the Perfect Career for You Through the Secrets of Personality Type.* New York: Little, Brown, 2007.

BOOKS ON RÉSUMÉS AND COVER LETTERS

Betrus, Michael. *202 Great Cover Letters.* New York: McGraw-Hill, 2008.

Enelow, Wendy, and Louise Kursmark. *Cover Letter Magic.* Indianapolis, IN: JIST Works, 2010.

Ireland, Susan. *The Complete Idiot's Guide to the Perfect Résumé.* New York: Alpha Books, 2010.

McGraw-Hill's Big Red Book of Résumés. New York: McGraw-Hill, 2002.

Whitcomb, Susan Britton. *Résumé Magic.* Indianapolis, IN: JIST Works, 1999.

Whitcomb, Susan Britton, and Pat Kendall. *e-Résumés: Everything You Need to Know about Using Electronic Résumés to Tap into Today's Job Market.* New York: McGraw-Hill, 2001.

Yate, Martin. *Knock 'em Dead Cover Letters: Great Letter Techniques and Samples for Every Step of Your Search.* Avon, MA: Adams Media, 2008.

WEBSITES ON RÉSUMÉS AND COVER LETTERS

Dummies.com, "Cover Letters," www .dummies.com/how-to/business-careers /careers/Cover-Letters.html.

Dummies.com, "Résumés," www.dummies .com/how-to/business-careers/careers /Résumés.html.

Purdue Online Writing Lab, "Cover Letters," http://owl.english.purdue .edu/engagement/index.php?category _id=34&sub_category_id=42.

The Damn Good Résumé, www.damngood .com.

The Riley Guide, "Help With Your Résumé and CV," http://rileyguide.com/resprep .html.

Wall Street Journal Careers, "How to Write a Cover Letter," http://guides.wsj.com /careers/how-to-start-a-job-search /how-to-write-a-cover-letter/.

BOOKS ON NETWORKING

Benjamin, Susan. *Perfect Phrases for Professional Networking: Hundreds of Ready-to-Use Phrases for Meeting and Keeping Helpful Contacts Everywhere You Go.* New York: McGraw-Hill, 2009.

Crompton, Diane, and Ellen Sautter. *Find a Job Through Social Networking: Use LinkedIn, Twitter, Facebook, Blogs and More to Advance Your Career.* Indianapolis, IN: JIST Works, 2010.

Directory of National Trade and Professional Associations. Bethesda, MD: Columbia Books, 2007.

Encyclopedia of Associations. Farmington Hills, MI: Thomson Gale, 2005.

Hansen, Katharine. *A Foot in the Door: Networking Your Way into the Hidden Job Market.* Berkeley, CA: Ten Speed Press, 2008.

Jacoway, Kristen. *I'm in a Job Search—Now What???: Using LinkedIn, Facebook, and Twitter as Part of Your Job Search Strategy.* Cupertino, CA: Happy About, 2010.

Levinson, Jay Conrad, and Monroe Mann. *Guerrilla Networking: A Proven Battle Plan to Attract the Very People You Want to Meet.* Bloomington, IN: AuthorHouse, 2009.

McKay, Harvey. *Dig Your Well Before You're Thirsty: The Only Networking Book You'll Ever Need.* New York: Currency Books, 1999.

Pierson, Orville. *Highly Effective Networking: Meet the Right People and Get a Great Job*. Pompton Plains, NJ: Career Press, 2009.

Vermeiren, Jan. *How to Really Use LinkedIn*. Charleston, SC: BookSurge Publishing, 2009.

WEBSITES ON NETWORKING

About.com, "Top 10 Social Media Dos and Don'ts: How (and How Not) to Use Social Media to Job Search" by Alison Doyle, http://jobsearch.about .com/od/onlinecareernetworking/tp /socialmediajobsearch.htm.

IP12's Resources by Subject, "Associations," www.ipl.org/IPLBrowse /GetSubject?vid=13&cid=7.

Kawasaki, Guy, "Ten Ways to Use LinkedIn," http://blog.guykawasaki .com/2007/01/ten_ways_to_use .html#axzz0nAh7w5bx.

Time, "LinkedIn Tricks for Networkers, Job Hunters and Hirers" by Lisa Cullen, http://workinprogress .blogs.time.com/2007/06/07 /linkedin_tricks_for_networkers/.

Weddle's Association Directory, www .weddles.com/associations/index.cfm.

WetFeet, "Blog Basics: How a Blog Can Boost Your Career" by Cara Scharf, www.wetfeet.com/Experienced-Hire /Getting-hired/Articles/Blog-Basics —How-a-Blog-Can-Boost-Your-Career .aspx.

WEBSITES ON RESEARCHING COMPANIES

Fortune, "100 Best Companies to Work for," http://money.cnn.com/magazines/fortune /bestcompanies/2010.

GlassDoor, www.glassdoor.com.

GuideStar, www2.guidestar.org.

Hoover's, www.hoovers.com.

Inc., "Top 100 Inc. 5,000 Companies by Industry," www.inc.com/inc5000/2007 /lists/top100-industries.html.

Jigsaw, www.jigsaw.com.

Quintessential Careers, "Guide to Researching Companies, Industries, and Countries," www.quintcareers.com /researching_companies.html.

The Riley Guide, "How to Research Employers," www.rileyguide.com /employer.html#tutor.

U.S. Securities & Exchange Commission, "Edgar Database," www.sec.gov.Vault .com, "Employer Reviews," www.vault .com/wps/portal/usa/companies.

Yahoo! Finance, http://finance.yahoo.com.

BOOKS ON INTERVIEWING

Beshara, Tony. *Acing the Interview: How to Ask and Answer the Questions That Will Get You the Job*. New York: AMACOM, 2008.

Burns, Dan. *The First 60 Seconds: Win the Job Interview before It Begins*. Naperville, IL: Sourcebooks, 2009.

Oliver, Vicky. *301 Smart Answers to Tough*

Interview Questions. Naperville, IL: Sourcebooks, 2005.

Schuman, Nancy. *The Job Interview Phrase Book: The Things to Say to Get You the Job You Want.* Avon, MA: Adams Media, 2009.

BOOKS ON NEGOTIATING

Fisher, Roger, and William L. Ury. *Getting to Yes: Negotiating Agreement Without Giving In.* New York: Penguin, 1991.

Garlieb, Stacie. *My Job Offer Negotiation Skills Are Solid (I Think) . . . So Why Didn't I Get Anything I Asked For?* Charleston, SC: CreateSpace, 2010.

Miller, Lee E. *Get More Money on Your Next Job . . . in Any Economy.* New York: McGraw-Hill, 2009.

Pinkley, Robin L., and Gregory B. Northcraft. *Get Paid What You're Worth: The Expert Negotiators' Guide to Salary*

and Compensation. New York: St. Martin's, Griffin, 2003.

Wegerbauer, Maryanne. *Next-Day Salary Negotiation: Prepare Tonight to Get Your Best Pay Tomorrow.* Indianapolis, IN: JIST Works, 2007.

WEBSITES ON NEGOTIATING

GlassDoor.com.

JobStar Central, "Salary Information," http://jobstar.org/tools/salary/index.php.

PayScale.com.

Quintessential Careers, "Salary Negotiation and Job Offer Tools and Resources for Job-Seekers," www.quintcareers.com /salary_negotiation.html.

Salary.com, "Negotiation Clinic," www .salary.com/Articles/ArticleDetail .asp?part=par186.

Susan Ireland's Résumé Site, "Salary Negotiation Skills," http://susanireland .com/interview/salary-pay.

PART 2

How to Write a Stellar Executive Résumé

PREFACE

As an executive conducting a job search, you might never have had to write a résumé before, and you might be feeling unsure of where to start. This book provides an easy-to-read, practical, and up-to-date guide on best practices for writing your Executive Résumé. *How to Write a Stellar Executive Résumé* takes you through the résumé-writing process step by step, from thinking through your approach to creating a professional format, crafting effective branding statements and bullets, and handling specific challenges.

Whether you are a résumé writer catering to executives or a senior-level job seeker, you will learn valuable tips to write a STELLAR résumé!

This book is a living document. When résumé trends change, I will be sure to update the book so you stay on top of current best practices. If you have a question about any part of the book, or think I've missed something, I'm always available to clarify points or add items that would add value. I look forward to having you as part of The Essay Expert's readership community at theessayexpert.com.

—BRENDA BERNSTEIN, THE ESSAY EXPERT
MADISON, WISCONSIN, 2017

INTRODUCTION

Recruiters spend only six seconds reviewing an individual résumé, and 80 percent of those six seconds is spent looking only at your name, current and previous title/company, current and previous position start and end dates, and education. A professionally formatted résumé is key to landing an interview.

Though technology is quickly changing the way hiring entities collect and review job search information, the résumé still reigns supreme. In a 2016 survey of four hundred US advertising and marketing executives, 78 percent "said they would rather receive traditional CVs in Word or PDF format from candidates applying for creative roles at their company," and that "far fewer executives today favored online profiles (14 percent) and video or infographic résumés (3 percent each) as their format of choice."

If you are a successful executive, it is likely you have never had to write a résumé before. Yet in today's market, job seekers at all levels are being asked to provide a résumé for consideration. You must either master the craft of résumé writing or hire someone who has mastered it.

I love writing résumés. I have spent many hours studying how to do it well and getting certified at the highest level in the profession, yet I am equally thrilled to see someone do a stellar job writing a résumé on his or her own. That's why I chose to write this book.

Now that you know that you have six seconds to grab the attention of your next employer, how are you going to do that? Perhaps the biggest challenge in résumé writing is that there is no one right way to do it. Seven people will give you seven opinions about your résumé's effectiveness. The good news is that you only have to impress one person: the person who hires you.

This book will guide you through writing and formatting each section of your résumé, providing examples for you to follow every step of the way. If at any point while reading this book, you realize that you prefer to hand your project to a résumé writer, please do not hesitate to contact us at theessayexpert.com. We would love to work with you!

Note on Company Guidelines and Style: If you know that a company follows specific writing guidelines, comply with those guidelines in your résumé and ignore anything in this book that contradicts them. This rule of thumb applies particularly to any style guides used by the company, such as the Chicago Manual of Style or the AP Stylebook.

If you are a grammar and style geek, you might notice that this book was edited according to the Chicago Manual of Style; however, every résumé in the book does not conform to those guidelines. Résumé formatting decisions are sometimes forced by line length and page length considerations, which might mean breaking some rules. However, don't break rules if you know the company abides by a specific set of rules. And be sure to maintain consistency throughout your résumé. In other words, if you break a rule in one spot, break it everywhere.

Note on Formatting Instructions: All instructions and images in this book are given using Microsoft Word. If you use another word-processing program, please follow the overall formatting advice given here and implement it according to your program's functionality.

1
CONTEXT

TIP #1:
WRITE FOR THE FUTURE

It is a misconception that résumés are about your past. Résumés are about your FUTURE. In other words, your résumé will work if you think about what a potential employer would want to know about how you WILL perform. What experience do you have that will enable you to make a contribution to their firm or organization?

If you are writing from the perspective of the FUTURE, here's what will happen:

1. You will write detailed bullets that demonstrate your capability to achieve measurable results. Your readers will infer that you can produce similar results for them.

2. You will think about the purpose and priority of each item on your résumé, then choose and place your sections and bullets accordingly.

3. You will delete anything that is irrelevant or of minimal importance to your future.

4. You will include positions from as many years back as necessary to share information that's relevant to your next position—there is no absolute rule about how many years to include!

Keep reading for more résumé tips that will help you write a well-formatted, attention-grabbing, future-based résumé!

TIP #2:
KNOW YOUR TARGET

If you're not sure what position you are aiming for, how are you possibly going to get it? Make sure you know what your ideal job is and write your résumé as if you are going 100 percent for that job. If there are two types of jobs you want, write two résumés. If there are three types of jobs you want . . . ? You guessed it!

ONE SIZE DOES NOT FIT ALL IN THE WORLD OF RÉSUMÉS!

If you try to write a "universal" or "general" résumé, you will almost always fail. You will feel scattered and unfocused as you write, and you will most likely not succeed in obtaining job interviews.

If you are applying to multiple types of jobs because you are not sure what direction you're headed in, take a step back and consider whether you might want to get some career coaching before you sit down to write your résumé or pay someone else to write your résumé. Clarity of purpose is key when you start your job search. You might still apply to more than one type of job; just be clear about your intention when doing so.

If you want a recommendation for a career coach, contact us at TEESupport@TheEssay-Expert.com. We will give you a list of people who can help.

You might want to try some exercises that you can do on your own. We recommend Mary Elizabeth Bradford's Award-Winning program, the Job Search Success System,[1] which provides worksheets and audio modules to support you through every step of your job search.

Once you know your target or targets, you can begin tailoring your résumé. Many of the tips in this book will help you think through how to match your experience to your desired job description(s)! Part of knowing your target is determining whether it is an appropriate fit for your skills and experience. Take an honest assessment of whether you are a match for the position. You might discover that you are not the best fit and that your energy would be better spent on a different application. An article in *Forbes* magazine covered this issue well: "3 Things That Will Get Your Résumé Thrown in the Trash."[2] While it's good to aim high, it's important to achieve a balance between reaching for the next challenge and barking up the wrong tree.

TIP #3:
KNOW WHAT MAKES YOU STAND OUT

Before you start writing your résumé, I recommend that you do some soul searching. Mary Elizabeth Bradford's Job Search Success System[3] provides questionnaires and forms to help you in that process. Here are some of the questions you will want to answer:

- What makes you unique? (What do you have that distinguishes you from the applicant sitting next to you with the same experience?)
- What are five characteristics that best describe you when you are at work?

---

1 http://theessayexpert.com/job-search-success -system/

2 http://www.forbes.com/sites /dailymuse/2013/01/24/3-things-that-will-get -your-résumé-thrown-in-the-trash/

3 http://theessayexpert.com/job-search-success -system/

- What is the biggest ROI (Return on Investment) an employer will get from you?
- What have you been complimented on at work?
- What do your friends and colleagues say about you when they compliment you?
- Describe an ideal workday. What tasks would you be doing? What would your interactions be like?

There are some work personality assessments you might consider doing, whether on your own or with an executive career coach. The Essay Expert administers the DISC Profile Assessment, which gives you a clear picture of your leadership strengths and challenges in the workplace based on four characteristics: **D**ominance, **I**nfluence, **S**teadiness, and **C**onscientiousness. The DISC profile pinpoints what your "natural" working style is versus the style you have adapted for the work environment. The assessment is very enlightening in evaluating your leadership style and potential.

Another assessment is the 360 assessment, which asks you to reach out to friends and colleagues who give their opinions about your strengths and challenges. This assessment is very valuable as well, as it provides outside perspective on what you truly have to offer. You might be surprised by what you find out.

If any of these assessments interest you, contact TEESupport@TheEssayExpert.com.

We will arrange for you to proceed with the assessment most appropriate for you.

Once you have a handle on what you have to offer a potential employer and what you seek in your work environment, you will have much more power in writing a résumé that brings forth your strengths.

TIP #4:
GATHER INFORMATION FIRST

Before you start writing your résumé, you need to gather information. Start with the basics: your company names (spell them right!), position titles, and dates. Then move on to what you accomplished in each of your positions. Here are some questions to ask and answer about each of your positions:

- How would you describe the company? How big is it? What is the size/value of accounts? How many clients served? What were annual revenues or profits?
- Why were you hired/what were you hired to do? What are/were your job duties?
- Did you have any notable clients?
- How much money did you make/ save your company? How much did you generate in sales? Did profits, revenues, sales, or customer numbers increase due to your efforts or programs you implemented? Did you break any records?

- Did you implement a program that improved something by a certain percentage? Did you save a certain amount of time with a process you created or redesigned (to make a process more efficient)? What did this area look like before, and what does it look like now?
- Which accomplishment(s) are you most proud of at this job? Be specific. You may want to write these in the following "CAR" format:

  C = Challenge (think of a challenge you faced or problem you had to resolve)

  A = Action (which action did you take?)

  R = Results (what were the results of the action you took?)

  Note: You might also have heard of these as "STAR" (Situation— Task—Action—Results) or "PAR" (Problem—Action—Results) stories.
- Did you receive any awards? What were they for?
- How did you grow and develop into a more valuable, more knowledgeable, more skilled commodity?

Once you answer these questions for all your positions, you will have most of the material you need to sit down and write your résumé.

For a more structured approach, you may want to try The Essay Expert's DIY résumé questionnaires. These questionnaires help you create a STELLAR executive résumé *for just a fraction of the cost of working directly with a résumé writer.* If you are ready to take on the challenge of writing your own résumé now, these services are available at theessayex -pert.com:

- General Résumé Questionnaire: $97 (VP and C-Level, Sales & Marketing, Accounting & Finance)[4]
- IT Résumé Questionnaire: $47

Do you like what you're reading? More news and updates are available from The Essay Expert Blog![5]

While you're at theessayexpert.com, you can sign up for our e-list[6] for a free preview of *How to Write a KILLER LinkedIn® Profile*!

---

4 http://theessayexpert.com/product/general -résumé-questionnaire/

5 http://theessayexpert.com/product/it-résumé -questionnaire/

6 http://theessayexpert.com/subscribe-to-the -weekly-blog/

2
GETTING STARTED

TIP #5:

HOW LONG SHOULD MY RÉSUMÉ BE?

And How Many Years Should I Include? A question that comes up extremely frequently with job seekers is whether their résumé can be more than one page—or more than two pages. During my Top 10 Ways to Make Résumé Writing FUN webinars, I am often asked questions such as "Can my résumé be automatically rejected by a company simply for being too long?" I am happy to report that these fears are for the most part unfounded.

Let's get it from the horse's mouth: Career Directors International conducted a survey of recruiters, human resource professionals, and hiring authorities titled "Global Hiring Trends 2012."[7] The report is summarized in my blog article "What Do Recruiters Want in a Résumé? Answers Within . . ."[8] I encourage you to read the entire report if you can. It is a quick read, full of illustrative graphs and charts. Many topics are covered, including recommended résumé length. The following is what the report found:

PAGE PREFERENCES FOR EXECUTIVE RÉSUMÉS (VP, GM, DIRECTOR, C-LEVEL)

In the survey, 37 percent of respondents stated that "length is not an issue as long as the résumé provides the right data to make decisions"—and 8 percent actually *preferred* a three-page résumé, versus 6 percent who preferred a one-pager! (Only 34 percent preferred a two-page résumé.) Perhaps most important, 58 percent of respondents stated that they would NOT penalize an executive candidate for having a résumé that did not meet their preferences (only 5 percent stated they would do so).

Ready for a surprise? Several respondents stated that five pages was the maximum length they would read! Did you hear that, ladies and gentlemen? A five-page résumé! This

---

7 http://www.careerdirectors.com/members/docs/hire_survlow.pdf

8 http://theessayexpert.com/blog/what-do-recruiters-want-in-a-résumé-answers-within/

reality check is a good one for any executives attempting to squeeze their résumé onto two pages. Clearly it is more important to include essential information such as achievements and experiences than to meet some mythical page requirement. A hard-hitting résumé with a compelling message about what the executive will do for a company will almost always be read, regardless of length.

Conclusion: It's not size that matters—it's content! A hefty 54 percent of respondents said the length would not really matter if the résumé were well written and highly focused. As one stated, "*As long as the person has a reason for several pages and I can find value in what is written, I don't care. However, if the résumé is filled with nothing but job duties on eighty separate lines, it is a waste of space and my time.*" (The same could be said of a one-page résumé that doesn't deliver the goods.)

A more important question than "How long should my résumé be?" is "How much should I include about my past positions?" The answer to this question depends on the relevance of those positions. It might be sufficient to reach back ten years and then stop. However, if your most relevant experience was more than ten years ago, don't hesitate to write about it. Some people write more about older positions than about more recent ones because they are targeting a type of position or industry they worked in many years ago.

There are no rules when it comes to length or how much to include . . . other than to present information in the most effective way for your specific situation.

TIP #6:
RÉSUMÉ TETRIS: WHICH ORDER SHOULD MY RÉSUMÉ BE IN?

Putting a résumé together is like a game of Tetris. You want to create a solid, impermeable block; and each piece must fall in the right direction, at the right time, in the right order. Here are some tips on how to win the game:

1. Every résumé starts with your CONTACT INFORMATION: Your name, city and state, phone number, e-mail address, and LinkedIn Profile URL. (See Tip #8 for more on the LinkedIn URL.) Do NOT put your contact information at the bottom of your résumé! Recruiters as well as ATS (Applicant Tracking System) programs prefer your contact information at the top, and may not bother looking for it at the bottom. This is not the place to get original! You do not need to include your street address; city and state are generally sufficient.

2. Choose a **HEADLINE** that states who you are (e.g., CEO, Director of Marketing, Supply Chain Executive, Asset Management Executive, VP Finance, #1 Ranked Medical Device Sales Leader). (See Tip #7 for more on how your headline might look.)

IMPORTANT NOTE: If you are submitting to online systems where your résumé will be read by a computer, you must put the word **SUMMARY** before this section so the computers will recognize the section.

3. Under the headline, you might want to write a brief paragraph, preferably no more than three lines, describing your most important qualifications and accomplishments. (Make sure not to use worn-out phrases like "proven track record" and "team player"! See Appendix C.) You might follow this summary with some bulleted HIGHLIGHTS of your accomplishments.

4. If appropriate, write a list of your **CORE COMPETENCIES** or **KEY STRENGTHS** or **AREAS OF EXPERTISE.** This can be a bulleted list if you wish, or you may list them with the pipe symbol (|) or inserted bullets of your choice between them. Use the TAB key to format these items. Here's what the top of a résumé might look like taking into account points 1–4:

VP FINANCE

Revenue-generating Finance Executive with 12+ years' diverse leadership experience. Change agent known for:

- **Adding value to organization:** Achieved **$145M** in funding increases through implementing new processes and software.

- **Tenacious problem solving:** Rocketed sales by **225%** in a declining revenue environment, overcoming obstacles and breaking paradigms to accomplish strategic initiatives.

- **Analytical thinking and clear communication:** Formulated grounded recommendations that **more than doubled** organizational revenue from **$35M to $79M** in one year.

- **Team Leadership:** Increased EBIT **$3.6M** by championing individual and team talent, motivating staff to outperform targets.

- **Customer Relations:** Reached **100%** customer satisfaction by anticipating customer needs.

EXPERTISE

- Business Strategy
- Financial Planning / Analysis
- Customer Relationships
- Risk Mitigation
- Change Management
- P&L Responsibility
- EBIT Analysis
- Earned Value (EVMS)
- Enterprise Resource Planning (ERP)
- Team Motivation / Development

5. Your **EXPERIENCE** section will almost always be the first section after the branding section. (Exception: for senior academic positions, Education will almost always come first—and you might want to *skip* the summaries and headlines at the top!)

6. You may then have sections such as **TRAININGS & CERTIFICATIONS, PROFESSIONAL ASSOCIATIONS, Volunteer Activities, Publications, Skills & Interests, TECHNOLOGICAL SKILLS, LANGUAGES, Additional Experience, Patents, BOARD MEMBERSHIPS,** or anything else relevant to who you are.

7. Do NOT include References unless specifically requested by the organization. Generally, references should not be on your résumé but instead should be listed on a separate document, formatted with your résumé header. There is no need for the line "References Available Upon Request" at the bottom of your résumé. It just takes up space. Companies will always request references when they want them!

The key: *Relevance*. Order things specifically for the position you're applying for, and you won't go wrong! For sample résumé arrangements, see The Essay Expert's sample résumés.[9] Having trouble organizing your résumé? Contact The Essay Expert at Résumés@TheEssay -Expert.com or 608-467-0067 and speak to one of our Certified Résumé Writers.

TIP #7:
CRAFTING YOUR RÉSUMÉ HEADER— DON'T USE AN OBJECTIVE!

As stated in Tip #6, Your résumé header should include your name, phone number, e-mail address, city, state, and LinkedIn URL. Under that should be your target job title or title describing who you are.

Do *not* use a traditional "Objective" statement that focuses on what you want rather than on what you provide. If you are in the U.S., do *not* include a picture unless you are seeking board positions—there are legal implications for companies who do not want to be accused of discrimination. Pictures remain standard in some countries, including France, Germany, Switzerland, and Austria.

Note: You may include your street address, but it is often unnecessary, since nowadays most employers do not send snail mail to applicants.

THERE'S NO NEED TO TAKE UP MORE THAN TWO LINES WITH YOUR CONTACT INFORMATION

Are you using five lines just for your header ("tombstone" style)? If you need to fill space,

---

9 http://theessayexpert.com/samples/résumés -cover-letters-samples/

that's fine. But once you have a lot of information to squeeze onto a page, why use up space unnecessarily? Here are some ways you can be efficient with your header:

You don't need an entire line for your address, then an entire additional line for your phone number and e-mail. Be creative about your formatting. Keep it professional, of course. Consider using diamonds or the pipe symbol (|) to separate items. (The pipe symbol is found on most keyboards just above the "Enter" or "Return" key, on the same key as your backslash. So hit SHIFT-\.)

A sample second line under your name might look like this:

3 Wood Chip Way | Flint, MI 99999 | jgirardxyz@gmail.com | 321-555-1234

If you are a more advanced Word user, you might use more creative formats, but remember to keep it clean and polished, not fussy or overdone. Check these options out:

Julie Girard

Flint, MI | jgirardxyz@gmail.com | (321) 555-1234 | linkedin.com/in/juliegirardoemsales

SALES EXECUTIVE

Julie Girard

Flint, MI | jgirardxyz@gmail.com
321-555-1234 | linkedin.com/in/juliegirardoemsales

SALES EXECUTIVE

JULIE GIRARD

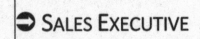 SALES EXECUTIVE

FLINT, MI | JGIRARDxyz@gmail.com | 321.555.1234 | WWW.LINKEDIN.COM/IN/JULIEGIRARDOEMSALES

Use one of these streamlined formats to maximize the space available to talk about what you've done! You'll notice that Julie's LinkedIn profile URL is included in the above examples. Why? Because every employer or recruiter will look you up on LinkedIn. Make it easy for them to find your profile!

THE LINKEDIN "BUTTON" OPTION

If you are submitting your résumé as an electronic attachment, you can use a LinkedIn button such as the following:

(160x33)

Or download a button from jobsearch.about.com/od/linkedin/qt/linkedin-button.htm. (Just right-click on the button and choose "Save Image As . . .") Once you've saved the image to your computer, insert it in the header of your résumé and hyperlink it to your LinkedIn profile! In Word, you'll find the hyperlink function under the Insert tab, Links section:

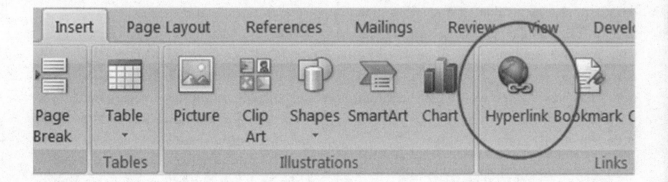

Here's what the final product might look like:

JULIE GIRARD my **Linked** in profile

Flint, MI • 321.555.1234 • juliegirardxyz@
gmail.com

Of course, you want to impress the people who visit you on LinkedIn. Get some help on writing a standout LinkedIn profile by reading my other book, *How to Write a KILLER LinkedIn® Profile . . . And 18 Mistakes to Avoid.* You can get a **free** preview when you sign up for The Essay Expert's e-list.[10]

OBJECTIVE STATEMENTS ARE NO LONGER COOL!

Employers care about what you have to offer them—not about what you want! Instead of writing an objective statement, write a branding statement that shows what you have to offer and at the same time makes your objective clear. More details on writing a branding statement are offered in Tip #11. For now, know that the best way to grab attention is simply to put your current or target job title at the top of the résumé. For instance:

GENERAL
MANAGER—MANUFACTURING
CEO | PRESIDENT
IT DIRECTOR
CORPORATE COUNSEL

---

10 http://theessayexpert.com/subscribe-to-the
-weekly-blog/

VP SALES

A job title is all it takes for a potential employer to understand your objective. If you haven't previously held the job title you are applying for, you can write a general title that encompasses both your past/current positions and where you are going. For example:

SENIOR
EXECUTIVE—MANUFACTURING
MARKETING INTELLIGENCE LEADER

Then you can include in your summary statement something like "Poised to take the reins as General Manager of growing automotive corporation." Your task is to provide just enough information to keep your reader engaged past the 6.25-second barrier. Ask yourself what will accomplish that goal and then do it!

TIP #8:
CUSTOMIZE YOUR LINKEDIN URL

Tip #7 recommended that you put your LinkedIn URL in your résumé header. Did you notice that the LinkedIn URL for http://www .linkedin.com/in/sandrasavvy does NOT have a bunch of messy letters, numbers and slashes at the end (e.g., http://www.linkedin.com/in /sandrasavvy/13/72a/a64)?

You can easily change your long, cluttered LinkedIn URL to a shorter, more easily memorable and professional one. To get rid of those extra letters and numbers, go to your profile and click on "Edit your public profile" in the right sidebar.

Add new profile section ▼

Edit your public profile ⓘ

Add profile in another language ⓘ

At the top of the right-hand column, you will see "Edit public profile URL."
Click on the pencil icon to reveal an entry field where you can customize away!

Public profile settings
When viewers haven't signed in, this is how your profile appears. You control what sections are visible and can update your URL.

Brenda Bernstein
Resume & LinkedIn Profile Writer, Author,
Speaker ★ Executive Resumes ★ C-Level
Resumes ★ Executive LinkedIn Profiles ★
College Essays ★ Law School Admissions
Essays ★ MBA Admissions Essays
Madison, Wisconsin Area | Writing and Editing

Current   The Essay Expert LLC, Kaplan, Inc., The
                 Essay Expert

500+
connections

Edit public profile URL

Enhance your personal brand by creating a
custom URL for your LinkedIn public profile.

www.linkedin.com/in/brendabernstein ✏

Customize Your Public Profile

Select what shows via searches on Bing,

Edit public profile URL

Enhance your personal brand by creating a custom URL for your LinkedIn public profile.

www.linkedin.com/in/**brendabernstein** ←

Is the name you want unavailable? Try your last name followed by your first name or use a credential or keyword. Find a solution that works for you. Keep in mind that the custom ending to your URL must be between 5 and 29 characters and may not include any spaces or "special characters," which include dashes, dots, and other symbols.

Important Note: Once you change your Public Profile URL to a custom URL, your previous URL will no longer work. If you have your Public Profile URL on your résumé, business card, e-mail signature, or any other materials, change it to your new custom link on all these documents.

**Keyword Tip: If you have room to add keywords at the end of your profile URL, you can get search engine optimization (SEO) mileage out of adding your top keyword directly after your name. For example,

johnjonescorporatecounsel or janesmithitdirector. Adding these keywords will not affect your search rankings within LinkedIn itself, but it will provide some leverage in Google searches.

**Résumé Tip: If you don't already own yourname.com for other purposes, such as a blog or other job search marketing materials, this option might be a good one for you. For example, instead of listing your profile at the top of your résumé as "https://www.linkedin.com/in/brendabernstein," you could write "LinkedIn profile: www.brendabernstein.com," which looks much cleaner and also shows that you are tech-savvy.

TIP #9:
USE A PROFESSIONAL E-MAIL ADDRESS
Unless you're applying for a very unconventional job, don't take the chance of rejection

based on your cutesy, political, or even playful e-mail address! Only an applicant for a clown position should have an e-mail like bozo44@ hotmail.com. Stay away from religious connotations (e.g. revivaltime@gmail.com) or e-mail addresses that imply you have another business (e.g., bookexchange@att.net). Use your full name, your first initial with last name, or something else straightforward.

It's easy to get a free e-mail address through Gmail, and these addresses are universally respected; alternatively, you might want to purchase a domain name like JohnSmith.com and create your own e-mail there. If you're in a technological field, some recruiters actually throw away résumés with yahoo.com, hotmail.com, and aol.com addresses because these addresses indicate you are "behind the times." See the article "Is Your E-mail Address Preventing You From Getting the Job You Want?"[11] So use gmail.com! It is important to be aware of any preferences of this kind in your field.

If you don't already have an e-mail address that you'd want an employer to see, sign up for a new one now. Doing so has the added advantage of keeping your job search efforts separate from your other personal and business e-mails, which keep you organized in your job pursuits.

While we're on this topic, make sure your outgoing voice-mail message is professional, too! You don't want employers hearing your cute kid's voice on your answering machine. You might consider getting a separate telephone number, or even using a message service or Internet number, for job search purposes. Do you want to wade through your usual twenty daily messages from friends and family to get to the one from a potential employer?

---

11 https://www.brazen.com/blog/archive/job-search /is-your-e-mail-address-preventing-you-from -getting-the-job-you-want/

3
CONTENT

TIP #10:
THE DANGERS OF "FUNCTIONAL RÉSUMÉS"—AND THE BENEFITS OF A "HYBRID"

Most résumés—and those preferred by recruiters and hiring managers—are organized with the most recent position first and go backward from there. Under each position is a bulleted list describing what the candidate accomplished in that position.

A "functional résumé" is organized as a list of accomplishments without dates, and often without attaching the accomplishments to a particular position. Recruiters and hiring managers are universally suspicious of these résumés, which are often constructed this way in order to hide something.

A much more accepted format is the "hybrid." In this format, you list all your employers, positions, and dates in one section on the first page of the résumé; this makes it clear that you are not hiding anything. Then you can choose what to expand upon and what to present first. Here's an example:

SELECTED EMPLOYMENT HISTORY

CARS R US INC., Flint, MI	August 2007 – Present
ABC PROMOTIONS, Flint, MI	March 2005 – June 2007
VANDERBILT WINDOWS & DOORS, Flint, MI	September 2002 – November 2004
FLINTSTONE REMODELING, Flint, MI	September 2001 – September 2002
CABINETS AMERICA, Charlotte, NC	March 1990 – April 1994

INDUSTRIAL SALES EXPERIENCE

CABINETS AMERICA, Charlotte, NC	March 1990 – April 1994

Private German firm; worldwide leader in design and innovation of cabinet hardware. Global sales of $100B+.

Senior Regional Industrial / Technical Sales Executive

Traveled 40+ weeks per year serving 30 accounts (OEMs and six two-step distributors) in 5½ states valued at $2.5M+. Identified new OEM sales opportunities and worked with client engineering and purchasing departments to secure specifications for products. Trained distribution sales people to sell to end user.

Notable Clients: Riverside Furniture, UNICOR – Federal Prison Industries, O'Sullivan Furniture, Bush Furniture, Bertch Cabinet Company, Pyramid Products, CDI.

This client's most relevant experience was from 1990 to 1994. We gave details about this remote position before providing details of more recent positions; and in order to allay any concerns that she was trying to hide something, we listed her entire work history before anything else. She was successful in obtaining a position in OEM, which was her goal.

There are many ways to present information on a résumé; the hybrid format is one option that provides a lot of flexibility. If you have a challenging work history, you would benefit from speaking with a professional to determine the best way to present your particular situation.

TIP #11:
CREATE A COMPELLING BRANDING STATEMENT AND SUMMARY STATEMENT!

The most important section of your résumé is the top third—the part the reader will read first. You must grab their attention in six seconds so that they will read further.

USING A TAGLINE

Tip #7 discussed some of how to craft the top third of a résumé. You want a clear headline that states who you are and tells your reader that you are qualified for the position. And you might follow that headline with a tagline or branding statement. Here are some branding statements my clients have used:

- Leading Teams to Performance When the Game Is on the Line

- Strategy Architect, Change Agent, and HR Business Partner who blends business acumen with distinctive understanding of people and HR Systems.
- Top-performing marketing executive—Creating compelling campaigns for print and online
- Decisive top performer with multi-faceted knowledge of Asian business culture and processes.
- Multicultural sensibility—Rigorous accountability—Rapid growth
- Success Formula for Operational Excellence and ROI: 80% Execution / 15% Position / 5% Strategy
- Change is the only constant and continuous improvement is the only path. Never accept "We have always done it that way."

In determining your branding statement, it might be helpful to answer the branding questions provided in Tip #3. Often when I work with clients, I am able to glean a branding statement from their questionnaire.[12] Work personality profiles are another source of information for branding statements.

One thing is clear: you don't want your branding statement to sound like anyone else's, and you don't want it to sound corny. So give

12 http://theessayexpert.com/résumé -questionnaires/

it some thought, brainstorm with some people you trust, and don't settle until you love it!

WRITING A UNIQUE, ACHIEVEMENT-ORIENTED SUMMARY STATEMENT

The summary statement is possibly the most difficult section of a résumé to write. Frankly, there is no requirement that you write a summary at all. If you are going to write one that includes general, puffed-up terms that make you sound like everyone else, you would do better not to write one.

Results-oriented executive with entrepreneurial spirit and proven track record of blah blah blah . . .

Don't do it!

Instead, pull in some actual accomplishments, actual names of companies, and as much detail as you can of your career highlights, right into the summary. Consider writing not one blocky paragraph, but some compelling bullets instead. As much as possible, tailor your summary to each job description by addressing the job qualifications requested in the job description. Here are some examples:

HUMAN RESOURCES EXECUTIVE ~ COMPENSATION, EMPLOYMENT, GENERALIST

Strategy Architect, Change Agent, and HR Business Partner who blends business acumen with distinctive understanding of people and HR Systems.

HR Director with versatile experience leading established domestic, international and governmental organizations, as well as subsidiary technology start-ups, to highly profitable results. Measurable contributions to diverse organizations such as Diagnostics Corporation and Major Pharmaceuticals, including launch of a global pharmaceutical and turning around an organization that had been unprofitable for 15 years.

- Conceptualize, design, operationalize and manage human capital systems to positively impact business unit performance.

- Employ innovative strategies to build organizational culture of collaboration, engagement and alignment.

- Committed to relevant and sustainable solutions that seamlessly align HR systems and business systems.

- Work vertically and horizontally with employees across all levels, internal stakeholders, senior management, boards of directors, and business partners.

Demonstrated HR Value

- *Organizational Development*
- *Compensation & Benefits*
- *Talent Acquisition*
- *Performance Management*
- *Employee Development*
- *Employee Engagement/Relations*
- *Succession Planning*

INTERNATIONAL (ASIA/CHINA) SENIOR EXECUTIVE
CEO | COO | GENERAL MANAGER – B2B MANUFACTURING, TRADING & RETAIL
Multicultural sensibility – Rigorous accountability – Rapid growth

Multi-faceted Manufacturing & Operations Executive who takes high-level, all-encompassing goals from Board of Directors, creates focused strategies and objectives, and executes with efficiency.

Poised to take the helm at a U.S. company based in and operating in one or more foreign markets, or foreign company based in and operating in the U.S. *Asia specialization.*

- **Business Expansion:** Managed ballooning sales ($300MM in 2009 v. $50MM in 2002) and 675% employee growth (to 6,000).
- **Supplier Management:** Created, implemented and maintained successful Supplier Management System for large furniture company's Asia expansion.
- **Business Development:** Founded and grew a leading boutique interior design and décor business in Shanghai market.
- **Systems Efficiency:** Overhauled sourcing team and supply chain to achieve significant improvements in all supplier areas.
- **Team Building:** Recruited and mentored best-in-industry multi-cultural management teams comprised of highly collaborative, results-driven and value-added risk takers.

SENIOR EXECUTIVE
CEO | President | Executive Vice President

Success Formula for Operational Excellence and ROI: 80% Execution / 15% Position / 5% Strategy

Change is the only constant and continuous improvement is the only path. Never accept, "We have always done it that way."

SNAPSHOT of VALUE OFFERED

Entrepreneurial business champion, motivated by challenge, willing to take fast and calculated action to execute and implement programs, processes and structure that drive innovation and growth. Passionate with ability to inspire and energize teams and organizations. Fluent Norwegian (Swedish, Danish) & English; Basic German.

- **BUSINESS DEVELOPMENT:** Key Player in transforming entrepreneurial start-ups into #1 market dominators.
- **TURNAROUNDS:** Reversed 1,8 MNOK loss to 14,1 MNOK profit in first year at company.
- **SALES LEADERSHIP:** Motivated teams to outpace all prior performance measures.

When you sit down to craft your summary (if you choose to write one at all), ask yourself: does this statement truly define who I am as a valued leader at any organization? If the answer is no, you're not done. If the answer is yes, then ask: Could someone else have written this summary? If the answer is yes, you're not done. Keep at it until you have described yourself in unique terms that wake up the person reading. It's not an easy thing to do, but it's worth it.

TIP #12:
DELETE THESE WORDS AND PHRASES FROM YOUR RÉSUMÉ

Are you spouting ineffective words and phrases on your résumé? The following is a list of commonly used words and phrases that will not serve you; eliminating them will encourage you to develop more productive alternatives!

RESPONSIBLE FOR

Do you have bullets on your résumé that start with the phrase "Responsible for"? Although it is important on some level to portray the level of responsibility you hold or held in your positions, "Responsible for" is a weak opener. Have you ever stopped to think that you can be "responsible for" something and not actually do it?! Employers care about what you *did*. Compare:

a. Responsible for establishing sourcing strategy.
b. Formalized sourcing with RFPs and metrics to monitor and manage the competitive process. Conducted 20 RFP events in 10 months.

Or:

a. Responsible for purchase of capital equipment.
b. Halved time to acquire approvals and issue purchase orders for capital equipment, from 7–10 days to 3–5

days, by designing and implementing process that eliminated redundancies.

Version b in both cases is more action-oriented and more powerful than version a. Yes they are longer, but the information is so much more persuasive that it's worth the extra line. There are many verbs that make it clear you held responsibility for certain functions or projects. For instance:

- Headed
- Directed
- Steered
- Led
- Managed
- Oversaw
- Piloted
- Orchestrated

Use these powerful verbs instead of listing your responsibilities. Overall, what you achieved is much more important than what your responsibilities were. If you can write a bullet that encompasses *both* your responsibilities *and* your achievements, you will pack the biggest punch. Compare:

a. Responsible for creating costing and pricing-related training materials for Operations and Sales.
b. Bridged previously existing gap between Operations and Sales through crafting of specific, relevant

costing and pricing-related training materials that elevated sales staff confidence and trust.

Notice the difference? Choice b contains responsibilities but doesn't emphasize them. The most important part is the results. In conclusion, please be "responsible for" choosing résumé bullets that reflect the true impact of your actions at your organization!

THE THROWAWAYS: VARIOUS, VARIETY, ETC.

Compare:

a. Created various reporting tools and business analysis processes.
b. Streamlined operations by creating reporting tools and business analysis processes including End-of-Month Performance Reporting, HR Staffing Plans, Investor Reporting, and KPI Reporting.

Version a leaves us with nothing to grab onto. Version b provides specifics. It's not a complete list, but it conveys a sense of variety without using the word.

I acknowledge that there might be exceptions to this rule. Sometimes it does work to use the word "various" or "variety." My recommendation is to take it out and see if the bullet works better. It probably will. Please report back what you discover.

"Etc." is just a variation on various. You might be tempted to put it at the end of a list of clients:

Before: Key clients: Home Depot, OfficeMax, Walmart, etc.

Don't use "etc." if at all possible. Pick your list of top clients and introduce it with "such as" or "including":

After: Key clients include giants such as Home Depot, OfficeMax, and Walmart.

OVERUSED BUZZWORDS

I think it's safe to say that I find at least one of the following phrases on every résumé that comes across my desk: Team player, Proven track record, Results-oriented, Detail-oriented.

What section do you think these phrases appear in? You guessed it: the Summary.

You need to get this: your Summary statement is intended to make you stand OUT from the crowd. Why ever would you choose to use the same words that everyone else is using and that ultimately because of their overuse say absolutely nothing about who you are?

Any generic language should be stripped, if humanly possible, from your Summary section. Some examples of powerful Summary statements were included in Tip #11. Here are two more, one from a for-profit and another from a nonprofit leader:

Influential, trusted advisor with deep Board and corporate governance expertise in energy, clean technology, banking, and manufacturing industries. Success raising billions of dollars in capital to catapult start-ups and growth companies into thriving, profitable entities. Position businesses for successful IPO or sale; restructure underperforming operations while gaining investor confidence and capturing up to 4x capital investment. Achieve measurable results by controlling hold periods and formulating exit strategies.

EXECUTIVE DIRECTOR
Nonprofit Executive and current CEO of ABC Inc. who transforms organizational challenges for local and national organizations. Talent for devising financial and programming solutions that rejuvenate fiscal health while empowering staff and constituents. Results achieved for children and families through unique relationships with academic, business, and government entities.

These professionals did not use the phrase "proven track record" to demonstrate their success. Got it?

The more you can describe your accomplishments and specific strengths in your Summary, the better. Do not rely on clichéd phrases that fail to distinguish you from the pool. Take care in crafting your Summary and every bullet of your résumé. It's worth the effort. (See Appendix C for more words and phrases to delete!)

TIP #13:
✶ MAKE YOUR BORING RÉSUMÉ BULLETS SPARKLE! ✶
Are you struggling to put some pizzazz into

your résumé? Do you think you don't have anything interesting to say? In addition to citing your accomplishments and providing the right level of detail, an easy way to inject interest into your résumé is to vary your language, especially your verbs!

For instance, how many ways can you say "Led"? Here are some examples:

- Piloted
- Oversaw
- Steered
- Propelled
- Directed
- Championed
- Dominated
- Architected
- Orchestrated
- Pioneered
- Drove

How about multiple ways to say "increased"? Here are some possibilities:

- Heightened
- Raised
- Elevated
- Upturned
- Accelerated
- Amplified
- Grew
- Enhanced
- Mushroomed
- Skyrocketed
- Multiplied
- Doubled
- Tripled
- Quadrupled

And "decreased"? Try these:

- Shrank
- Slashed
- Shortened
- Reduced
- Diminished
- Minimized
- Lessened
- Lowered
- Contracted
- Condensed
- Cut
- Compressed
- Divided
- Halved

Imagine a résumé where each bullet starts with new and different verbs. This could be *your* résumé! If you're getting bored by your résumé language, infuse it with life. Your thesaurus is your friend. By changing your verbs from bullet to bullet, you will have more fun writing your résumé . . . and make things more fun for the person reading it! For more ideas for snazzy résumé verbs, see Appendix A and Appendix B!

TIP #14:
FOCUS ON ACCOMPLISHMENTS
Many Executives, despite their impact on their organization, make the mistake of filling their résumé with job duties and responsibilities.

Your responsibilities will not get you your next job—they do not distinguish you! To spark the interest of decision makers, you need to show them what you accomplished.

Questions to Answer: What did things look like before you got there? What did you do to make a difference? What were the results? Which challenges did you face, and how did you conquer them?

FIND THE TREASURE: QUANTIFIABLE ACHIEVEMENTS

When writing about any accomplishment, dig for the numbers. Write about revenue increases, cost and time savings, and percentage increases. Write about the size of your accounts. Write about the big-name clients you served. If you are in a VP, Director, or C-Level position, and you tell me you have no numbers or names to report, I won't believe you.

If the numbers are confidential, speak in terms of percentages instead of dollar amounts. If client names are confidential, describe the companies in terms of size and industry. There is always a way to quantify your achievements!

The more you can quantify what you've done, the more you will come across as a contributor who will be valuable to your next organization. Let's be realistic here: your next employer needs to know that you will make and/or save the company more money than the company will be paying you.

Here are some examples from a range of industries with quantifiable achievements included:

- Enabled company to keep pace with **doubling sales every 12 months**—$0 to $30MM in 3 years with sales projected to reach $60MM in 2013.
- **Grew business sales from $50MM to $300MM** in 6 years to become world's largest upholstery cutting & sewing manufacturer. **Achieved 5% ($15MM) cost reduction/year while expanding business by 500%.**
- **Spurred a $900K influx in revenue and 34% program ROI** by creating customer champion show sites, based on research that increased sales closings and secured an additional four deals annually.
- **Increased EBIT $3.6M** by negotiating cost incentive clause and motivating workforce to contain expenses; turned around project experiencing cost overruns to an **$11M** surplus, a **28%** improvement.
- **Eclipsed largest competitor, driving organization from #2 to #1 worldwide.**
- **Territory Growth:** Propelled district from **$2.3M to $9.6M** and region to **1st of 4** in revenue production through strategic sales initiatives.

CONTEXT IS EVERYTHING

Simply reporting numbers is not sufficient. You must also provide context for these numbers. Note in the last example above (Territory Growth) that if the bullet had the result $9.6M but not the starting number $2.3M, we would not know the significance of the growth. In fact, many of the above examples provide both before and after numbers. Generating a surplus is more impressive when there were previous cost overruns; and achieving profitability is more impressive when the company was previously operating at a deficit.

Read your bullets carefully and be rigorous about framing your accomplishments in an appropriate context; that way, you can make your achievements sound as impressive as they truly are. Go over each of your bullets carefully after you write them. Have you put the most important part of the bullet at the beginning? For instance, in the final bullet above about territory growth, we did not start with "Implemented strategic sales initiatives"—we started with the facts about the numbers. Don't wait to share results until the end of the bullet—put them right up front!

This point is so important that I am providing additional examples below. Look at the "Before" example: does it remind you of any of the bullets on your résumé? If so, stop, reflect, and rewrite. How can you make it look more like the "After" examples?

EXAMPLE #1 (GENERAL MANAGER)
Before:
- Sales leader spanning responsibilities of inside sales team, field team, and value-added reseller network; team

responsible for software sales to independent physician offices and hospital systems

After:
- **Closed $1.4M and $2M deals, breaking product sales records;** spearheaded technology and healthcare services bundle to best position Healthcare IT software solutions to independent physician offices and hospital systems.

EXAMPLE #2 (SOURCING EXECUTIVE)
Before:
- Developed sourcing strategies to drive cost reduction and improve supplier performance.

After:
- **Achieved 60% reduction in unit costs** by developing company's first manufacturing scorecard.
- **Culled $400K off working capital expenses** and ensured better performance from contractors and CMO by converting to new payment schedule.
- **Shaved volume of catalyst inventory 80% and slashed recycle time from 15 weeks to 6 weeks, reducing working capital requirements by $4M.**

(It took several bullets to adequately explain what this Executive had put into one generalized line.)

EXAMPLE #3 (EUROPEAN BUSINESS DEVELOPMENT EXECUTIVE)

Before:

- Responsible for top-line revenue and global sales.

After:

- **Led 1-year turnaround of 1,8 MNOK loss to 14,1 MNOK profit.** Team set new revenue records monthly, including record sales and profits Q4 2011 and Q1 2012. **On track to reach 500+ MNOK within next 2 years.**

What made the difference between the lackluster "before" samples and the more enticing "after" bullets? Details of accomplishments! You might have thought "less is more" when it comes to résumé bullets. Perhaps you kept your bullets to a list of responsibilities so that you could convey the scope of your position and not give away so much that you wouldn't have anything to talk about in the interview. Please reconsider! First of all, you'll never be able to put in a 2–3 page résumé every detail about how you performed your job, impacted your company, or reached your achievements. Second, you'll just shoot yourself in the foot if you don't entice employers with your actual accomplishments.

Unless you want to be looked over for the next person who gets a "Wow" out of company decision makers, include details of your accomplishments. Our Résumé Questionnaire[13] is a good place to start if you're not sure what to include. Once you complete the questionnaire, if you want us to write your résumé for you, contact us at Résumés@TheEssayExpert.com.

TIP #15:
TAILOR YOUR RÉSUMÉ BULLETS

In Tip #2, I told you that résumés must be tailored to each job application. The summary at the top is the first section to tailor; and ideally you will customize the order and emphasis of your bullets, as well.

If you are applying for a position with a published description, go through that description item by item. If you have done something that matches the listed responsibilities or requirements, put it on your résumé.

EXAMPLE #1:

The position description says you will be engaging in strategic planning, executive oversight, and management of problem resolution, process/efficiency improvement, and employee relations.

Your current résumé does not contain these phrases.

Solution: Divide your bullets into sections titled Strategic Planning, Executive Oversight, Problem Resolution, Process Efficiency, and

---

13 http://theessayexpert.com/résumé -questionnaires/

Employee Relations; then group relevant bullets under each one of those headers.

EXAMPLE #2:

The position description says: "We have a great new opportunity for a Vice President of Procurement to provide direction and oversight of the procurement department and ensure that daily operations are performed in a consistent and high-quality manner."

Your current résumé talks all about sourcing and operations, but you did not emphasize procurement.

Solution: Think about your procurement experience and weave it into your résumé. If possible, add the phrases "oversight of the procurement department" and "daily operations" into your résumé bullets.

EXAMPLE #3:

The position description says: "You will play a key role in collaborating with senior functional leads to establish both short and long-term business objectives as well as identify, develop, and manage strategic business relationships to enable implementation of the corporate growth strategy, revenue achievement, and new product development initiatives."

Your current résumé says you collaborated with senior team members and cultivated relationships with key stakeholders. It mentions long- and short-term planning and alignment with organizational growth strategies. The words are not the same, but the concepts are.

Solution: Your résumé will be perfect for a

human being as is. A human will know that you have met the requirements of the position. If you are giving your résumé to a human being, your tailoring job is done.

A computer, however, will not understand that you have the requisite skills and experience for the position. Therefore, you may need to create multiple versions of your résumé. See Tip #42 on ATS systems to find out how to do this and give yourself a much-improved chance of obtaining interviews if you are applying to jobs online.

Again, if you are applying for an advertised position, look at the position description and find ways to integrate the words and phrases you find into your résumé.

Important: Prioritize your bullets with the most important and relevant items for that particular position first! To grab the reader's attention, you must provide examples of the skills and accomplishments they care about most.

If you want professional help in targeting your résumé to give you the best chance of being invited to meet with the company, please contact the Certified Résumé Writers at theessayexpert.com/contact-us/.

TIP #16:

SHOULD I HAVE A SKILLS & INTERESTS SECTION?

At the Executive level, it is rare to see a list of activities and interests at the bottom of a résumé. However, there is always a possibility that rapport can be established by writing about your interests in aerospace, golf, orchids, or NASCAR. If you are extremely passionate and/or involved in one of your hobbies, and if you have room to spare, you may choose to include an Interests section. Winning an Ironman triathalon, for instance is a feat worthy of a résumé mention!

If you have advanced or unusual computer skills that are required for your position, list them along with your level of proficiency under Skills. You can list your foreign languages, as well.

Things to watch out for:

Sports: Be careful about listing your favorite team, especially if the job is in a city with a competing team! And only list a team if you can recite some stats.

Politics & Religion: Generally, politics and religion are not brought up, either at the interview or on the job. In most cases, it is advisable not to reveal too much on your résumé.

For Executives, generally your most important activities will be Board or volunteer roles, which you can list in a Board Memberships, Volunteer Activities, or Civic Contributions section. According to Link Humans, "42 percent of hiring managers surveyed by LinkedIn said they view volunteer experience as equivalent to formal work experience." If you choose to include a Skills & Interests or an Activities section, list only things that are likely to catch someone's attention in a positive way, and about which you can speak in depth.

TIP #17:
SHOULD I HAVE A SEPARATE LANGUAGES SECTION?

If you speak several languages and this aspect of your profile is important for the type of work you are seeking, you may choose to have a separate Languages section. If languages play a less significant role, or if you do not have enough room to devote an entire section to them, you can include language skills under the Skills & Interests section.

In the Skills & Interests section, you can simply have a bullet that says something like:

- Proficient in French (written and spoken)

Or you can have a Languages sub-header under Skills & Interests, for example:

Skills & Interests
Languages: Fluent in Mandarin Chinese (written and spoken); Basic knowledge of Korean
Computer: . . .
Other: . . .

HOW SHOULD I DESCRIBE MY LANGUAGE SKILLS?

If you speak a foreign language at a conversational level or above, list it on your résumé and tell us the level at which you speak and write. These are possible ways to describe your language skills:

Basic | Proficient | Conversational | Advanced | Fluent

... or whatever is appropriate. Keep in mind: If you list fluency in a language, make sure you are prepared for an interview conducted in the foreign language! That means don't *ever* overstate your level of proficiency. EVER.

TIP #18:
CONSIDER INCLUDING A CHART, GRAPH, OR TESTIMONIAL

If you are an executive, you might choose to create a chart or graph as a pictorial representation of your accomplishments. If you're a receptionist or a nursery school teacher, a graph would be overkill. Here's a sample of a graph included in a résumé:

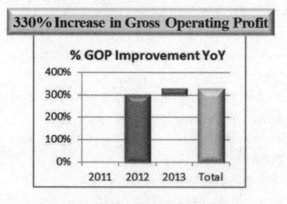

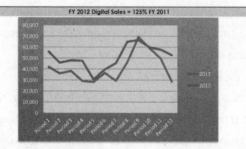

% Growth YOY 2011-2012		
	Q1 2012 V. 2011	Q2 2012 V. 2011
Data	211.44%	227.51%
New Vessels	233.33%	200.00%
Revenue	121.30%	130.32%
Profit	191.51%	144.50%

Only use a graph if appropriate for the position to which you're applying. In Career Directors International's survey Global Hiring Trends 2012,[14] 33 percent of respondents reported that they still have not received a résumé with a chart or a graph. Of those who had seen charts and graphs, 24 percent found them helpful or very helpful, while 22 percent found them distracting. These results are rather inconclusive but indicate that if you work in a conservative industry (such as insurance or finance), it might be best to stick to the tried-and-true bullet format; in more innovative industries, or for marketing and sales positions, charts and graphs are a great fresh approach. For someone climbing the ladder within the same company, charts and graphs might also be very effective. When in doubt, keep it simple!

TESTIMONIALS
You might be tired by now of tooting your own horn, and frankly, some things are much more

---

14 http://www.careerdirectors.com/members/docs/hire_survlow.pdf

credible when said by people other than your-self. If you have received recommendations on LinkedIn, positive feedback in evaluations, or testimonials in any form, consider putting them on your résumé! Here's what a testimonial might look like:

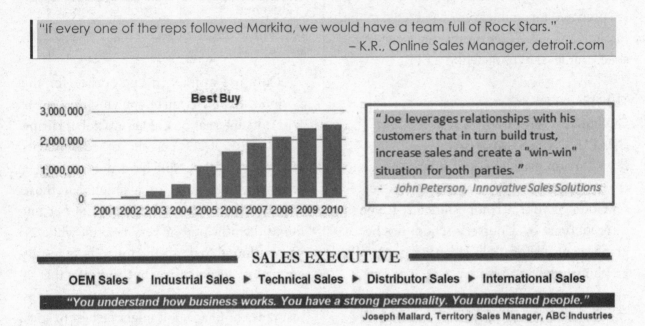

"If every one of the reps followed Markita, we would have a team full of Rock Stars."
– K.R., Online Sales Manager, detroit.com

"Joe leverages relationships with his customers that in turn build trust, increase sales and create a "win-win" situation for both parties."
- John Peterson, Innovative Sales Solutions

SALES EXECUTIVE

OEM Sales ▶ Industrial Sales ▶ Technical Sales ▶ Distributor Sales ▶ International Sales

"You understand how business works. You have a strong personality. You understand people."
Joseph Mallard, Territory Sales Manager, ABC Industries

The use of testimonials is becoming more and more common on résumés. In Global Hiring Trends 2012,[15] 29 percent of those sur-veyed said a testimonial would influence their decision positively. So take advantage of this trend and let your potential employer know what key players at your past organizations have to say about you! You may place the tes-timonial in the top third of the résumé, near the relevant position, or anywhere that makes sense and is visually appealing.

TIP #19:
"I" VERSUS "WE"

As an Executive, many of your accomplish-ments are team accomplishments, yet you still need to take credit for your role in achieving those results.

Many executives say "we" when they mean "I." In doing so, they risk underplaying their contributions and weakening their value prop-osition. An alternative to giving credit to your

15 http://www.careerdirectors.com/members/docs /hire_survlow.pdf

team for all your accomplishments is to distinguish what *you* did from the results achieved by your team.

Perhaps you were the one who discovered the problem and began taking action to solve it so that it was addressed before it was too late. Perhaps you initiated a brainstorming system and your team devised potential solutions under your guidance. Was it your insight that led to the most effective solution being chosen? Who was responsible for the productive nature of the conversation and the collaborative climate that permitted across-the-board buy-in? Were you the person who presented the ultimate solution to senior management?

Here is an example of bullets from a Supply Chain Executive résumé that shows the executive at the source of his teams' successes:

FACTORY OVERSIGHT/QUALITY CONTROL & ASSURANCE

- **Sourced sales to ABC of $2–3M/year** for one product after prior trading company dropped project. Took reins at factory, ensuring proper QC while interfacing with product development and manufacturing.
- **Developed QA team** that achieved **consistent passing of factory audits and shrank quality rejects to <1%.**
- **Drafted supplier agreements** with Chinese manufacturers, clearly setting forth expectations for quality, on-time delivery, and product pricing in climate of widely fluctuating raw material costs and exchange/labor rates.

PRODUCTIVITY/PROFITABILITY THROUGH TALENT MANAGEMENT

- **Spurred $4M sales increase** by leveraging team in Asia, turning weak link into relied-upon unit.
- **Empowered previously unproductive employees,** accomplishing unprecedented culture transformation.

Part of your challenge as a high-powered executive will be to balance the presentation of your own contributions with those of your team. Don't sell either yourself or your valued staff short.

TIP #20:
SPECIAL ISSUE—FILLING A "GAP"

If you have a gap on your résumé, perhaps from caring for children or a sick or elderly relative, you will be faced with the question of how to treat this situation on your résumé.

The first question to ask yourself is what you were doing during this "gap." Often people say they were doing "nothing," whereas in reality, they were taking leadership in a school or nonprofit organization, taking classes, or homeschooling their children. It might be more appropriate to write on your résumé exactly what you were doing during the so-called gap.

Here is one example of a résumé for a "stay-at-home mom":

First, the top third of her résumé:

SARA D. LEES, MBA

Austin, TX 77777 | 512.555.5555 | linkedin.com/in/saradlees1 | saradlees@austin.rr.com

SENIOR PROJECT MANAGER – REGISTERED ARCHITECT

GLOBALLY SAVVY, AWARD-WINNING LEASE MANAGER AND SITE DEVELOPER

⇒ VALUE TO ORGANIZATION

15+ YEARS DRIVING ROI THROUGH EXECUTION OF SITE DEVELOPMENT PROJECTS AND EXPANSIONS WORLDWIDE:

◆ Saved millions while delivering $100M+ in capital projects for BIG BIZ over 5-year period.
◆ Oversaw successful, deadline-driven construction of $56M new TTT/Big Biz Corporate Headquarters (US) and international sales offices (US, Asia, Latin America).
◆ Winner: National Leadership in Environmental and Energy Efficient Gold Award.

It would be impossible to identify this candidate as a stay-at-home mom from reading the top third of her résumé. She passes the six-second test.

Here is how she presents her most recent experience:

PROJECT MANAGEMENT HISTORY & PERFORMANCE

Contributing experience in positions including: **Real Estate Project Manager and Director of Real Estate / Facilities** – *BIG BIZ* ➲ **Management Consultant** – *Realty Co.* ➲ **Partner Design and Construction Team** - *Blackbird Company* ➲ **Architect and General Contractor**

ARCHITECT, GENERAL CONTRACTOR, CONSULTANT – Austin, TX   2008|to present

⇒ *Provided powerful artistic and financial leadership for residential and commercial projects.*

♦ **Commercial:** Brought new life to Montessori School kitchen by spearheading $40K new facility design and construction (2011-2012).
♦ **Residential:** Transformed lackluster kitchen, living room, dining room, and outdoor covered living space of a residence to a modern paradise. $140K budget (2008-2010).
♦ **Financial:** Successfully managed investment portfolio during down economy by following trends and engaging in continuing education; focused on energy as viable investment sector.

Note that this job seeker has accomplished quite a bit while raising her children. She was able to present some powerful achievements up front without showing an obvious gap.

Whether you've taken two years or ten years away from the traditional workforce, you face the issue of how to handle this gap on your résumé. Here are nine strategies for handling this type of gap:

1. **Take stock.** What have you been doing during your "gap" years? Whether it's building an addition to your home, freelancing, or volunteering for the PTA or a non-profit organization, you have gained valuable experience while you've been away from the traditional working world. Put it on your résumé. Emphasize leadership roles.

2. **Have confidence!** You are a valuable employee and have skills and talents to offer. Don't ever apologize for your life choices!

3. **Keep up your skills.** Have you been taking any classes during your employment gap? Put those on your résumé. If you haven't been keeping current, now's the time to start!

4. **Put a title at the top of the résumé that states who you are.** This title should be a match for the job you're applying for. For instance, "Nonprofit Executive" or "IT Director." Similarly,

write a summary that highlights your skills and accomplishments.

5. **Use a cover letter.** You may choose to mention that you are excited to reenter the workforce in your cover letter. The cover letter is a great place to more fully explain a gap (the résumé is not the best place for it).

6. **Consider a hybrid format** for your résumé. It deemphasizes the gap. See Tip #10.

7. **Stay connected!** Your most likely source for your next job is someone you know. If you get a job through networking, gaps in your work history become much less important.

8. **Participate on LinkedIn.** Join LinkedIn groups where your employers might be lurking. Participate in group discussions and reach out to people you want to get to know. LinkedIn is a great place to develop networks and to find job opportunities. Check out *How to Write a Killer LinkedIn® Profile*[16] for easy-to-follow tips on writing a LinkedIn profile that gets you noticed!

9. **Polish up your job search skills.** They might be rusty! Get a friend or a professional to do mock interviews with you. Practice answering tough questions, especially questions about

---

16 http://theessayexpert.com/how-to-write-a-killer -linkedin-profile-e-book/

an employment gap, so you feel confident you can answer in a positive light. Videotape yourself to find out how you are coming across. Keep it up until you would hire yourself!

Everyone with an employment gap has a unique situation that needs a unique approach. If you are unsure of how to handle your set of circumstances, it is advisable to obtain professional advice. You might want to get help from the Certified Résumé Writers at The Essay Expert.[17] You might also like my interview on BlogTalkRadio, Résumés for Relaunchers.[18]

TIP #21:
SPECIAL ISSUE—FOR "OLDER" JOB SEEKERS

What to Do If You're an "Older" Job Seeker—or If You're Just Frustrated in Your Search!
For many executives, age is not an issue. If you are seeking a consulting role, for instance, you might be trusted more if you are over sixty. However, let's not pretend that age discrimination does not pervade today's job market, even, sometimes, in the executive realm.

One surefire way to circumvent age discrimination is to work with an executive talent agent. These agents are extremely well connected and will market you in a way that

makes you shine. You will have companies coming after you because a buzz has been created about what you offer; any concerns about your age will be negligible.

The two Executive Agents I recommend are Fred Coon (fcoon@stewartcoopercoon.com / 480-245-5904) and Debra Feldman (DebraFeldman@JobWhiz.com / 203-637-3500). If you are willing to invest from $5,000–$10,000 to find your next position faster and at a higher compensation, contact them to find out what they offer.

There are also steps you can take to mitigate the effects of age discrimination. Two of my blog followers over fifty agreed to share their success stories with you. I hope their success inspires job seekers of all ages to keep on taking action! Becky S. shared the following about how she obtained a Senior IT position:

- Your **webinars and e-book** were a real encouragement and a definite part of the process. Thanks for sharing and encouraging all job seekers!
- Took a **3-month contract position** which lasted a year. I am so thankful to have had this opportunity.
- **Posted updates on LinkedIn** when attending classes, announcing the approaching contract end and my desire to be the newest member of your team.
- My **new boss maintained contact through LinkedIn.** He even downloaded my résumé and

---

17 http://theessayexpert.com/about-us/

18 http://www.blogtalkradio.com
    /backinforce/2011/03/22/résumés-linkedin-for
    -relaunchers

considered me an applicant. **Three interviews** later I had an **offer**!

Note that Becky used social media to her full advantage, demonstrating that even though she is older, she is computer-savvy and on top of current trends. Note that she was open to contract positions and accepted one that gave her valuable experience while she was actively looking for other work.

Steven A. provides the following wisdom stemming from his successful search for a senior-level accountant position:

- **Volunteering** was a great confidence-lifter and networking tool. I did that at North Shore Long Island Jewish Medical Center for six months. It was extremely fulfilling; met new professional contacts/links and helped fill the gap in the résumé while looking for next position.
- Strong **perseverance**, applying for jobs that may not necessarily been 100 percent qualified for (i.e., taking chances).
- **Strong LinkedIn profiling** & participation in **group discussions** there.
- Having **good contacts** (such as yourself, Brenda) that help you with strategies and point you in a good direction.

- **Supportive job search services** such as Connect-To-Care (Little Neck, NY, & other New York locations; FEGS and other channels) were great support groups.
- **Networking** helps, but unless it is properly targeted, it won't always work (e.g., job fairs predominant in sale promotions or solicitations/advertising will not help an unemployed, experienced, professional accountant).
- [Steven also warns:] Employers, recruiters, & HRs will never ever admit it, but age is a negative running factor if the applicant is in fact older (i.e., as myself, over fifty). Many agencies (I recall approaching at least a dozen) don't ever get back to applicants. Only two in twelve ever gave me leads in a year's unemployment time. Job searches must be predominantly independently pursued.

Steven's insights hammer home the message that being active online and pursuing multiple networking opportunities are two keys for the older job seeker. LinkedIn can be used in multiple ways, from researching whom you might know at a particular company in order to network your way in, to participating in groups, highlighting your volunteer activities, and attracting recruiters with targeted keywords.

In LinkedIn's blog article, "5 Steps for Older Workers to Succeed in the Job Hunt,"[19] author Kerry Hannon advises to use a professional e-mail address (with your full name if possible, preferably at Gmail or a paid provider), join LinkedIn, network, and start a Twitter account. And use these platforms to their utmost capabilities! In her words, "don't be a wallflower." Let your contacts know what you are looking for and who would be great to talk to about your search.

By joining LinkedIn, you announce yourself in the job market and can leverage its features to get the best results. Note that Becky and Steven used LinkedIn to its max, and both of them found new positions. *How to Write a KILLER LinkedIn® Profile*[20] is a great place to start.

Fully utilize your networks both on LinkedIn and in person. Hannon points to a new, free service from AARP called Work Reimagined,[21] which leverages LinkedIn's API to help job hunters find information and job openings. You can sign up for customized job alert postings in your field of interest.

In her advice about starting a Twitter account, I defer to Hannon: "Follow people or companies where you might want to interview. For your username, use your actual name or a shortened form. Include a bio—where you live and what kind of work you do . . . 160 characters. By following tweets, you can get the scoop on people you may wind up interviewing with and stay on top of a potential employer's news. You can also share ideas and tips with other job seekers. Plus, you're expanding your network."

Hannon's last piece of advice—don't be a wallflower—is valuable both on the job as well as when you're searching for a new job. Just like you need to exercise your body to build muscle, you need to participate in discussions online and in person, and keep doing your research, to build your job-search success muscles. Looking for a job is a full-time job, so create a plan and get into action!

Using a combination of tips from Becky S., Steven A., and Kerry Hannon, you can win the job search game regardless of your age.

TIP #22:
SPECIAL ISSUE—MORE THAN ONE POSITION AT THE SAME COMPANY

It is likely that you received promotions over time if you spent more than a year at any company. There are a couple of ways to handle this situation:

1. List each position as a completely separate entry under "Experience." I don't recommend this solution on your formatted résumé, as it takes up more space than necessary and

19 http://blog.linkedin.com/2012/09/26/5-steps-for -older-workers-to-succeed-in-the-job-hunt/

20 http://theessayexpert.com/how-to-write-a-killer -linkedin-profile-e-book/

21 http://www.aarp.org/work/job-hunting/info-08 -2012/connect-with-AARP-and-work-reimagined .html

makes it challenging to convey the full length of time you were at a company. However, in the version of your résumé that you create for ATS systems, you must list multiple positions this way.

2. List the company with the full range of dates you worked there. List your most recent position, with the dates of that position in parentheses, and bullets conveying your accomplishments in that position. Follow with the same information for the position you held before the most recent one. You would choose this option if you had distinct accomplishments at each of your positions. For example:

MAJOR PHARMACEUTICALS, New York, NY   January 1996-December 2000
Senior Director of Human Resources (March 1997-December 2000)
- **Key Responsibility:** Facilitated 1st-ever launch of global product, Product Name®, that generated $1.5B in revenues in first 18 months. Supported Executive VP of Global Operations, senior staff, and 3500 global employees in 12 international manufacturing facilities (Europe, Russia, Latin America, and Puerto Rico).
- **Organizational Development:** Led HR due diligence and integration of 200-employee plant in Puerto Rico and 150-person plant in Italy; built and staffed 60-employee plant in Russia.
- **Compensation & Benefits; Performance Management:** Led global implementation of highly innovative corporate-wide Development / Performance / Reward system. Eliminated salary ranges and merit pay by providing stock ownership and annual cash incentives for all employees.

Director of Human Resources for Subsidiary Start-Up (January 1996-March 1997)
Managed all human resources activities for subsidiary start-up after acquisition by Major Pharmaceuticals.
- **Organizational Development:** Led development of company's vision and principles, culture, and organizational design through move to new facility and launch of major new product.

3. First list the company with the full range of dates you worked there. Underneath, write each title with dates in parentheses, most recent first. Then follow with accomplishments from all the positions, without necessarily distinguishing for which position you did what. Choose this option if you have significant overlap in the accomplishments for your various positions. Here are two examples:

HAMILTON SUNDSTRAND
Division of United Technologies (UTC) Business, a Fortune 500 Company.

Business Unit Financial Controller, Houston, TX (2009–Sept 2011) **Business Manager / Program Manager,** Cape Canaveral, FL (2005–2009)

2005–2011

Supervised staff of seven handling 100% of finance closings, corporate and customer reporting, pricing, accounts payable, and audit functions. While executing program management duties for HS Shuttle contract, selected to establish and lead Field Office and assume Shuttle Program Manager duties for 18-month interim basis.

PROJECT & PROGRAM LEADERSHIP

▸ Increased EBIT **$3.6M** by negotiating cost incentive clause and motivating workforce to contain expenses; turned around project experiencing cost overruns to an **$11M** surplus, a **28%** improvement.

▸ Leveraged experience by implementing project cost and schedule status, establishing baselines and estimate to complete processes.

▸ Developed key program metrics, including variance to cost and schedule, and variance at completion.

▸ Presented and led program reviews for leadership and customers.

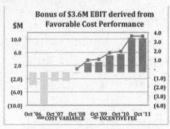

CHANGE MANAGEMENT

▸ Implemented pricing software for **$130M** proposal across multiple locations, allowing for an integrated deliverable with seamless reporting capabilities. Demonstration led to software's selection for transition to entire business unit.

CUSTOMER SATISFACTION ACHIEVEMENT

▸ Achieved multiple **100%** Customer award fees scores, up from 85%.

▸ Received awards for Earned Value Implementation, Customer Focus, and restoring office operations following Tropical Storm Faye.

BIG Machine Corp., Dollar Tree, OH

2000-2007

$20M designer and manufacturer of packaging and product handling equipment, serving Bayer, HP, Procter & Gamble.

Managed $5.5M budget and 16 staff, including Accounting/Finance, Human Resources, IT/IS and Materials departments, representing substantial portion of company's operations. Saved $500K+ over tenure.

CFO (2005-2007)
DIRECTOR OF FINANCE, INFORMATION & MATERIALS (2001-2005)
CONTROLLER (2000-2001)

COST REDUCTION & CONTAINMENT

• Saved $40K+ in annual internal audit costs by preparing additional schedules in-company and automating submission; 22% saved through competitive bidding between accounting firms.

• Restructured Accounting and Administrative Support areas to realize annual savings of $200K+.

• Established metrics to identify subtle "cost creep" in raw materials for fabricated parts, and locked in pricing early. As industry costs for stainless steel were reported at 200+%, held cost increase to 18%.

• Realized annual savings of $130K through reduction in Material Control staffing.

• Outsourced fabricated/machined parts domestically and internationally, saving 17% annually and capturing 6,000 square feet of floor space to build machinery. Enlarged capacity 15% without cost of additional leased space or fixed overhead.

PROCESS IMPROVEMENT

• Transformed uncontrolled stockroom to a closed environment with dedicated staff, slashing staggering annual inventory variances from 56% of inventory value to <2%; dropping parts shortages in staging from 18% to 4%; and strengthening on-time-start percentage from a disappointing 64% to 83%.

• Championed lean/continuous improvement project in Cartoning and Case Packing group to eliminate wasted time and materials, reducing "bad parts" by 81%, improving on-time-start percentage from 83% to 88%, and shrinking number of days to complete from 102 to 46.

As with all the choices you make on your résumé, implement the solution that works best for your particular situation. Always show your résumé to an objective reader or two to give you feedback on whether the way you organized your résumé makes sense to them!

4
FORMATTING YOUR RÉSUMÉ

TIP #23:
WHY CARE ABOUT THE FORMAT ANYWAY?

I'll tell you a story. Not long ago, The Essay Expert worked with a client (I'll call him Jim) on his Executive résumé. We gave Jim a nice looking format, and he had success in obtaining interviews. Jim's wife (I'll call her Mary) saw Jim's résumé and liked the format. She liked it so much, in fact, that she decided to "steal" it and reformat her own résumé, using her husband's résumé as a model. The year before, Mary had applied for a job at a university. She was not asked for an interview. Mary submitted her newly formatted résumé for the same position she had applied for the year before. Guess what.

Yep, you guessed right. She got an interview. Was it her new format that did the trick? It's certainly a possibility. Remember, it's not just computer scanners that read résumés. Humans read them, too. You convey a certain attitude and impression to your human readers with your résumé format. Take the time necessary to create a format that you like and that will make the right impression on the humans who read it. Giving your format the attention it deserves can make all the difference.

There are many samples of winning résumé formats from The Essay Expert.[22] If you are applying to jobs online through companies that use ATS (Applicant Tracking System) programs, format matters a lot! I have included formatting tips for ATS software in Section 6 (Technology and Social Media), Tip #42.

TIP #24:
DON'T USE TEMPLATES!

Microsoft Word has many choices of résumé templates. I encourage you to LOOK at them. Do **not** use the templates unless one of the following is true:

---

22 http://theessayexpert.com/samples/résumés
-cover-letters-samples/

1. You want your résumé to look like everyone else's who is using a Microsoft Word template (I hope you do not fall into this category!).
2. You are VERY skilled with MS Word and can take the template and change it so it doesn't look like the template.

Option 2 is tricky. The templates in Word are often filled with complex code, tables, columns, etc. For example:

One of my clients had used a template from Monster.com. The second page had someone else's name on it, and the lines forming the border did not intersect properly. Why risk these deadly snafus?

As you have probably gathered, I highly encourage you **not** to use templates. Instead, create your own résumé format. You will avoid the risk of an employer's recognizing the template. You will also be able to edit your résumé yourself, which will allow you to tailor it for each job application.

You can find sample résumé formats on various sites such as Monster.com. Most often, these formats are professional but **not** unique. If you do use a résumé template, you MUST understand the formatting tools used on the résumé so you can easily edit it yourself. User beware!

For more sample résumé formats, look at the "After" résumé examples on The Essay Expert's website.[23] Find one that meets your experience level and the image you want to portray, and feel free to create something similar.

TIP #25:
DON'T USE A COLUMN FORMAT

(Unless You're Trying to Fill Up Space—or You Have a Creative Idea)

A common résumé format is the column format. In the left-hand column are the words "Education," "Experience," "Skills," etc., and the dates of employment. In the right-hand column are the names of your employers, your job titles, and your résumé bullets. I recommend against this format unless you have a truly inspired and creative idea of how to use the left-hand column that does not waste space and it is well executed.

Here's an example of a column format (from Word templates) that I would NOT recommend:

---

23 http://theessayexpert.com/samples/résumés-cover-letters-samples/

YOUR NAME

OBJECTIVE	To get started right away, just tap any placeholder text (such as this) and start typing to replace it with your own.
SKILLS & ABILITIES	You might want to include a brief summary of certifications and professional skills.
EXPERIENCE	**COMPANY NAME, LOCATION** Dates From-To This is the place for a brief summary of your key responsibilities and accomplishments. **COMPANY NAME, LOCATION** Dates From-To This is the place for a brief summary of your key responsibilities and accomplishments.
EDUCATION	**SCHOOL NAME, LOCATION, DEGREE** You might want to include your GPA here and a brief summary of relevant coursework, awards, and honors
COMMUNICATION	You delivered that big presentation to rave reviews. This is the place to showcase your skills.
LEADERSHIP	Are you head of the condo board, or a team lead for your favorite charity? This is the perfect place to let everyone know
REFERENCES	**REFERENCE NAME, COMPANY** Contact Information

Why do I recommend NO columns? For one thing, format-wise, columns and tables are very difficult to work with on a résumé. You might find that when you delete one thing, you accidentally end up deleting an entire section; or you may find that you are trapped by the format with no way to do what you want to do. It's a recipe for résumé anxiety.

Second, columns take up more space than their alternatives. If you don't have a lot of information to put on your résumé, you might want to use columns. But if you have significant amounts of information to share, this format will just waste space. Use columns cautiously!

IMPORTANT: Applicant Tracking Systems (the software that reads your electronically filed résumé) often skip over information in columns or tables—so you **must have an alternate version** for submission to online systems to avoid this risk (see Tip #43 for more about ATS).

In conclusion, choose a crisp, clear format that you like, with formatting techniques you understand. If you're struggling with the format (for instance, if things keep changing or disappearing when you attempt to make changes in the text), use a simpler format, find a friend who can teach you word processing skills, or hire a professional!

The Essay Expert can help you create a businesslike format that really pops and displays your accomplishments in the best light. Contact us at Résumés@TheEssayExpert.com or see our Executive Résumé and Cover Letter Writing services.[24]

TIP #26:
KEEP IT SIMPLE

It's important to create a résumé that looks professional and is appropriate for your industry. If you think you're getting too fancy, you probably are.

CHOOSING A FONT

Résumé writing experts universally warn job seekers not to use curly (serif) fonts for their names on résumés. Use the KISS principle (Keep It Simple, Stupid). Choose a font that is crisp and clear, like Calibri, Arial, or Corbel. For serif fonts, choose Garamond or Georgia. The once-ubiquitous workhorse, Times New Roman, is losing popularity as newer fonts come into common use. Do NOT write your name like this or anything like it on the top of the résumé:

You might succeed with using two different fonts in your résumé, such as Garamond for your name and section headings and Calibri for the rest of the résumé; however, I recommend never using more than two fonts in one résumé.

---

24 http://theessayexpert.com/services-rates /résumé-and-cover-letter-writing/#tab-1

Brenda Bernstein

Regarding font size, different fonts show up differently. My recommendation is to print out your résumé and do the "squint" test. If you are squinting or your eyes are straining to read the text, make it bigger. As a general rule, your font size should be between 10 and 12 point. It can be bigger for your name and any other headers you want to stand out.

MINIMIZE THE GRAPHICS

Be very careful about including any graphics on your résumé. It might be appropriate to use light shading, simple borders, and possibly maroon, dark-blue, or dark-green lines across the page. A tasteful logo or a graph or chart might also work well depending on your industry. Here's an example of an eye-catching résumé that you can achieve with some relatively simple formatting:

SETH DIAMOND ~ RECORD-BREAKING SALES LEADER – ELECTRONIC PAYMENTS ~

7712 Electronic Drive | Pay Day, CA 00000 | (415) 000-0000
sd@live.com | LinkedIn: http://www.linkedin.com/in/sd

DIRECTOR OF SALES

Consistently exceed revenue and profitability goals in multiple sales channels

Forward thinking leader in electronic payments industry. Develop sales channels and processes that ensure unprecedented profitability and performance. Turn underperforming teams into record breaking sales generators. Winner of Payment Systems Co.'s' Pinnacle Award and Strategic Partner Channel MVP.

AREAS OF EXPERTISE

- ✓ Sales Channel Development
- ✓ Self Prospecting
- ✓ Lead Generation
- ✓ Performance Turnaround
- ✓ Relationship Management
- ✓ Investor Relations
- ✓ Financial Analysis
- ✓ New Business Development
- ✓ Budgeting
- ✓ Social Media Networking
- ✓ Sales Team Management
- ✓ R&D

If you have a bit more graphic design talent, you might experiment a bit with simple shapes (diamonds, circles, and arrows), text boxes, and shadowing. For example:

SARA D. LEES, MBA

Austin, TX 77777 | 512.555.5555 | linkedin.com/in/saradlees1 | saradlees@austin.rr.com

SENIOR PROJECT MANAGER – REGISTERED ARCHITECT

GLOBALLY SAVVY, AWARD-WINNING LEASE MANAGER AND SITE DEVELOPER

➡ **VALUE TO ORGANIZATION**

15+ YEARS DRIVING ROI THROUGH EXECUTION OF SITE DEVELOPMENT PROJECTS AND EXPANSIONS WORLDWIDE:

- ◆ Saved millions while delivering $100M+ in capital projects for BIG BIZ over 5-year period.
- ◆ Oversaw successful, deadline-driven construction of $56M new TTT/Big Biz Corporate Headquarters (US) and international sales offices (US, Asia, Latin America).
- ◆ Winner: National Leadership in Environmental and Energy Efficient Gold Award.

Your résumé formatting must be clean and consistent and must be a match for your industry. If you are a finance, insurance, or legal professional, I recommend very straightforward formatting. Other industries, especially sales, call for more catchy layouts.

When in doubt, keep it simple!

Want more résumé tips? Sign up for The Essay Expert's blog.[25]

TIP #27:
USE THE BORDERS FUNCTION TO CREATE LINES

A common résumé formatting technique is to insert lines that span the width of the page.

25 http://theessayexpert.com/subscribe-to-the -weekly-blog/

CAREER PROGRESSION

CORE COMPETENCIES

EXPERIENCE

How do you create those great-looking lines? Use the border function. It looks like this:

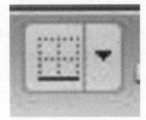

Click on the border icon, and you'll get a line that extends from one side of the page to the other and adjusts when you adjust the margins. Or, from the Format menu, go to Borders and Shading, where you can choose the placement and style of both section and page borders.

Using this menu, you can control the style, color, width, and location of your borders.

I won't give a complete tutorial on borders here. For more detail on how to use the border function, I recommend going to the Microsoft Word help site.[26] Play around with it and create something you love! If you choose to insert a line, be careful not to end up with a line that looks like this:

Eek! This line is not straight AND it runs off the page. I know you think this would not happen to you, but I can't even count the number of times I've seen these squiggly lines in a résumé. Although inserting a line as a shape does give you some good options, it can end up backfiring. When in doubt, stick with borders: they are simpler, easier to control, and reliably professional!

TIP #28:
HOW TO LIST DATES OF EMPLOYMENT
If you're following my advice and not using up a whole column for your dates of employment, you will be left with the natural question "How should I format my dates?"

26 https://support.office.com/en-US/article/Add
-borders-to-text-D7A74500-EF35-43C0-8215
-6B358B565A04

The most important rule about placement of your dates is to put them to the right of the company name. The reason for this is that the ATS (Applicant Tracking System) programs look for the date in that location.

Paragraph ? ✕

Indents and Spacing | **Line and Page Breaks**

General

Alignment: [Left ▾]

Outline level: [Level 3 ▾] ☐ Collapsed by default

Indentation

Left: [0.5" ▲▼]

Right: [0" ▲▼]

Special: [Hanging ▾] By: [0.25" ▲▼]

☐ Mirror indents

Spacing

Before: [Auto ▲▼]

After: [Auto ▲▼]

Line spacing: [Single ▾] At: [▲▼]

☑ Don't add space between paragraphs of the same style

Preview

Previous Paragraph Previous Paragraph Previous Paragraph Previous Paragraph Previous Paragraph
Previous Paragraph Previous Paragraph Previous Paragraph Previous Paragraph Previous Paragraph

Line up the dates with the Right Margin. The best way to accomplish this is by inserting a Right Tab using the Tab menu (the tab menu is found under Paragraph):

1. Put in the location where you want the tab stop;
2. Click "Right" in the options;
3. S

[Tabs...] [Set As Default] [OK] [Cancel]

My preferred date format is to line up the dates with the Right Margin. The best way to accomplish this is by inserting a **Right Tab** using the Tab menu (you will find the Tab menu under the Format, then Paragraph menu, in the lower right-hand corner):
Click on the "Tabs . . ." button to get to the tab menu.

1. Put in the location where you want the tab stop (probably 6.8, 6.9, or 7.0, depending on your margins);

2. Click "Right" in the options;
3. Save the tab; and
4. Hit the Tab button to move your dates over to the tab you have set.

Note: When you do this, a date might disappear off the page. If that happens, just go to the line where it should be and start hitting the delete button. You probably have some tabs in there that need to be deleted. Eventually the date will reappear! Here's what the final format might look like:

Tabs

Tab stop position:

Default tab stops:

0.5"

Tab stops to be cleared:

Alignment

- ● Left
- ○ Center
- ○ Right
- ○ Decimal
- ○ Bar

Leader

- ● 1 None
- ○ 2 ....
- ○ 3 -------
- ○ 4 ____

Set   Clear   Clear All

OK   Cancel

BEST HR CONSULTING LLC, San Francisco, CA February 2009–present
Managing Director

DIAGNOSTICS CORPORATION, Hayward, CA June 2001–February 2009
Senior Director of Human Resources (**March 1997–December 2000)**

MAJOR PHARMACEUTICALS, New York, NY January 1996–December 2000

Senior Director of Human Resources (**March 1997–December 2000)**

However you choose to format your dates, be consistent! Consistency makes your résumé easily readable and proves to the reader that you truly are detail-oriented.

TIP #29:
DON'T FORMAT WITH THE SPACE BAR!

Too many résumés are formatted using the space bar. When you use the space bar to format anything, you end up with a squiggly, inconsistent, and *unprofessional* format. Don't do it!!

1. Do NOT use the space bar after your bullets. Use the bullet function—that's what it's there for!

Do not get it into your head to insert a bullet as a symbol and then put spaces after it. You'll end up wasting time, and your bullets will wiggle down the page rather than line up straight.

2. Do NOT use the space bar to create columns. You will end up with a big mess and lists of items that are nearly impossible to edit!

3. Do NOT use the space bar to jump five spaces ahead—that's what the TAB bar is for!

I don't have to explain this one do I? It's just so much cleaner and simpler to tab out several times than to insert twenty-seven spaces.

4. One exception to my rule: if you want your dates to be flush against the right margin, you can either insert a right tab (see Tip #28) or you can tab out as much as possible and then hit the space bar until your dates are lined up with the right margin.

Be aware, however, that if you change your font style or size, you'll need to reformat the dates. User's choice.

TIP #30:
HOW TO CREATE DISTINCTIVE, PROFESSIONAL BULLETS

One way to put some pop and distinction into your résumé is with nonstandard bullets. If you click on the arrow next to the bullet function, you will see at the bottom of the list "Define New Bullet." Here's where to find the arrow:

You will be taken to the following menu:

Define New Bullet

Bullet character

[<u>S</u>ymbol...]   [<u>P</u>icture...]   [<u>F</u>ont...]

Alig<u>n</u>ment:

[Left   ▾]

Preview

[OK]   [Cancel]

From there, have a field day (within reason, of course). You can choose check marks, square boxes, arrows, or any *professional*-looking bullet from the Bullets and Numbering menu, found under the Format dropdown menu. You can use these bullets for the list of key strengths or core competencies, or for the items in your experience section. For example:

BUSINESS DEVELOPMENT & TEAM LEADERSHIP
- **Secured Top Health Insurance account** that had not advertised with City Newspapers for 10+ years. Conducted multi-media campaign that **increased Top's membership 200K.**
- **Made recommendations that secured $295K** new revenue in print and online products.

▶ Grew territory sales from $700K to $2.1M. Named Salesperson of Year for largest sales volume increase.
▶ Promoted from Regional Sales for excellent performance in evaluating manufacturers' requirements.
▶ Captured business from strong competitor that had been in market for over three years.

Managing Director
- **Compensation; Performance Management (150-employee organization):**
  ○ Redesigned 31-level step pay salary structure to 10-level pay-for-performance system.
  ○ Created common performance review form (reduced from 8) and a single performance rating system (reduced from 3). Revised form to value content and process of work equally.

As long as you don't go overboard and do keep your résumé formatted as your profession demands, you can really spice it up with creative bulleting. Have fun!

TIP #31:
GUIDELINES FOR MARGINS

How big or small should your margins be? Some of you have default margins set to 1.0" on top and bottom and 1.25" on left and right. These are huge margins for a résumé. Some of you have 0.5" left and right margins; these are tiny margins for a résumé that make it seem as if you don't have enough space.

If you really need to fill up space, use 1.0" margins all around. There's no excuse for 0.5" margins; you would do better to add an extra page or cut out some material. Here's what The Essay Expert recommends:

1. Top Margin: 0.6"or 0.5" are nice small margins that look good above the header you created after reading Tip #2.
2. Bottom Margin: It's best if it's just a little bigger than the top margin. 0.6" tends to work well.

3. Left/Right: These should be the same width. Do not have a skinny left margin and a fat right margin, or vice versa. Do not go below 0.8", as it starts to look like you're trying very hard to squeeze things in.

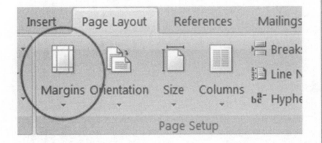

It's sometimes hard to tell on a computer screen whether your margins are reasonable.

ALWAYS print out your résumé before sending it to make sure you haven't created something that looks great on a computer screen and horrible on paper. If for some reason you can't print it, AT LEAST look at the Print Preview before sending. You will very likely discover something that needs adjustment!

TIP #32:
HOW TO USE PAGE BORDERS

A simple border can be a great way to give your résumé a professionally formatted look. You will find this function under the Format menu, dropdown item Borders and Shading. Make sure to click on the Page Border button at the top.

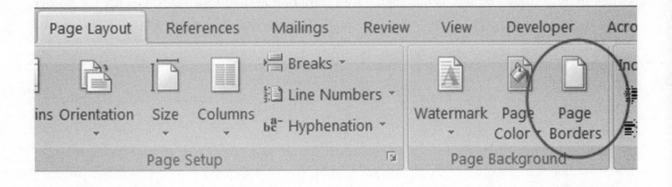

Once you click on the Page Border icon or tab, you will see the following menu:

As you can see, you have many options of how to proceed from here! You can change the color of your border (I recommend black or gray, nothing else), the width of the border, and the style of the border. In most cases, I would recommend only a solid border. Don't get fancy. Just use the border to add some "pop" and contain the text on the page. Here's an example of how a border changes the look of a résumé:

WITHOUT BORDER

WITH BORDER

Which do you prefer? If you like the border, consider using a border to frame your résumé. I generally prefer no border, but the choice is yours.

Are you in a creative field? The Essay Expert offers graphically designed résumés. One of these[27] was nominated for a TORI Award for Best Creative Résumé (TORI =

Toast of the Résumé Industry).[28] The awards are administered by the national organization Career Directors International.

Contact us at theessayexpert.com if you want a well-designed résumé with graphics that have pop and pizzazz, without being overdone.

---

27 http://theessayexpert.com/pdf /GraphicDesignerRésumé-AFTER.pdf

28 http://www.careerdirectors.com/tori_2012 .htm

TIP #33:
SPACING (OR HOW TO MAKE YOUR THREE-PAGE RÉSUMÉ FIT ON TWO PAGES)

Can't get rid of that one line that spills over to the third page of your résumé? Don't want your résumé to look squashed? There are always choices to make about which content to include, and these issues will be addressed in the next section. For now, here's one formatting trick that can help fit your résumé into the allotted space and preserve coveted "white space" at the same time.

Take a look at your résumé. You might have a full line of space between sections that you don't need. Thankfully, there are options that can make just enough difference to get your résumé back onto one page (or two). One way to reduce the height of the space is to put your cursor there and reduce the font size by clicking CTRL+SHIFT+>. The line will magically shrink! Here's another way to do it that I usually prefer:

1. Delete the unwanted full space between lines.
2. Put your cursor on the line above which you want to insert space.
3. Go to the Paragraph menu, Indents and Spacing submenu.

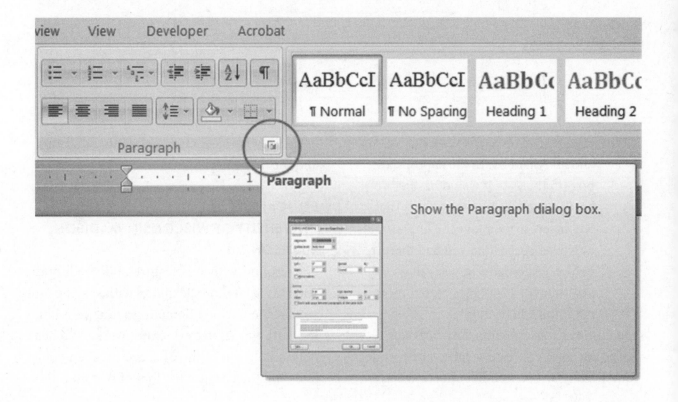

Show the Paragraph dialog box.

Paragraph

Indents and Spacing | Line and **P**age Breaks

General

Alignment: `Left` ▾

Outline level: `Body Text` ▾

Indentation

Left: `0"` ⬍   Special: `(none)` ▾   By: ⬍

Right: `0"` ⬍

☐ Mirror indents

Spacing

Before: `0 pt` ⬍   Line spacing: `Multiple` ▾   At: `1.15` ⬍

After: `6 pt` ⬍

☐ Don't add space between paragraphs of the same style

Preview

Previous Paragraph Previous Paragraph Previous Paragraph Previous Paragraph Previous Paragraph Previous Paragraph Previous Paragraph Previous Paragraph Previous Paragraph Previous Paragraph

Sample Text Sample Text Sample Text Sample Text Sample Text Sample Text Sample Text Sample Text Sample Text Sample Text Sample Text Sample Text Sample Text Sample Text Sample Text Sample Text Sample Text Sample Text Sample Text

Following Paragraph Following Paragraph Following Paragraph Following Paragraph Following Paragraph Following Paragraph Following Paragraph Following Paragraph Following Paragraph Following Paragraph

Tabs...   Default...   OK   Cancel

4. Under Spacing, you'll see a Before box and an After box. In the appropriate box (in this case it would be "Before"), hit the arrow until it says "6pt." That will insert space above the line—a narrower space than you had there before. (Alternatively, you can insert 3pt or 12pt of space, but most common will be 6pt.)

You can use this trick not just between sections, but also to create a little space under your headings. For example, here's what 6pt of space looks like between the title Education and the first entry:

EDUCATION
UNIVERSITY OF WISCONSIN-MADISON, MADISON, WI

Play around with this feature and you'll find you have a lot more flexibility with spacing on your résumé. Note: Sometimes, due to a bug in Word, this strategy does not work. Another option is to put a line of space between your lines and then reduce the font of that line. The easiest way to do this is to hit CTRL-SHIFT-< (on PCs). Your line will magically shrink! You might want to go down to 5pt font.

Whichever spacing choices you use, make sure to be consistent! Consistency in formatting is one of the keys to a professional-looking résumé.

Still having trouble getting your résumé onto one page? The Certified Résumé Writers at The Essay Expert can help! Contact us today at 608-467-0067 or Résumés@TheEssayExpert.com.

TIP #34:
HYPERLINKS ARE WELCOME—AND SO ARE WORD DOCUMENTS!

You may have heard rumors that recruiters and hiring managers never click live links because of the possibility of viruses. The results of Career Directors International's survey on global hiring trends tells a different story. Although 17 percent of respondents never click on links, 62 percent reported that they sometimes or always click on hyperlinks when provided. Places you might link to:

- Your LinkedIn profile
- Your website
- A video you created
- A website with examples of your work
- A document you wrote
- A site mentioning your name as an award recipient

Regarding format, the survey found that Word (.doc or .docx) is the preferred format for receiving résumés by far, although 23 percent preferred PDFs. It is acceptable to send your résumé in two formats if sending via e-mail; if submitting online, choose Word.

5
COVER LETTER TIPS

TIP #35:
YES, YOU NEED A COVER LETTER!

Just about every client I work with lately brings up the rumor they've heard that no one reads cover letters anymore. With the possible exception of highly technological fields and internal promotions, this is *only* a rumor. If you take action based on it, you may shoot yourself in the foot.

In an article posted on Work Coach Cafe, "15 Job Search Tips from a Guy Who Just Got a Job,"[29] a successful job seeker named John relates how the CEO of a company personally reached out to him to thank him for sending a cover letter! In fact, John was the ONLY candidate to send a cover letter, most likely because everyone else believed the rumor that cover letters never get read. John made an impression.

This topic is also covered in my article "Job Search Myth: You Don't Need a Cover Letter."[30] The cover letter is your opportunity to showcase strengths that you could not highlight within the confines of your résumé. Write a unique letter to the company about who you are and the difference you would make for that company. Begin building a relationship right from the start. Imagine yourself in a leadership role at this organization and write down what you will bring to the position. Sell yourself.

You do need to know your target audience. You might need to keep your letter very short and to the point, or you might have room to share more about yourself and your accomplishments. If in doubt, keep your cover letter short, sweet, and focused.

---

29 http://www.workcoachcafe.com/2010/06/01/15
-job-search-tips-from-a-guy-who-just-got-a-job/

30 http://theessayexpert.com/blog/job-search
-myth-you-dont-need-a-cover-letter/

TIP #36:

THREE COMPONENTS OF AN EFFECTIVE COVER LETTER

Your ability to present yourself in a cover letter is a test of your ability to communicate effectively as a leader. Here are some pointers for presenting a professional image and for conveying a clear statement of the value you would add to an organization:

1. Instead of starting the letter with something about yourself, state what you know about what the company needs. For example:
   For a corporation to succeed and expand in Asia, it is essential to have smart decision making and global supply chain expertise in place. The complex Asian environment requires a person of high integrity to lead business strategy—someone fluent in Mandarin, Cantonese, and Chinese culture, with an understanding of Chinese labor laws and business structures. Someone who can be trusted to handle every facet of the supply chain to create value and growth for the company. I offer all the qualities necessary to take on the General Manager position at Company, strategically formulate a vision and business plan, then execute that plan with detail and precision.

Do you have a gap in your résumé? Explain it in the cover letter:
   It takes a fighter to battle "terminal" cancer and come back to run five Iron Man triathlons. I'll fight for your company with the same gusto I fought for my life.[31]

2. After you prove you know what the company needs, state why you are a match. List *briefly* the major reasons you are the right candidate for the job. This task can be done in just a few sentences. Yes, really, it can! For example:
   My management style has paid huge dividends in Asia for the manufacturing companies I have served for the past ten years. Through assessing and identifying people's strengths, I match them to a need in the company and encourage them to take ownership and make a contribution. Value is added. Loyalty is created.
   The reader shouldn't have to wonder whether you've got the training and experience for the position. Make it clear right away and give your audience a reason to read further.

3. Provide bullet points of your top three accomplishments—the ones

---

31 From Donald Burns, http://www.donaldburns.com/

most relevant to THIS position. List them briefly so the reader can get a snapshot of what you can provide to their organization.

My clients have great success getting interviews, and I know at least part of that success is due to their effective, engaging cover letters.

TIP #37:
DELETE THESE WORDS FROM YOUR COVER LETTER!

Certain words appear in almost every cover letter. Below I explain why you don't want to use four of these too-common words and what some alternatives might be.

If you want to make your cover letter stand out, do some editing and make sure to avoid these words completely. You might be surprised at the result.

HOPE
e.g., I hope to hear from you soon.
OR
e.g., I hope to be able to contribute my skills to ABC company.

Why not?
Hope springs eternal. The company doesn't care about your hopes and dreams. They care about what you can do for them.

Alternatives:
I look forward to speaking with you further regarding my qualifications.

OR
My ability to take clear, decisive action will allow me to make an impact at ABC company from day one.

OK, now we're talking!

HONE
e.g. This summer, I honed my research and writing skills through a position at XX law firm.

Why not?
You and every other person honed something. It's an outdated and overused expression. Tell them what you did, and they will figure out that you honed your skills. If you absolutely must, use "strengthened," "developed," or even "sharpened."

Alternative:
My research regarding constitutional rights violations culminated in a report and recommendations that guided the ACLU in future actions. It's obvious this person is using some powerful research and writing skills.

DRAWN
e.g., I am drawn to ABC company because of its outstanding reputation and high quality service.

Why not?
You get drawn to a person across a crowded room. Companies don't care to hear that you are drawn to them. And a bonus tip:

Companies with outstanding reputations don't need to be told that you want to work there because of their outstanding reputations.

Alternative:

The relationship management skills I built while working in a state office are a match for ABC company's commitment to outstanding customer relationships.

That's so much better, isn't it?

FEEL

e.g., I feel the relationship management skills I built while working in a state office are a match for ABC company's commitment to outstanding customer relationships.

Why not?

Can you see how adding "I feel" at the beginning of this sentence killed it completely? Tell a psychologist how you feel. Tell a company what you can do for them. If you must, use the word "believe" instead of "feel." But see if you can avoid this type of mushy, maudlin language altogether.

Alternative:

The relationship management skills I built while working in a state office are a match for ABC company's commitment to outstanding customer relationships.

Delete these four words from your cover letters, and I promise you more creative and powerful language will arise.

TIP #38:

"TO WHOM IT MAY CONCERN" DOESN'T CUT IT

Do not address your letter to "To Whom It May Concern." Whenever humanly possible, find out the name of the person who will be reading your résumé, and write the letter specifically to that person.

Use your networks to conduct whatever research is necessary. Whom do you know on LinkedIn who is connected to someone in the company you are approaching? What research can you do online to identify the organization's leadership?

If you don't do your research, it is quite possible you will not be seriously considered for a position. How well you are connected is a big component to your value as a senior leader. Leverage your connections and demonstrate to your potential new company that you are taking your application seriously. Your letter will certainly stand out among the others that say, "To Whom It May Concern" or "Dear Sir/Madam."

TIP #39:

WRITING A VALUE PROPOSITION LETTER

If you are approaching a company cold, it might be most effective for you to include a value proposition letter (VPL). Here's an example of what a VPL might look like. Note that the impetus for the letter was an accomplishment achieved by the company. The candidate proves that he has been following the industry and this company in particular:

Dear Mr./Ms.:

I recently noticed your accomplishment of _____ in the _____.
I am an experienced Vice President of Operations who has recently worked for a nationally recognized top 25 Home Builder, where I drove the division to an unprecedented 35% market share while increasing productivity 140%.

My accomplishments include:

- Piloted restructure of product types and land positions that **limited risk potentials by 27%, increased closings by 51%,** and ensured continued growth and improvements in volume, revenue, and customer satisfaction.
- Maintained highest profit margin in company **(26.3%)** while overseeing developments comprised of Condo, Villa, Row-Home, Single Family, and Single Family Luxury product.
- Enriched customer relations through Sales and Construction Manager personal follow-up; designed a referral program resulting in a **30% increase in willingness-to-refer rating**.

If you would like to achieve and sustain results like these, let's talk. My company recently restructured their operations, and I would like to explore challenging opportunities in operations management.

I will follow up in a few days with a phone call and would be happy to forward you my résumé upon request. I look forward to speaking with you.

Sincerely,

If you are reaching out to Executive search firms, you might write a brief VPL something like the following:

Subject: CPG Executive 10+ Years of Double- and Triple-Digit Growth in China/Asia and US
Dear Ms. Recruiter:

If you are engaged in a search for a Senior Executive in CPG industry based in the U.S. or Asia, you may be interested in the depth of knowledge and experience I offer. With 10+ years in B2B consumer products, I am available and well situated to contribute to an organization with a growing international/China presence.

Some quick highlights of my qualifications in growing international organizations include:

- Led furniture giant Yangtze to **500% growth,** selling to large retailers that included ABC Carpet & Home and Costco.

- Instituted groundbreaking QC and efficiency measures that carried Yangtze to **#1 industry leader** worldwide.
- Expanded sourcing operations from 10% of ABC Furniture's overall business ($95MM) to **20% ($200MM)**.

My attached résumé provides more information about my background and accomplishments. I would greatly appreciate the opportunity to speak with you and am available by phone, Skype [Skype address], or e-mail to arrange a mutually suitable time for a conversation. Thank you.

Best regards,

John Paul Jones
Shanghai, CHINA ■ +86-555-5555-5555 ■ jpjoneschina@yahoo.com ■ cn.linkedin.com/in/jpjoneschina

As demonstrated by the above examples, it doesn't take pages and pages to demonstrate your value to a company. The faster you can do it, the better.

6
TECHNOLOGY & SOCIAL MEDIA

TIP #40:
GOOGLE RESULTS ARE THE NEW "RÉSUMÉ"

A simple résumé just doesn't cut it anymore. You need to build a strong online presence so you look good when someone punches your name into the Google search bar. Ways to do this:

1. Have a 100% LinkedIn profile that is professional and full of keywords. Learn more in *How to Write a KILLER LinkedIn® Profile.*[32]

2. Clean up your Facebook page. That means no pictures of you within 100 yards of a beer! (Did you know that studies show people are judged as less intelligent when holding an alcoholic beverage?!)

3. Establish a Twitter account and tweet useful information about your field of work.

4. Create a website for yourself! Post your online résumé there and stock it with keywords.

5. Create a PowerPoint-based résumé and upload it to SlideShare. See CareerCloud's "3 Great PowerPoint Résumés"[33] for some inspiration.

6. Start a blog and write something at least once a week. People with blogs are seen as leaders and doers. The topic is up to you as long as it's professionally appropriate.

7. Post a professional video on YouTube. YouTube has high search rankings and will have your video show up in Google searches.

8. Search for yourself on Google and see what happens. Is there anything there that looks less than pristine? If so, clean it up. It *will* keep you from getting hired.

---

32 http://theessayexpert.com/how-to-write-a-killer-linkedin-profile-e-book/

33 https://www.careercloud.com/news/2015/7/25/3-great-powerpoint-résumés

Yes, you still need a résumé. Just about every hiring entity will ask for one in some form or another. But build your Google brand, too. Check out The Essay Expert's Google results.[34] The results change every day!

TIP #41:
POWERPOINT AND VIDEO RÉSUMÉS

Calling all armchair graphic designers and creative people of all sorts!!! I've got great news for you: you can create a PowerPoint or video résumé in addition to your standard "vanilla" résumé! How cool is that?

If you read the previous tip, you know that Google results are the new résumé. How can you get your résumé to show up on Google results? That's where PowerPoint, SlideShare, and YouTube come in.

POWERPOINT

For more samples of PowerPoint résumés, read "4 Steps to Creating a Visual Résumé That Stands Out."[35] These folks have used uniquely creative methods to market themselves by means of their résumé. Through a combination of language and graphics, they have set themselves apart from the competition: they have shown they are willing to go the extra mile to get noticed and produce outstanding results.

Don't you want to be one of them? If so, don't wait another second. Open up Power-Point on your computer and get to work!

NEED HELP PUBLISHING YOUR PPT PRESENTATION TO SLIDESHARE?

Read LinkedIn Help Center's "SlideShare—Frequently Asked Questions."[36]

VIDEO RÉSUMÉS

Video résumés are becoming more and more viable as a way to present yourself to potential employers. Many hiring managers would rather watch a three-minute video than read through yet another résumé. However, according to a September 2015 article by Recruiter.com,[37] a stand-alone video résumé will not get you hired on its own. It's important to present a consistently branded multimedia package to succeed in leveraging the power of video and other technology in your job search.

Branding expert Alex Kecskes states in his article "Video Résumés: Should You Use Them? Do They Work?"[38] that "once the CD disk, thumb drive or other media is viewed, your personality, poise, speaking skills and

34 https://www.google.com
/search?q=the+essay+expert

35 http://blog.slideshare.net/2013/10/14/4-steps-to
-creating-a-visual-résumé-that-stands-out/

36 https://www.linkedin.com/help/slideshare
/suggested/53164

37 https://www.recruiter.com/i/is-a-standard
-résumé-enough-to-get-you-an-interview
-anymore/

38 http://www.care2.com/greenliving/video
-résumés-should-you-use-them-do-they-work
.html

overall demeanor are evident immediately." This can be both good and bad. Mistakes can be edited out, but if you're not comfortable in front of a camera, awkward body language could cost you an interview, and although illegal, potential discrimination based on appearance or dialect may also occur.

If you do choose to create a video component to your job search profile, make sure to keep it clear and short (ideally, about two minutes) and point to that video clearly from your résumé and LinkedIn profile. Use consistent imaging and branding: Say or show something that differentiates you. "Multimedia résumés work best when they are part of a broader campaign," according to the *Boston Globe*, paraphrasing John Wilpers, founder and chief executive of Degrees2Dreams. This campaign "should include a blog about a niche in your professional field, personal marketing through social media, and a series of informational interviews."

While you may feel that technology has begun to outclass paper when it comes to résumés, don't be too hasty: 78 percent of hiring entities still prefer a traditional résumé over any other format—that's up 8 percent from 2013, according to a 2016 survey of four hundred U.S. advertising and marketing executives.[39]

So be careful if you jump on the multimedia bandwagon. It's not for everyone, it takes a lot of work, and it must be done well to pack a punch. Also keep in mind that many large companies won't accept video résumés, preferring to utilize résumé scanning technology to prefilter the best candidates. For more help on deciding whether to use a video résumé, see Robert Half's article "Is a Video Résumé Right for You?"[40]

TIP #42:
BEAT THE SCANNERS PART 1—ELEVEN ESSENTIAL RÉSUMÉ KEYWORD TIPS

You've probably heard about the importance of keywords in your résumé. Your résumé might go through a scanner and not even make it to a human being unless it has the requisite keywords to match the capricious desires of the hiring manager.

What's a job seeker to do? Here are my top eleven tips for optimizing keywords in your résumé:

1. Look at the job description (obvious, right?). In the job listing, you will find the secret to what the company is looking for. Just incorporate the important terms into your résumé. For instance, if they want someone with social media experience, you MUST have the words Social Media,

39 http://www.prnewswire.com/news-releases /the-best-résumés-get-back-to-the -basics-300263320.html

40 https://www.roberthalf.com/blog/writing-a -résumé/current-résumé-styles-and-trends-you -need-to-know

LinkedIn, Twitter, Facebook, and Google+ in your résumé, IF you can honestly say you have expertise in those areas. Don't lie! Just make sure that if you can put the keywords in with integrity, you do it.

2. Look on the company website where you are applying and use the company's or organization's language. You might find keywords in an annual report, as well.

3. Use O*Net[41] to help target your résumé keywords:

   - On the website, copy the text in your résumé (CTRL-A) and paste (CTRL-C) into the "job description" box (keep the job title box CLEAR). Click Search. The target job title your résumé codes toward will appear at the top of the result box with a score next to it. Anything **above 70** is good. Scores above 70 percent will be recognized as a "positive match" by computer screening technologies.

   - To find the O*Net job description for a specific job title, **CLEAR** the results, type in your target job title, for example, "Compliance Manager," and you will see the O*Net job title listed. Click

on the job title to see the full description. **Utilize the words in the O*Net description to better tailor and customize your résumé.** You can add appropriate sections to your résumé in order to incorporate these words and phrases.

4. Check keywords for your industry by looking at multiple job descriptions and by looking at the lists in an excellent guide published by The Ladders: Guide to Crafting the Professional's Résumé.[42] This book is written by writers at the top of their game and has excellent industry-specific advice for professional résumés.

5. Search for your position on these websites:
   - MyNextMove.org[43]
   - Occupational Outlook Handbook[44]
   - Dictionary of Occupational Titles[45]

6. Use Wordle.net or Tagul.com. You can cut-and-paste the job description, the home page of your target company, and any other relevant language into

41 http://www.onetsocautocoder.com/plus /onetmatch

42 https://cdn.theladders.net/static/pdfs/Crafting _The_Professionals_Résumé.pdf

43 http://www.mynextmove.org/

44 http://www.bls.gov/ooh/

45 http://www.occupationalinfo.org/

Wordle to see what words show up the most often. The words that show up biggest in Wordle give you big hints about what to include in your résumé.

7. Try the Google Keyword Planner.[46] Type the keywords you've identified into the search bar, and you will get a list of similar words and phrases.

8. Don't stop with the keywords you find. Look for synonyms, too.

9. Put keywords at the TOP of your résumé. The sooner the better. And see #5.

10. If you put keywords in your Core Competencies or Key Strengths section, make sure you ALSO put them in bullets. It will NOT work to claim expertise in a list at the top of your résumé and then fail to support your claims in the body of the résumé. The scanners are sophisticated enough to catch it when you don't back up your claimed competencies.

11. Don't put your keywords in text boxes or tables. Some scanners won't pick them up.

These tips will help you get past the evil scanners (ya ha ha . . .). If you followed all my other tips, you'll also have a good chance of making it past the human being who will ultimately be your judge.

---

46 http://adwords.google.com/keywordplanner

court review responsible
Organizational Preparing
Team Locks investigations CCTV
reports Requirements Job
Coordinating experience
alarms Conducting
required compliance
Supervising system
policies inspections
EAS May Accounting standards
security installation
protection Strong
Prior appear Enforcing
Protection
checks Asset Utilizing
assets
Investigating asset Ensuring
high bad
attention
Club skills preferred
responsibilities limited
detail Additional
shrink procedures
include interpersonal Follow
safety merchandise
Members
equipment Manager

TIP #43:
BEAT THE SCANNERS PART 2—FORMATTING TIPS

Here are some formats that the ATS software understands. Keep the section headings basic, e.g., Summary, Experience, Education, Certifications. If you diverge from these standards (e.g., Career Progression) or combine section headings (e.g., Certifications & Memberships), the scanners might not recognize the sections at all. The information following the section header could be ignored.

Format #1

First Last

Street Address • City, ST ##### • ###—####: mobile • e-mail@e-mail.com

SUMMARY

Insert summary here

EXPERIENCE

Company name
Location, Dates
Company description

Job Title

Subheader
- Bullet 1
- Bullet 2
- Bullet 3
- Bullet 4
- Bullet 5

Company name Location, Dates
Company description

Job Title

Subheader
- Bullet 1
- Bullet 2
- Bullet 3
- Bullet 4
- Bullet 5

EDUCATION

Name of School, City, ST: **Degree,** Date (optional)
Name of School, City, ST: **Degree,** Date (optional)

Format #2

First Last

Street Address, City, ST #####
e-mail@e-mail.com (###) ###-#### (Cell)
(###) ###-#### (Home)

Insert Summary here.

Company name, City, ST **Dates**
Job Title
- Bullet #1
- Bullet #2
- Bullet #3

Company name, City, ST   **Dates**
Job Title
- Bullet #1
- Bullet #2
- Bullet #3

EDUCATION

Degree, University, Date
Degree, University, Date
Degree, University, Date

CERTIFICATIONS

Certification, School, Date
Certification, School, Date
Certification, School, Date

BONUS TIP

You may have heard that people copy the job description into their résumé in white type so that they "secretly" match the keywords in the job description; or that they simply copy and paste the job description as part of the résumé without hiding it at all. I do not recommend either of these strategies. The first is blatantly deceptive, and companies have started to convert text into black to catch this tactic. The second, although there were rumors of its working in the past, is not proven to be effective and could backfire. I always recommend remaining on the up-and-up, writing the best résumé you can with as many keywords as possible, and not trying to "beat the system" in underhanded ways.

TIP #44:
LINKEDIN–SAVVY

DON'T COPY YOUR RÉSUMÉ SUMMARY INTO YOUR LINKEDIN SUMMARY SECTION! DO LINK YOUR RÉSUMÉ TO YOUR LINKEDIN PROFILE

Why not to copy your résumé summary into your LinkedIn Summary:

1. Often your résumé summary is laden with overused phrases like "Results-oriented team player with a proven track record . . ." or "Dynamic, motivated self-starter with extensive experience . . ." If your résumé summary looks anything like the above examples, please rewrite it and hire a professional résumé writer if necessary! This type of language belongs neither on your résumé nor in your LinkedIn profile.
2. You have two thousand characters at your disposal for a LinkedIn Summary, vs. three to four lines maximum for your résumé summary. Why not use all that real estate to say something—really say something—about yourself?
3. Your LinkedIn Summary is an essential place for you to insert keywords if you want to be found on LinkedIn. By inserting a three-line summary, you lose out on your chance to build keywords into your profile.

For more on this topic, and for an example of how to write a LinkedIn Summary, see "3 Reasons Not to Copy Your Résumé Summary into Your LinkedIn Summary Section."[47]

HOW TO ATTACH YOUR RÉSUMÉ TO YOUR LINKEDIN PROFILE

Recruiters and hiring managers who find you on LinkedIn will likely be interested in viewing your résumé. If you try to upload your résumé

into your LinkedIn profile itself using the résumé tool prompted by LinkedIn, you will end up with a mess. Don't do it!!

In your Summary and Experience sections, you can add files or links to documents or presentations by clicking on the pencil icon in the corner:

47 http://theessayexpert.com/blog/3-reasons-not -to-copy-your-résumé-summary-into-your-linkedin -summary-section/

Scroll down and you will see the following:

Edit experience   ✕

Media

Add or link to external documents, photos, sites, videos, and presentations.

| **Upload** | **Link** |

⑦ Supported formats

No ⬤○ **Share profile changes**
       If enabled, your network may see this change.

Delete   **Save**

Presto! Your résumé will be attached to your LinkedIn profile.

SPECIAL ISSUE

If you're targeting two different job types, consider whether it makes sense to attach a résumé that is generalized to qualify for both types of positions, or to attach two versions, or to skip this option entirely.

For a comprehensive tutorial on crafting a KILLER LinkedIn Profile, consider purchasing the #1 Best-Seller *How to Write a KILLER LinkedIn® Profile*,[48] another one of my titles, which is available in PDF, Kindle, and paperback.

TIP #45:
QR CODES ON RÉSUMÉS?

You may have heard about a trend toward putting QR, or "Quick Response," codes on résumés. QR codes are links to a website, and they look like this:

The scanner on a mobile phone can take a picture of this image and take the viewer to a website.

---

48 http://theessayexpert.com/how-to-write-a-killer
    -linkedin-profile-e-book/

To create a QR code, go to a free QR creator like QRCode-Generator,[49] enter the URL of the site you want the code to link to, and the program will create a QR code for you.

For a QR code to be worthwhile, it must link to a site that is worthwhile. If you are in a technical field, graphic design, or communications AND you have a website with robust information about yourself and your projects, you might want to put a QR code on your résumé. It's more noticeable than a link, so it might entice more people to scan and click.

Note that if you're sending your résumé electronically, a QR code won't be that useful. If someone is already on a computer reading your résumé, they might not scan the code and you might do better by highlighting a URL or inserting another clickable image. If you think about it, the code is only useful for someone who has a hard copy of the résumé and wants to investigate further by scanning the code into their phone.

A Boston Globe article in January 2013[50] told the story of Igor Kharitonenkov. Igor included a QR code on his résumé that linked to a site with his "work history, letters of recommendations, and samples of his work, including a video about Bootstrap Compost, a Boston recycling firm, that he shot for his blog on sustainable businesses."

---

49 http://www.qr-code-generator.com/

50 https://www.boston.com/jobs/jobs
    -news/2013/01/13/multimedia-résumés-can
    -help-candidates-stand-out

He was hired as communications coordinator for the nonprofit City Year Boston out of 200 applicants. It wasn't the QR code that got Igor his job; it was his website. But the QR code sure helped.

TIP #46:
SEND A HARD COPY!

Even with all the technology available today, and really *because* of it, it is very unusual for a hiring manager to receive a hard copy of a résumé. If you have the address of the hiring manager or the company you're applying to, send a hard copy! Online résumé submissions of course are required by many companies. Nevertheless, you can make an impression by sending a cover letter and résumé on nice bond paper. You will have very little company in doing so, and you will stand out by making this extra effort to impress and put care into your application.

Off-white or white paper is acceptable, and white is generally preferred. Don't use other colored paper, and do not use paper that has an image on it (other than a graph or simple logo that you've created). The only reason to have any other image on your résumé is that you are a designer of some sort and are sharing your own artistic design!

Another advantage to printing and sending your résumé and cover letter is that you will be forced to print your résumé and see what it looks like. Many people never print out their résumés, an omission that can lead to an end result with some very strange formatting issues or a font that is so small it is barely legible.

So print your résumé. Make sure it looks good and does not have any errors; and use a good old-fashioned envelope or hand-deliver the document to your target company. You might be surprised by the response you receive.

7

THE #1 MOST IMPORTANT TIP SET!

TIP #47:
HOW TO AVOID EMBARRASSING EDITING MARKS ON YOUR DOCUMENTS

MS WORD'S TRACK CHANGES PROGRAM
Have you ever gotten a document back from an editor with tons of red or blue lines (maybe even some green ones) and have no idea how to get rid of them all, or view the document the way it's supposed to look? This tip is for you!

DON'T SUBMIT A DOCUMENT THAT LOOKS LIKE THIS!

WHY I LOVE TRACK CHANGES

Microsoft Word has a very useful feature called "Track Changes" that keeps track of changes that an editor makes to a document and allows subsequent readers to see which changes were made. When the "Track Changes" feature is turned on, anyone who opens the document can see every change made to the original document, whether to fonts, page formats, margins, or text. Track Changes also has a "Comments" feature that allows explanations and suggestions to be entered in the margins of your document.

The value of Track Changes to me as an editor is that my clients can see what I've changed, and I can see the changes they make. I do not then have to go through their résumé word by word to see which alterations have occurred. Accepting or rejecting changes is easy and does not require changing individual fonts or colors. Gone are the days of manually inserting a strikethrough to indicate a deletion!

If you are working with someone on your résumé and they send you a set of edits, I recommend accepting them and then tracking the changes you make. This system makes it easy for both parties to keep track of what's being changed and avoids the necessity of reading the entire résumé to find any changes.

THE DANGERS OF TRACK CHANGES

Track Changes can be troublesome, too. You don't want to send a document with lots of red lines and bubbles all over it to an employer or a school (many people have embarrassing stories of doing this)! The recipient then sees all the suggestions, changes, and possibly the original language and mistakes that needed changing.

As part of proofreading and preparing the final draft of a résumé, cover letter, or essay, take the following steps to ensure that you do not inadvertently send a marked-up copy to an employer:

DIRECTIONS FOR MS WORD 2007/2010

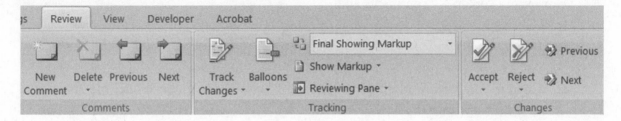

Review Tab

1. Check to see if there are any comments or tracked changes in the document:
   - Go to the "Review" tab and click on the window that says "Final Showing Markup." Go to the "Show Markup" menu and make sure there are check marks in all the boxes (otherwise, you might not see the comments or formatting changes when you look at "Final Showing Markup").
   - **NOTE:** If the window says "Final" and you do not see any red lines, this does not mean they are gone! Make sure you are viewing the markups before determining that your document is clean.

2. If you do not see any changes or comments and you do not make any other changes to the document, you're good to go.

3. However, if you do see comments and tracked changes, you can do one of two things:

   a. Change "Final: Show Markup" to "Final" and save the final document as a PDF. This solution works if the place to which you're submitting your résumé accepts .pdf files.

   b. Accept all the tracked changes and delete all edits and comments (unless you only want to accept some of them, in which case see Step 4). NOTE: You need to delete edits SEPARATELY from comments!
   - Under the "Review" tab, go to "Accept" icon and accept all changes.
   - Under the "Review" tab, go to the icon that says "Delete" (next to the "New Comment" icon) and click "Delete All Comments in Document."

4. If you want to accept some changes and delete others, you can accept or reject changes and comments one at a time by right-clicking on them individually. You will get a drop-down menu with choices of what to do.

5. Repeat Step 1.

DIRECTIONS FOR MS WORD 2003

1. Check to see if there are any comments or tracked changes in the document.
   - Go to the "View" menu and click on the "Markup" option. This feature can be switched on or off. On the Reviewing toolbar, click Show and then make sure that a check mark appears next to each

of the following items. If a check mark does not appear next to an item, click the item to select it.

1. Comments
2. Ink Annotations (Word 2003 only)
3. Insertions and Deletions
4. Formatting
5. Reviewers (point to Reviewers and make sure that All Reviewers is selected)

- When on, you will see all the comments and changes. When off, you will see the document in its final form. **Note: The default setting may be set to "off." Therefore, never assume your final Word document does not contain any hidden comments or changes**!!!

2. Get rid of all the redlines and comments (you must delete edits and comments separately). Do this in one of two ways:

a. Turn off the View Markup option and convert the final form of the document into a PDF. You can use a program such as Primo PDF.[51]

b. In the View menu, point to Toolbars, and then click Reviewing.

- On the Reviewing toolbar, click Next to advance from one revision or comment to the next. Click Accept Change or Reject Change/Delete Comment for each revision or comment. Repeat until all the revisions in the document have been accepted or rejected and all the comments have been deleted.

OR

- To accept all the changes, click the arrow next to Accept Change and then click Accept All Changes in Document. If you know that you want to reject all the changes, click the arrow next to Reject Change/Delete Comment and then click Reject All Changes in Document.
- THEN, to remove ALL comments, click the arrow next to Reject Change/Delete Comment and then click Delete All Comments in Document.
- If you want to accept SOME changes and delete others, you can accept or reject changes and comments one at a time by right-clicking on them individually. You will get a drop-down menu with choices of what to do.

---

51 http://www.primopdf.com/

3. Repeat Step 1.

IMPORTANT NOTES FOR BOTH MS VERSIONS OF WORD:

1. If you accept all changes before reviewing the document and there is a comment in the middle of your document like "(dates?)," then that change will be accepted and become a part of your document! Make sure you respond to all questions and make any revisions needed inside your document before accepting all changes.

2. *ALWAYS* proofread your final document at least three times! As much as The Essay Expert and other editors attempt to ensure that your documents are perfect, final approval is ultimately your responsibility.

3. If you don't want all your future edits to show up as marked on your document, turn Track Changes off by clicking on it. It's a toggled function. Click it on, click it off.

4. Finally, when you receive an edited document, whenever possible accept or reject the changes before making your own edits! This practice will make it much easier to look at the NEW edits you have made to the document.

TIP #48:
PROOFREAD, AND PROOFREAD AGAIN!

Yes, this is the grand finale! You would be amazed how many grammatical and typographical errors show up in "finished" résumés. I reread every résumé I write multiple times, and have my client and another résumé writer look over the document, as well. There is a LOT of information in a résumé, and just as many opportunities to get something wrong. Here are eleven essential spots to examine carefully before submitting your résumé to an employer:

1. **Address, phone, and e-mail.** Although it's unlikely you have misspellings in any of these key areas, it can happen, so check them carefully! Perhaps you changed a phone number or e-mail address and forgot to change it on your résumé? Make sure your address, phone, and e-mail are all correct and up-to-date! If you are in a technology field, use a Gmail address or paid account and stay away from Hotmail and Yahoo.

2. **Section headings.** Have you checked the spelling of the word Achievements (I have seen senior executives' résumés where the heading is spelled Acheivements)? How about Experience and Activities? Are there any extra letters floating around? Did you correctly spell Extracurricular (I have seen Extracaricular). Not

only could errors like these turn off a hiring manager who notices them, but they could prevent an ATS system from recognizing an entire section of your résumé.

3. **Job titles.** One of the most commonly misspelled words on résumés is "Manager" (often spelled "Manger"). Check your job titles to make sure they are spelled correctly! Also, in all your correspondence, make sure to refer to the exact job title listed in the job announcement. Do not abbreviate! Why take chances?

4. **Verbs.** "Led" is the past tense of "Lead" (many people mistakenly write "Lead"). Make sure you've spelled it correctly. If you are repeating your verbs over and over in your bullets, see what you can do to vary your verbs. Your résumé will truly start to shine. Finally, make sure your past jobs use past tense verbs. Often when someone converts a present job to a past job, some of those verbs remain in the present tense. This applies to ALL verbs in the section, not just the ones that start each bullet.

5. **Format.** Do all your bullets and dates line up with one another? Do you use the same font and font size throughout your résumé (unless you have an artistic, consistent reason for using two different fonts)? Is your spacing even? Are your headers all

formatted the same way? If not, you have some cleaning up to do!

6. **Dates.** Line up all your dates format-wise and use consistent formatting (don't write 1/06 to 2/05 in one spot and 3/2008–4/2011 in another; don't write December 2004 in one spot and Dec. 2006 in another). Check that all dates are accurate, with proper months and years, listed in reverse chronological order.

7. **Document Properties and Tracked Changes.** If someone else assisted you with your résumé, there might be tracked changes and document properties still lurking. To clean up tracked changes, accept all changes and delete all comments. Want more detailed instructions? Check out Tip #49, or my article "How to Avoid Embarrassing Editing Marks on Your Documents!"[52] To delete document properties such as Author, go to the File tab, click on Check for Issues and then Inspect document. Follow the prompts, and your document will be cleaned of whatever information you choose.

8. **Consistency between cover letter and résumé.** Match your cover letter format, including header and font,

---

52 http://theessayexpert.com/blog/how-to
-avoid-embarrassing-editing-marks-on-your
-documents-ms-words-track-changes-program/

to your résumé format. Consistency matters to recruiters and hiring managers!

9. **Additional instructions.** Did you supply all the information and documentation requested by the employer in the job description, in exactly the way it was requested? Following instruction is one of the most important parts to a successful job application!

10. **How does it look in PRINT?** Yes, I suggest PRINTING out your résumé and reading it on paper. You might be surprised what you find.

11. **Style guide.** The Chicago Manual of Style and the AP Stylebook are two of the most popular guides on how to write in the English language. These guides govern whether to write out numerals to the number ten or use the Arabic numeral 10; whether to use the % sign or "percent"; and whether to put spaces on either side of an em dash (—). When writing a résumé, the most important thing is to be consistent throughout the résumé. Don't put spaces before and after the em dash in one spot and leave them out in another. Don't put periods between your B.A. and not between your MA [*sic*]. Of course, if you're applying for a job at a publisher, please conform to the style guide used by that publisher. That goes without

saying. Other than that, most decision makers will care much more about consistency than about adherence to a particular set of style rules.

Once you are absolutely sure there are no errors in your résumé, go through the checklist in Appendix D one item at a time. Then run it by at least three trusted friends and colleagues to see if they find anything you missed! Once they've approved of the résumé, start applying for your dream jobs!

TIP #49:
GET YOUR RÉSUMÉ OUT THERE!
Your résumé won't do you much good sitting there on your computer or even sitting there on your LinkedIn profile. It's up to you to get your credentials in front of the people who matter.

NETWORKING
A former hiring director at Hallmark shared some advice at a career professionals' conference I attended: "The best way to get an interview is to take advantage of your networks. Get out there and talk to people!" Networking is essential to connect to people who might lead you to a job opportunity. Most important, networking will lead you to the "hidden job market"—the jobs that are not advertised but that are waiting for you to fill them!

If you want coaching on how best to find the jobs that are a fit for you, contact TEESupport@TheEssayExpert.com, and we'll give you the names of some career coaches who can steer you in the right direction.

RÉSUMÉ DISTRIBUTION

One way to get your résumé distributed widely is through a résumé distribution service. This type of service will send your résumé to hundreds of recruiters who have positions available that match your skill set. If you are interested in taking advantage of a résumé distribution service, contact TEESupport@TheEssayExpert.com, and we will assist you in setting up the distribution. The cost of this service ranges from $275 to $375 depending on industry.

TIP #50:
IT DOESN'T END HERE. ON TO THE INTERVIEW!

Your résumé will get you in the door, but won't get you a job. That's what the interview is for. Here are ten tips for interviews and negotiations that will help you land a job offer. These come straight from the mouth of a hiring director!

1. Prepare! Know everything you can possibly find out about the company. Come prepared with questions that prove you've done your research.
2. Bring one copy of your résumé (on white bond paper), and portfolio if applicable, for each person who will be interviewing you. You never know when you might be requested to provide these materials.

3. Arrive on time! Plan to arrive an HOUR EARLY so if *anything* goes wrong, like your cell phone falls in a puddle, you get a speeding ticket, you copied the address wrong, or the subway breaks down, you'll still arrive on time—calm, cool, and collected.
4. Be friendly to the gatekeepers like the receptionist or secretary who greets you. You are being interviewed the moment you walk in the door.
5. Confidence is key. The most important thing you can do is exude confidence, regardless of how long you've been unemployed or which "weaknesses" other people might think you have.
6. It's essential to have a short statement at the ready (your "elevator pitch") that identifies your unique strengths and what you offer.
7. How you carry yourself physically is extremely important. Confidence shows through your posture, facial expressions, and handshake. Look the interviewer in the eye.
8. You must exhibit a willingness to learn and adapt, over and over again. Come prepared with examples of how you embraced change and excelled.
9. Do your salary research. Educate yourself on payscale.com and salary.com so that you can back up your salary request with knowledge about

industry standards and cost of living in the relevant geographic area.

10. Remember the 5 Ps: Positivity, preparedness, professionalism, perseverance, and persistence.

Those 5 Ps apply to every aspect of your job search! How are you living up to them? Are you staying positive? Preparing diligently? Remaining professional and never giving up? I hope so! I want to know how you're doing! Please send me an e-mail at BrendaB@TheEssayExpert.com to update me on how your résumé has improved and how your job search is going.

APPENDIX A
POWER VERBS FOR RÉSUMÉS

SOME OF BRENDA'S FAVORITES, GROUPED BY TOPIC

The following list of résumé verbs is meant to get the wheels in your mind turning. It is by no means complete. Please be creative and use verbs to convey your accomplishments in the most effective way possible.

Although I have organized this list by categories, please do not limit yourself to the categorical headings. For instance, "promoted" could fall under just about any of the categories provided. If you like a word, take it and run with it!

LEADERSHIP

Achieved / Advised / Architected / Championed / Conducted / Directed / Drove / Energized / Engineered / Enlivened / Evaluated / Headed / Hired / Led / Managed / Orchestrated / Organized / Oversaw / Piloted / Propelled / Ran / Reorganized / Steered

INITIATIVE

Began / Birthed / Brought / Built / Conceived / Conceptualized / Created / Designed / Developed / Discovered / Entered / Established / Founded / Ignited / Infused / Initiated / Instituted/ Introduced / Launched / Pioneered / Sparked / Started

SALES & ROI

Accelerated / Amplified / Blasted / Captured / Doubled / Eclipsed / Elevated / Exceeded / Expanded / Exploded / Gained / Generated / Grew / Heightened / Improved / Increased / Landed / Lifted / Maximized / Monetized / Multiplied / Mushroomed / Outperformed / Populated / Pushed / Quadrupled / Raised / Rallied / Realized / Rocketed / Soared / Sold / Sourced / Sustained / Tripled / Turned around / Upturned / Yielded

COSTS

Averted / Avoided / Budgeted / Condensed / Contracted / Curtailed / Cut / Decreased / Diminished / Divided / Halved / Lowered / Minimized / Negotiated / Reduced / Reversed / Saved / Shortened / Shrank / Slashed / Trimmed

EFFICIENCY / PROCESS

Channeled / Compressed / Consolidated / / Eliminated / Enhanced / Implemented / Organized / Overhauled / Repurposed / Streamlined / Transformed

STRATEGY & IMPLEMENTATION

Acquired / Addressed / Aligned / Analyzed / Assessed / Brainstormed / Chose / Decided / Delivered / Differentiated / Executed / Focused / Identified / Implemented / Leveraged / Marketed / Measured / Navigated / Penetrated / Planned / Plotted / Positioned / Prioritized / Recommended / Repositioned / Repurposed / Retooled / Strategized / Targeted / Zeroed in

RELATIONSHIPS

Coached / Collaborated / Cultivated / Empowered / Engaged / Forged / Fostered / Mentored / Nurtured / Partnered / Smoothed / Teamed with

COMMUNICATION

Communicated / Corresponded / Drafted / Edited / Educated / Instructed / Presented / Revised / Taught / Trained / Wrote

RECOGNITION

Awarded / Certified / Credentialed / Designated / Earned / Excelled / Honored / Ranked / Received / Recognized / Rose / Won

OTHER

Argued / Met / Provided / Served / Strengthened / Transported / . . . and more!!

APPENDIX B

397 FAVORITE RÉSUMÉ VERBS

REPRODUCED WITH PERMISSION OF THE RÉSUMÉ WRITING ACADEMY

This list is much longer than the one in Appendix A, presented in alphabetical order. Have fun choosing your best options!

Accelerate
Accentuate
Accommodate
Accomplish
Achieve
Acquire
Adapt
Address
Adjudicate
Advance
Advise
Advocate
Align
Alter

Analyze
Anchor
Apply
Appoint
Appreciate
Arbitrate
Architect
Arrange
Articulate
Ascertain
Assemble
Assess
Assist
Augment
Authenticate
Author
Authorize
Balance
Believe
Bestow
Brainstorm
Brief
Budget
Build

Calculate
Capitalize
Capture
Catalog
Catapult
Centralize
Champion
Change
Chart
Clarify
Classify
Close
Coach
Collaborate
Collect
Command
Commercialize
Commoditize
Communicate
Compare
Compel
Compile
Complete
Compute

Conceive	Develop	Engineer
Conceptualize	Devise	Enhance
Conclude	Differentiate	Enlist
Conduct	Diminish	Enliven
Conserve	Direct	Ensure
Consolidate	Discern	Entrench
Construct	Discover	Equalize
Consult	Dispense	Eradicate
Continue	Display	Establish
Contract	Distinguish	Estimate
Control	Distribute	Evaluate
Convert	Diversify	Examine
Convey	Divert	Exceed
Coordinate	Document	Execute
Correct	Dominate	Exhibit
Corroborate	Double	Exhort
Counsel	Draft	Expand
Craft	Drive	Expedite
Create	Earn	Experiment
Critique	Edit	Explode
Crystallize	Educate	Explore
Curtail	Effect	Export
Cut	Effectuate	Extricate
Decipher	Elect	Facilitate
Decrease	Elevate	Finalize
Define	Eliminate	Finance
Delegate	Emphasize	Forge
Deliver	Empower	Form
Demonstrate	Enact	Formalize
Deploy	Encourage	Formulate
Derive	Endeavor	Foster
Design	Endorse	Found
Detail	Endure	Gain
Detect	Energize	Generate
Determine	Enforce	Govern

Graduate	Launch	Obfuscate
Guide	Lead	Obliterate
Halt	Lecture	Observe
Handle	Leverage	Obtain
Head	Liaise	Offer
Hire	License	Officiate
Honor	Listen	Operate
Hypothesize	Locate	Optimize
Identify	Lower	Orchestrate
Illustrate	Maintain	Organize
Imagine	Manage	Orient
Implement	Manipulate	Originate
Import	Manufacture	Outsource
Improve	Map	Overcome
Improvise	Market	Overhaul
Increase	Marshall	Oversee
Influence	Master	Participate
Inform	Mastermind	Partner
Initiate	Maximize	Perceive
Innovate	Measure	Perfect
Inspect	Mediate	Perform
Inspire	Mentor	Persuade
Install	Merge	Pilot
Institute	Minimize	Pinpoint
Instruct	Model	Pioneer
Integrate	Moderate	Plan
Intensify	Modify	Position
Interpret	Monetize	Predict
Interview	Monitor	Prepare
Introduce	Motivate	Prescribe
Invent	Navigate	Present
Inventory	Negotiate	Preside
Investigate	Network	Process
Judge	Nominate	Procure
Justify	Normalize	Produce

Program	Regulate	Sold
Progress	Rehabilitate	Solidify
Project	Reinforce	Solve
Project manage	Rejuvenate	Spark
Proliferate	Remedy	Speak
Promote	Render	Spearhead
Propel	Renegotiate	Specify
Propose	Renew	Standardize
Prospect	Renovate	Steer
Prove	Reorganize	Stimulate
Provide	Report	Strategize
Publicize	Reposition	Streamline
Purchase	Represent	Strengthen
Purify	Research	Structure
Qualify	Resolve	Study
Quantify	Respond	Substantiate
Query	Restore	Succeed
Question	Restructure	Suggest
Raise	Retain	Summarize
Rate	Retrieve	Supervise
Ratify	Reuse	Supplement
Realign	Review	Supply
Rebuild	Revise	Support
Recapture	Revitalize	Surpass
Receive	Sanctify	Synergize
Recognize	Satisfy	Synthesize
Recommend	Schedule	Systematize
Reconcile	Secure	Tabulate
Record	Select	Target
Recruit	Separate	Teach
Recycle	Serve	Terminate
Redesign	Service	Test
Reduce	Shepherd	Thwart
Reengineer	Simplify	Train
Regain	Slash	Transcribe

Transfer	Unify	Verbalize
Transform	Unite	Verify
Transition	Update	Win
Translate	Upgrade	Work
Trim	Use	Write
Troubleshoot	Utilize	

APPENDIX C
WORDS TO AVOID IN YOUR RÉSUMÉ!

You can get away with using one or two of the following words, but be careful not to rely on them. Go for detail and concrete statements instead!

Assisted
Helped
Energetic
Ambitious
Accomplished
Dedicated
Dependable
Confident
Highly qualified
Results-oriented
Results-focused
Results-driven
Goal-oriented
Detail-oriented
Competent
Innovative
Hard-working

Strong work ethic
Effective
Highly motivated
Successful / successfully
Capable of
Able
Qualified
Suitable
Proven track record
Proven ability
Extensive experience
Responsible for
Has talent for
Duties included
Self-starter
Professional
Seasoned professional
Team player
Multitasker
References available upon request
References furnished upon request

APPENDIX D
RÉSUMÉ & COVER LETTER CHECKLISTS: DON'T SKIP THESE!

the essay expert

RÉSUMÉ CHECKLIST PART 1 OF 2: SUBSTANTIVE/CONTENT/GRAMMAR ISSUES

1.	Have you matched the keywords in the résumé to your job descriptions?	☐
2.	Have you conveyed your unique selling proposition/branding statement in a way that makes you shine—three lines MAX in a block/paragraph?	☐
3.	Have you crafted an effective tagline—or chosen not to?	☐
4.	Are there any unexplained gaps? Have you considered how to address those?	☐
5.	Are the verbs starting each bullet varied and powerful?	☐
6.	Are verb tenses consistent throughout (present for current jobs, past for all others)?	☐
7.	Are bullets prioritized in order of importance?	☐
8.	Does every bullet contain quantifying information?	☐
9.	Does every bullet under a skills category (subheader) belong in that category?	☐
10.	Is the most important information visible in the top 1/3 of the résumé?	☐
11.	Have you placed a testimonial or graph/chart on the résumé (or chosen not to)?	☐
12.	Are additional skills and outside activities included if appropriate? Have you added an Awards, Affiliations, Certifications, or Publications section if appropriate?	☐
13.	Have you eliminated as many instances of "a" and "the" as possible?	☐
14.	Is GPA included if 3.4 or above? OR major GPA included if higher than overall?	☐
15.	Is year of graduation included if within ten years?	☐
16.	Does EVERY word count?	☐

17.	Have you checked and double-checked for parallel structure throughout?	☐
18.	Have you checked/Googled spelling, capitalization, and exact language for company names and technology/software?	☐
19.	Are the summary statements under your positions three lines or less?	☐
20.	Have you shown your résumé to at least three trusted friends and colleagues for review?	☐

RÉSUMÉ CHECKLIST PART 2 OF 2: FORMATTING

1.	Have you printed the résumé to check for readability and visual appeal?	☐
2.	Are fonts and font sizes consistent throughout?	☐
3.	Is the font size big enough given the font you are using (see #1)?	☐
4.	Are margins NO less than 0.8" left and right, 0.5" top, and 0.6" bottom?	☐
5.	Are there any double spaces between words?	☐
6.	Is there consistent spacing between sentences? There should be only ONE space after each period, comma, semicolon, question mark, exclamation point, and colon!	☐
7.	Is there consistent spacing between all lines and paragraphs?	☐
8.	Have you made sure your page breaks are logical?	☐
9.	Is there a period at the end of every bullet?	☐
10.	Are numbers consistent throughout? E.g., 1M/3MM or 3,000/75,000	☐
11.	Are numerals consistently either written out or written as numerals?	☐
12.	Is the description of the company directly under the company name and not under the job title?	☐
13.	Are all company and school names in a consistent font and typeface, and all job titles and degrees in a consistent and different typeface?	☐
14.	Are the dates formatted consistently, including consistent dash sizes?	☐
15.	Have you deleted any unnecessary tab stops and widows and orphans? Have you inserted hard page breaks?	☐
16.	Is there a header on the second page that includes name, phone, and "Résumé Page 2 of 2"?	☐
17.	Is there a line that says, "Experience (Cont'd)" and/or "Company Name (Cont'd)" at the top of the second page?	☐

COVER LETTER CHECKLIST PART 1 OF 2: SUBSTANTIVE/CONTENT ISSUES

1.	Does the letter begin with a "hook"? Remember to keep the first paragraph more about the company than about yourself.	☐
2.	Have you addressed the key points in the job description?	☐
3.	Have you minimized use of the word "I"?	☐
4.	Do you state what you know and respect about the company?	☐
5.	Have you used a testimonial in the cover letter (or chosen not to)?	☐
6.	Is the addressee's name spelled correctly in both the address line and the greeting?	☐
7.	Have you checked for repetition of ideas and phrases, and eliminated repetitive language?	☐
8.	Have you shown the letter to at least three trusted friends and colleagues?	☐

COVER LETTER CHECKLIST PART 2 OF 2: FORMATTING ISSUES

1.	Does the header on the cover letter match your résumé header?	☐
2.	Is the font consistent with the résumé font?	☐
3.	Is there consistent spacing after each period and paragraph? Use ONE space after each period, comma, semicolon, question mark, exclamation point, and colon!	☐
4.	Is there a colon (not a comma) after the greeting?	☐
5.	Is there a call to action in the last paragraph along with a value proposition?	☐

APPENDIX E
SERVICES & SPECIAL OFFERS

Are you ready to start writing your résumé? If you are, congratulations! If not, remember you might get some useful guidance from The Essay Expert's Résumé Questionnaires.[53]

- General Résumé Questionnaire[54] (VP and C-Level, Sales & Marketing, Accounting & Finance)
- IT Résumé Questionnaire[55]

Plus . . . We are always here to help you. Here is the link to our Executive résumé packages (click to learn more). Book purchasers receive specials discounts! Use the following coupon codes for up to $150 off our executive résumé services:

RÉSUMÉ150 ($150 Discount): Any résumé package worth $2,397 or more.

RÉSUMÉ100 ($100 Discount): Any résumé package priced between $1,447 and $2,396.

---

53 http://theessayexpert.com/do-it-yourself/

54 http://theessayexpert.com/product/general -résumé-questionnaire/

55 http://theessayexpert.com/product/it-résumé -questionnaire/

APPENDIX F

RECOMMENDED RESOURCES

Want to read more about résumés and job search? Here are some great resources:

- Guide to Crafting the Professional's Résumé: https://cdn.theladders.net/static/pdfs/Crafting_The_Professionals_Résumé.pdf
- Career Thought Leaders: Free Career & Leadership Advice: https://www.careerthoughtleaders.com/jobseekers
- Résumé-Specific Grammar Tips: Articles on Résumé Writing from the Résumé Writing Academy: https://résuméwritingacademy.wildapricot.org/writing-articles
- Job Seeker Resources including Finding a Career Professional, Award-Winning résumés, Career Podcasts, and Résumé / Interview / Career / Job Search Advice: http://www.careerdirectors.com/jobseeker.htm
- Career Jam 2015: https://www.careerthoughtleaders.com/resources/Documents/Papers%20and%20Journals/CTL-White-Paper-2015.pdf

APPENDIX G

IMPORTANT OPPORTUNITIES TO GIVE & RECEIVE

WE WANT YOUR FEEDBACK!

We hope you've enjoyed *How to Write a WIN-NING Résumé*! Did you find this book helpful? Please share a review on Amazon and let others know about the value you received.

CHECK OUT OUR SERVICES

If you are still stuck on how to write your résumé, consider The Essay Expert's Résumé Writing services. Contact us at TEESupport@ TheEssayExpert.com or through our web form at TheEssayExpert.com, or call us at 608-467-0067. We look forward to working with you.

Book purchasers receive special discounts on résumé services from The Essay Expert.

See Appendix E **for coupon codes** you can use right now.

GET ON MY LISTS

Want news and updates from The Essay Expert? Sign up for my Job Search list. You will receive a free e-book preview that you can give to a friend!

CONNECT WITH THE ESSAY EXPERT ON FACEBOOK

"Like" our Facebook Fan page now to connect with other readers and additional resources . . . And of course, please Connect with me, Brenda Bernstein, on LinkedIn!

ACKNOWLEDGMENTS

Many special thanks go to Laura DeCarlo, whose spot-on résumé coaching has made me into the writer I am today. I could never have earned the recognition or certifications I have without her tough yet supportive mentorship.

For editorial help, I thank my good friend Beth Garner, who kept asking me when my book would be ready so she could edit it, then spent many hours of her valuable time making incisive comments and edits. Her contributions made a good book even better!

Additional editors and brainstorming partners include résumé writer and career coach Kristin Johnson, as well as career trainer/job developer Darlene Morse and employment counselor Kelly Mitchell, who commented on one of my posts to a group on LinkedIn and sparked a cascade of ideas.

My Virtual Assistant, Jeanne Goodman, provides amazing technological support on everything from creating a table of contents to uploading my book to all the right places. I would be lost without her!

Jeri Hird Dutcher, one of my past subcontractors, designed one of the coolest-looking résumés in this book! Judith Monaco, another subcontractor, was primary author of another one of the résumés included as a sample.

I must always thank my publicity man, Scott Becher, who has been relentless in connecting me with media opportunities. And finally, thank you to the University of Wisconsin Law School's Career Services Office, where I received excellent training through writing dozens of résumés for law school students.

Thank YOU for reading my book! You are my inspiration.

ABOUT THE AUTHOR

Brenda Bernstein, founder and senior editor at The Essay Expert LLC, is a #1 bestselling author, an in-demand speaker & consultant, and one of only a handful of career professionals worldwide with both the Certified Master Résumé Writer (CMRW) and Certified Executive Résumé Master (CERM) credentials. Her #1 bestselling book, *How to Write a KILLER LinkedIn® Profile*,[56] was featured in *Fortune* and *Forbes* magazines and commanded the top ranking in Amazon's business writing skills e-book category for two years straight. Brenda espouses the belief that résumé writing does not have to be a drag, as evidenced by her signature presentation, Top 10 Ways to Make Résumé Writing FUN!

Brenda realizes that many people struggle when it comes to writing about themselves. Her services, which include résumé writing, LinkedIn profile writing, professional bio writing, and coaching on personal statements for college, enable clients to break through their resistance and look great on paper!

An English degree from Yale University and a J.D. from the NYU School of Law have given Brenda fantastic training in targeted writing. She has used her skills for the past fifteen years to coach professionals and companies on their writing projects. For help today

---

56 http://theessayexpert.com/how-to-write-a-killer
-linkedin-profile-e-book/

with your Résumé, LinkedIn Profile, Personal Statement, or Business Writing Projects, contact The Essay Expert.

- E-mail: BrendaB@TheEssayExpert.com
- Web: TheEssayExpert.com
- LinkedIn: Linkedin.com/in /brendabernstein
- Facebook: Facebook.com /TheEssayExpert
- Phone: 608-467-0067

PART 3

Moving Forward
in Mid-Career

INTRODUCTION

Being fired or laid off is one of the most devastating events one can experience. For trauma, it ranks up there with divorce, loss of a loved one, and permanent personal injury. It is no longer that which happens to someone else. Most likely it will happen to you, too, when you least expect it . . . like in midcareer, when you thought your job would last forever. Today, it is no longer thirty years with one company, a retirement dinner, a goldplated Apple Watch, and a fat pension.

It goes by different names: fired, bounced, riffed, sacked, whacked, downsized, canned, rightsized, laid off, let go, or whatever it might be called tomorrow. Regardless of what the process is called, the result is the same: you are no longer employed, which means that going forward you will have no paycheck, no bonus, and no benefits. And the title *Director of Marketing for Microsoft* will be gone, too. Henceforward, you are just plain *Mary Jones*. When an employer decides that you are expendable, you are going, regardless of social status or length of time with the company. Not fair? Sorry. That's just the way it works.

The most serious error one can make after starting a new job, whether it is an entry-level position or a presidency, is to assume the job will last throughout the work cycle. In reality, how long will the job last? It could be six days, six weeks, six months, or six years. In today's workplace, all workers must prepare for the day when their jobs might end. For example, if you had been working with Ford in May 2017, you would have been facing a layoff because Ford had missed its quarterly revenue goal and subsequently announced that it was planning to cut 10 percent of its global workforce.

Many workers believe their jobs are secure and will last forever because of social status. They might think, "I'm a veteran. My employer won't let *me* go." Or "*I'm* a woman, and if they fire me, that's gender discrimination." Or "I'm sixty years old and they will never fire me and risk an age discrimination lawsuit." Or "*I'm* African American, and if they lay me off, that's racial discrimination." Dream on! This is not your grandparents' generation. Anyone is subject to being sacked on any given day for any reason.

How does it happen? Assume you have been on the payroll for two years. One ordinary workday, your boss calls you in for a chat. In the past, she has given you high fives for performance, but now she says your job has been eliminated because your division is not profitable. She has been ordered to reduce her staff by 50 percent. The company gives you a severance check and a folder of benefits, and you are escorted from the building by a security guard. You return home, seeking answers and wondering how you are going to survive.

Adding to the concern of losing a paycheck and benefits is the psychological trauma that accompanies being fired or laid off. Now you are just another human being trying to make it in a seemingly unfair world. Your thoughts and feelings run wild. You feel humiliated. You are angry. You blame everyone but yourself. You enter a period of deep grieving and possibly serious depression. You feel pressure to get a job, sometimes *any job*, to relieve the pain.

Losing your job will crush your ego like no other event because in our culture self-esteem and a positive self-image are closely tied to a job title and a company name. Working through the aftereffects of job loss and rebuilding a career is a serious matter. It involves more than crafting a dynamite résumé and sending it off to numerous job boards and career pages. It's a process with many moving parts.

Job loss will negatively affect any worker regardless of rank, title, age, or time on task. However, midcareer workers suffer the most because they have the most to lose. They have high personal expenses like mortgage payments, car payments, various insurance premiums, student loans, and childcare. For them, losing a job has life-changing ramifications.

How does one cope with the trauma and begin the rebuilding process? How does one redefine persona? How does a discharged worker tread through the grieving process? Most important, how does one find new employment opportunities to make the bottom line black again? After we cut through the hype about fulfillment, purpose, and mission, this thing called *work* has a universal purpose—to make money in order to survive. No salary? No food, no shelter, no clothing. The bottom line is this: *work is all about the paycheck*, as crass as that might sound. Mission, fulfillment, and purpose are important but secondary.

Based on my experience in the staffing industry and on research from various sources, I have identified the major issues resulting from job loss. They are the basis for the six major themes that run through *Moving Forward*:

1. Losing a job is a major life crisis. Frequently, it comes unexpectedly, catching one unprepared to deal with its trauma and ramifications. Coping and rebuilding involve working through humiliation, denial, anger, blame, and grief, and finally accepting responsibility for your life and career going forward.

2. The majority of workers will have a series of jobs over the course of their working life. The era of "thirty years with AT&T, a retirement party, and a new smartphone" is over. On average, workers will change jobs six times during their working years.

3. Workers are fired or laid off for a variety of reasons, most of which are not related to their personal work productivity.

4. Fired workers must learn to fine-tune character and redefine persona independently of company affiliation or job title.

5. Searching for new career opportunities is productive only after recovering from the initial trauma of losing a job and after redefining career and life goals.

6. Secular and spiritual help can be instrumental in recovering and moving forward.

Moving Forward will guide your search for meaning and understanding while providing solutions for the challenges at each stage of the process, from the initial shock and humiliation of being let go to rebuilding your persona, examining your character, crafting a new résumé, and seeking new employment opportunities. The book has two major objectives:

- To provide timely support for workers who have lost their jobs and are in process of rebuilding their careers.

- To provide job-hunting rubrics for workers reentering the job market.

The writing style of *Moving Forward* is informal, encouraging, conversational, and instructive. Each chapter concludes with two important features:

1. **Chapter Takeaways,** a series of succinct rubrics in bullet-point format.

2. **Print and Digital Resources,** a list of books and Internet references that extend the chapter content.

Throughout the book are personal stories of fired or laid-off workers that detail how they managed their job loss and what they did to move forward. They reflect a broad spectrum of the workplace: editors, sales representatives, marketing directors, presidents, video producers, and information technology managers.

You can read *Moving Forward* sequentially or proceed directly to chapters that have immediate appeal. Either way, the contents of this book will help you through the trauma, lead to a better understanding of who you really are, and help you through the process of building a new career.

So why did I decide to write this book? For two reasons:

1. In my job as an executive recruiter, I witness firsthand the trauma that workers experience when let go in

midcareer. This book is my solution to guide them through their crises and help them move forward into other careers.

2. I was laid off in midcareer myself, so I know from personal experience the many ramifications of this life event. When I was laid off, I had a huge home mortgage, car payments, insurance payments, and tuition expenses for three children in college. I was laid off in a company-wide conference call with the CEO. I was given two days' notice, three weeks' severance pay, and two weeks of outplacement services. All other company employees suffered the same fate. Laid off in a conference call in midcareer? Does that really happen? Yes, it does, but I never thought something like that could happen to me. After my outplacement time, I vowed never again to work for someone else and started my own entrepreneurial business as an executive recruiter focusing on the education industry. That was twenty years ago, and I have never looked back.

PART I

Coping with the Ramifications of Job Loss

It takes 20 years to build a reputation and five minutes to ruin it. If you think about

that, you'll do things differently.

—Warren Buffett

CHAPTER 1

HOW AND WHY WORKERS ARE FIRED OR LAID OFF

A typical day goes something like this for most workers. Wake up at six. Breakfast at seven. Report to work at eight. Do your thing until noon, with a break for coffee at ten. Lunch at twelve. Return to work at one and slug it out through the rest of the afternoon. Leave work at five and return home. Alternatively, on some days you might go shopping or for a drink with friends. Dinner at six. Then spend some quality time with the children, watch TV, or read a book. Maybe go to a movie with your spouse or partner. Go to bed between ten and eleven. This routine continues indefinitely until *something else* happens at work, usually late in the afternoon, near quitting time.

HOW THE LAYOFF PROCESS WORKS

That *something else* emerges like this. At 3:00 p.m. your boss invites you to the office of the human resources director for a chat. *A bit unusual but nothing to worry about*, you think. You know the HR director: nice woman, understanding, supportive. They call her Mrs. Friendly. Nothing to worry about. Probably some change in office routine or maybe a

new office. Maybe an out-of-sequence performance evaluation. Maybe a promotion. Maybe a change in health benefits. She is all smiles, and so is your boss who closes the door. Mrs. Friendly asks you to sit down in the chair in front of her desk. Your boss sits down beside you. Here's what happens next.

Your boss begins the chat saying something like this. "Joe, you have really made a solid contribution to the company, and we appreciate it. You were great. Always on time. Job requirements fulfilled. Good leadership potential. Nice job, Joe!" So far, so good. But why are your palms feeling a bit clammy? And what did the boss mean by "*were* great"?

Mrs. Friendly says, "Yes, Joe. I echo all of what your boss said. And I do like your last performance review. Nice job, and we thank you." *Hey*, you think. *How nice of them to single me out for some well-deserved recognition after three years on the job.*

She continues, "Joe, don't take personally what I'm going to say next because it has nothing to do with you. And I really mean that. However, the CEO and the president believe the company needs to cut expenses as we head into the next quarter. Unfortunately, the highest company expense is employee compensation. In order to save money and maintain profitability, we are having a reduction in force. So, Joe, we have to make some cuts, and it really pains me to tell you that we have decided to eliminate your position." Your boss nods his head in agreement. "And so, today is your last day working here, Joe. I'm truly sorry."

Then Mrs. Friendly hands you an envelope and says, "Joe, enclosed are your severance benefits that include your COBRA options, a check for your two remaining paid holidays for this year, and a check for three weeks of base salary, one week for each of the three years you worked with us. I know you will be happy with that. Your wife will be, too."

Now your boss chimes in: "Joe. I could not be more upset to see you go, but it happens sometimes. I'll give you a good recommendation. You will probably find something else very soon. Look, it's only 3:30, but you can leave early today. I'll walk you back to your office and wait while you collect your personal belongings and then escort you out of the building. Oh, by the way, we have already eliminated your company e-mail address and shut down your company cell phone. And Ed, the security officer, will walk us to your car. Nothing personal. Just company procedure. Routine, Joe."

You don't know what to say to your boss or Mrs. Friendly. You are shocked into silence. In addition, you are humiliated because you feel the eyes of your coworkers sneaking peeks at you from their cubicles. You collect your personal items, including pictures of your wife and fifteen-month-old daughter, and walk out of the building in a daze, accompanied by the security officer and your former boss. You are hurt . . . hurt so much that your hands are trembling and you are mad as hell and humiliated in the extreme.

And you wonder out loud, "Why didn't my colleague, Marsha, get sacked like I did? And what about Bill? He's still there. All of us had comparable jobs in the marketing department. What am I going to tell my wife? I didn't do anything wrong, so why did they let me go? Was I fired? Laid off? What's going on here? Maybe I should get an attorney to sort this out."

Does it really happen like that? Count on it. On any given day, thousands of workers will be fired just as you were. Use any euphemism you want, but when your employer tells you to leave the premises, consider yourself fired. However, you can use *laid off* or *let go* if it makes you feel better.

So what's next, Mr. Fired? First, it means finding another job in order to put food on the table for you, your wife, and your kid. And a roof over your head for you, your wife, and your kid. And clothing for you, your wife, and your kid. In addition, it means collecting your unemployment compensation check each month, with embarrassment. By God, you never imagined that you would be on welfare! A college degree was supposed to prevent this from occurring. Now what, food stamps? Section 8 housing? A government cell phone? Medicaid? Asking friends and family for a long-term, no-interest loan?

The first next step means finding another job—any job, you believe, to stop the nightmare. This means going through the job-hunting process again, a hated activity that keeps you awake nights. Résumés? Interviews? Rejection? Who needs it! You get advice from everyone: your spouse, your friends, your industry network, your neighbors, and those irritating bloggers who tell you that finding another job is just a matter of crafting a *dynamite résumé*, which they will do for a price. And so you sit at your computer day in and day out scouring the job boards and firing off your brilliant résumé to places like Box 21, Position 47, and Employment Manager. The result? Nothing. Might as well send your brilliant piece of dynamite to the third ring of the planet Saturn.

Finding new employment is not just a matter of creating a résumé and firing it off to multiple job boards. It is a multistep process that requires your patience, time, and understanding.

WHAT TO DO AND NOT TO DO AFTER LOSING YOUR JOB

In a *US News and World Report* article, Alison Green lists ten things to do immediately after being let go:

- Don't panic.
- Don't freak out.
- Don't do anything rash.
- Don't sign a severance agreement immediately.
- Negotiate how your departure will be described.
- Look over your finances.
- File for unemployment.
- Plan to keep in touch with clients and coworkers.
- Remain objective.
- Remember that you're not alone.

This list is a good starting point to rebuilding your career. Consider it a bit of first aid to get past the initial trauma. The last bullet point is something to always keep in mind as you navigate the rest of your working years. Today, as you are reading this page, thousands of workers will get laid off just as you did . . . through no fault of their own. Being laid off, being fired, and being hired are just impersonal events in the world of business. (This brings to mind my experience, being laid off in a company-wide conference call. Laid off by phone? It does not get more impersonal than that.)

We hear so much from the pundits, financial gurus, and national media about companies letting go thousands of workers at a crack. One might think that the US economy is in a constant state of recession. Reality, however, is much different. Workers are let go for a number of reasons, all of which have to do with the numbers. A look at the reasons why workers are laid off will set the record straight.

WHY MIDCAREER WORKERS LOSE THEIR JOBS. IT'S ALL ABOUT THE NUMBERS

Learning *why* workers are laid off is important not only for those out of work now, but also for those still working because one never knows when the ax will fall. Going forward, you will be looking for *good* job opportunities, not just *any* job. This requires information about how employers operate, why they do what they do—like lay off ten thousand workers at a crack. The last thing you need is to jump into another job that will disappear in six months. To avoid that potential tragedy, you need to do your homework while you are unemployed, or still employed and preparing for what could happen on any work day at 3:30 p.m.

One could argue night and day about why workers are laid off or fired. You hear one story from the academics, another from business executives, another from the talking heads on the financial channels, and still another from politicians. And do not forget the chatter on social media. To cut through the hype, let's go to the numbers.

Workers are constantly being downsized, reorganized, or rightsized. For example, data from the Bureau of Labor Statistics indicate that approximately 55,000 workers are fired or laid off each day. *That's approximately 20 million per year!* On the plus side, millions of workers will be hired each day. Because of this constant churning in the workplace, workers will change jobs an average of six times during their working years.

The American workplace employs over 155 million workers, making *our workforce alone* the world's eighth largest "country." There are many moving parts in the workplace, some working in sync and others fighting against one another. Employers are constantly revising plans, merging, acquiring competitors, moving operations to another country, going into bankruptcy, and going out of business. All of this means that workers are going to lose their jobs. For you, the laid-off worker, it is important to remember that being let go is usually *not about you personally*. It's about an employer fighting to survive and remain profitable.

THE UNEMPLOYMENT RATE

Daily, we hear the pundits, talking heads, and media gurus screaming about one of their favorite topics—the unemployment rate. To hear them talk, one would think that America is heading for financial disaster with unemployment taking a leading role. The numbers help us sort fact from fiction. And they will help you understand why you got that sorrowful "good-bye, Joe" from the human resources director at 3:30 p.m. on a day you were not expecting it.

The average rate of unemployment in the United States since the Great Depression has been approximately 6 percent. Many economists interpret that to mean that an employment rate of 94 percent is truly full employment. Since 1970, our lowest rate of unemployment was 3.8 percent in 2019, and the highest was 10 percent in 2009.

The three main causes for unemployment are *seasonal* unemployment, when workers are laid off because of bad weather; *structural* unemployment, when workers are laid off because their jobs are replaced by technology; and *cyclical* unemployment, when workers are laid off because of changes in the economy, such as a recession that weakens consumer demand for products and services. These three causes of unemployment will always be present. There will never be such a thing as 0 percent unemployment.

The numbers tell us that America has an average *employment* rate of 94 percent. If workers in America claim they can't find work, it is not the fault of the president, elected officials, their teachers, or their mothers and fathers. The fault lies with them alone. If you really want a job, it is there for the taking—if you use the rules for job hunting in this book and other resources.

FACTORS THAT CONTRIBUTE TO JOB LOSS

Six major factors are responsible for the large number of job losses each year.

1. ***Reduction in force.*** Businesses exist to make money. If they make money, they remain in business and grow, which results in more hiring. This applies to *for-profit* and *nonprofit* businesses alike. If a company does not make money after deducting expenses and taxes, it will go out of business and workers will lose their jobs. To maintain profitability, companies are constantly adjusting the size of their staff. For example, when a fast-food company like McDonald's experiences a downturn in profits over a period of two or more quarters, it will downsize its staff. The result? Massive layoffs. This process is frequently called a reduction in force, an *RIF*. Those laid off in this process are referred to as having been *riffed*.

2. ***Mergers.*** Tens of thousands of companies combine forces each year for a variety of reasons. When two companies merge their operations, workers are laid off. For example, when company A and company B merge, the new company C will need only one vice president of sales. The result? One of the VPs from A or B will be laid off.

3. ***Acquisitions.*** You hear it every day. "Company X buys company Y." Again, when two companies are combined into one, workers are laid off to prevent duplication of services. Also, businesses sometimes sell only their products or services. The result? Massive layoffs occur because the acquiring company

does not take the employees, only the products. It is called an asset acquisition.

4. ***Trade deals that send jobs overseas.*** Staff employees are usually the last to hear that their American employer cut a deal to have their products manufactured in a foreign country. It is only after the layoffs that workers learn their jobs were lost because the company's products can be made more cheaply outside of the United States. The same applies to services. For example, when was the last time you spoke to an American-based customer service worker? And what is the country of origin of your new pair of Nike shoes?

5. ***Bankruptcies.*** When a company is consistently unprofitable, it uses the business tactic called bankruptcy to pay off creditors. When a company files for bankruptcy, what usually follows is a reorganization, which results in massive layoffs.

6. ***Reorganizations.*** Periodically, companies reorganize to improve day-to-day operations. For example, General Electric moved its corporate home office from Connecticut to Massachusetts. GE offered to relocate workers with key positions, but this was not acceptable for those firmly rooted in Connecticut. Those who did not accept that offer were laid

off along with workers in support positions. The same thing happened to workers employed by Merck in some of its New Jersey offices. When the company decided to relocate some operations to other states, many workers were laid off. Frequently, it is less costly for companies to lay off workers and hire new talent in the new location.

When you are seeking a new job, it is prudent to learn as much as you can about a potential employer's plans going forward. This information is available from company press releases, from TV interviews with company executives, and from company hiring managers during interviews for a new position.

MOVING FORWARD

Being fired or laid off is a traumatic experience, one like no other for a midcareer worker with financial and family responsibilities. All workers who have been let go, regardless of the reason, experience several stages of grieving, and it is of paramount importance to deal with this process as soon as possible. In the next chapter, we will identify the various stages of grieving and provide help for moving through them as quickly as possible.

CHAPTER TAKEAWAYS

- Working for someone else is a hazardous occupation.

- No job is forever. Always remain is a state of readiness to look for another job.
- Companies lay off workers primarily for business reasons, not personal reasons.

PRINT AND DIGITAL RESOURCES

Berman, Karen, and Joe Knight. *Financial Intelligence: A Manager's Guide to Knowing What the Numbers Really Mean.* Harvard Business Review Press, 2013.

Doyle, Alison. "The Difference Between Getting Fired and Getting Laid Off." *The Balance*, December 6, 2016. https://www.thebal-ance.com/difference-between-getting-fired-and-getting-laid-off-2060743.

Molly's Middle America. www.mollysmid-dleamerica.blogspot.com.

US Small Business Administration, SBA, www.sba.gov.

US Department of Commerce, www.com-merce.gov.

CHAPTER 2
WORKING THROUGH THE GRIEVING PROCESS

When I was laid off in midcareer, I thought that finding another job would be a quick and easy process. After all, I had been in the educational technology business for quite some time working with the likes of Apple Computer. Write a résumé, make some phone calls, and a job will follow, fast. However, I was caught off guard when I entered the grieving process after losing my job because of an asset acquisition. Everyone goes through a period of grieving after a significant loss, which could be the death of a loved one, loss of a spouse by divorce, loss of a physical function through permanent injury, *or loss of a job*. Losing a job frequently triggers a period of grieving as severe as that caused by death or divorce. For verification, ask anyone who has been let go.

The severity of the grieving process caused by job loss is proportionate to the separated worker's rank, compensation, and age. Midcareer workers usually suffer the most because they have the most to lose in terms of status, rank, and compensation. They are likely to have significant mortgage or rental payments, automobile payments, credit card payments, childcare expenses, college tuition payments, insurances payments, and more. Being forced to deal with all of those responsibilities will throw most laid-off workers into the classical stages of the grieving process.

CLASSICAL STAGES OF THE GRIEVING PROCESS

Swiss-born psychiatrist Elisabeth Kübler-Ross worked with terminally ill patients and their loved ones and noted certain patterns that emerged in the dying process. In her book *On Death and Dying*, she states that there are five stages in the grieving process:

1. Denial
2. Anger
3. Bargaining
4. Depression
5. Acceptance

The length of time one stays in the grieving process is proportional to the closeness of the bond between the two individuals. The closer the bond, the longer it takes to move ahead and restore normal life balance. Most people work through the grieving process using their own resources, but others require professional help from a psychologist, psychiatrist, clergy member, or career counselor.

THE GRIEVING PROCESS EXPERIENCED BY LET-GO WORKERS

In my work as an executive recruiter, I have seen laid-off workers go through a grieving process parallel to that experienced by death of a loved one. However, it is usually abbreviated because workers quickly become preoccupied with finding another job, a time-consuming task that pushes the worker through the grieving process. I have noted the following stages of grief when counseling, and consoling, job candidates who have lost their jobs, especially those in midcareer.

DENIAL

After hearing those torturous words from the boss or the human resources director, "We have to let you go," most workers say aloud or silently, "This can't be happening to me. I've given my blood, sweat, and tears to this company, and there is no reason why I should be laid off." Many workers refuse to believe they were asked to leave the premises and petition the boss and HR director for reinstatement. If that does not work, they persist in seeking reasons for dismissal that make sense to them. They want more than "We're having a reorganization." Some take it to the next level and demand to see their boss's boss

or the president or CEO. Usually, the appeal to a higher authority bears no fruit, and the laid-off worker leaves the premises dejected but still in denial.

After leaving the premises, some workers take it to the next step, seeking help from a colleague in the company. Some ask a company friend to intercede with the boss or human resources director to reinstate their jobs. Others seek the help of a lawyer to have their employment reinstated. These initiatives are rarely successful.

HUMILIATION

A person who has just been told that their presence in the company is no longer needed feels a great sense of humiliation. When it happens, it seems that the eyes of all coworkers are on you. You feel that *they* know that you were sacked. Word travels fast. The most humiliating event is being walked out of the workplace accompanied by a security officer as though you committed a crime. It hurts like nothing else and sets you up for the next stage, anger.

ANGER

A worker enters the anger stage of the grieving process when attempts to become reinstated have failed, and when the humiliation continues as more people become aware that you were let go. Anger is usually directed at three sources: the company, the boss, and the human resources director, the one who frequently delivers the bad news. If not resolved quickly, the anger stage will prevent the fired worker from thinking clearly and planning the next step, rebuilding their career. Usually, workers in the anger stage will hurl epithets at the boss and the company to anyone who will listen. Some will curse using language heretofore unused. Some will lose it completely and resort to violence by physically injuring the human resources director or the boss. When you find yourself in a prolonged stage of anger, do everything possible to move forward, like seeking counseling from a psychologist, a career coach, or a clergy member.

DEPRESSION

Fired or laid-off workers lose that sense of professional identity that sets them apart from the rest of the pack. Frequently, laid-off workers enter a stage of pessimism, inadequacy, helplessness, and despondency, which is manifested by constant complaining to family members, friends, colleagues, and anyone who will listen to their tale of woe. Unfortunately, for some workers it goes beyond constant complaining, and they enter a state of depression that requires clinical help from a psychiatrist. However, most work through this stage of the grieving process by activating their network of family and friends for support and encouragement.

ACCEPTANCE

Acceptance is the final stage of the grieving process for those who have lost their jobs. In previous stages of the process, you may have tried to resolve the problem but to no avail. You are not going to be rehired. Period. You must put the past behind you and move forward, but on your own terms. Acceptance is a liberating process. It closes the grieving stage and enables you to move forward to rebuild not only your career, but also your entire life. In a sense, being fired or laid off can prove to be one of the best things that has ever happened to you. When you accept your situation, you take total ownership not only of your career, but also of your entire life.

> Put aside your regrets of the past.
> Put away your fear of the future.
> Move forward with confidence.

FIVE SOLUTIONS FOR WORKING THROUGH THE GRIEVING PROCESS

Workers at every rank can move through the grieving process using these resources: the Internet, print and digital books and magazines, a career coach, a friend or family member, faith-based resources, an outplacement service, and common sense. I have witnessed let-go workers use some or all of these resources to move forward successfully. Here are five initiatives to hasten your trip through the grieving process:

TAKE A BREAK

The first thing most let-go workers do is plunge into the job-hunting process, and that is a huge mistake. First, take a well-deserved break. Consider beginning the process by going out to an upscale restaurant or pub today or tomorrow, preferably with a trusted friend. Go out and let loose. Have a good time. Lift your glass and get it off your chest shouting the title of a song made famous by country singer Johnny Paycheck, "Take This Job and Shove It!" Pay in cash and leave a generous tip. While you are at dinner, begin planning the next step—leaving the house and having more fun.

The day following your night on the town, make a written list of activities for the next seven days that you can do alone. Do not include anything work-related. You will have time for that later. Include in your list all of those things you could not do when you were working because your job sapped all of your time and energy. (Remember those irritating text messages at 10:00 p.m.?) Plan to leave the house each day to participate in physical activities such as visiting museums and art galleries, playing golf, swimming, hiking, skiing, biking, mountain climbing, and exploring locations that arouse your curiosity. Make sure they take place away from home. At the conclusion to this week of physical activity, move forward to the next step, leaving town.

If you have enough discretionary income, leave town for a week, preferably alone, to a faraway national or international destination. You can find attractive and reasonably priced travel deals with a bit of research. How would you like six days in Ireland? London? How about nine days touring the Grand Canyon,

Sedona, Monument Valley, Bruce and Zion National Parks? Getting out of town is the best remedy I know to forget about the past, particularly about that nasty employer who had the temerity to let you go. The hell with them! Move on. You can live without them. Truth be known, you never really liked working there. Other jobs are out there, as you will discover upon returning home from your vacation.

TAKE A PERSONAL INVENTORY

Make a list of all of the good things that you still have: your spouse or partner, children, family members, friends, intelligence, job skills, energy, and education. Your former employer could not take all of that away from you. Most of all, you still have your attitudes and opinions, which you will use moving forward. You are still intact.

In addition, record the personal possessions that your work has enabled you to acquire (i.e., the best of the basic three: food, shelter, clothing). While millions in the world will go to bed hungry tonight, you will not. Be thankful for what you have and remember that you are among the most fortunate people in the world, a worker in the United States. While millions of people from around the world are banging on the door of America in order to get a job, you are already here. As a midcareer worker, most likely you have reached an income level in your previous job that placed you in the upper 15 percent of the income bracket. Looking at the numbers always puts things in perspective.

STUDY THE NUMBERS

When you are out of a job, there is a tendency to hear only the bad news. Tune out the media babble about the dire state of the economy and conduct your own research. Study the numbers from the Bureau of Labor Statistics, the Department of Commerce, and the Pew Research Center.

Also, look at the employment rate (as opposed to the unemployment rate) in America and others countries. As I discussed earlier, we have had an average employment rate of 94 percent over the past seventy years. Look at European countries, like Greece, where the employment rate is a mere 75 percent, and you will count your blessings. It does not get better than living in America when you are looking for a job.

EVALUATE YOUR WORK-LIFE BALANCE

For some fortunate workers, work-life balance was never a problem. Their employers were cognizant of the fact that life existed away from the office, storefront, or construction site and planned the workday accordingly. However, for others, especially those whose jobs were technology-driven, work never seemed to go away. Tweets at 10:00 p.m. on a Tuesday from the boss. Texts at 8:00 a.m. on a Saturday requesting a work-flow summary for a meeting on Monday morning. An e-mail at 7:00 p.m. on Friday "asking" you to show up for an emergency meeting the next day. What did you usually do after work? Did your last job, where you worked sixty hours a week,

leave you so exhausted that you can't recall when you last visited an art museum or seen a movie? Were there any "afterwork" hours, or were work and personal life one and the same?

Define your life priorities beginning with family responsibilities: spouse, children, parents. Next, write down what brings you pleasure and satisfaction in your life *outside of work* and after fulfilling family responsibilities. In your last job, how much time did you devote to those strictly personal pursuits? One hour each day? Maybe a few hours on the weekend after the usual household chores? Vow that you will never again permit an employer to control your life. This is *your* life. Define it on your own terms.

EVALUATE YOUR WORK HISTORY AND OBJECTIVES

Did you really like your last job or did you go there every day solely for the money? Do you want to continue working in your specialty or would you be happy to move forward to something else? Many workers fall into a specific area in the workplace for which they really have no particular liking. It may have been the need to pay off the student loan after graduating with a master's and the most easily accessible job that had an above-average compensation level was one in sales, first as a territory sales rep, then as a district manager, and most recently as a regional sales manager. You were on the road more than 50 percent of the time, rushing from one airport and hotel to another. You were constantly making pipeline reports and evaluations of your subordinates. Did you really enjoy that? If not, define and write down your five ideal jobs. Are you ready to move to a new career? Will one of your five ideal jobs provide the compensation you need to maintain your desired style of living and meet current living expenses?

If your financial situation is such that you can make a change, do it now. Why wait until you are thinking about retirement?

MOVING FORWARD

Transitioning to the acceptance stage of the grieving process is a prerequisite for moving forward to defining a new you, independent of job rank or title. However, it is important to evaluate your financial situation to make sure that you can meet obligations related to your own personal well-being and that of your family and your dependents. In succeeding chapters, we'll examine the financial ramifications of job loss and what you can do to minimize the impact. Stay tuned.

CHAPTER TAKEAWAYS

- All let-go workers experience a period of grieving.
- Accepting the fact that you were laid off and that having no chance of having your job reinstated is a liberating experience.
- Put away the regrets of the past.
- Forget your fears of the future.
- Move forward to another career in America, the breadbasket of the world where jobs are always available for those who know how and where to find them.

PRINT AND DIGITAL RESOURCES

Froehls, Michael. *The Gift of Job Loss*. Peitho Publishing, 2011.

"Job Loss and Unemployment Stress." HelpGuide.org. www .helpguide.org/articles/stress/job-loss -and-unemployment-stress.htm.

Kyosaki, Robert. *Rich Dad. Poor Dad*. Plata Publishing LLC, 2012.

Warrell, Margie. "Bouncing Back from Job Loss: The 7 Habits of Highly Effective Job Hunters." Forbes, June 12, 2012. https://www.forbes.com /sites/womensmedia/2012/06/12 /bouncing-back-from-job-loss-the -7-habits-of-highly-effective-job -hunters/#240b15147b70.

Willink, Jocko, and Leif Babin. *Extreme Ownership: How U.S. Navy Seals Lead and Win*. St. Martin's Press, 2015.

CHAPTER 3

PROTECTING AND MAINTAINING YOUR SAVINGS, INVESTMENTS, AND IRA

When the paycheck stops, there might be a knee-jerk reaction to begin liquidating savings and other assets in order to continue your lifestyle as though you were still on the payroll. Nothing could be riskier. Even though you are out of work and have no regular paycheck, it is important to evaluate, monitor, and preserve the financial gains you have made. Make this a priority.

Remember that your out-of-work situation is temporary. The paycheck will return when you move forward with another job. While redefining your persona and rebuilding your character, evaluate all of your assets and decide what you are going to do to preserve them.

PROTECTING ALL OF YOUR INVESTMENTS

An investment is anything that has monetary value: savings accounts, individual retirement accounts, non-IRA brokerage accounts, credit cards, mutual funds, real estate holdings, and personal possessions.

Financial investments should be monitored constantly because of the cyclical nature of our economy. The last thing you need is to see your investments lose significant value overnight. It happened in the Great Recession of 2008, and it can happen again. Remember that two consecutive quarters of negative gross domestic product (GDP) herald a recession, a time to move your money to a safe haven like cash, which can be reinvested when the economy emerges from the recession. (You can learn more about how to monitor the economy by tuning in to financial TV channels like CNBC, Fox Business, and Bloomberg Business.)

PROTECTING YOUR CASH SAVINGS

Being let go usually comes when you are least expecting it. The first thing that the laid-off worker may think about is how much money they have in the bank to carry them through the period of unemployment. Is the cash you have in the bank enough to cover expenses until you have a new income stream? According to a study conducted by the Financial Industry Regulatory Authority (FINRA), 56 percent of US workers do not have enough in their cash accounts to cover three months of necessary expenses. Alarmingly, a new study reveals that seven out of ten American workers have less than $1,000 in their savings account. This borders on a national tragedy and reveals that the majority of adult workers have not learned the basics of money management. Every worker, regardless of income level, should keep enough money in a cash account to cover at least six months of expenses. My recommendation is to keep an extra margin for safety and make it twelve months at all times during your working years.

ESTABLISHING A SIX-MONTH EMERGENCY FUND

To determine where you stand financially after losing your job, make a list of all *necessary* monthly expenses. Do not include money that you would spend on items like going out to dinner; going to concerts, ball games, or shows; and purchasing the latest fashion items advertised on TV or social media, the latest clothing and digital apps for the children, new cell phones, new pets, and new furniture. Include on your list only those items that are absolutely necessary, such as

mortgage payments, car payments, children's tuition, insurance premiums, utility bills, tax payments, food, and critical clothing needs for yourself and family members.

After determining your monthly expenses, multiply by six to learn what you will need to carry you through a six-month period of unemployment. If you do not have a sufficient amount in your money market or savings account to cover necessary expenses for six months, the average length of time it should take to find a new employment opportunity, establish an emergency fund. Do this by transferring money from other sources, like your personal investment portfolio.

Transfer only what you need to cover these expenses. For example, if you determine that your estimated six-month expenses are $24,000 and you have just $15,000 in ready cash, transfer only $9,000 from your personal investments to cover costs. This might require selling favorite equities or mutual funds. In extreme situations, it may require withdrawing from your IRA, but remember that this carries a 10 percent IRS tax penalty if you are under the age of 59 ½.

Protect your newly created cash emergency fund by resisting the temptation to buy unnecessary items. When you find another job, rebuild your emergency fund to the $24,000 level, the amount of money required to pay for six months of expenses. Your newly created cash emergency account will build the confidence you need to make the right employment choices moving forward.

PROTECTING YOUR IRA

This is an opportune time to reevaluate your entire financial position. If you were enrolled in a company-sponsored IRA with your previous employer, you had a certain amount withdrawn from your paycheck and invested in an IRA mutual fund. Most workers believe the company and the fund looked after your best interests but . . . did they? Now is the time to evaluate the mutual funds in your IRA. What kind of funds are they? Bond funds? Equity funds? ETFs? Money market funds? Domestic funds? International funds? How much does the mutual fund company charge in annual fees? How much do they charge for making changes to your account? A 1 percent fee could add up to thousands of dollars over the lifetime of your IRA. You do not have to leave your IRA with the company used by your former employer. You can easily transfer the IRA to another company. The move is transparent, and you lose nothing in the process. Usually the transfer can be completed by phone in a few minutes.

There are a number of reputable companies to consider for your IRA. Two of the most popular are Vanguard and Fidelity. They have very low administrative fees and buy/sell fees. Most of their funds do not have a front-end load, which is a fee assessed for buying into a specific mutual fund.

If you have dependent children, consider establishing a 529 College Savings Account, a plan that offers many advantages. Your IRA provider will help you either online or by phone to establish the 529.

Moving forward in the second half of your career, I recommend that you assume total control over your IRA rather than permitting your employer to make the decision for you. Evaluate all of your options and select those that best meet your objectives.

MONITORING COSTS OF THE BASICS

This in-between-jobs time is ideal to make an objective review of all your possessions. Begin by making a written inventory of everything you own. Place a value beside each item. Decide whether it is a short-term item that you can modify downward or live without.

AUTOMOBILES

Transportation-related expenses are likely to be included in your list of necessary items. However, it is advisable to examine your current situation to see if changes can be made to cut down the costs. If you live in the middle of the city, for instance in Chicago, New York, Boston, San Francisco, or Washington, DC, maybe a car is unnecessary because you can walk or take public transportation to and from work. If you want to leave town on weekends, you can always rent a car or use Uber. Choosing this option will save thousands of dollars in car cost, insurance, parking, and maintenance.

If you do need a car, evaluate the make and model of car you are driving. Did you ever consider why you need that particular car to get from point A to point B? Downsizing your car or moving to a hybrid model could result in savings totaling thousands of dollars.

FOOD

Like transportation, food is a necessary expense, but you can control its cost. Pay close attention to your food-spending habits. Do you go to the supermarket and just load your basket with things you like regardless of cost? You can save a bundle by evaluating every item you pick up. For example, take the traditional box of corn flakes. Recently, I went to my local supermarket and purchased an eighteen-ounce box of corn flakes. I had two choices: the Kellogg brand at $4.17 or the store brand at $1.99. I selected the store brand and saved $2.18. Multiply savings like this over time, and you save thousands on food purchases. By the way, the store-brand corn flakes looked the same and tasted the same as the Kellogg brand.

Another stealth expense can be food purchased at restaurants. For example, the cost for a burger and fries is approximately $13. Add $3.00 for a beverage, $1.00 for tax, $3.00 for a tip, and you have chalked up $20.00. Do that five times a week and you spend $100; for a month, it's $400, a lot of money for a load of cholesterol. The same applies to eating upscale. Go to a medium-grade restaurant, and the average price for an entrée is $22.00. Add a beverage at $8.00, a dessert at $8.00, tax at $1.80, and a $7.00 tip, and your total bill is $46.80. Do that four times a month, and you spend $187.20. Over six months, the average length of time you could be out of work, your restaurant bill is $1,123.20. When you are out of work, you do not need to eat out every week.

When you do, allot a certain amount of money for your meal before looking at the menu.

SHELTER

Next, consider the item that has become a national obsession—housing. Why is it that we spend so much of our time and money on shelter? Why is it that we are constantly "moving up" the shelter chain to something larger and more luxurious? Do you really need a house or apartment of the size that you live in now?

Rethink your housing needs considering the risk of losing your job. It is possible, in fact probable, that you will face another layoff as the economy changes. I am not implying that you should downsize immediately after being laid off. It is just something to consider when rebuilding your career and lifestyle.

CLOTHING

The cost of clothing is huge. The next time you are dressed in business attire, add up the cost of everything on your person, from underwear to jewelry. For men, the cost will be at least $500. For women, it will be approximately the same if the cost of jewelry is added. If you have children, make a cost inventory for them, as well.

Clothing is a stealth cost because we have gone online to purchase much of it. It is so easy to do. A skirt from Talbots. Shoes from Nordstrom. Nike shoes for the kids from Amazon. We charge these online purchases to credit cards. When you had a paycheck on a regular basis, you thought nothing of paying that bill online. In the entire process, you never touched money, paper or coin. When you spend money in the cloud, you lose track of value. Now, when you receive the bill at the end of the month, you are shocked at the total.

While unemployed, set a strict budget for clothing. Buy only what you need for yourself and family members. Go back to brick-and-mortar stores and pay for clothing using real money, not credit cards. The high cost of this basic necessity will once again become a reality and enable you to control your clothing costs.

EDUCATION

What can you do to cut expenses if you have children moving toward college when you have just been laid off? A year at a middle-ranked private college will cost at least $40,000 per year. An Ivy League university will set you back at least $60,000 per year. Even your state college will cost $20,000 or more per year. Why send your kids off to a high-priced college now when they do not have the slightest clue about what they would like to do with the rest of their lives? While you can't tell your children to stop their education while you are unemployed, you can be creative and consider these short-term alternatives that will work to their benefit and save money for the family:

- Have your child take a year off after high school, a gap year as it is called, and work to learn what this world is all about. After that, send your child genius to a community college for two

years to learn what a college education means short and long term. It may be that your child/student will discover that a hands-on job like carpentry or photography is more in line with their interests and aptitude.

- Another alternative is studying for an online degree while working part-time. We are slowly learning that the traditional four years of bricks-and-mortar college immediately following high school makes little sense for many of our teenagers.

MOVING FORWARD

The most important thing you can do while out of work and out of a paycheck is to protect your finances. But what happens after you cut to the bone and still need money to carry on? How do you replace the income you lost? There are common-sense ways to survive this temporary monetary crisis. I'll tell you what to do and how to do it in the next chapter, "Replacing Income."

CHAPTER TAKEAWAYS

- Always keep six months of expense money in cash reserves.
- Constantly monitor your expenses and financial assets.
- Take total control of your IRA.
- Your possessions are investments. Evaluate their usefulness and cut back if they are expendable.

- Once you have found a new job, prepare for the next crisis, which may be losing your job again.

PRINT AND DIGITAL RESOURCES

Bloomberg Business News TV, 6:00 a.m.–10:00 p.m.

Bureau of Labor Statistics, www.bls.gov.

CNBC Financial News, CNBC TV. 6:00 a.m.–7:00 p.m.

Fox Business News, Fox Business Channel. 6:00 a.m.–8:00 p.m.

Mad Money with Jim Cramer, CNBC TV, 6:00 p.m.

CHAPTER 4
REPLACING INCOME

Replacing the paycheck after losing a job is an immediate and serious challenge for all workers. There are few events more jarring than losing your source of income, which we need not only to supply the basics needed now, but also for future security. Every worker grapples with this issue regardless of income level. When the paycheck stops, the fun ends, as well. Here are some viable options to deal with this mess.

TAPPING INTO FIVE SOURCES OF INCOME WHILE UNEMPLOYED

Usually, employers provide let-go workers with severance packages, which vary in form and content from one company to another. To make sure you are receiving what is owed to you by the company, check the offer letter you received when you joined the company. It is common for companies to award one week of severance pay for each year worked to those in midlevel management positions. Workers at the director level and up will receive greater severance pay.

The severance package is an important benefit. Use it wisely while you continue through the process of rebuilding your career. It is akin to receiving a paid vacation. Use this period of respite to plan your strategies for replacing income while you are unemployed. Here are five ways to ensure that you will have sufficient financial resources during your period of unemployment:

IMMEDIATELY APPLY FOR UNEMPLOYMENT COMPENSATION

Some call it the safety net system. Others call it welfare. Whatever the term, it is the best system we have to help unemployed workers through a difficult time. It is referred to as unemployment compensation, unemployment benefits, or unemployment insurance depending upon the jurisdiction and the type of separation from the employer. The system originated in 1935 when President Franklin Delano Roosevelt signed into law the Social Security Act. It has had many iterations over the years. Always check to see what is owed to you.

Do not confuse workers' compensation with unemployment compensation. They are two different programs. Workers' compensation provides benefits for workers who suffer injuries while on the job. Unemployment compensation provides benefits for workers who are laid off.

Unemployment compensation comes from the joint federal and state operation that was devised to provide substitute income for workers who lost their jobs. It is administered by each individual state. There are well-defined requirements that must be met in order to collect these benefits. The employer who terminated you must disclose your unemployment benefits before you leave the premises. If this did not happen, immediately contact the human resources director of your former employer for an explanation of how the benefits apply in your situation and what the procedures are to apply for benefits. In addition, contact your local unemployment office for advice and guidance. You can do that by phone, but the best way to get immediate results is to make a personal call at the nearest office.

Some workers are hesitant to tap into the system because of embarrassment, arrogance, or fear of hurtful gossip. However, remember that the system was created to help unemployed workers provide for the basics for a limited period of time and is funded in great part by unemployment insurance paid for by the employer and the worker through payroll tax deductions. You have paid for this insurance. Use its benefits whether your income was $5,000 per month or $20,000 per month.

Stereotypes abound depicting the "type" of person collecting unemployment benefits. They are frequently thought of as uneducated and holding low-skill jobs. Think again. I learned firsthand about people collecting unemployment compensation when I was laid off after the company I was working for was sold. I had a mortgage payment, a car payment, insurance payments, and college tuition bills for three of my children. Soon after being laid off in a companywide conference call, I visited my local unemployment insurance office. It was a bare-bones environment crowded with hundreds of unemployed workers applying for benefits. Some were dressed in upscale office attire, some in casual clothing, and others in clothing worn for hands-on jobs. While waiting my turn to meet with a counselor, I spoke with a physician, a sales rep, and a truck driver, all unemployed, like me. All of us were in the same boat—let go and needing a short-term fix to survive. It was a humbling experience, and from it I learned something that you could not find in a textbook or an Internet search. My benefits lasted for three months. I used this time to explore my career path and decided to start my own business, executive recruiting in the for-profit education industry. Without the unemployment benefits to carry me through a very challenging period of my life, my future may have taken an unwanted direction.

SEEK PART-TIME WORK WITH YOUR PREVIOUS EMPLOYER

Occasionally, the employer who let you go will hire you back to undertake a specific task on a contract basis. Why? Because it saves the employer money. This arrangement has benefits for both you and the employer. For you, it keeps the paycheck coming in, and for the employer it eliminates the added cost of benefits, usually about 30 percent of base salary. To make this happen, you must take the initiative and make a proposal to the employer. For example, employers who exhibit at trade shows need company-knowledgeable workers to administer the operation with the convention centers, display companies, and transportation companies such as FedEx, in addition to coordinating schedules of company employees who will staff the exhibit booths. Sometimes the company has one of the marketing staff handle these tasks, but when workers are let go, the job of coordinating trade shows is outsourced to reduce costs. Who better than a laid-off employee who knows the company's products and operations to coordinate trade shows on a part-time basis? To initiate the process, contact your former HR director or marketing director and present them with a proposal to manage trade shows on a per-event basis. An added benefit is that you will meet numerous potential employers at the convention center hosting the event you coordinated.

SEEK PART-TIME WORK WITH A NEW EMPLOYER

While you are looking for new employment opportunities, you have the option of seeking a part-time job with an entirely new employer, maybe in an entirely new business. Job hunting can be a full-time activity, but you can allocate a certain number of hours to working on weekends. Remaining active in the workplace will build your network, enable you to explore alternate job opportunities, and keep you mentally alert.

MAKE REALLOCATIONS TO YOUR PERSONAL INVESTMENT PORTFOLIO

If you need serious extra money and have a personal portfolio of investments in equities, consider selling some or all of them and using the money to purchase income-producing bonds. Use the monthly dividends as income. You can purchase individual bonds or buy into a bond mutual fund, which is my recommendation. Corporate bond funds will have a much greater yield than government bond funds. Caution! Do not tap into your IRA, because you will be charged a hefty penalty for a premature withdrawal. The IRS watches this like a hawk. Once you have secured another job, reevaluate your investment portfolio. You may consider reinvesting your bond dividends instead of moving them to a money market fund, or you may consider exiting the income-producing bond funds and purchasing equities.

SECURE A LOAN FROM FAMILY MEMBERS

If all else fails and you really do need the cash to survive, seek a short-term loan from family members. Use this initiative as your last resort. Parents or grandparents are usually the best sources for personal loans. If you must go this route, prepare a formal written loan agreement stating the amount of the loan and the terms for repayment after you secure another job. Do not assume this is a family jackpot. Repay the loan on time.

MOVING FORWARD

The concern over financial matters after being let go does not stop here. We're talking about reducing risk through the purchase of insurance to protect against mishaps of every kind that cost money, sometimes *serious* money. In the next chapter, I will walk you through the types of insurance that you will need, not only during your period of unemployment, but also when you are employed again. Stick around.

CHAPTER TAKEAWAYS

- Seeking alternate income while unemployed is a common practice.
- Replacing income while unemployed is a short-term strategy, not a permanent solution.
- Frequently, employers will hire back laid-off workers on an hourly or per-job basis.
- Tap into family money as a last resort.
- Do not tap into your IRA, because the penalties are extremely high.

DIGITAL AND PRINT RESOURCES

Social Security Administration, www.ssa.gov. Go to the search box and enter "unemployment benefits" for helpful information.

Unemployment Assist, www.unemploy-ment-assist.com. This site provides assistance for accessing benefits.

CHAPTER 5

INSURANCE MATTERS: MEDICAL AND COBRA, DENTAL, HOMEOWNERS, AUTO, LIFE, DISABILITY

Insurance matters are of great importance, and all let-go workers must address them as soon as it is practicable. Life goes on after you lose your job, and *so do the risks that you face every day*. Untoward events never get laid off or take a vacation. On any given day, you could contract a life-threatening disease like pancreatic cancer, come down with a long-term debilitating and costly illness like Lyme disease, or have a car accident resulting in serious personal injury and substantial property damage. Your house or apartment is at risk, too. A hidden electrical malfunction could burn your dwelling to the ground and destroy all of your personal possessions in the process. Risk is omnipresent, and insurance is the only way to hedge against it. Many workers think insurance matters are boring, but when it comes to reducing risk, boring is good. In today's world, insurance has become a necessity.

Every person, regardless of social status or employment status, needs protection that insurance offers. The most important classes of insurance are medical, dental, homeowners, automobile, life, long-term disability. Having adequate medical insurance is of the utmost importance for every laid-off worker and should be addressed when the termination takes place or shortly thereafter. We'll examine each classification beginning with medical insurance and the insurance option known as COBRA.

COBRA: THE CONSOLIDATED OMNIBUS BUDGET RECONCILIATION ACT

COBRA is a federal government program that enables workers to continue their medical insurance coverage after being let go. However, there are strict rules governing its implementation. For example, workers who are fired for gross misconduct are not eligible. Also, companies that employ fewer than twenty workers cannot participate in the plan.

While COBRA is a helpful risk-lowering federal government medical insurance plan, you must pay the entire cost of the plan plus an administrative fee after you are laid off. If your company group medical insurance premium was $5,000, split equally between you and your employer, now you are responsible for paying the *entire* premium plus a 2 percent administrative fee. Generally, you must apply for COBRA benefits within sixty days after being separated. Benefits will last for eighteen months and will cover you, your spouse, and your children. However, as with all government programs, the rules and regulations are constantly changing, so act immediately if you elect to choose COBRA benefits. For other rules and regulations regarding COBRA, review the Department of Labor website.

Caution! Do not assume that you will find another job with medical insurance benefits and pass up the chance to use COBRA. Your period of unemployment could go on for six months or more, and you cannot be without medical insurance for that long a period.

MEDICAL INSURANCE

Medical insurance is important for all workers, but especially for laid-off or fired workers whose COBRA coverage is coming to an end. You cannot risk being without medical insurance to cover costs for routine or extended care by a physician and costs for hospitalization. Before your COBRA coverage expires, research individual medical insurance plans and be prepared to act. If you have no job prospects and COBRA is coming to an end, by all means purchase medical insurance for you and your dependents regardless of cost. Why? Tomorrow at this time you could be in the hospital with serious personal injury suffered in an accident. The natural tendency is to think, "It will never happen to me." That is nothing short of delusional. If you want verification for the uncertainty of life every day, just visit the emergency room at your local hospital. Sit in the waiting room for an hour or two and observe what happens. It will be a life-changing experience. Guaranteed.

Your options for purchasing medical insurance are limited by both state and federal rules and regulations. To determine what your options are, contact the human resources director at your former employer and the person in your doctor's office who handles insurance matters. Also, go online to research your options.

DENTAL INSURANCE

I speak from personal experience on this matter. One fine day, I was taking an early morning bike ride when I unexpectedly hit a patch of damp road. Down I went, striking my face on the pavement. The result? Two front teeth were cracked beyond repair and had to be replaced with dental implants. The cost? Five thousand dollars. And I had no dental insurance—an expensive mistake.

People often focus on health insurance and forget that it will not cover most dental work. Dental problems can arise without notice on any given day. We are always at risk for infections that require costly root canals, and for teeth damaged by accidents. For a realistic account of what can happen unexpectedly, talk with your dentist.

If you had dental coverage in your last job, by all means try to extend coverage while you are out of work. If you did not have it, go online and look for reasonably priced dental insurance. Most dental plans are limited to group coverage through an employer, but there are a handful of dental insurance companies offering individual plans.

HOMEOWNERS INSURANCE

When out of work, many workers try to minimize expenses by cutting insurance coverage on their homes or apartments. They say, "It will never happen to me. I'll cut my coverage while unemployed and pick it up after I get another job." Don't buy into that narrative. Homeowners carrying a mortgage do not have a choice because the mortgager requires coverage and, in most cases, it is factored into the monthly mortgage payment. However, if you own your property outright or live in an apartment, coverage is optional. Do not eliminate this coverage. On any given day, your residence could burn to the ground and take all of your belongings with it. On another given day, someone could trip over a rug in your apartment, fall, and incur serious personal injury. You will be responsible for payment of all medical expenses and possibly be sued for negligence. Homeowners insurance may seem optional when you are out of work, but it is not. It is a necessity in today's world.

AUTOMOBILE INSURANCE

Automobile insurance is required if your car is financed, and the premium is usually built into your monthly payment. In all states, proof of financial responsibility (i.e., automobile insurance) is required. You must present proof of coverage when you apply for or renew your license plates every year. Do not even think about skirting the rules and discontinuing premium payments believing that you will never get into an accident if you drive extra carefully. Once again, risk is with you 24/7. Automobile insurance is a necessity.

LIFE INSURANCE

"Why life insurance?" you might ask. "I'm in the prime of my life, and I'm not going to die in the foreseeable future." Think again. Your life could end at any time during the day or night, regardless of your age, leaving your dependents or extended family with expenses that could reach beyond their means. Burial expenses come to mind. Today, the average cost of a funeral, including the cemetery grave plot and headstone, is $13,000, sometimes more. Add some upgrades like a fancy coffin and elaborate headstone, and the cost of your good-bye will run closer to $15,000.

The following true story illustrates the fact that life is risky and that death takes no holidays. It does not care if you are in midcareer and have children and a spouse, or that your income is an integral part of the family budget.

LINDA'S STORY

I recruited Linda for a job as a reading consultant with an educational publisher where I was the regional sales manager for the Northeastern United States. Linda excelled in her job and was sought after by school districts implementing their new reading programs.

Linda belonged to a number of fine and performing arts organizations in Boston. She was an officer in the Junior League and performed volunteer work for the Museum of Fine Arts. Her teenage daughter was the pride and joy of her life and attended only the best schools.

As Linda entered midcareer, she and her husband frequently took skiing trips to Aspen and Vail in addition to vacations in Europe and the Caribbean. Life was good for Linda. In February 2008, they went on a five-day ski trip to Vail and returned home tired and happy. However, Linda seemed more tired than usual after five days on the slopes and scheduled an appointment with her doctor to see if she needed a dose of vitamins to keep up her energy level. As a precaution, Linda's doctor ordered lab tests and an abdominal CT scan. He called these tests "routine." However, the "routine" tests indicated that Linda had pancreatic cancer. Surgery followed and so did death, seven weeks after diagnosis. Linda possessed intelligence, energy, and passion beyond the ordinary, but death does not play favorites. To this day, Linda is missed by her husband, daughter, friends, and coworkers. They still ask, "How could she have died in the prime of her life without forewarning?" Rest in peace, Linda.

There are several forms of life insurance. The most common, and the lowest in price, is called "term life insurance," which is what most employers provide for their employees. It terminates as soon as you are fired or laid off. When you walk out the door after being let go, you are no longer insured. Purchasing term life insurance should be a priority for all let-go workers. It is readily available from any number of life insurance companies at reasonable cost for midcareer workers. Conduct an online search for low-cost term life insurance and purchase it immediately.

LONG-TERM DISABILITY INSURANCE (LTD)

The story goes something like this. "I don't need LTD insurance because 'it' will never happen to me." Most of us delude ourselves into thinking that accidents resulting in long-term or permanent disability always happen to the other guy. I fell into this trap in midcareer, too, and but for the guidance of an extraordinary insurance saleswoman, I would not have survived financially.

CHICKEN MAN

I was riding my bike past a farm in a rural section of Bucks County, Pennsylvania. Suddenly, a bantam chicken darted from weeds growing along the side of the road into the front wheel of my bike, and down I went. I suffered a concussion, a torn rotator cuff, and a fractured hip and was disabled for eight months following surgery and a two-week stay in the hospital. During this time, I had no income, but the bills kept rolling in: mortgage payments, car payments, property taxes, and college tuition bills for the children. I survived only because my insurance agent, Joanne, had badgered me into purchasing LTD insurance. The policy became effective just a week before the accident and provided income to survive this ordeal. Thank you, Joanne, for educating me about risks we face each day when we get out of bed.

Many insurers provide LTD coverage, but most are group plans for employers. Two companies that provide individual LTD insurance are Northwestern Mutual and Unum. Go online and check out their LTD options and prices.

MOVING FORWARD

Most people consider insurance a boring topic, one to be avoided at all costs. The unexpected illness or accident always happens to someone else. Don't fool yourself. Consider the insurances detailed above as much a necessity as food, shelter, and clothing. In today's world, you cannot live without it. Insurance is a family matter, too, as it protects those dear to you not only from temporary financial challenges, but also from catastrophic loss.

There is something else you must do concurrently to ensure your future employability. It is something that most laid-off workers bypass entirely because there is so much going on. I'm talking about your reputation, which will be the subject of the next chapter, "Safeguarding Your Reputation."

CHAPTER TAKEAWAYS

- Apply for COBRA medical insurance immediately after being separated from your company.
- Consider purchasing a private medical insurance policy as an alternative to COBRA, which is available to you for only eighteen months after termination.
- Death and accidents take no holidays.
- According to the National Highway Traffic Administration, an automobile accident occurs every sixty seconds.
- LTD and life insurance are equally important for midcareer workers.

PRINT AND DIGITAL RESOURCES

For detailed information on COBRA, see www.COBRAinsurance.com.

For current information about disability insurance policies, see www.insure.com /disability-insurance.

CHAPTER 6
SAFEGUARDING YOUR REPUTATION

Reputation is one of your most valuable possessions, and it is in your best interest to safeguard it after being let go. Word travels fast through social media, e-mail, and phone messages. Even before you are officially notified that you are being laid off, your boss and the human resources manager know what is happening. And so does everyone in their respective networks, like the company president and CEO.

The reason for your layoff usually involves company finances. When a company needs to show better bottom line, frequently workers are eliminated. It has nothing to do with your work ethic or personal behavior, but when colleagues see you walk out the door escorted by a guard, they might assume the worst.

RUMORS SPREAD QUICKLY

With so many people knowing that you have been let go, rumors can spread fast about the reason for your departure. Speculation abounds. Human nature being what it is, some of that speculation could reflect negatively on your reputation. Idle chatter could go something like this:

- "Wonder why Mary got axed. Bet it was because she was late for work so many times."
- "Seems that Bob's home remodeling business always left something to be desired. Remember when his workers left the house in a mess after installing the kitchen cabinets?"
- "Her interpersonal skills were not so great. She always seemed to say something that ticked off the boss. I guess they did not feel she was trustworthy."

Before long, idle talk could tarnish your personal and professional reputation and impede your chances of finding another job. To head off any assaults on your reputation, time is of the essence.

STRATEGIES FOR PROTECTING YOUR REPUTATION

Preemptive strikes are the best way to quash rumors that could begin inadvertently or by design from detractors. Here are some strategies to begin the process of protecting what you have worked so hard to achieve:

TERMINATION LETTERS

The dismissal event usually catches workers off guard. They gather their personal possessions and walk out the door, never even thinking about having the boss and the human resources director state the reason for dismissal in a written termination letter. If you did not receive a termination letter, contact your former human resources director and request a signed termination letter that includes the following items:

- Your name
- The beginning date of your employment and the date of termination
- Specific reasons for termination, like a major company reorganization, reduction in force because of economic conditions, sale of the company, or any other reason that caused your position to be eliminated
- Signature of the human resources director

The termination letter is an important document to keep in your personal files as verification for the reasons why your job was eliminated. When applying for a new job, you may want to present the termination letter along with your résumé.

LETTERS OF RECOMMENDATION

When requesting your termination letter, always ask for a letter of recommendation signed by your former boss and/or the human resources director. Usually they will be more than obliging if the request is made in conjunction with your being let go or shortly thereafter while your good work is still fresh in their minds. There is a certain amount of sympathy for a terminated worker, and on most occasions the former boss will honor your request. However, your request may be denied or forgotten if you wait months to act, so do it now.

Frequently, letters of recommendation, or letters of reference as they are sometimes called, are nothing more than happy talk. They say nothing meaningful about who you are and what you can do professionally. The letter should address two traits: your public image (your *persona*) and your personal traits (your *character*). When you request someone to write a letter of recommendation, suggest that the letter address the following points about your character and persona:

- Trustworthiness
- Your industry and company reputation
- That you abided by the rules established by your employer
- Punctuality
- Physical and mental energy level
- Passion for completing any task on time

- Ability to get along with subordinates and superiors
- Leadership skills

These are the personality and character points that every prospective employer examines when evaluating you for a job.

We suggest that you acquire additional letters of recommendation or reference from company coworkers and customers you have worked with. Timeliness is of the essence, as memories fade quickly. Strike while the iron is hot and request these letters as soon as possible after being terminated.

PROTECTING YOUR ONLINE REPUTATION

When prospective employers see your name in a list of candidates for a specific job, the first thing they do is Google your name to learn more about you personally and professionally. Usually the first stop is LinkedIn, to compare what they see on your résumé with your online profile. Start the process by asking workers in your network to provide a LinkedIn recommendation attesting to your character traits and work expertise. Don't hesitate to ask your contacts to address specific traits that you want potential employers to notice.

If you have not yet done so, update your LinkedIn profile. Provide the dates you were employed with your last employer and add the heading "Accomplishments at Saturn Software, Inc.," followed by three or four key items. For example, a regional sales manager wants everyone to know that she attained or surpassed her sales goals. State that accomplishment like this: "Exceeded multimillion-dollar revenue goals for the past five years in my twelve-state region while managing a staff of fifteen outbound, full-time sales representatives."

MAKING A GRACEFUL EXIT

While the layoff is hurtful in the extreme, being let go provides an opportunity to enhance your character and reputation. Soon after leaving the company, send a thank-you letter or e-mail to your boss, the human resources director, and the president. It could go something like this: "Leaving was very difficult, but I enjoyed my stay with the company, and thank you for giving me the opportunity to learn and grow in my career. When you have another opportunity, I would appreciate your keeping me in mind. I wish your company the best going forward."

You want your former employer to think and speak well of you personally and professionally. It does you no good whatsoever to maintain a negative attitude toward your former employer. Your former boss or president could move on to another company and be the hiring manager when you apply for work with that employer. Never burn bridges.

MOVING FORWARD

In addition to protecting finances and reputation, the midcareer worker faces additional challenges related to family issues that could prove distracting and add an additional burden to the budget. We'll identify family challenges and offer solutions in the next chapter.

CHAPTER TAKEAWAYS

- Do not trash your former employer.
- Have your former boss or human resources director write a termination letter specifying the reason for your departure.
- Ask colleagues to post positive reviews about your work on LinkedIn.
- Solicit letters of recommendation from your previous employer and from colleagues as soon as possible after being let go.

PRINT AND DIGITAL RESOURCES

"How To Manage (and Protect) Your Online Reputation." *Forbes*. www.forbes.com. Go to the website and enter the title of this article in the search box.

CHAPTER 7
FAMILY CHALLENGES AND SOLUTIONS

Our workforce is almost evenly divided between men and women. Both face the same workplace challenges, and both are subject to losing their jobs periodically throughout their careers. Approximately 55,000 workers lose their jobs every day, and, contrary to popular opinion, women and men lose their jobs at the same rate. When employers need to shed personnel, gender is not an issue.

Women and men face similar challenges after being let go. The issues frequently center on childcare, aging-parent care, separation or divorce, and education. Let's examine each challenge and explore solutions.

THE CHILDCARE CHALLENGE

When a parent is laid off, family lifestyle is altered because of childcare responsibilities. Even though there might be a continuing income stream coming from a spouse's job, something has to give. Expenses across the board must be adjusted. Usually, the person at home, the husband or wife, picks up the slack. Caring for kids is a time-consuming process that begins when they wake up and get ready for school and continues until they finish homework and go to bed. Adding these responsibilities to the process of finding another job is frustrating because there are only so many hours in a day. The parent looking for another job has résumés and cover letters to write, personal interviews away from home that might require an overnight stay, phone interviews, networking calls, attendance at trade shows or job fairs, and the list goes on. Looking for a job is a full-time job in itself, but when added to caring for the children, the challenge to make it work can be overwhelming.

Specific challenges include transporting children to and from school, making sure they complete homework assignments, meeting with teachers to discuss the children's progress or problems, and driving them to and from recreational events. All of these responsibilities are in addition to caring for their day-to-day physical and emotional needs. So how does the laid-off parent handle childcare responsibilities and look for employment concurrently?

THE CHILDCARE SOLUTION

Nothing happens without a plan. Your first initiative in solving this problem should be to sit down at your computer or notepad and make an hourly written plan that you can refer to every day. Block out those hours you will spend seeking new employment, even if it means letting household chores take a backseat. If your spouse has questions about how you can care for the kids while job hunting, construct a plan for him or her to pick up the slack. The employed spouse might not like doing routine childcare chores like driving the kids to school, and that is understandable. But you are in this together. Construct a plan that is equitable for both.

During this unemployment hiatus, you can't possibly do it all yourself. What happens when you are going to a trade show or meeting with a network contact, or when you go to an interview? Again, we get back to the plan. When it is necessary to leave the house, you will need a backup to handle the childcare responsibilities. The key is to plan for these outside-the-home events at least a week in advance. Seek help from your spouse, neighbors, friends, parents, or grandparents. Most people, including your spouse, are willing to lend a hand to someone in need as long as the request for help is on a timely basis. When you need help, say so.

If you can't resolve the childcare issues with "free" help, sit down with your spouse and make a financial plan that includes paying for outside help with the children. This could mean a reallocation of discretionary dollars to childcare dollars, which may be uncomfortable, but remember that this is temporary. When you find another job, you can reconstruct your budget to include formal childcare payments.

Some laid-off workers with considerable childcare responsibilities elect to seek employment that can be done *at home*, a very attractive alternative to full-time work away from home. In fact, a report by the National Bureau of Economic Research revealed that the average worker values working from home and is willing to give up about 10 percent of their wages to exercise this option.

THE AGING PARENT CHALLENGE

All of us can cite examples where a midcareer worker is faced with caring for an aging parent or a parent who has developed a debilitating illness such as Alzheimer's. Unfortunately, illness has no respect for your time or the fact that you are temporarily unemployed.

THE AGING PARENT SOLUTION

When the unemployed spouse has this responsibility in addition to shouldering some of the childcare responsibilities and is looking for a new job, there are not enough hours in the day to get it all done. Something has to give. Other family members must help the unemployed person make all of the moving parts come together.

If the parent in need is at home and requires transportation to and from the doctor or hospital, build that into your plan. If this is in conflict with your eighth-grade son's basketball schedule, he may need to cut some practice sessions or competitive games. It's a good opportunity to counsel your son that taking care of family members is everyone's responsibility. Bring him into the picture by prioritizing events in order of importance. Counsel him that caring for a family member comes before basketball, no exceptions.

If the aging-parent situation becomes too time-consuming while you are unemployed and looking for new full-time opportunities, a viable solution is to seek only part-time employment. (According to research conducted by the Pew Research Center, 27 percent of the respondents surveyed said they left their full-time jobs permanently to care for an ill parent or child.) Implementing this alternative could make all the moving parts—parent care, childcare, income stream, work-life balance—work together.

THE DIVORCE OR SEPARATION CHALLENGE

While exiting an unhappy marriage is a liberating experience, it can pose a challenge for a midcareer worker who has been fired or laid off. When this event occurs, two factors come into play: dealing with the trauma accompanying divorce and dealing with the trauma of losing a job. It's a double challenge, but there are solutions.

THE DIVORCE/SEPARATION SOLUTION

A top priority for divorced or separated laid-off workers is to maintain self-confidence.

Such workers need to reaffirm their ability to move forward and rebuild their career into something that will provide income, job satisfaction, and work-life balance, all while trying to sort out the divorce or separation.

The best way to find a job while divorced or separated, and avoid depression, is to leave the house and attend trade shows at nearby convention centers. There you will find hundreds of potential employers under one roof and opportunities to make new friends, build your professional network, and expand your work horizons. Even if the trade show is not focusing on your area of expertise or interest, attend just the same. A new environment frequently reveals interests and abilities never before imagined.

But what about the divorce itself? Dealing with a double whammy, divorce and job loss, is a real bummer because both are calling for your attention. We suggest focusing on the job first because in our culture, a job confers self-esteem and a sense of identity, both of which are necessary to resolve uncomfortable issues. When you have a job, even a job that is not exactly what you would like, you will be better able to work through the divorce or separation with confidence and resolve. When you are out of work, you are just plain vanilla James Jones. When you have a job, you are James Jones, Director of Marketing for Ajax Software. There is a world of difference. A job with a title and a paycheck confers self-esteem, respect, dignity, and financial independence.

MOVING FORWARD

Even though various family responsibilities and job-hunting activities are time-consuming, use this period of unemployment to begin improving your character and redefining your persona. Allot a certain amount of time each day for this project. This is an interesting task in the rebuilding process, and we'll help you with it in the next chapter. Keep reading.

CHAPTER TAKEAWAYS

- Family responsibilities continue after being laid off. Plan accordingly.
- Childcare, aging parents, and divorce/separation present challenges, but by using your intelligence, energy, and creativity, you can find solutions.

- Part-time jobs frequently offer a viable temporary solution when a laid-off worker is overwhelmed with family-care responsibilities.
- Sales jobs frequently offer flexible hours and work schedules.
- After losing your job, create a daily agenda to meet your responsibilities.
- Plan your work. Work your plan.

PRINT AND DIGITAL RESOURCES

Best Companies for Working Mothers. www .workingmother.com/best-companies.

Morris, Virginia, and Jennie Hansen. *How to Care for Aging Parents: A One-Stop Resource for All of Your Medical, Financial, Housing, and Emotional Needs.* 3rd edition. Workman Publishing Co., 2014.

PART II

The Process of Moving Forward in Your Career

Believe in yourself! Have faith in your abilities! Without a humble but reasonable confidence in your own powers you cannot be successful or happy.

—Norman Vincent Peale

CHAPTER 8

RESHAPING YOUR PERSONA AND IMPROVING YOUR CHARACTER

We develop our character and persona over time without thinking about who we are becoming. Character traits are something learned from first influencers, parents, and teachers. We develop our persona as we grow and present ourselves to the public. We seldom realize that these traits are what lead us to do what we do and how we do it. Often we settle into patterns and do not reflect on them. For example, you may have been at your last job for a number of years, and after two promotions, your interest waned and going to work each day became a chore. It seemed that your head was somewhere else, but you could not determine why. Then one day you were laid off in a massive company reorg, and you asked, "What am I going to do now? My last job put bread on the table and gave me status and respectability, but I did not like it, and it never felt like the right fit. There has to be a better way."

Being fired or laid off is traumatic, but it does have benefits, two of which are:

1. It opens the door to reviewing and possibly reshaping your persona.
2. It provides an opportunity to learn who you really are by examining your character.

RESHAPING YOUR PERSONA

The word *persona* derives from the Latin, where it originally referred to a theatrical mask. In theatrical terms, it is an assumed personality. In today's world, it refers to that part of your personality exposed to the public. It is the *apparent* you that people see, and it may be different from your character, the *real* you. It is you who created your persona, either consciously or subconsciously, and it may have resulted in your being a dynamic leader or a loyal follower.

People in the public eye such as company presidents or CEOs, TV personalities, actors, and politicians frequently assume a certain persona that appeals to their target audience. Take politicians, for example. They want to be viewed by constituents as caring for their welfare and the needs of the country as a whole, but sometimes their character flaws are revealed and they fall from grace. The disconnect between the two, once it has emerged into the public view, can lead to the politician's being perceived as unreliable and dishonest.

Persona is equally important in the private sector. Let's review the persona of a well-known deceased CEO, Steve Jobs, cofounder and CEO of Apple Computer. When I worked with Apple in its early days, Steve's persona was that of the good, kind, caring, and generous boss. However, behind his mask, Steve could be a ruthless guy, one who might greet you in the morning and say a polite "Good Morning" or look at you with fury in his eyes and say, "You're fired!" for no apparent reason. Nobody quite knew who Steve really was, and for that reason many workers left Apple or declined offers to work there.

Bring this to a more personal level and look at your persona in the workplace. Focus on the role you played in your last job, the one that disappeared one day when you were least expecting it. If you were in a leadership position (i.e., the boss), what was your persona? Was it in conflict with the real you? Did you think of yourself as the good, compassionate, helpful, caring boss dedicated to making the company great? Did you assume this persona, this mask, to hide your real motivation: to oust your boss and move up in rank and compensation? Could it have been the reason why you were let go from your job as regional sales manager in a staged "reorganization" while your friend Mary, another regional sales manager, was kept on the payroll? Only you can answer that after a private, honest meeting with yourself.

Before making the big move toward serious job hunting, discover who you really are. Were you the one who used every chance to derail your boss while playing Mister Good Guy? If your introspection reveals a difference between your persona and the real you, take measures to make these two competing entities one and the same. How do you begin? With honesty. If you have any doubts about how you are seen, ask your former boss and coworkers what they thought of you, no holds barred.

IMPROVING YOUR CHARACTER

Character can be defined as the aggregate of traits and features that form and identify the real you. Your character is the set of values and sense of ethics that you hold dear. They determine not only what you might say, but also how you act.

This period of downtime affords an opportunity not only to see where you've been and where you want to go, but also to learn who you really are now that you can't hide behind a corporate title or affiliation. Looking back, you might find that the real you became lost in the corporate culture or was disguised by a preoccupation with political correctness. In the course of your previous job, you may have forgotten what you truly think or how you feel. It's time for a homecoming with yourself to find out who you really are.

To begin the process of rebuilding character, you need a foundation upon which everything else rests. I like best the foundation stones posited by Character Counts!, a nonprofit organization dedicated to character education. One of their constructs is the Six Pillars of Character, which act as the foundation for exploring character education and character building. These pillars are trustworthiness, fairness, respect, caring, citizenship, and responsibility. Review this material at www.charactercounts.org.

The next step is to determine who you truly want to be and how you can build character traits to fulfill your mission. For example, assume that your goal is to secure a leadership position in a management job where you can help your staff grow professionally by acquiring new skills and by working as a team. This mission requires you to develop character traits that include teaching and mentoring skills, learning how to assess an individual's strengths and weaknesses, accepting total responsibility for your role in the company, and becoming a sympathetic listener.

The rebuilding process is not for the timid. The easiest path is to do nothing and just hope that *something* will happen in the future. Chose this path, and you will stay where you are now, the same old you who lost a job quite possibly because you did not have those character traits to be an effective leader or a loyal and productive follower.

MOVING FORWARD

Redefining your persona and improving your character will prepare you to move forward with confidence to the next phase of the rebuilding process, establishing objectives for the remainder of your career. It's just ahead in the next chapter.

CHAPTER TAKEAWAYS

- Persona is the face you present to the public at large.
- Character is who you really are.
- Persona and character must work in harmony for growth in your new career.

PRINT AND DIGITAL RESOURCES

Brooks, David. *The Road to Character*. Random House, 2016.

Character Counts! www.charactercounts.org.

CHAPTER 9

DEFINING OBJECTIVES FOR THE REMAINDER OF YOUR CAREER

Recently I reviewed the résumé of an interesting midcareer worker. Under "Professional Employment," which covered the past five years, I saw "US Peace Corps, English Teacher." Following that was a string of twelve jobs in different industries spanning twenty years. It was one year here, six months there, two years at a different company, and so on. When I interviewed this candidate, he told me he had been fired from the last corporate job he held as associate marketing manager for a publishing company. This was the catalyst that prompted him to embark on an extended period of reflection to find his real self. As a result, he learned that he was driven not by status, power, and money, as so many workers are in the for-profit corporate world. His new objective was to be instrumental in the lives of people studying to reach their full potential. After a period of introspection, he decided that the ideal job to accomplish that objective was teaching. He took online courses that awarded teaching certification and subsequently found work with the Peace Corps. The job provided enough money for him to be self-sufficient and gave him the sense of mission he had been

seeking. Making the transition from the Peace Corps to the "civilian" world was easy for this candidate. He found a job teaching at a local high school. The objective he established after his last corporate job provided direction for the remainder of his career.

Many midcareer workers who have been let go worked in one industry in similar departments, like sales or marketing, for the first half of their careers. For example, take Claudia, a midcareer woman who came to me seeking help finding new employment after losing her job. She was working in the pharmaceutical industry since attaining her BS in biology. All of her jobs were in sales or marketing. The money was good, but the job satisfaction was zero. When she was let go in a reorganization, Claudia thought about her work history and realized that she did not like working in sales and marketing, so she asked, "What's next? More of the same? How can I get out of this sales and marketing game and still make enough money to survive?" During her period of introspection, she learned that she really did not care for the business world. Going after the sale was not in line with her character. She was caring and compassionate and had the ability to impart information objectively. She remembered that her first love was teaching others about the world of living things, biology. She went back to school, online and at a bricks-and-mortar college, and earned a minor in education, which qualified her for a public school teaching position. After teaching biology at a local high school, Claudia found a job as an editor with an educational publishing company where she works now editing high school science texts and digital materials. She is not making as much money as she did on the corporate side, but she earns enough to live a comfortable life, and she has something that money cannot buy—job satisfaction. For workers like Claudia, being fired or laid off is often a blessing in disguise because it gives one time to pause, reflect, and reset before moving forward to another career.

SEARCHING FOR CAREER OBJECTIVES

Redefining your career goals is a process that you can accomplish in the classroom of your own mind. You do not need multiple sessions with a shrink, nor do you need to attend every conference advertised by motivational speakers trumpeting, "Find Yourself in Three Easy Steps." You have the intelligence and energy to accomplish this mission yourself. Here are strategies to begin the self-defining process:

FOUR STEPS IN THE REDEFINING PROCESS

1. Write your career vision statement, one that defines what you believe will fulfill career expectations. It might read like this:

    Moving forward in the second half of my working years, I wish to find a career that combines my interests with my aptitudes and abilities, and that will provide income to sustain a middle-class style of living.

2. On a sheet of physical or digital paper, draw two lines down the middle of the page to create three columns. Title the left-hand column "My Interests" and make a list of five things that interest you most. One word or a phrase is sufficient. For example, your first five written entries may be:

    Music, primarily show tunes;
    Sports, especially baseball;
    Finance, especially insurance;
    Laws/rules/regulations that make for a safe and secure America;
    Environmental conservation to create a clean and healthful climate.

3. Title the middle column on your page "My Aptitudes/Expertise." Beside each of your five interests, write your aptitude and experience corresponding to each of your five interests.

4. Title the right-hand column, the third column, "Jobs." Record a job corresponding to your interests and abilities in the first and second columns.

My Interests	My Aptitudes/Experience	Jobs
Environmental	Audubon Society	Ecologist
Conservation	Volunteer Work	Teacher

Assume that your primary interest is in the broadly defined field of environmental conservation, but you don't know what jobs are available in this field. You can go to the Internet to conduct a search, or you can consult the online or print version of one of the best sources available for career information. It was developed by the United States Department of Labor, and job seekers have purchased millions of copies. It is revised every year and is available from booksellers like Amazon and Barnes & Noble. It is the *Occupational Outlook Handbook*, which is cited below under "Print and Digital Resources." Look for jobs in your area of interest, environmental conservation. You will find them in the sections titled "Green Occupations," "Education," and "Life/Physical/Social Science." Each section lists related occupations, the forecast for such jobs, education and skill requirements, advancement opportunities, work environment, and average earnings. The thousand-page *OOH* is a valuable resource for workers redefining their career goals. Have a copy near at hand while exploring new career paths. After consulting the *OHH*, your record sheet might look something like this:

SEARCHING FOR EMPLOYERS WHO MEET YOUR OBJECTIVES

Following this exercise, search for employers who offer jobs in environmental conservation. The most expeditious way to find a plethora of such companies is to conduct a Google search. Enter "companies with jobs in environmental conservation." When I did that, I found numerous employers active in such pursuits. Some of those were CWM Environmental, Watts Architecture and Engineering, North Cascades Institute, Packaging Corporation of America, and State of North Carolina.

For additional prompts on opportunities in the field of environmental conservation—or whichever field you might be interested in—consider federal government jobs, which are often overlooked by workers seeking new career goals. To begin the process, we recommend consulting what is considered the bible of government jobs, *The Book of U.S. Government Jobs: Where They Are, What's Available, and How to Complete a Federal Résumé*. Expand the process by reviewing the corresponding website: www.federaljobs.net. When I reviewed the book, I found an interesting reference to the "Environmental and Natural Resources Division" of the US Department of Justice. This Division develops and enforces civil environmental laws that protect US natural resources.

When you have found posted job opportunities with an employer who meets your objectives, continue the process by establishing a relationship with the hiring manager for the position that interests you or with the human resources director. Present your candidacy for the position of interest using the rubrics in this book for résumé writing, interviewing, and negotiating a job offer.

CONTINUING IN YOUR PRESENT CAREER PATH

Not every laid-off worker seeks a new career path. Many wish to continue working in their present careers, but with an employer who provides opportunities for work-life balance, community outreach initiatives, and job satisfaction. Such workers can move directly to seeking potential job opportunities in their chosen industry. For example, a worker in the food industry who had been working in managerial positions with fast-food providers may now look for more health-conscious companies in the food industry like Whole Foods or Wegmans.

Workers in the technology industry frequently reach a point where they need more than a big paycheck and less than a sixty-hour work week. Take one of my family members, Andrew, for example. He was riffed from his tech company where he had nine direct reports and worked long hours. He wanted to remain in technology and used his downtime to find employers engaged in a socially conscious business. After almost a year of searching, he hit pay dirt with a national pharmacy company. In his new job, Andrew supervises a department using robotic technology to fill prescriptions for people needing continuous refills of life-sustaining medications. He manages the entire process using his many technology skills and takes home not only a paycheck, but also job satisfaction resulting from his work in a life-sustaining business.

WHERE AM I GOING?

Now that you are ready to activate your search for another job, what can you expect? Based on my experience working with let-go workers and anecdotal reports, I predict that three to six months from now you will be gainfully employed in one of four ways.

FOUR OPTIONS FOR FUTURE EMPLOYMENT

1. Employment with a company in an industry you like and that pays more than your previous position.
2. Employment in a *meaningful* job that brings you personal satisfaction in addition to an income that provides for your needs.
3. Employment as an entrepreneur by starting your own business.
4. Employment as a worker in an entirely different industry pursuing what you

always wanted to do but could never before find the courage to try.

MOVING FORWARD

Now that you have diligently used your intelligence and skills to define your objectives, you are ready for the next step in the process, crafting a résumé that reflects the *new you*. The following chapter will guide you through the résumé-writing process.

CHAPTER TAKEAWAYS

- Redefine career objectives on your own or with the help of resources like the *Occupational Outlook Handbook*.

- A meaningful career provides job satisfaction in addition to power, status, and money.
- Workers can transfer work skills from one industry to another.

PRINT AND DIGITAL RESOURCES

Damp, Dennis. *The Book of U.S. Government Jobs*. Bookhaven Press, 2011.

Federal Government Jobs. www.federal-jobs.net.

The US Department of Labor. *Occupational Outlook Handbook*. JIST Publishing, 2016–2017.

CHAPTER 10

CRAFTING A RÉSUMÉ AND DIGITAL PROFILE TO REFLECT THE NEW YOU

Crafting a new résumé is not everyone's idea of a good time. In fact, I have witnessed many midcareer workers struggle with this task because they have not updated their résumés for five years. The résumé created five or more years ago does not include your recent accomplishments. Adding these accomplishments and additional information, like professional development, education, and community outreach activities, gives you an entirely new look. It is really a new you in writing. In addition, crafting a new digital profile for LinkedIn should be a concurrent effort. The digital profile and the résumé must be in sync because potential employers and executive recruiters review both items.

THE PURPOSE OF A RÉSUMÉ

You craft a résumé in order to interest a potential employer in your candidacy and to motivate the hiring manager to schedule a personal interview. However, no matter how great your résumé, if it does not get to the right person, your candidacy will go nowhere. Many job candidates sit at home and send résumés by the hundreds to job boards and company career pages. The result? Nothing.

Companies do not hire résumés. They hire living, breathing, walking, talking, thinking candidates who have the smarts to leave the house and meet hiring managers and human resources directors, in the flesh, to begin building a relationship.

GENERAL GUIDELINES FOR WRITING YOUR RÉSUMÉ

Job candidates frequently spend hundreds of hours writing the *perfect* résumé based upon advice from peers, spouses, college professors, and a variety of online resources. When you say "résumé," everyone provides suggestions and advice believing their way is the best way. While some of this input could have value, most of it is redundant or based on personal experience, which may be outdated. Even college professors get into the act and give advice that has no relevance in the business world. For example, they call the résumé *curriculum vitae*, a term used only by the academic establishment. Do not refer to your résumé as a CV. In the business world, it is a *résumé*.

Résumé guidelines vary with the times. Today's résumé has certain major components and a certain style. Gone are the days of block paragraphs to describe previous jobs and their responsibilities.

My experiences as an executive recruiter working in the staffing industry every day is the basis for the direction I offer. If you follow my instructions, you will design a first-class résumé that reflects what is current and acceptable in today's business world. However, if you want general résumé-writing advice, review websites like Career Confidential, www.careerconfidential.com. The CEO, Peggy McKee, is one of the best in the business, and I suggest that you attend one of her many webinars, the cost of which is very attractive—*free*.

What about those professional résumé-writing services that charge $50 to $300 for designing your résumé? If these résumé-writing gurus sell their services, they must be good. Right? Save your money. Spend that money to attend a trade show or conference where you will find hundreds of hiring managers in person. This would be money well spent because landing a job is a matter of building a personal relationship with hiring managers and other influential company workers like the director of human resources.

Still, there are some rules and guidelines that are important to keep in mind. I have reviewed thousands of résumés in my recruiting business. Few are outstanding; many are just okay; and some are too cute. Cute résumés contain too many unnecessary stylistic features like a nonstandard typeface, multiple colors, clip art, photos, borders, and other design features. The basic rule is this: *Keep it simple. Keep it clean.* Remember this is business communication, not a promotion piece for the Super Bowl and certainly not a menu for a French restaurant.

Recruiters working in the staffing business know how a résumé should look, and they can tell you what mistakes to avoid. Executive recruiters say these are the five most common mistakes candidates make on résumés:

FIVE COMMON RÉSUMÉ MISTAKES

1. *Typos.* Correct spelling is your responsibility, not the spell-checker's. Nothing will send your résumé to the trash heap faster than a misspelled word.
2. *Grammar mistakes.* Hiring managers expect grammatically correct résumés from everyone. Make a mistake, and you are finished. There is no second chance.

3. *Inconsistent formatting and style.* Use only one typeface and type size. The current preferred typeface is 12 pt. Times New Roman.

4. *Missing metrics.* Quantify as much as possible. Generalities say nothing about your expertise or accomplishments.

5. *Gaps in employment history.* You do have a work history, which consists of full-time professional experience and possibly significant part-time work in college or even high school. Make sure your work history is in chronological order beginning with your last job and going back to your first job.

RÉSUMÉ FEATURES YOU MUST GET RIGHT

One could write pages listing the most important rubrics for résumé writing. Do this. Don't do that. Do it this way. No, do it my way. It's not that complicated. Here are the items you must get right to produce a credible résumé:

- *Résumé File Name.* This is one of the most important parts of your résumé, and you must get it right. The file name must be brief and to the point so the reader will understand without hesitation who you are and what the file is about. State the file name like this:

"Jerome Michael's Résumé. Marketing Associate Candidate for General Electric."

- *Résumé Length.* The résumé for an entry-level candidate and a résumé for a midcareer candidate will differ in length. Appearance, style, and format, however, are the same for all candidates. Length of résumé for all entry-level candidates should be no more than two pages. However, the résumés for midcareer workers with ten to twenty years of experience that includes executive-level positions and possibly publications could be three or four pages, or even more.

- *Résumé Appearance.* Your résumé is your personal appearance in written form. Think of it as the way you would dress for a live interview: uncluttered and neat. Hiring managers are not interested in your picture, graphs, boxed items, borders, charts, shading, or clip art. If they want to see how you look, they can always go to LinkedIn, Facebook, Twitter, or other social media.

- *Résumé Formatting.* Consistency is key from beginning to end. Use bullet points consisting of only one line instead of paragraphs in the body of the résumé. Use only one typeface and size. Use uppercase bold for major headings and lowercase regular type for text. Do not use a script typeface, like Segoe Script, under any circumstances. The typeface is not the tool to differentiate your candidacy from the rest of the pack.

- **Résumé Style.** Résumé styles change over time. Today's readers view content in small bits and pieces. They lose interest when confronted with long paragraphs. Save that for your first novel. The way we convey information is by using bullet points instead of paragraphs, with one exception. The first major heading of your résumé, "Objective" or "Summary," should be in paragraph form but not to exceed about ten lines. List every other item in bullet points. Use "Objective" when you are applying for a specific job. Use "Summary" if you are submitting your résumé to a human resources director to make this key person aware of your search for an unspecified position in the company.
- **Résumé Metrics.** One of the most common mistakes candidates make is listing their achievements using broad generalities like "Treated a large number of patients at the emergency room at Chicago Hospital." The statement means much more to the hiring manager if it reads, "Treated an average of thirty patients per day over a three-year period at Chicago Hospital."

MAJOR HEADINGS OF YOUR RÉSUMÉ

Here are the major parts of your résumé. Include all of them on your résumé in this order:

1. Personal Identification
2. Objective or Summary
3. Military Work Experience (if applicable)
4. Work Experience
5. Awards, Recognition, Community Service
6. Technology Skills
7. Education

Do not include "References on Request" or "Hobbies and Special Interests." Here is a review of each major heading with an explanatory note:

PERSONAL IDENTIFICATION

The first items on your résumé, at the top of the page and centered, are your name, address, phone number, and e-mail address. Use only one phone number, the one that you use most frequently for both inbound and outbound calls. Remember that calls regarding employment matters come at all hours. The 9:00 a.m. to 5:00 p.m. window is no longer valid. Your address must include your street number, town, and zip code. Your name should be first, in uppercase bold. Beneath your name is the address, phone number, and e-mail address in lowercase regular type.

I have received résumés without an address, only a name, phone number, Twitter hashtag, and an e-mail address. This is the result of a mistaken notion of tech gurus who believe that in a digital world, where you live is not important. Tell that to a human resources director, and you are history. Do not buy into the hype. Use common sense. Always include your full address.

OBJECTIVE OR SUMMARY

This is nothing more than a marketing piece about the product you are selling: your candidacy. Write this in paragraph format and limit your self-advertisement to ten lines. Write a custom "Objective" for each job application reflecting the contents and requirements in the job description. Specifically, state your work expertise in terms that reflect the job specifications and using key words from the job description. Remember that the reader, the hiring manager or the human resources director, is thinking, "What can this person do for our team and the company going forward?"

If there is only a general statement on a company website under "careers" that reads, "Customer Service Representative Manager," think about what this position requires: excellent verbal and written skills, patience, punctuality, understanding, and courtesy. Build your objective statement around the job description.

State specifically the position for which you are applying (e.g., "I am applying for the Finance Manager position."). If appropriate, quantify your experience. For example, if you are applying for a position requiring writing skills, state, "My written communication experience includes ten years as housing industry writer for *Forbes* magazine." In your cover letter, you can elaborate on that experience.

In this section, you may want to include specific competencies in a list of single words or phrases following the "Objective" or "Summary" paragraph. Here is an example:

CORE COMPETENCIES

*PowerPoint Excel Database Social Media
Personnel Management Field Manual Writing
Logistics Editing Research*

Including such a list will give you a plus mark if the company is using key-word scanning software.

MILITARY WORK EXPERIENCE (ONLY IF APPLICABLE)

List your military experience chronologically beginning with your most recent service assignment and rank. List each MOS (Military Occupation Specialty) under a major heading followed by specifics in bullet point format. Do not use acronyms and write using civilian-speak, not military jargon.

WORK EXPERIENCE

Make this a chronological listing beginning with your most recent work experience. To explain what you did at these companies, state your responsibilities in bullet-point format. In the following example, note that each contains a specific responsibility, not a broad generality:

MCGRAW-HILL K-12 EDUCATION, 2000–2020

- Regional Sales Manager with six direct reports covering fifteen Midwest States, 2014–2020.
- District Sales Manager with three direct reports covering Illinois, Wisconsin, and Indiana, 2007–2013.
- Sales Representative covering Wisconsin and Illinois, 2000–2006.

While you were in college, you may have had a number of part-time positions related to the specific job for which you are applying. For example, if you are applying for a technology position and in college you designed websites for local small businesses, this should be included under work experience. It indicates that your passion for using technology is more than a passing fancy. In addition, it tells the hiring authority, like the technology director, that you have an interest and aptitude for work in technology.

AWARDS, RECOGNITION, COMMUNITY SERVICE

This is a section not often found on résumés, but I encourage its inclusion based on my experience with hiring managers. I have noted that one of the first things that a hiring manger will notice when scanning a résumé is a major heading listing awards and recognition for outstanding achievement.

What do you include? Awards for performance from previous employers, like "Employee of the Year Award." Also, go back to your college years and list notable achievements like making the Dean's List or graduating cum laude.

Another noteworthy item is your outreach experience, because many employers are community conscious. Hiring managers and human resources directors will give you a big plus mark for your give-back to those in need. Many small businesses and large corporations like Starbucks, Microsoft, Bank of America, and General Electric are community conscious and encourage their employees to participate in outreach efforts.

TECHNOLOGY SKILLS

In today's world, employers assume that candidates have the technology skills required to be productive workers. However, hiring managers have been burned many times because of this false assumption. If your tech skills are outdated, take an online course from HigherNext or another online organization as verifiable proof to a hiring manager that you are up to speed. Also, you can find technology courses at universities, local community colleges, and online.

No matter what the job or industry, you will be required to use technology to meet your job requirements.

EDUCATION

This is the last major heading on your résumé, and it is very straightforward. Chronologically list college and military (if applicable) education. Also, if you attended a prestigious college prep high school, list that, too. Include other professional development courses and certifications. This is how your education section might look:

- The Lawrenceville College Prep High School, Lawrenceville, NJ. Diploma. 1995.
- Elon University, BA. Major: Events Management. Minor: Communications. 2000.
- Elon University Study Abroad. Art History Program. Florence, Italy. 1999.
- The International Culinary Center, New York City. Graduate-level courses in Pastry Arts and Cake Design. 2001.
- Strayer University, Completion of online Web Design course. 2006.
- HigherNext, Online Certified Business Laureate Degree. 2019.

If you authored books or published articles, add a new major heading titled "Publications." Chronologically list all publications in bullet-point format.

Don't add anything after the "Education" section (such as references, favorite sports, ethnicity, gender, religion, or age). If pertinent, you can address these topics during your interview with the hiring manager or human resources director.

WRITING A DIGITAL PROFILE

Always write a digital profile for media such as LinkedIn. It is an important tool that hiring managers, human resources directors, and recruiters use to verify what is on your résumé and to read references from colleagues or customers. Therefore, it is important to make sure that your résumé and digital profile are in sync. Write your résumé first and then create your digital profile.

The digital profile need not be a verbatim repeat of your résumé. Extract the most important features of your résumé and place them in the appropriate place on the digital profile.

COVER LETTERS

When you send your résumé to a named person, always include a one-page cover letter. The cover letter is a summary of your candidacy and explains why you are interested in that particular job and company. It is a business document, so format it as such. Include the following five items in your cover letter:

1. Your source of information for the position. Include the name of the person who referred you if applicable.
2. The reason for submitting your résumé.
3. A compliment about the company.
4. A brief statement of your background and experience and how it relates to the job description.
5. A post script (PS) suggesting the next step, like scheduling a date for a personal interview.

If you are submitting your résumé by e-mail, make the cover letter a part of the e-mail text and attach the résumé. If submitting your résumé by FedEx or UPS, include a formal typed cover letter rather than a handwritten note on a plain sheet of paper.

MOVING FORWARD

Crafting a résumé and digital profile in keeping with today's style is necessary to move your candidacy to the next step, a personal interview with the hiring manager.

Where and how to find these decision makers and the companies they represent is key. You will learn all of this in the following chapters.

CHAPTER TAKEAWAYS

- Your digital profile and résumé must be in sync. One must reflect the other.
- Spelling and grammar mistakes on your résumé will end your chances for employment.
- Today's employers are community conscious. List all outreach activities on your résumé.
- Always list awards and special recognitions from past employers, schools, colleges, and civic organizations.

PRINT AND DIGITAL RESOURCES

Career Confidential. www.careerconfidential.com.

Higher Next/Proctor U. www.highernext.com.

CHAPTER 11

HOW TO FIND DECISION MAKERS AND HIRING MANAGERS

The most serious mistake a midcareer worker can make in the job-hunting process is to believe that writing a "dynamite" résumé and e-mailing it to multiple job boards and career pages is the best way to find a job. What chance do you have when the average medium-sized company receives more than two thousand résumés each month? Who is going to see your résumé at Google when the company receives an estimated twenty thousand per day? When you send your résumé to Southwest Airlines, it is just one of ninety-eight thousand received each year. Writing a résumé is just one step in the job-hunting process. Submitting it to hiring managers and human resources directors is another step, but the process does not stop there. There are additional steps in the process for midcareer workers that I call the Big Ten.

THE BIG TEN STEPS IN THE JOB-HUNTING PROCESS

1. Learn who you are and the role you want to play in your new career.

2. Find employers in your chosen industry.
3. Craft a résumé reflecting your new career goals and updated skills.
4. Learn what jobs are available with employers you have identified.
5. Find the name of the hiring manager and human resources director for a specific employer and connect personally.
6. Activate your industry and personal networks.
7. Attend trade shows and job fairs.
8. Conduct a successful phone or Skype interview.
9. Conduct a successful personal interview.
10. Negotiate a job offer.

THE PROCESS FOR FINDING DECISION MAKERS

Midcareer workers can fall into complacency when it comes to job hunting. A common error is believing that time in the workplace and a network of contacts will make the process a no-brainer. Making a few phone calls to colleagues and sending out a dozen or so résumés will result magically in finding job opportunities and job offers. Nothing could be more delusional. Employers do not come looking for you at home while you are sitting at your computer sending résumés to job boards and career pages. You must seek them out yourself. If this sounds like a daunting task, fear not, because there are certain tried-and-true methods for finding employers.

The people you need to contact personally are hiring managers and human resources directors. These are the people in large companies or small businesses who decide who is hired and who is not. If you are seeking a job in sales, the person you need to reach is the sales manager. If you are pursuing a marketing job, the person you should see is the marketing director. If technology is your focus, the person you need to see is the chief technology officer (CTO) or chief information officer (CIO). If you are seeking a position in finance, the person you need to reach is the chief financial officer, the CFO. If you are not sure what role you would like and are seeking opportunities generally, the person you need to see is the human resources director.

Sometimes people at the highest departmental rank will refer you to a subordinate who evaluates all new hires, regardless of rank. See the person to whom you are referred and do not consider this a put-down. Be assured that the department head approves all workers hired at any level. For most positions, the first interview is usually with the human resources director, who will send the best candidates to the hiring manager, who ultimately will make the final decision.

How do you go about finding the people who have the authority to hire you? How do you learn their names and contact information? You may have had the disappointing experience of calling a company and asking for the director of sales only to have the receptionist tell you that all job applicants must go through the human resources department. When that happens, take it to the next level and ask for the name and contact information of the human resources director.

HOW TO FIND THE NAMES OF HIRING MANAGERS

You can learn the name and contact information for the human resources director, a department head, or a hiring manager using these proven methods.

STRATEGIES FOR LEARNING THE NAMES OF HIRING MANAGERS

- Google the company and the department head's title, e.g., "VP Sales for Walmart."
- Review the company website for the names of its key staff members.
- Network with friends, neighbors, and relatives who are employed.
- •Call the company customer service

- department and ask for the name of the hiring manager.
- Use LinkedIn by entering the name of a company and a position.
- Leave the house and attend conferences and trade shows that take place almost every day in most large- and medium-sized cities across the country.
- Make cold calls at companies located in office and industrial parks.
- Use "old-fashioned" methods like the Yellow Pages and newspapers when seeking employment opportunities with local or neighborhood businesses.

PROACTIVE JOB HUNTER

People with the authority to hire you are lurking everywhere. You can find them in airports, on airplanes, in restaurants, bars, Starbucks, sports events . . . any location where people gather. However, just being in a crowd is not enough; you must be proactive.

FINDING HIRING MANAGERS AT RESTAURANTS AND COFFEE HOUSES

When you're at Starbucks ordering a grande cappuccino, most likely the first thing you will do is look for a table that is unoccupied so you can whip out your smartphone or iPad and begin texting or scrolling through the news. This is not the way to find your potential boss. Select a table occupied by those dressed in business attire because they are the people you want to know. Instead of tweeting your life away, begin a conversation with the woman who is dressed for success and pounding away on her laptop. How do you begin the conversation? Begin with that all-time favorite, the weather. "It's really hot out today. Good thing this place has air-conditioning. By the way, you look like the president of a company. What do you do?" Another tactic is to make a comment about Starbucks's successful business model and its college scholarship program for employees. You have just opened the door, and who knows what is inside.

One never knows the status of the person in business attire, but it's your job to find out. Contrary to hype, the world of work has not gone entirely casual. Business executives who are on the job customarily dress in business attire. Even in the technology world, executive-level people are dressed a cut above the people working in the trenches. Look for the people in business attire, and you will find hiring managers.

LOOKING FOR EMPLOYERS AND HIRING MANAGERS IN THE YELLOW PAGES

Another way to find employers and their hiring managers may shock you. It is using the Yellow Pages, particularly for jobs with small businesses in your local area. Prior to 1990, people used print books to find just about everything, including employers. One of the most useful books was the Yellow Pages phone directory. It is still being published for every location in the United States, and it is a fascinating book to review. The Yellow Pages are online, too.

The Yellow Pages for a large city like Chicago, Dallas, or New York City can run over a thousand pages. It lists all businesses alphabetically under industry headings. For example, I just clicked on www.yellowpages.com and then entered "insurance companies in New York." The result? Hundreds of companies by name with detailed contact information. For example, I selected Aflac and went to their website and clicked on "Management Team." There I found the name, title, and picture for every key executive including the CEO, marketing director, human resources director, CIO, CTO, and so on down the line. If I were looking for a marketing job with Aflac, I would send my résumé and cover letter directly to the named marketing director.

Could anything sounding so *yesterday* really help you find a job in today's digital world? According to Richard Bolles, author of the bestselling job-hunting book *What Color Is Your Parachute?*, workers who use the Yellow Pages to identify potential employers and find the names of hiring managers have a success rate exceeding 50 percent.

You can use either the print or the digital editions. If you know the industry you want to explore, just go to that major heading and you will find many companies. Finance. Education. Banking. Publishing. Retailing. Agriculture. Automobiles. Insurance. Healthcare. It's all there . . . in the Yellow Pages.

Back to the Future . . . Again. Using Newspapers to Find Employers.

Reading the print or the digital versions of local, regional, or national newspapers is still a productive way to find potential employers and the names of their key personnel. One of the best newspapers to source is the *Wall Street Journal*. I call this daily newspaper America's most honest publication because its agenda makes no bones about its purpose—helping people make money.

Newspapers like the *Wall Street Journal*, the *New York Times*, the *Washington Post*, the *Chicago Tribune*, and the *Los Angeles Times* carry ads for workers at the managerial, director, and vice-president levels, the sweet spots for midcareer workers. Employers spend serious money to advertise these job openings, so you will rarely find ads for entry-level positions. Both print and online weekend editions carry the job ads for midlevel workers and listings of businesses for sale. Be sure to check them out regularly.

NETWORKING

The primary purpose of networking is to connect personally with someone who can help you secure a job. Who are these people? Everyone who is presently employed by a company or who owns a business is a networking source. Where do you find them? They are as close as your next-door neighbor or a former boss. These individuals can direct you to a named person with a job title in their own place of employment.

YOUR FORMER BOSS

Contact all former bosses and seek their help. Ask for the names of hiring managers at their present employers, and in other companies. Bosses usually know other bosses. Also, you might ask that person for a letter of recommendation. Do not overlook this obvious source. Most people are willing to help let-go workers in their job searches.

USING THE COLD-CALLING PROCESS TO FIND HIRING MANAGERS

Midcareer workers who have been out of the job-hunting loop for a number of years tend to forget about protocols, like befriending workers in support positions. You need to be mindful of the importance of workers like receptionists and administrative assistants, "gatekeepers," who control access to the people you want to see. There are gatekeepers in every company, one of the most important being the receptionist at the front desk. When cold-calling, the receptionist is the first person you will meet. These individuals can make or break you, and you must treat them with respect and build a relationship quickly. Your appearance and introductory remarks are critical. The receptionist will dismiss anyone who disregards basic business protocols.

The process begins when you enter an office without an appointment. You tell the receptionist that you are seeking a job and would like to meet with the human resources director or hiring manager for a specific department. If you are focusing on a specific position, maybe associate marketing manager, ask to see the hiring manager in charge of marketing. If you are seeking a position in sales, ask for the sales manager. Your introductory statement to the receptionist, accompanied by a smile, might go something like this: "Good morning, Ms. Jones. My name is William Foster. I'm seeking a position in information technology. May I please speak with your technology director?" The receptionist will respond in one of several ways:

1. "Our technology director is Mrs. Deborah George, and I'll see if she's available." Your response might be, "Thank you. I would appreciate only a few minutes of her time. I know she's a busy person."
2. "Our technology director is Mr. Adams, but he's out of the office today." Your response might be "Thank you. In that case, may I speak with his administrative assistant to make an appointment to see Mr. Adams?"
3. "We do not have a technology director." Your response might be, "Thank you. In that case, may I speak with the human resources director?"
4. "I'm sorry, you need an appointment to see any of our staff members." Your response might be, "Thank you. May I please have the name of your human resources director and the e-mail address and phone number? I'll call for an appointment, as you suggested."

Note that your response should always begin with a "thank-you." Also, note that you never just say "thank you" and walk out. That is not the way it works in the business world, because the company is always looking for new talent, like you. Be professionally assertive, but courteous, until you get what you want and need.

COLD CALLS ARE ALWAYS IN STYLE

Some consider making personal calls on potential employers without an appointment something out of yesterday's playbook. Wrong! The purpose of the cold call is not to be hired on the spot; its purpose is to arrange a personal meeting with a hiring manager.

Cold-calling is not easy at first, but the more calls you make, the easier it will become. Of course, you risk rejection when you make a cold call. Do not take it personally. Over time, your technique will improve and you will learn that rejection is not a personal insult, but part of the business process.

The odds of something happening are in your favor, as the numbers will show. Assume that you make fifteen cold calls per week on potential employers in an industrial or office park. At the end of one month, you will have made sixty calls where you spoke with a real person.

Assuming a success rate of only 10 percent, at the end of one month you will have met personally with six influential people. Compare that to the number of personal interviews you will have had if you stayed at home and fired off résumés to unknown entities.

WORKING WITH EXECUTIVE RECRUITERS

Another productive way to reach employers is to connect with recruiters. These are individuals who work alone or in partnership, or who are employed by large national or multinational search firms. They are located in every part of the country and abroad.

Most recruiters specialize in a particular industry and job level. For example, recruiters who work for the multinational search firm Heidrick & Struggles, which is based in Chicago, specialize in managerial-level jobs and up. The firm has been successful conducting searches for C-level executives with companies like Coca-Cola. It is one of the giants in the industry and is listed on the New York Stock Exchange. It has offices in every major US city and in many cities abroad, as well. Another multinational search firm is Los Angeles–based Korn Ferry. It specializes in C-level and midlevel searches. Both of these search firms have sterling reputations among both employees and customers. Both undertake searches for midcareer managerial candidates for multiple industries.

Individual recruiters and boutique search firms employing several recruiters specialize in a particular industry. Some conduct searches for only one level of employment, like entry level or midlevel. Some work only local job searches, and others work nationally or internationally. In addition, some conduct searches only for contract workers, such as computer programmers, who are employed for a stipulated period of time, say twenty-four months.

Recruiters work for employers, not job candidates. They conduct searches for candidates like you, the midcareer worker, to fill a specific job identified by an employer, which could be a small business or a large publicly traded company. Usually the employer pays a fee to the recruiter based on the job's base salary. Most career recruiters work on retainer, which means they are paid a fee in specified increments by the company even if the search is not successful, an infrequent occurrence. Other recruiters work on a contingency basis. They earn a fee only if they provide a candidate who is hired by the company. Recruiters never ask a job candidate for a fee.

Even though recruiters are paid by the employer, their success derives from presenting qualified candidates to the company. Job candidates, like the laid-off midcareer worker looking for new opportunities, are in effect their "products." They want and need job seekers like you to maintain their businesses. They find candidates through networking, attending trade shows, and by using social media such as LinkedIn.

HOW TO CONTACT A RECRUITER

Midcareer workers in a particular industry can find a recruiter by accessing their industry network or by using the Internet. If using the latter method, go online and enter your location, industry, and job level. For example, Google "Regional sales manager recruiters in St. Louis" or "Recruiters for trade publishing editors in New York." Always enter the industry and the job title. Another tactic is to use LinkedIn. Enter "executive recruiters" and add your industry or job specialty.

To connect with a recruiter in one of the large multinational firms like Heidrick & Struggles, call the company and ask to speak with a recruiter specializing in midlevel jobs in a particular industry.

PROCEDURES FOR WORKING WITH RECRUITERS

Consider the recruiter a friend who is working for you. Tell her or him how and why you have been laid off or fired and what kind of new opportunities you are seeking. Do not hesitate to disclose your compensation history and what you would like going forward. Recruiters are the best source you can find for information about compensation levels and qualifications because they are in touch with the workplace every day.

The recruiter will ask for your résumé. Prepare it using the rubrics in this book and always ask for advice to enhance your résumé. For phone, Skype, or personal interviews, follow the advice in this book. Just as you would when working with a potential employer directly, make every effort to meet the recruiter personally. After the vetting process, the recruiters will submit your candidacy for a particular job with a particular company. They will do that by sending your résumé and a written review of your interview and qualifications to the company's human resources director or directly to the hiring manager.

Your relationship with the recruiter should be based on honesty and trust. The recruiter is one of your best sources for finding new opportunities. Make every effort to contact a recruiter in your selected industry as soon as you have prepared a viable résumé.

MOVING FORWARD

This chapter reviewed *how* to find decision makers and hiring managers using tried-and-true methods. There is another important step for reaching the Promised Land—learning *where* to find potential employers. In the next chapter, I'll tell you how this is done. Stick with us.

CHAPTER TAKEAWAYS

- Treat the gatekeepers with respect.
- Meeting hiring managers personally is a key step in the process.
- Cold-calling on companies in office and industrial parks is an effective strategy to find hiring managers.

PRINT AND DIGITAL RESOURCES

"Job Search Strategies." Lynda.com. www.lynda.com/Business-Skills-tutorials/Job-Search-Strategies/97580-2.html.

Sandberg, Sheryl. *Lean In: Women, Work and the Will to Lead.* Knopf, 2013.

Standard & Poor's 500 Guide 2013: America's Most Watched Companies. McGraw-Hill, 2013.

CHAPTER 12
WHERE TO FIND EMPLOYERS

Finding employers in your chosen area of the workplace is a task that will prove interesting and successful if you use tried-and-true strategies. Two of these are using digital technology, which you can do from home, and the other is tearing yourself away from home to attend trade shows, conferences, and job fairs.

GOING ONLINE TO FIND EMPLOYERS

Using online resources creatively can yield positive results, but it is necessary to proceed with caution because online job hunting can steal your time like nothing else. Studies show that using digital media is the least effective way to find employment with one exception—LinkedIn.

USING JOB BOARDS

Job boards have yielded disappointing results for many job hunters. My assessment of the boards is that most fail to connect you with a named person, a hiring authority, and, in many cases, even with a named company like Microsoft, Raytheon, or McDonald's.

REVIEWING CORPORATE WEBSITES

To learn what's happening at consumer goods companies, like Procter & Gamble, review their websites and check out their career pages. However, do not assume that all available jobs are posted on company websites. Many jobs, from entry level to midlevel to executive level, go to job boards and recruiters.

When you do respond to a company career page listing, make sure that you respond to a named person with a title. Sending it to "Employment Manager" is a waste of time. The most expedient way to find the name and title of that person is to call the company customer service department and ask for help.

FINDING EMPLOYERS AT OFFICE AND INDUSTRIAL PARKS

In every metropolitan area, you will find office, business, and industrial parks, places where hundreds of companies locate their local offices, regional offices, or home offices. Some parks specialize in one particular industry, while others host companies from different industries. For example, an industrial park in Langhorne, Pennsylvania, specializes in medical offices for both physicians and dentists. An industrial park in Portland, Maine, hosts a diversified group of companies including J. Weston Walch Publishing Company, a ninety-year-old educational publisher.

How do you contact companies in a business or industrial park? Easy. You leave the house at 8:00 a.m. in your business attire and armed with business cards and a dozen résumés to distribute to hiring managers and human resources directors. You go from door to door and request a personal meeting with the hiring manager in charge of your field of interest.

One might ask "Do I make a cold call on every business in the business park?" If you are job hunting for any kind of job regardless of industry, the answer is *yes*. If you are interested only in positions with insurance companies as an underwriter, sales representative, or claims adjuster, narrow your cold calls to insurance companies. You learn where these companies are by reviewing the online directories for that particular business or office park.

USE THE INTERNET TO FIND BUSINESS PARKS

There are many business, office, and industrial parks in every area of the country, and the best way to learn where they are is to Google an entry like "business parks in Denver, Colorado." I did just that and found the Denver Tech Center, an area along the I-25 corridor southeast of Denver. This business park is home to more than sixty companies spanning a number of industries. The list includes Agilent Technologies, Boeing, Cargill, Centex Homes, JP Morgan, Kodiak Petroleum, Morgan Stanley, Nissan Motor Corp., Time Warner Cable, and Western Union. These are either home offices or regional offices and are potential employers. If you live in the Denver Metro Area, start cold-calling at the companies located at the Denver Tech Center.

Here is another example of what you will find. I searched for "industrial parks in Houston, Texas" and found the Beltway Industrial Park, where light manufacturing companies are located. Industrial parks in other locations host large manufacturers as well as warehouses and regional offices. If manufacturing is your thing, you can't go wrong by cold-calling on companies in an industrial park dedicated to manufacturers.

To see what is available in the Pacific Northwest, I Googled "Seattle business parks" and found enough potential employers, and their locations, to keep me busy job hunting for the next six months.

No matter where you live in the US, you will find office parks and industrial parks located near your home. Does it get any easier?

FINDING EMPLOYERS AT JOB FAIRS

There is a mistaken notion that job fairs are only for entry-level workers. In fact, companies in certain industries conduct job fairs whenever they have a critical need for experienced workers who have managerial talent. For example, financial companies and technology companies need hundreds or even thousands of workers when they develop new products, and one way to attract potential candidates is to conduct a job fair. Go online to learn the date and location of a job fair in your location or your area of interest and expertise. Midcareer workers have an excellent chance to connect because of the experience and expertise they can offer. Laid-off workers have another advantage—they can start work immediately. Attending job fairs is an excellent way to meet potential employers and their hiring managers. There are hundreds available throughout the year at a location within driving distance from your home.

The managers you will meet have one thing in mind—to find the best candidates for job openings. It is all business, so you must go prepared, just as you would for attending a trade show. That means bringing a dozen résumés and calling cards, and dressing appropriately. How you dress could take you to the top of the heap or put you in the trash can.

FINDING EMPLOYERS AT CONFERENCES AND TRADE SHOWS

The best places to find potential employers, in the flesh, are convention centers where conferences and trade shows are held. Here you will find a multitude of potential employers, all under one roof. Attending conferences at major convention centers like McCormick Place in Chicago or the Javits Center in New York City is the best use of your job-hunting time. I know from firsthand experience that many candidates have met their potential employers on the floor of a convention center; in fact, candidates have even been hired on the floor. You will not find a better way to make productive use of your job-hunting time and effort.

WHAT IS A TRADE SHOW?

A trade show is a gathering of workers representing companies in a specific industry. The purpose of a trade show is to give companies an opportunity to display their products and advertise their services in exhibit booths located on the floor of a convention center.

Trade shows go by different names—conventions, conferences, exhibits, expos, trade fairs, or trade exhibitions. All mean the same thing. Usually they are held at convention centers, which are located in large cities or state capitals, but occasionally they meet in hotels or resorts that have large rooms for hosting exhibit booths and smaller rooms to host "breakout sessions," where industry experts present new products or discuss research and industry trends.

Industry professional organizations sponsor these shows, which can be very costly. Some of those costs are defrayed by member dues and by conference attendance fees. An example of a trade show is the world's largest technology show called the Consumer Electronics Show (CES), which convenes every January in Las Vegas. In 2017, attendance at this show exceeded one hundred and fifty thousand, including thirty-five thousand people from foreign countries. More than three thousand companies attended and hosted exhibits. Can you imagine three thousand potential employers under one roof? If you are interested in technology, you cannot afford to miss CES.

For those let-go workers who were office-bound and did not attend trade shows, here is another example of what to expect at a trade show hosted at a major convention center. Book Expo America (BEA) is the largest trade show in America for the book publishing industry. BEA held its 2017 annual convention at the Javits Convention Center in New York City. More than twelve hundred companies hosted exhibits on the conference center floor, all staffed by publishing company employees. Some held editorial positions, some were marketing managers, some came from sales, others from finance, and still others from information technology. Where in the world could you find so many potential employers and hiring managers under one roof?

Attending trade shows is the most productive strategy for job hunting. However, what do you do once you are in the convention hall? Once again, attending a trade show is a process.

PREPARATION CHECKLIST FOR ATTENDING A TRADE SHOW

One does not just show up at an exhibit and expect miracles to happen. In order to reap maximum benefits, plan for it in advance. Here is a checklist and suggestions for planning purposes:

- Your primary purpose for attending these events is to visit the many exhibit booths where you will find hiring managers. Many shows hold exhibits only on specific days and at specific hours. For example, the dates listed for CES, the technology conference in Las Vegas, may be January 10–16, but the exhibits could be open only on January 11–15, from 10:00 a.m. to 6:00 p.m. You can find this information online, or by calling the conference center or the organization hosting the show. This is important because you are attending the conference primarily to visit the exhibit booths where you will find the hiring managers. There is no need to attend the conference on days when the exhibits are not open.

- The organization sponsoring the conference publishes a list of exhibiting companies in the printed conference program. Frequently, the directory will include the names of the representatives who will be attending along with their contact information. Obtain this list either online or at the conference center because it will provide the names and contact information for key executives and hiring managers.

- Bring at least one hundred business cards and twenty résumés to the show each day. The exchange of business cards is still the accepted way to build your list of networking contacts. The résumés are for hiring managers you will meet in the exhibit booths or on the convention center floor.

- When you enter the conference center to attend the show, first go to the registration desk to pay the exhibit fee, obtain your name tag, and pick up the conference program, which is usually tucked in a tote bag. Make sure you get the conference program. Always wear your name tag while in the convention center.

- Almost all shows charge a fee for attendance. Many large trade shows, which are open to the public, charge very low admission fees, in the $25 to $50 range. Fees may vary with the number of days you will attend, your affiliation, and your work status. As an example of fees to attend specialized conferences, a technology education industry trade show called EdNET charges up to $900 for admission, but the fee is worth it. The reason is that six hundred hiring authorities attend this annual convention, including CEOs; presidents; vice presidents for sales, marketing, and product development; chief technology and information officers; and human resources directors. During this three-day conference, you will meet keynote speakers and participate

in breakout sessions. Also, you will have an opportunity to present your candidacy for two minutes in front of six hundred hiring authorities. It does not get better than that. Negotiate the lowest entrance fee for this and every conference. Always ask for discounts when you register.

- If you are coming from a distance and plan to stay overnight near the conference center, make hotel reservations well in advance. If the conference center is in a large city like Los Angeles, local hotel rates will be quite steep. Find a hotel or motel just out of town at a more reasonable room rate and then drive to the conference center each day. In addition, some conference organizations negotiate lower room rates with hotels and motels in the area, so always check this out online several months in advance.

- Dress at trade shows is usually casual, but as a job candidate you should always be dressed as though you were going for an interview. You are there to sell your candidacy, and you should dress with that in mind.

WHAT YOU DO AT A TRADE SHOW

Are you ready for a bit of fun? This is where you will have a good time in a very relaxed environment and meet hundreds of full-time company workers, many of whom will be hiring managers. Exhibit halls are crowded with customers who are there to get product information and to visit company representatives. This is a place where workers conduct business in a pleasant way. Workers in the various exhibit booths will be dressed informally, many times wearing a casual shirt or top bearing the name of the company and the company logo. Remember, however, that you are not a worker here and you should be in business attire.

After you register and get your name tag, enter the exhibit hall and begin visiting each booth. You can start your booth visits in the first aisle and proceed around the hall until you have stopped at each booth. If there are hundreds of exhibits, this may take two or even three days.

WHAT DO YOU SAY AFTER YOU SAY "HELLO"?

When you enter an exhibit booth, view the products on display and ask one of the representatives to explain what the company does. Establish a personal relationship by learning what the person's job is and how he or she likes working for the company. After you establish the relationship, tell the person you are job hunting and ask to speak with a hiring manager who may be there. If you are interested in marketing and the director of marketing is not there, ask for that person's name and contact information, and follow up with a phone call or e-mail when you return to your home office.

If all of this is new to you, here is a script you might use to break the ice when visiting an exhibit booth. Establish the relationship by addressing the worker by name, which is always on the name tag. Here is a sample script:

SCRIPT FOR TALKING WITH A COMPANY REPRESENTATIVE AT A TRADE SHOW

"Hello, Tom. My name is Jennifer, and I'm here for two reasons and would appreciate your help. First, I would like to know more about your company and what you do. Second, I'm seeking employment and would like to see the hiring manager for marketing if this person is attending the conference. If not, would you please write his or her name and contact information on the back of your business card for me? Also, could you give me the name and contact information for the company human resources director? Thanks, Tom."

Before you leave the exhibit booth, give your business card to your new contact and write on the back, "Seeking employment and would appreciate your help."

If a hiring manager you want to see is in the booth, request a few minutes for an informal interview and give that person your résumé. The way to get this moving without feeling awkward is to say something like this:

"Bill, here's my résumé and if you have the time now, maybe you could take a minute to review it. I'm looking for a job opportunity in marketing, and, being in midcareer, I have a wealth of experience. If you don't have time now, could we make an appointment to chat for a few minutes, maybe over a cup of coffee or lunch? My treat, of course."

WHERE THE HIRING MANAGERS AND RECRUITERS HANG OUT

The big guys, the hiring managers, always attend trade shows and conventions in order to meet their key customers, to keep up with industry trends, *and* to recruit workers for all levels of employment. Recruiters, too, often attend these shows to prospect for new clients, to seek workers for open positions, or to look for qualified candidates to place in their database for future reference. I have attended hundreds of conferences to recruit job candidates and seek new clients and have never been disappointed. In the job-hunting world, trade shows and exhibits *are* the Promised Land. Visiting these shows is the best way to search for a new job as you rebuild your career after being fired or laid off.

HOW TO RECOGNIZE A HIRING MANAGER

In exhibit booths and on the convention center floor, you will see people dressed in formal business attire. Often, these are the company executives, the people you need to meet. Lacking an introduction, you just have to wing it. Walk up to that person and say something

like this: "I can tell by the way you're dressed that you must be running the show here. My name is John, and I'm here job hunting. I'm looking for a sales position. Could you steer me in the right direction? I would really appreciate your help." This person will appreciate your sense of humor and the subtle note of respect and recognition.

LUNCH IS A TIME FOR NETWORKING

On the convention center floor, there will be formal restaurants, kiosks selling hot dogs and soft drinks, and sometimes bars selling alcoholic drinks. This is another place to meet people. After you buy a burger and a Coke, find a table that is partially occupied. Take a seat, introduce yourself to the person next to you, and go into your sales pitch. Lunch is not just lunch; it is a networking opportunity. You never select an empty table, whip out your smartphone, and begin texting. Never. Why waste your time and money when you could be meeting potential employers?

THIRSTY FOR A COLD BEER?

Convention center restaurants frequently sell alcoholic drinks. *Never* buy them. Do not even think of it. A cardinal rule is never to drink anything alcoholic while job hunting, even if others around you are. You are here on business, not to throw down a beer or a Malbec. Many of the people here are hiring managers, and they could be sizing up your personal habits. Company managers do not hire candidates who drink while job hunting. The same rules apply to using any form of controlled substances.

FINDING JOBS WITH CONVENTION CENTERS

When you review the conference center website, always check out the career postings. Convention centers, such as the Cobo Center in Detroit, are profit-making organizations and employ many workers across all specialties. These are good full-time jobs in sales, marketing, technology, finance, and human resources. In addition, go to the conference center offices and inquire about job opportunities when you attend the conference.

HOW TO FIND A TRADE SHOW CATERING TO A PARTICULAR INTEREST

There are many sources to find conventions matching your interests: industry journals, both print and digital; local newspapers; and convention center schedules. In addition, you will find a trade show directory on the website of Events in America (www.eventsinamerica .com/tradeshows). This organization tracks and publicizes the names and locations of industry trade shows across the country.

MOVING FORWARD

Attending trades shows is the best strategy for finding hiring managers in the flesh. Trade shows convene every week in large metropolitan areas. To learn the who, when, and where, search the convention center websites. For a directory of major convention centers and a review of the top convention centers and trades shows, refer to appendix A and appendix B of this book. I suggest doing this now, because this information will save you hours of time and lead you to places where you will meet hiring managers.

The next step in the process is the interview, which some consider an intimidating event. In the next chapter, I'll provide guidelines for navigating your interview.

CHAPTER TAKEAWAYS

- The best place to meet hiring managers and key executives is at conferences, trade shows, and job fairs.
- Access the convention center website for a list of upcoming trade shows.
- Dress in business attire while attending trade shows.

PRINT AND DIGITAL RESOURCES

Events in America. www.eventsinamerica .com/tradeshows.

The appendices of this book. Here you will find a list of major convention centers by state and the names of important trade shows by industry.

CHAPTER 13
INTERVIEW RUBRICS FOR MIDCAREER WORKERS

Millions of words have been written about interviews. For example, Google "job interviews," and you will get thousands of hits. Go to the business and career sections at a Barnes & Noble bookstore, and you will find dozens of books on interviews. All of us have read Internet hits titled "Ten tips for killer interviews," or "Ace the interview in three easy steps," or "Interviews for dummies." All of this tells us that the interview is an important part of the job-hunting process and that we should prepare for it carefully.

THE PURPOSE OF THE INTERVIEW

Before we get into the heart of the interview process, let's reconstruct the bigger picture. The interview is a part of the process that enables both you and the company to determine if the relationship will work to the advantage of both the company and the candidate. When that happens, everyone wins. The company makes money from your productive work in order to pay your salary and benefits, expenses, taxes, and perhaps contribute to charitable causes, and still

have enough left over to be a profitable business. You win because you make money to become self-sufficient, take care of your family, and give back money and time to the community.

WHO'S HOLDING THE ACES?

Even though the interviewer appears to hold all of the cards, it really is not so. The hiring manager needs someone like you to fill an important position and is under pressure to find the right candidate as soon as possible.

While the hiring manager is evaluating the person across the desk, smart candidates are sizing up the hiring manager, as well. It is important that the hiring manager be someone you respect, someone who shows courtesy and honesty. If you find that the interviewer lacks these qualities, erase that company from your list. You may need a job, but you do not want it at the expense of working on a ship of fools. If, for some reason, you think that this listing ship might change once the company hires you, remember this rule: *you can't fix crazy!*

LISTEN AND LEARN

All candidates, especially midcareer workers, want to tout their accomplishments and general work experience to anyone who will listen. They tend to smother the interviewer with a recitation of what's on the résumé. The interviewer has most likely checked out who you are and what you have done and is not interested in your retelling it. The person sitting across the desk from you is forward-looking. Keep that in mind when the interviewer begins the conversation by asking questions. Listen and comprehend, because it is how you respond that really counts.

In his well-known book *The Seven Habits of Highly Effective People*, Stephen Covey says, "Most people do not listen with the intent to understand; they listen with the intent to reply. They are either speaking or preparing to speak."

A good example that supports Covey's theory is the TV interview. Interviewers are often more concerned with presenting their own agendas than with listening for responses to questions they ask. Why don't they permit the person to complete the answer? Before the response is even completed, the interviewer interrupts with her own statement.

Your interviewer, too, might have the same tendency, so be sure to maintain the integrity of the interview to make your point. If the interviewer interrupts before you have the last word out of your mouth, you need to make an appropriate response to keep the interview on an even keel, even though your gut reaction might be, "Shut up. Let me finish my answer to your question."

Here is what you might say when this happens: "To complete my response to your first question, here is what I was going to say . . ." That should keep the interview on the right track and make for a fruitful exchange of ideas and courteous discourse.

The interview is a conversation where two people listen, comprehend, and then respond. There are two basic rules for interviews.

THE TWO GOLDEN RULES FOR INTERVIEWS

1. Be courteous.
2. Be honest.

These two rules build the foundation for all personal relationships. This holds true no matter how young, how old, or how senior the interviewer is. And it applies if you have been laid off or fired from your last job. If the interviewer asks you why you left your previous job, be honest and say that you were let go. If you were laid off, state the circumstances: a reorganization, downsizing, rightsizing, or bankruptcy. If you were fired, don't talk around it. Be forthcoming and state why you were fired: that you did not meet the job expectations, or that you and your boss were on different pages. Admit it and follow by saying that you have learned your lesson and that you have resolved to move forward using your new-found persona and your reconstructed character. (As a matter of fact, the interviewer most likely learned that you had been fired for cause after some preliminary background checking before you came for the interview, so do not try to hide it.)

THE INTERVIEWER'S AGE AND RANK

The person sitting across the desk from you may be older than you are and may be at the director or vice president level. To reach that point in the corporate hierarchy, this person has been doing something right.

On the other side of the age situation, the interviewer may be ten years your junior and display arrogance that is nothing short of irritating. Suck it up, because you cannot do anything about it. Build the relationship by expressing interest in this person's rise to a position of responsibility.

Regardless of the situation, the only way to deal with these variables is to be prepared to answer the questions in a mature manner and on your own terms. When you prepare for the interview, resolve that you are going to look at the hiring manager as a potential friend.

HOW THE INTERVIEWER JUDGES YOU

Three important items on an employer's checklist appear so self-evident that candidates overlook them. However, if you fall short on any of the three, your chances of moving ahead in the process are diminished.

APPROPRIATE DRESS

Your appearance is the first thing a hiring manager notices. If you come to an interview dressed inappropriately, you are history. Case closed. No second chance. With the workplace becoming more casual, there is a tendency to dress down, even for an interview. We see midlevel and executive-level workers in casual dress when on the job, but an interview is a different occasion. I have asked human resources directors about this, and their advice is to dress a cut above casual for an interview. In fact, several told me that many experienced candidates, midlevel and executive level, dress too casually for interviews, and it does not help their candidacy. Their advice is to wear business attire for an interview.

APPROPRIATE LANGUAGE

After dress, the most important checklist item is verbal communication, which includes vocabulary. Avoid clichés and slang terms. Answer questions using business-speak that you have learned throughout your working years. The hiring manager expects no less. For example, one of the question most frequently asked is "Why do you want to work here?" Deliver your answer in business language such as this:

I want to work with your company because I'm impressed with your record of generating revenue. For example, in the last quarter your revenue was up 10 percent over a comparable quarter a year ago. This tells me that you have a viable business model. I would like a chance to work for such a company and contribute my time and talents to help the company continue to grow.

APPROPRIATE BODY LANGUAGE

There are two parts to the interview: what you say and how you say it—content and delivery. The content part of the interview should reflect your research on the company's finances, your interest in the job opportunity at hand, and your qualifications for helping the company move forward. The delivery part of your conversation includes the unspoken word—body language—which reflects your level of confidence and your interest in the job and company.

Many words have been written on this subject, but it still comes down to a few basics. Sit straight, make eye contact, relax, smile, and display your personality. If you are not accustomed to using your hands to make a point, do not make an awkward attempt to do this in an interview. You are having a conversation about how you can help the company going forward, not auditioning for a part in a movie. To learn more on this general topic, conduct a Google search on body language.

Here is a real-life situation that I encountered recently while conducting a search for a vice president. This story demonstrates that delivery, particularly the body language part of it, is just as important as content.

FRED FROM CALIFORNIA

Fred had a personal two-hour interview with the CEO of a major company located in Los Angeles. The position, vice president for international

sales and marketing, required the candidate to live in the home office area, and Fred met that requirement. He did not need to relocate. This was a huge problem out of the way. On paper, he met every job requirement and more. So far, so good. However, something untoward happened during the interview process. The CEO rejected his candidacy citing two reasons. One, "Fred's answers seemed shallow." In other words, the CEO did not buy the content. Two, "Fred appeared insecure, lacking confidence, and appeared to be distracted." His body language told the CEO that there was a disconnect. His eyes were wandering during the interview, his posture was strained, his arms were folded much of the time, and his legs were crossed during the interview. Fred's body language told the CEO that he was not buying into the conversation.

I counseled Fred on the basics of body language and persuaded the CEO to have a second interview with Fred. Specifically, I told Fred to sit erect facing the interviewer, make direct eye contact throughout the interview, sit with hands resting in his lap rather than folded, rest legs on the floor rather than tightly crossed, and avoid fidgeting and letting eyes wander if there are interruptions from office sources, like a ringing phone. Also, I told Fred to relax and maintain a friendly smile during the interview. The CEO obliged by granting Fred a second interview, and the results were startling. The interview proceeded as a conversation, and the CEO and Fred learned they had much in common on a personal level. Both were star performers on their college swim teams, and both had similar current interests. After another round of interviews with company executives, Fred was hired.

PREPARING A WRITTEN INTERVIEW AGENDA

I am always impressed when a candidate comes to an interview with a written agenda that includes questions about both the position and the company. I'm equally impressed when the candidate hands me a written agenda and requests a brief discussion of each topic if time permits. A written agenda sends a powerful message that you have carefully prepared for the interview and that you are pursuing *this* particular opportunity, not just any job. Here is a sample agenda that you can use as a model for crafting your own, which you can then print on your letterhead and hand to the interviewer before beginning the interview:

SAMPLE INTERVIEW AGENDA

Subject: Agenda for Interview with Amazon

Position: Director of Inside Sales

Candidate: Lisa Hopkins

Human Resources Director: Joseph Kowalski

Date: June 7, 2018

I would appreciate the opportunity to discuss the following questions during my interview with Mr. Kowalski:

1. Why is this position open?
2. If someone else had this job, why did that person leave the company?
3. Why are you considering me for this position?
4. Would superior performance in this position lead to a promotion?
5. What are the three major expectations for the Director of Inside Sales?
6. To whom does this job report, and what is that person's management style?
7. What is the background of the person to whom this position reports?
8. What is the company's revenue goal for this fiscal year? How much of an increase is that over the previous year's revenue?
9. What has made this company a leader in the industry?
10. Does the company participate in community outreach programs?
11. Does the company require ongoing professional development courses?
12. Why should I join Amazon?

I thank you for discussing these issues during our interview.

Sincerely,

Lisa

Lisa Hopkins

Answers to these questions are a tool for evaluating the position and company. You need this information to determine if you want to continue the process or decline. Using the written interview agenda will separate you from the rest of the pack. Do not hesitate to use this technique for every interview.

THE INTERVIEW PROCESS

The interview process has four sections, each with its own set of procedures:

1. The beginning of the interview. This is the introductory phase, which sets the tone for the interview.
2. The body of the interview, which takes place after the greetings are completed.
3. Interviewing the interviewer.
4. The ending of the interview, a critically important action item.

Before each interview, write your plan detailing how you will deal with each section. Let's explore each part in detail.

HOW THE INTERVIEW BEGINS

After you exchange hellos and informal chit-chat, like "This is just a beautiful day. I'm happy spring has finally come after such a harsh winter," it is showtime.

Trying to anticipate what the interviewer will ask can be a never-ending game. To level the playing field and keep this a true give-and-take rather than an interrogation, plan to incorporate some or all of these five topics into the interview:

- You are here because you have learned there is a specific employment opportunity.

- You have researched the company and would like to work there for several reasons. State what they are. Some reasons could be your interest in their product, company profitability, glowing reports from company workers, or the steady increase in the price of the company stock.
- You would like an opportunity to increase company profitability by using your talents, intelligence, energy, and passion.
- Highlight your successes and awards for achievement. Verbalize the key points on your résumé under the major heading "Awards, Recognition, Community Service."
- State your career goals and do not be shy. If you really would like to be the company president someday, say so. Tell your interviewer how and why you believe you could work your way up to that position.

One never knows where an interview will go, and it is really up to the candidate to set the direction and tone of the interview. Your written agenda will help accomplish this. Naturally, the interviewer has a certain number of questions, but you do not know these in advance. However, the interviewer will ask one question in almost every situation: "Would you tell me about yourself?" It appears to be a trivial question, but that's just the way it is, and you have to prepare for it.

If you are caught off guard, you might end up reciting your family history or rendering a chronological account of your life from birth to the present. What the hiring manager really wants to hear is what you might do for the company if you are hired, rather than hearing that you like a latte better than a cappuccino.

How do you answer that question? It could go several ways, but here is a script that you might use. It gives direction to the interview and sets the tone for a dialogue instead of a Q&A session.

SCRIPT ANSWER FOR "WOULD YOU TELL ME ABOUT YOURSELF?"

I'm the kind of person who takes responsibility for my own life, and that includes having a position that will give me income to continue to be self-sufficient and accomplish my career goals. I'm here because I believe that your company can provide that opportunity. My research indicates that your last quarter generated revenue that exceeded expectations and that your past three years were profitable. I want to be part of a company with that kind of track record because it means that you are doing something right. I would like to build on that success by applying my intelligence, energy, and passion to make this company even better and more profitable. Also, my career vision includes a vice president–level position, and hopefully I can that find that here.

Read this aloud several times until you make it your own. Modify it to include some hard numbers and specifics from your résumé.

THE BODY OF THE INTERVIEW AND FREQUENTLY ASKED QUESTIONS

Candidates, understandably, are curious about what the interviewer will ask. The kinds of questions asked in an interview follow a somewhat standard format. Here are questions the interviewer may ask regardless of the company or position:

1. Would you tell me something about yourself?
2. How did you find out about us?
3. Why do you want to work here?
4. What are your major qualifications for this position?
5. Are there any areas where you think you need to improve?
6. What is your career goal?
7. Can you tell me about a work problem you encountered and how you resolved it?
8. What are your compensation requirements?
9. When could you begin work with us if we agree this is the right job for you?
10. Have you participated in community outreach programs?
11. What is your main academic interest?
12. What books have you read recently?

13. Can you give me an example of how you use social media like YouTube, Twitter, Facebook, and LinkedIn?
14. What do you want to know about the company and the job?
15. Why did you leave your last job?

You don't know how many of these questions the interviewer will ask, but be prepared to answer all of them. Conduct a rehearsal before the interview by having a trusted friend ask you these questions, and then deliver your responses. Practice until you feel comfortable with your answers. Remember to quantify as much as possible.

INTERVIEWING THE INTERVIEWER
You can begin evaluating the hiring manager by asking a question like "Could you tell me about your job experience, such as how long you have been here, what your responsibilities are, and what you did before taking this job?"

Such dialogue permits the hiring manager to brag a little and tell you some success stories. Your expressed interest in the hiring manager's accomplishments helps build the relationship and provides valuable information to evaluate this person. In addition, it makes the interview conversational rather than interrogative.

Remember, this is *your* interview, and you are entitled to ask as many questions as necessary to learn about the company and its people. Do not be intimidated by the interviewer's status or title. This is your interview, your time, your career, your life.

Most likely, you will have your own list of questions, but here are five you should always ask, according to Jeff Haden, a very successful executive recruiter and author of many articles and a book on job hunting and interviewing. This material appeared in his article "Five Questions Job Candidates Should Ask," which appeared in an issue of *INC.* online magazine:

1. *What really drives success for the company?* Every profitable company has rubrics that account for its success. Learn what these are, and you will know much about the company and what it expects from its workers. If you hear something like, "Everyone here works like crazy, even coming in on Saturdays and Sundays," consider it a yellow flag. You should not have to spend seven days a week meeting job expectations, and you should not be expected to be on call via texts and e-mail 24/7, unless you are a medical professional or a law enforcement officer . . . or president of the United States.
2. *What do employees do in their spare time?* This might be a difficult question for the interviewer to answer, especially in a large company. However, the answer will tell you much about the kind of people the company hires, and if these are

your kind of people. Do they spend off-work hours at a sports bar? Do they volunteer their off-work hours for company-sponsored outreach programs? Do some of them take graduate-level courses to improve their work skills?

3. *How do you plan to deal with . . . ?* The blank part of this question could be any number of items that aroused your curiosity while doing your research on the company and the industry. The question could be, "How do you plan to deal with lower margins for your technology products?" The answers to these questions will tell you if the company recognizes its problems and how it plans to deal with them going forward.

4. *What do you expect me to accomplish in the first sixty to ninety days?* This question lets the interviewer know that you are no slouch. You want the company hiring manager to know that you are ready, willing, and able to be productive immediately. You are job-ready.

5. *What are the common attributes of your top performers?* The answer to this question will tell you much about the corporate culture, the company expectations, and what workers are willing to do in order to be successful there.

ENDING THE INTERVIEW

There is a definite way to end the interview. Salespeople ask for the order after making their product presentation instead of just saying, "Thank you for your time," and leaving. The same holds true for the interview. Close by saying thank you and, if you are interested in the job and the company, ask, "What are the next steps in the process? I really would like to work here based upon your answers to my questions and my research about the company. When can I start?"

If the interviewer gives a nebulous answer to your closing statements, counter with an action item like, "Thanks for your time. I'll follow up with you by phone or e-mail to check on the status of my candidacy. May I please have your business card? And by the way, what is your hiring deadline?"

If you are not interested in the job, say so and leave after saying, "Thank you for your time. I really do not think this is a good fit. I'm sure that you will find a candidate better suited for this position."

Remember to send a follow-up letter even if you are no longer interested in the job. Always maintain the relationship regardless of the results of the interview.

PANEL INTERVIEWS

Occasionally, a panel instead of just one person will conduct the interview for the company. The panel interview may sound intimidating, but it can work to your advantage.

Panels usually consist of the hiring manager, the company human resources director, and a worker from the department where the job is located. For example, if you are interviewing for an editorial manager position with a publishing company, the worker may be an associate editor.

The purpose of the panel interview is to save time, not to intimidate the candidate. When you walk in the door, you don't know if the interview will be with one person or with a panel, so be prepared mentally for both. Usually a panel interview means that the company is seriously interested in your candidacy. It's a positive sign for you. Be reassured and confident that the interview is going to work to your advantage. After the interview begins, determine the person who appears to be most friendly and supportive and make an effort to build a relationship with him or her.

Interviewing with a panel is advantageous for a number of reasons. In the one-on-one interview, if you do not connect with the person across from you, there is nobody else you can turn to for help. In a panel interview, you have options for building strong relationships with more than one person.

BREAKFAST, LUNCH, OR DINNER INTERVIEWS

Occasionally, the hiring manager will invite you to interview over breakfast, lunch, or dinner. The reason is not hunger. Rather, this type of an interview gives the manager an opportunity to observe your behavior in a real-life setting. Candidates for customer-contact jobs in sales or marketing are frequently subjected to interviews over a meal. There are several basic rubrics for such interviews:

- Table manners should be scrupulously observed. That means chewing with your mouth closed, not leaning on the table, and not slurping your soup or coffee.
- Never lick your fingers.
- Never drink alcoholic beverages at meal interviews, even if the interviewer does.
- Never take calls on your smartphone. In fact, turn it off and put in your pocket or purse.
- Treat the wait staff and clean-up crew with respect.
- Remain focused regardless of circumstances.

These may sound like adolescent suggestions, but I have included them because I have observed violations of basic manners on a number of occasions while interviewing midcareer candidates. On one occasion, I was interviewing a candidate for the presidency of a publishing company, and she licked her fingers after finishing her entrée. In effect, she licked her way out of a job. I have interviewed many job candidates over breakfast and lunch. Most observed our rubrics, but a number did not, with devastating results—loss of a job opportunity. Here's just one example that highlights the benefits of adhering to the rules:

PHONE AND SKYPE INTERVIEWS

The phone/Skype interview is a standard part of the job-hunting process because of the large number of candidates applying for posted jobs, and because of the distance between candidate and interviewer. When a human resources director has a hundred applicants for one position, he makes the first cut using the candidate's résumé and information from other sources like social media. After the list is narrowed to a handful of candidates, the next step is to evaluate them with a phone or Skype interview. The process is sometimes called a "phone screening." Company execs claim the phone and Skype interview process is cost-effective.

These interviews usually are not conversations, but interrogations leaving candidates with little time to do more than answer rapid-fire questions. The interviewer has a list of questions on her desk and wants to run through them as quickly as possible. It is akin to a robotic procedure. The candidate is rarely given time to ask questions or offer more than a perfunctory answer to questions posed by the interviewer.

Try to avoid the phone screening by volunteering to come in for a personal interview, even if this means driving three hours each way to the company location. Face-to-face communication is what you need to move forward in the search process, and the phone interview gets in the way.

THE PURPOSE OF THE PHONE OR SKYPE INTERVIEW

The only purpose of the phone interview is to move your candidacy to the next step, the personal interview with the hiring manager. Nobody is ever hired because of a phone or Skype interview. It's just another step in the process. It permits the interviewer to screen out unqualified candidates and select finalists for personal interviews. It does not seem fair because the hiring manager or human resources director is holding the cards, but that's the way it is. You cannot change some things, so you must learn to live with them and do your best. The phone/Skype interview is one of them.

PHONE AND SKYPE INTERVIEW PREPARATION CHECKLIST

Talking on the phone comes naturally to some people, but most of us have a less-than-winning phone personality. However, with adequate preparation, anyone can accomplish the mission successfully. Prepare for the interview just as you would for a personal interview using this checklist:

- Find a private location for the interview, preferably your home office, where there will be absolute quiet.
- Eliminate traffic noise, barking dogs, crying babies, and music playing in the background. If there are two phones in your location, turn off the one not being used. The last thing you want is your alternate phone ringing during an interview.
- Avoid holding the interview in casual settings such as a restaurant, car, bar, or train. This is a business call, not a casual call. If there are barking dogs or clinking glasses in the background, surely the interviewer will hear the background noise, and you will be history. There are no second chances.
- Take the call at a table or desk where you can spread out documents for reference. You cannot do this while driving your car.

- Have your résumé, the job description, company information, and a written interview agenda listing your questions in front of you during the call. Also, have a tablet or notebook and a pen for note-taking. Handwrite notes instead of entering them on your desktop or laptop computer or smartphone. With today's sensitive audio technology, keyboard noise is distracting to the person on the other end of the line.
- Stay focused. On a separate sheet of paper, write the name of the company, the name and title of the person with whom you will be speaking, the date, time, and location of the interviewer.
- If the interviewer is located in another time zone, make the adjustment. If you are in New York and the interviewer is in Denver, there will be a two-hour time difference, so plan accordingly. If the call is scheduled for 9:00 a.m., Mountain Time, it will be 11:00 a.m. in New York. If you miscalculate the time difference and the caller gets your voice-mail instead of your voice, you will be history.
- Take the call dressed in business attire, because the way you dress sets the stage for your behavior. If you are dressed in a yoga outfit, your conversation could easily become too casual. The same applies to your body language. If you take the call with bare

feet resting on the top of your desk, you could slip into casual mode and begin using words like "awesome."

- Prepare to answer the question "Would you tell me something about yourself?"
- Select the three most important questions from your written agenda. Usually phone interviews are time-sensitive, so you want to make sure you have covered what is important *to you*. If the interviewer permits you to continue, go beyond the first three questions. Phone and Skype interviews, like personal interviews, should be a two-way conversation, which entitles you to be a proactive part of it. Your time is just as valuable as that of the interviewer.
- Have your laptop or desktop computer running with the company website on the screen.
- Smile during the interview. A smile on your face will relax you and make the tone more conversational. Think of the phone smile as virtual body language.
- If you are using a smartphone for the interview, conduct a test run to make sure the connection works.

NAVIGATING THE PHONE OR SKYPE INTERVIEW

Etiquette is everyone's concern. Should you address the interviewer by first or last name? Is it Mrs., Ms., Mr., Dr., or Mary? It is important to get it right. Here are some guidelines that follow the "listen first" rule.

If the interviewer introduces herself as "Mrs. Smith, human resources director," then you address her as Mrs. Smith throughout the interview. If she introduces herself as "Barbara Smith," call her Barbara. Never, under any circumstances, address a person using a nickname like "Barb" if she introduces herself as Barbara.

If the interviewer introduces himself as "Dr. William Ford," call him "Dr. Ford" throughout the interview. If the interviewer introduces himself as "Bob Ford, sales manager," call him Bob. If the interviewer introduces himself as "John Cupcake," call him John, not "Jack." A common error is to assume it is permissible to call a person by a shortened version of his or her name. I have found that the most frequently abused first name is "Robert." Why does everyone revert to "Bob"?

AFTER YOU SAY "HELLO"

The first thing to ask after you say hello and make introductory chitchat is "How much time do we have?" Knowing this will tell you how much time to spend answering questions, and how much time you have for asking questions that are on your interview agenda. Write the end time on a piece of paper and refer to it throughout the conversation. After learning the amount of time you have, tell the interviewer that you have several questions you would like to ask and find out when it would be appropriate to do so. It could be the last thing on the agenda, or the first.

CLOSING THE PHONE OR SKYPE INTERVIEW

The close is the same for the phone interview and the Skype interview. Learn the interviewer's phone number and e-mail address, say thank you for the interview, and ask for the job. The script for closing all interviews is the same: "Thank you for your time and consideration. What are the next steps in the process? I really would like to work here based on your answers to my questions and my research about your company. When can I start?"

After the interview, follow up by mailing or e-mailing a thank-you note.

FOLLOW-UP LETTERS

Courtesy dictates that you send a follow-up letter or e-mail to the interviewer(s) after every personal, phone, or Skype interview. This is a business document, so format it accordingly. Include the following items:

- A thank-you for the opportunity to interview for the position.
- A reaffirmation of your interest in the position and the company.
- A statement asking for the job.
- A post script (PS) after your closing signature. This is an action item such as "I will call you on Wednesday, March 10, to continue the conversation and answer any questions

you might have about my candidacy. What is the best time to call?

Send the follow-up letter by e-mail *and* by FedEx or UPS. I recommend using traditional services because hard copy has a tendency to stay on the recipient's desk. An e-mail doc disappears with a quick click, never to be seen again.

MOVING FORWARD

All types of interviews have one purpose: to see if you and the employer are on the same page for continuing the process. If you believe you are, pursue the job until you get an offer or a definite rejection. Do not let the process hang unresolved.

Midcareer workers come to the interview with a work history and an idea of what they need for compensation. The most frequent objections to one's candidacy are overqualification, compensation requirements that are too high, and lack of certain education requirements. In the next chapter, I'll discuss all of these issues.

CHAPTER TAKEAWAYS

- Build a friendly relationship with the interviewer. Friends hire friends.
- Body language is crucial nonverbal communication.
- Observe basic manners during interviews at restaurants.
- Control the interview process by

preparing a written agenda to share with the interviewer.

- Practice reciting answers to possible questions.
- The purpose of the phone or Skype interview is to move your candidacy to the next step, the personal interview.

PRINT AND DIGITAL RESOURCES

"12 Job Interview Tips for Women." www.EducatetoAdvance.com.

Covey, Stephen. *The 7 Habits of Highly Effective People: Powerful Lessons in Personal Courage.* Simon & Schuster, 2013.

Inc. magazine. www.inc.com/author/jeff-haden. Articles by Jeff Haden dealing with the interview process.

Kuhnke, Elizabeth. *Body Language for Dummies.* Wiley, 2012.

CHAPTER 14

OVERCOMING OBJECTIONS TO YOUR CANDIDACY

Job candidates who have been fired or laid off frequently report that potential employers voice three objections to their candidacy:

1. Sorry! You are overqualified.
2. Sorry! Your compensation requirements are too high.
3. Sorry! You do not have the education requirements for this job.

Sometimes these are unrealistic or perceptual objections. Sometimes they are accurate. Whatever the case, you must be prepared to deal with these three objections during interviews.

SORRY! YOU ARE OVERQUALIFIED

The overqualification objection is usually raised during the personal interview, and most candidates never see it coming. They assume that the hiring manger would be delighted to have an experienced candidate who could be productive on day one.

A typical situation finds the candidate, a let-go worker at the director level, interviewing for a job titled "director." It seems to be a lateral move, so the candidate feels confident that this will work. Toward the end of the interview, the hiring manager says, "Mary, you have all of the qualifications listed in the job description, and there is no doubt you can do the job. However, you have more experience than we need for this job. In short, I think you are overqualified." This jarring statement leaves you scrambling for a lucid response. Here are possible responses you can offer to the hiring manager when this happens to you.

RESPONSES TO THE OVERQUALIFICATION OBJECTION

Your first reaction might be disappointment and a gut verbal response and body language that seal your fate: "That's ridiculous. Why should my experience disqualify me? My twenty years in this industry should put me at the top of your list."

Here are some more productive responses that might overcome this objection and keep the conversation moving forward:

- "Thank you for recognizing my background and experience. Moving forward, I think the depth and breadth of my experience would be valuable to your cause. I could help take some of the pressure from your job and make your life easier. Combine your knowledge of the company culture and operations with my depth and breadth of experience, and together we could take this department to a higher level. I think we would make a great team."

- "I understand why you might feel that I'm overqualified, and I'm flattered that you have given that much thought to my candidacy. However, rest assured that I will not use my experience to steamroll your status and authority in the department. I'm not after your job. I'm looking for work-life balance and believe that I can find that here. I think we would make a great team."

- "I might bring more to the table than you need right now, but I assure you that I'm not looking for just another paycheck until I find something better. I've targeted your company for its stability, profitability, and employee-friendly culture. I think we would make a great team."

- "I'm looking for more than a paycheck and job title. And my overqualifications? You could use my experience to your advantage. In addition, I like you personally, and I think we could make a great team."

- "I can understand why you might feel that way. However, my qualifications, particularly in the technology sphere, could be of value to the company going forward. Technology is moving at lightning speed, and I can help the company keep up with the rest of the pack. In addition, I reviewed your profile on LinkedIn and believe our tech skills are complementary. I think we would make a great team."

You may have noticed that each one of the responses is positive and includes a statement of working together as a team. When a potential boss is confronted by a candidate whose background, experience, and qualifications exceed hers, the survival instinct kicks in. Unknowingly, she could see you as a competitor for her job. Human beings are in survival mode every waking hour without even realizing it.

The best way to allay fears of the potential boss is to research her background and experience to search for common and complementary attributes and interests. Articulate that at the beginning of the interview to begin building a friendly relationship. Remember one of the cardinal rules of job hunting: friends hire friends.

SORRY! YOUR COMPENSATION REQUIREMENTS EXCEED OUR BUDGET

Compensation is a serious issue for let-go workers who are job hunting. The expectation is that you should get what you had in your last job, or more. Assume the base salary in your last job, business development manager, was $95,000. Going forward into job-hunting mode, that is the number you have in mind when you begin talking with potential employers. However, is this a realistic expectation?

FACTORS AFFECTING COMPENSATION

Research indicates that salary expectations can be age-related. Workers under forty-five, those in early midcareer, are more optimistic than older workers that they will find acceptable compensation packages. The reason is related to the amount of compensation in question. Younger workers usually have lower daily expenses and can afford to take a lower salary. Their tendency to take less makes their candidacy more appealing to potential employers. Workers over forty-five have more expenses and require more compensation to meet their needs.

For laid-off or fired workers seeking new employment, there is another factor at play, ego. Being let go is a devastating event, and laid-off workers subconsciously make every effort to salvage their self-respect. For example, when a midcareer worker is laid off from his manager-level job paying a base of $110,000, he expects to make that much or more going forward. His pride will not permit him to think it is okay to accept a job paying $90,000.

When my job candidates are evaluating an opportunity, I counsel them to be reasonable, not greedy, to remember that compensation is negotiable, and to accept the fact that nothing is guaranteed.

RESPONSES TO THE COMPENSATION OBJECTION

Facing reality will save much time and angst and will hasten the job-hunting process. There is nothing that will jeopardize receiving a job offer more than believing "I will not take less than $105,000, no matter what. That's what I made in my last job, and that's what I'm entitled to get in my next job." That attitude reflects an entitlement mentality and does not match the reality of the workplace. Here's a true-life example of what can happen if you are delusional about compensation.

JANET FROM PHILADELPHIA

One day in early January, Janet, a midcareer worker, came to my office. She was well dressed, articulate, and exuded an air of confidence. After pleasant introductory remarks, she told me that she had been working for a software company as an outbound sales representative for the past ten years and thought that she had earned a ticket to long-term employment. However, one afternoon the human resources director called her in for a chat. She told Janet the company was being purchased by a competitor. It was an asset acquisition, and therefore her job was being eliminated. Janet was laid off that day and never saw it coming. Now she was on the street looking for another sales position. Her base salary was $130,000, and commissions averaged $80,000 per year. She asked me to help her find a sales position in the technology industry.

I asked Janet about her compensation expectations, and she told me she would not accept a penny less than her previous base. She expected a base of $130,000 and commissions that would average $80,000 per year, the same package as her last job. Knowing compensation numbers for such a position with companies in the area, I told Janet that her expectation was unrealistic because positions of that type were paying an average base of $100,000 and that commission plans varied greatly. She did not like what I told her and gave me a litany of reasons for her expectations. Four months later, Janet called to see what was happening. I told her that I did not have anything meeting her expectations and urged her to become more reasonable. In December of that same year, she came to my office again to inquire about job opportunities. It was almost a full year since she had been laid off, and she was still unemployed. Once again, I told her what the market was paying, and once again she would not lower her compensation demands. I could not persuade Janet to become more reasonable. After implying that I did not know my job, she left the office in a huff. She was still unemployed after almost a year of job hunting because she was delusional about her worth in the job market at that time.

Janet's story illustrates two points: that workers must be prepared to make compromises on compensation based on market conditions, and that workers must do their homework about compensation levels for their type of job. What Janet forgot is that the job market had changed since she joined her last employer ten years earlier.

Here are three compensation rubrics for all let-go workers to follow as they enter job-hunting mode:

THREE KEY COMPENSATION RUBRICS

1. Be open to compromise on compensation.
2. We do not live in an entitlement business culture. There is no guarantee that you will maintain or exceed rank, title, and compensation once you have reached a certain point in your career. It does not work that way in America.
3. Research compensation levels for your job type and rank remembering that compensation frequently varies with geography. A managerial position might average $150,000 per year in California, where the cost of living is very high, and $120,000 in Maine, where the cost of living is much lower.

SORRY! YOU DO NOT HAVE THE EDUCATION REQUIREMENTS FOR THIS JOB

It happens like this. You graduated from college with an AA, BA, or MA and proceeded to an entry-level job in your field of expertise. You work with this employer for five years and receive two promotions. Now you are working at the managerial level. Unexpectedly, one of your competitors comes to you with a job offer for a senior management-level position and an increase in compensation that puts you in the low-six-figure income bracket. "Nice," you think. "All of this without an MBA. Getting that college degree was a smart move on my part." So far, so good. You get married and have two children whose care takes all of your nonworking hours. Ten years later, you are still with the same company, have been promoted to a director-level position, and are making a base salary of $135,000, plus bonus and eligibility for the company profit-sharing program. Life is good. Then one ordinary day it happens. Your company is purchased by a competitor, and your position is eliminated.

Now you are out looking and have had only two interviews after three months of job searching. During an interview, the hiring manager tells you that your education background, especially in technology applications and project management, is very weak compared to other candidates. He asks if you have taken any professional development courses over the past ten years. Your negative answer seals your fate. It is not that you were unaware of changes taking place in job requirements. You saw it coming, but you just did not have the time to update your skills.

THE EDUCATION SOLUTION

Much has changed since you received your last college degree, especially on the technology front. Younger and less experienced candidates have education credentials reflecting the change in workplace requirements. As soon as possible after being let go, begin taking certified online courses to plug the gap, particularly in the technology area. Make sure that your coursework provides written certification that you can present to potential employers. You can find certified online courses by conducting a Google search.

In my recruiting business, I have noted that many employers are requiring candidates for senior-level management positions to have project management professional training. It is commonly called PMP certification. PMP training is available online from a number of sources. One is the Project Management Institute (PMI), the world's largest source for training. It boasts having five hundred thousand members and 280 local chapters. Another online source for certification is Villanova University.

MOVING FORWARD

Before having your first phone or personal interview, plan how you will deal with the three most frequently encountered issues for midcareer job candidates: overqualification, compensation, and education. Do your homework on all three issues, because one or all could be part of your discussion with a hiring manager.

When you reach the job-offer stage after overcoming objections to your candidacy, you could be confronted with issues spanning everything from base salary to noncompete requirements. We'll review all of this in the next chapter and provide guidelines about how to negotiate all parts of a job offer. This is an important part of the process, so stick around.

CHAPTER TAKEAWAYS

- Compensation levels for similar jobs will vary with geography.
- Overqualification is frequently a matter of perception on the part of the hiring manager.
- A certain compensation level is not guaranteed because of your experience or what you made in your last job.
- Technology moves fast in the workplace. Stay updated by taking online courses that carry certification.

PRINT AND DIGITAL RESOURCES

Bureau of Labor Statistics, www.bls.gov. Check this site for general compensation information.

Economic Research Institute, www.erieri.com. See ERI for compensation analysis by job and geography.

Profound Marketing Intelligence, www.profound.com.

Project Management Academy, www.projectmanagementacademy.net. The Academy offers online PMP certification.

The United States Census Bureau, www.census.gov. This site will keep you updated on job demographics and requirements.

Villanova University, www.villanovau.com/PMP. Villanova offers online PMP certification.

CHAPTER 15
NEGOTIATING A JOB OFFER

How many times have you heard on the street, "It costs too much"? This refrain usually pertains to the cost of goods and services. Sometimes it signals the beginning of the bargaining process. Take the street vendor in a big city like Chicago, Los Angeles, London, or New Delhi selling knock-off products like Ralph Lauren-labeled clothing or Coach-labeled purses or wallets. You don't pay the asking price. You negotiate. The process is much the same when talking with a hiring manager or human resources director about a job offer. Many let-go candidates leave money on the table because they do not realize that the compensation part of a job offer is negotiable, except for government jobs that have a grade level and a corresponding compensation level. Moreover, let-go candidates are under pressure to bring home another paycheck and are inclined to accept whatever the first offer might be.

THE PROCESS FOR NEGOTIATING BASE SALARY AND BONUS

Think of the employer's office as a street vendor's stand where everything is negotiable: base salary, bonus, and possibly benefits. When you walk into the employer's office, whether it's a formal corporate office or a contractor's trailer at a commercial building site, imagine you are back on the street bargaining with a vendor of knock-off products. Here's what can happen.

BASE SALARY

The employer's HR person makes a base salary offer for a sales director's position. The human resources director says, "Tom, we are thrilled at the prospect of your joining us. I know you will be happy here. We'd like to make you an offer that consists of three parts: base salary, bonus, and benefits. Your starting base salary will be $120,000. Your bonus is 25 percent of base salary for exceeding your revenue goal by more than 10 percent. Your benefits include term life insurance equal to your base salary, three weeks of paid vacation, shared-cost medical and dental insurance for you and your family, long-term disability insurance, and a contributory IRA plan that becomes effective after ninety days. It's a generous offer, Tom.

Here it is in writing. Could you let us know tomorrow when you can start?" You thank the human resources director and tell her you will come back tomorrow at ten after reviewing the offer.

Knowing the offer is low, you begin to compose a counteroffer. You have done your homework and know that comparable jobs in the area pay more than what was offered. In your last job, you had been making $140,000 base, plus a 10 percent bonus for meeting revenue goals, and benefits comparable to those in your new offer. Your research confirms that your evaluation is valid.

You really like the new job, the company, and its culture. This is a good place to be, and you decide to work out a compromise. You decide that you will try to negotiate a minimum base of $130,000, all factors considered, *including the fact that you have been laid off and the missing paycheck is beginning to take its toll on your pocketbook.* You are okay with the bonus and benefits. However, you would like to take an online course for PMP certification, the cost of which is $3,000.

You arrive at the office at ten and sit down with the HR director. Here is how you might present a counteroffer:

I am flattered that you made me an offer to join the company. However, I have some thoughts about the base salary and one of the benefits. Based on my research for comparable jobs

and considering my experience, I believe that a $150,000 base would be equitable. I'm okay with the bonus. Also, I would like to continue my professional development by taking an online course for PMP certification, which would benefit the company. The cost is $3,000, and I would appreciate your including that in my compensation package.

The HR director can do one of three things: reject your counteroffer entirely, offer a compromise on your proposed base and the tuition, or concede entirely on your proposed base and tuition request. You must be prepared ahead of time for all subsequent counteroffers. Before you go into the office to negotiate, have a number in mind for the base you would accept, and a compromise on the tuition. If the HR director counters with a base of $125,000 and $2,000 on the tuition, you must be prepared to accept, counteroffer, or decline.

Does it really happen that way? You bet. Just a week before writing this, I presented a candidate to one of my clients for a director-level job that carried a base of $120,000, a $5,000 sign-on bonus, and $10,000 for relocation expenses. The candidate counteroffered, and the company hiring manager came back with this final package: $125,000 base, a $10,000 sign-on bonus, and $15,000 for relocation expenses. He had offered the max that the company salary structure would allow. The result? The candidate said, "No, thank you," and accepted a job from another company offering a $150,000 base.

BONUS

Like base salary, a bonus can be negotiated. In fact, companies could be more flexible on bonus than on base salary. In some companies, certain workers receive a fixed bonus based on total company performance; in other companies, the bonus is based on individual or departmental performance. An exception is a bonus, or a commission as it is frequently called, for workers in sales.

Workers in sales receive a commission based on attaining revenue goals. For example, an outside full-time sales representative selling into the school market for John Wiley Publishing Company might receive 5 percent on all sales after reaching an established revenue quota of $2,000,000. If the sales rep delivers $2,800,000 ($800,000 over the revenue goal), the commission would be $40,000. If the sales representative's base salary was $60,000, the total income from base salary and commission would be $100,000, plus the value of the benefits, usually 30 percent of base, making the total package $118,000.

There are as many bonus and commission plans as there are companies. In small- to medium-sized companies, the bonus or commission plans are frequently negotiable. Large companies are usually not open to negotiation. The bottom line is this: always try to negotiate a higher bonus or commission. If the offer says the bonus or commission plan is 5 percent, ask for 8 percent. If the employer says no, ask for 6 percent. There is nothing to lose by asking. Your potential employer will probably appreciate that financial reward is an incentive for you, as it should be.

Everything monetary in a job offer is negotiable. In all of my experience in the staffing industry, I have never experienced a situation where the company did not have some flexibility on the money part of an offer.

BENEFITS PACKAGES

Traditional company benefits include medical and dental insurance, term life insurance, disability insurance, retirement plans such as an IRA (Individual Retirement Account), paid vacations, paid sick days, paid holidays, paid family leave, professional development education costs, tuition assistance for children, and unemployment compensation insurance.

Candidates often forget that benefits add to their compensation and to company expenses, as well. Benefits are not "free." The entire benefits package must be monetized and added to the base salary in order to determine the *true* value of the offer. The current accepted price of all benefits to the employee averages 30 percent of base salary. For example, assume the base salary is $100,000. Add 30 percent for benefits, and your job is really worth $130,000. And if there is a stock option benefit and a company contributory IRA plan, you must include those items to arrive at your true compensation.

WHICH BENEFITS ARE NEGOTIABLE?

A retirement program such as a company-sponsored IRA or Roth IRA will most likely become effective after you work with the company six to twelve months and cannot be negotiated. Paid holidays, paid sick leave, family leave, life insurance, disability insurance, and medical/dental insurance will not be negotiable. If they were, the company conceivably could have a different plan for each employee. However, vacation time is sometimes negotiable, or it can be used as a trade-off for other benefits.

Your most important benefits are medical insurance and disability insurance, because one never knows when illness or an accident will strike. Medical and long-term disability insurance benefits are almost as important as base salary. Of course, these benefits have even greater importance if you are married and have children.

HEALTHCARE

Prior to March 23, 2010, when the Affordable Care Act (Obamacare) became effective, a company would say, "Here is our medical and hospital plan. The plan is through Aetna, and your benefits and costs are contained in this booklet." That is no longer the case. Multiple rules and regulations have been imposed on companies depending on their legal status, revenue, number of employees, and other factors. It's no longer one size fits all.

ACA has become a highly politicized piece of legislation, and as such there will be revisions going forward. A prudent thing to do now, however, would be to go online and research this important topic yourself because new information is becoming available every day through a number of different sources. Review the official website at www.healthcare.gov. Also, Google "Obamacare" and "Affordable Care Act," and you will find a number of sites providing valuable information.

Healthcare benefits are a matter for serious discussion with potential employers, so do not hesitate to ask for explanations about your options. The human resources director will be familiar with the provisions and will share them with you. Healthcare benefits, which include medical, dental, and eye-care insurance, will not be negotiable.

PROFIT SHARING

Some companies offer profit sharing in addition to, or in lieu of, a bonus plan. The higher the company profits in any given fiscal year, the higher the profit sharing for each employee. Some companies have a profit-sharing program based on total company revenue. If you do not see "profit sharing" in the job offer, always ask if you might be eligible to participate in the program. Most companies have a profit-sharing plan for their key executives but might offer it as an incentive for midcareer workers who are applying for a management position. Some companies, like Starbucks or Texas Instruments, offer profit sharing for all employees regardless of rank.

STOCK OPTIONS

Another benefit in publicly traded companies is the stock option plan. This benefit permits workers to purchase shares of company stock below market price. The number of shares an employee receives is directly proportionate to rank and length of time with the company. Presidents get more that vice presidents, who get more than directors, who get more than managers, and so on.

Companies offering attractive stock option plans usually have a workforce that is stable and long-lasting. I have noted that companies offering stock purchase plans retain workers for longer periods. For example, Apple provides a discounted stock purchase plan for its workers, which has created many millionaires. I know Apple employees who joined the company in 1980 and are still there, primarily because of the stock purchase plan.

Negotiating stock option plans is easier with a smaller company than it is with an established company like Google or Apple. The risk of continued long-term employment with a start-up or small company is greater than that with an established company. For this reason, such small companies are more amenable to offering generous stock options to compensate workers for the added risk.

TUITION FOR PROFESSIONAL DEVELOPMENT

Going forward, every worker will need to update their skills through professional development courses. They may be certification courses, MA degrees, or even MBAs. Companies are usually open to including tuition reimbursement for such professional development because they benefit from your added knowledge and skills. Always ask for this benefit.

WHAT IS YOUR JOB REALLY WORTH?

Salary fluctuates with the economic cycle, workforce demand for a particular skill, and geography. For example, in a very robust economy where annual GDP growth is near 4 percent, compensation in a high-demand field, like information technology, will be higher than it would be when the country is in a steep recession.

One cannot reliably predict what a particular job will be worth in the future because of these variables, but there are many resources, both print and digital, for midcareer workers to use as a guide. On the print side, the most valuable resource is the *Occupational Outlook Handbook,* which lists average salaries for jobs in a particular industry.

Periodically, conduct online searches for salary information because numbers change and new sources of information are always emerging. Review the following sites, remembering that the numbers you find are *estimates,* not firm and final data:

SOURCES FOR DETERMINING COMPENSATION

Salary.com, www.Salary.com.
PayScale, www.PayScale.com.
Bureau of Labor Statistics, www.bls.gov.

SIX-FIGURE BASE SALARY JOBS

To put the compensation factor in context for midcareer workers who are negotiating job offers, I studied numbers released by the Bureau of Labor Statistics and confirmed by the *Wall Street Journal*. Here are the top twelve jobs paying six-figure base salaries:

MEDIAN ANNUAL WAGES FOR OCCUPATIONS WITH SIX-FIGURE BASE SALARIES

1. Physicians and Surgeons: $187,200
2. Chief Executive Officers: $175,110
3. Dentists: $158,310
4. Nurse Anesthetists: $157,140
5. Architectural and Engineering Managers: $132,800
6. Computer and Information Systems Managers: $131,600
7. Petroleum Engineers: $129,990
8. Pharmacists: $121,500
9. Natural Sciences Managers: $120,160
10. Podiatrists: $119,340
11. Marketing and Sales Managers: $119,280
12. Financial Managers: $117,000

Remember that these are median income numbers, which means that half are below and half are above the median income number stated.

Only twenty-seven occupations pay six-figure incomes. Management, healthcare, and engineering jobs account for twenty-two of the twenty-seven highest-paying occupations. Variables that still come into play are geography, total company revenue, education, and number of years of experience.

COMPANY COMPENSATION PARAMETERS

When negotiating base salary, bonus, and benefits, it is important to remember that the company must work within established parameters in order to keep peace in its workforce and maintain profitability. For example, assume that a company has a staff of twenty customer service representatives working from offices in Scottsdale, Arizona, all making a base salary in the $45,000 to $55,000 range depending upon length of service, experience, expertise, and education level. In that situation, it would be impossible to negotiate beyond $55,000. There would be a breakdown of trust if a customer service rep with two years of experience and making $40,000 learns that a new employee is making more. How will you learn the salary range for a particular position? Ask the director of human resources or the hiring authority with whom you are negotiating.

EVALUATING THE SMALL-PRINT CLAUSES IN A JOB OFFER

Frequently job offers contain a number of clauses that are overlooked because they are written in small print and in legal jargon. They just don't *seem* that important. However, it is critically important that you read and understand the small-print provisions. They could affect your employment status, both short and long term. Here are the most frequent small-print provisions found in a job offer:

TERMINATION-AT-WILL CLAUSE

Many job offers contain this provision. It means that the company, for no reason whatsoever, can terminate your employment. It can happen any day of the week when your boss or the human resources manager calls you into the office and says this is your last day working there. The real reason why you are being sacked could be that you did not perform up to expectations, and the most expeditious way to terminate your employment is to use business-speak, euphemisms like "downsizing," "rightsizing," or "reorganizing." Your job is not an entitlement, and in addition, you have no statutory right to your job.

Provisions of the termination-at-will clause will vary by state. Research the issue by Googling "Termination at will" and adding the state in which your company is located. If you want to be absolutely sure about how this provision will affect you, consult an attorney.

You can refuse to sign a job offer containing this clause, but your candidacy could be rejected because of it. I advise you to sign the offer agreeing to this clause and move on.

NON-COMPETE CLAUSE

This clause means that you agree not to take a job with an employer that would be in competition with your company after you leave the company voluntarily or after being fired or laid off. Like the termination-at-will clause, state law governs the non-compete provision. Some states, like California, prohibit employers from using the non-compete clause in employment agreements.

Usually, this provision is time-sensitive. Read the clause carefully. The non-compete time period could be limited to one year after separation from the company, or it could be forever. There is a geographical component to this clause, as well. For example, the clause may prohibit you from working for a competitor located within a three-mile radius of your employer, or throughout the United States.

There is a disconcerting trend for employers to include stringent non-compete clauses and to increase strict enforcement by filing lawsuits against former employees who violate the agreement. Unfortunately, courts in a number of jurisdictions have ruled in favor of the company, resulting in a severe fine against the employee. A recent article in the *New York Times* cited research about this controversial employment clause. The most disturbing news is that employers using the non-compete have expanded its scope to prohibit an employee from taking a job with another company working in the same or a related industry, or an employer whose operating procedures and infrastructure are similar. This means that if a worker is employed as an editorial director for a publishing company located in New York City, that worker is prohibited from taking a similar job with another publisher located anywhere in the United States for a stipulated number of years . . . or forever! Opponents of the non-compete argue that an employer has no right to control a worker's career and income, and we agree. The *Times* research cited a number of instances where an employee left the company for another job because it offered an increase in compensation and a move up the corporate hierarchy only to be served with a lawsuit to enforce a non-compete agreement. What such unscrupulous employers attempt to do is freeze workers into one job with one company during their entire working life.

If a job offer includes a non-compete clause that prohibits you from ever moving on, *do not sign it*. If the employer will not negotiate this out of the offer, walk away from that company. However, if the job, the company, and compensation are in sync with your plans and you really do want the job, consult an attorney for advice.

There is an entire body of law governing the non-compete agreement. Google "Non-compete agreement" and add your state for current legislation.

DRUG AND ALCOHOL TESTING CLAUSE

There is a growing trend for companies to require a drug and alcohol screening as a condition of employment. Employers outsource these preemployment tests. The potential employer always pays the bill for these screenings.

Refusing to submit to the preemployment drug or alcohol screening will jeopardize your chances of employment. If you have nothing to hide, agree to the screening. However, what about Alaska, California, Colorado, Maine, Massachusetts, Nevada, Oregon, Washington, and the District of Columbia, where recreational use of marijuana is legal? Employers in these states still require the preemployment screening and do not permit or condone use of federally defined illegal drugs and alcohol while on the job. If you live in one of these states, do not assume that employers permit the use of controlled substances. If you test positive for marijuana or any other controlled substance, you will not be hired.

Employers are very serious about this. For example, a sign written in bold letters on the entrance door of every Home Depot store in every state reads:

Federal law controls the use of recreational marijuana and other controlled substances, not state law, even though some states passed legislation permitting it. There is pending federal and state legislation on this. Don't test the waters. Agree to the drug provision, or you will not be hired.

THE CREDIT-CHECK CLAUSE

The credit-check clause could be in the job offer for a number of reasons, the foremost of which is that employers do not want to deal with wage garnishment requirements. In addition, an employer may believe there is something lacking in a candidate's sense of responsibility if they have a history of unresolved debt or bankruptcy. If you have any long-term debt or substantial credit-card debt, try to resolve these issues while in the search process. Do not object to the credit-check clause. It could cost you a job. Just sign it and report to work.

THE STARTING-DATE CLAUSE

A job offer will contain a start date. For example, assume you received the job offer on December 5 and it contains a start date of December 10. It sounds so official that you could be afraid of rejection if you do not agree to report on December

10 . . . even though you had a prepaid trip scheduled to see your ill mother halfway across the country. Do not fear the start-date clause. All employers consider this a negotiable item.

THE RELOCATION CLAUSE

If a company offers you a job based in another location, the job offer may contain a relocation clause. The terms vary widely from company to company, but usually they state how much the company will pay to relocate you, your dependents, your spouse or partner, and your household goods. There is much flexibility here, and companies are willing to negotiate the terms of relocation. Relocation is a highly negotiable item, and most companies will permit working remotely, even if the job is a presidency or vice presidency.

HOW TO REJECT A JOB OFFER

There is no rule that says you must accept a job offer, even if you have been laid off or fired. Some employers believe they can pick up a midcareer, laid-off worker "on the cheap" and will make a ridiculous offer. When that happens, reject the offer, because there are always other employers who will treat you fairly. How do you reject an offer? There are two ways to reject an offer after negotiations reach an impasse;

1. Tell the hiring manager that the job sucks and that you would be dumb to accept it.
2. Thank the hiring manager for considering your candidacy and

wish him success finding an alternate candidate. Close the conversation by telling him that your rejection is nothing personal; it just does not provide what you need at this time.

The downside of using the first method is that you have severed the possibility of ever being considered for a future job opportunity at that company. In addition, the person on the other end of your message could move on to another company, and guess what. You will find no job opportunities at his new company.

The second method is the route to select when declining a job offer. It says that you have a sense of business etiquette, maturity, and good judgment. Your candidacy for another job opportunity will remain alive if you use the second method.

MOVING FORWARD

The cost for most products and services we purchase is negotiable. The same is true for base salary, bonus, and certain benefits found in job offers. American workers tend to believe that what is stated in a job offer is firm and final and never think to negotiate a better deal. Just the opposite is true.

Dr. Chester Karrass, author of four books on negotiating, tells how you can negotiate a job offer in his book *In Business As in Life, You Don't Get What You Deserve, You Get What You Negotiate*. Make time to read this book and two others by Karrass, titled *Give and Take* and *The Negotiating Game*. These are classics, and

Dr. Karrass will tell you what can be negotiated, how much can be negotiated, and how it is done.

Another step in the career-rebuilding process is to determine where you would like to work. There are options like working in a large multinational corporation or a small neighborhood business. As an alternative, you could start your own business or purchase a franchise. All are viable options, and we'll explore them in Part III, "Finding Your Spot in the Workplace." It's coming up next.

CHAPTER TAKEAWAYS

- The base salary part of the job offer is always negotiable.
- Drug and alcohol screenings are not negotiable.
- Make negotiations a friendly event.
- Be reasonable, not greedy.
- Decline a job offer politely.
- Do not sign a job agreement if it contains a highly restrictive non-compete clause. Walk away from the job or consult an attorney for advice.

PRINT AND DIGITAL RESOURCES

Carnegie, Dale, and Associates. *How to Win Friends and Influence People*. Simon & Schuster, 2012.

Karrass, Chester. *In Business As in Life, You Don't Get What You Deserve, You Get What You Negotiate*. Stanford St. Press, 1996.

The official United States healthcare site is www.healthcare.gov.

PART III

Finding Your Spot in the Workplace

I can get plenty of first violinists. But to find someone who can play the second fiddle with enthusiasm . . . that's a problem. And if we have no second fiddle, we have no harmony.

—Leonard Bernstein, the late conductor of the

New York Philharmonic Orchestra

CHAPTER 16

WORKING FOR A LARGE COMPANY OR A SMALL BUSINESS

Moving forward in the process of rebuilding your career, you have several choices: to work for a large company or a small business in the private sector, or to work in a government job. Working in a local, state, or federal government job has its own rules and challenges, so I have devoted Chapter 18 to that topic. In addition, you have the option to start your own business or to purchase a franchise. Each initiative has its own challenges. Accordingly, I devoted all of Chapter 17 to these topics.

Most laid-off workers lacking professional experience in specialized areas like medicine, law, or education, or who have no desire to start their own businesses, will in all probability exercise the default choice: working for a large company like Boeing, General Electric, or Facebook; or for a small business, one with fewer than five hundred employees. One is not better than the other. Large companies, called corporations if they have publicly traded stock, have much to offer including generous salaries and benefits like a contributory IRA and stock options, while small businesses require less work experience and formal education and provide a more relaxed work environment. Pursuing one or the other is a matter of personal preference.

When midcareer workers are laid off or fired, they can continue working in the same industry or explore other industries. Workers usually exercise the second option when the industry where they spent the last fifteen years or more is undergoing a cyclical or structural change. For example, many editors, sales managers, marketing managers, and IT directors working for K-12 or higher-education publishing companies have been laid off as instructional materials are moving from print to digital delivery. Rather than continuing to pursue jobs in a changing industry, these midcareer workers have changed focus, opting to seek employment in other industries. Take Judy, a regional sales manager in Chicago for a prominent K-12 publisher. When her job was eliminated, she came to me for counseling on the

K-12 publishing industry and to explore sales manager positions with companies in other industries. After conducting her own due diligence and exploring industries in Chicago where she could transfer her sales skills, Judy decided to enter the real estate business, part of the broadly defined shelter industry. Now she is selling condos in the high-end market in downtown Chicago. She loves her new job in the shelter industry and is making a substantial six-figure income.

Contrary to street opinion, the majority of civilian workers are employed by small businesses, not large corporations like Amazon (647,000 employees) or Walmart (2.3 million employees). Regardless of their size, however, all companies fall into one of the major industries that keep our workforce employed. What are some of these industries? What are some of the companies in each industry? How large, or small, are they? Let's have a look at some of the major industries, broadly defined, because they provide plentiful job opportunities for midcareer. Here are some of the industries employing a large number of workers:

MAJOR US INDUSTRIES

- The Clothing Industry
- The Education Industry
- The Energy Industry
- The Financial Industry
- The Food Industry
- The Healthcare Industry
- The Insurance Industry
- The Petroleum Industry
- The Shelter Industry
- The Technology Industry
- The Transportation Industry

In addition, there are other fast-growing industries to explore, like the "Green Industry," which is concerned with making our local environment and planet Earth a more healthful and desirable place to live. The *Occupational Outlook Handbook* lists the following jobs associated with this industry:

- Biofuels Production Workers
- Biomass Energy Production Workers
- Energy Auditors
- Geothermal Energy Production Workers
- Hydroelectric Energy Production Workers
- Methane/Landfill Gas Production Workers
- Solar Energy Production Workers
- Weatherization Installers and Technicians
- Wind Energy Production Workers
- Environmental Restoration Planners
- Redevelopment Specialists and Site Managers
- Fuel Cell Technicians
- Industrial Ecologists
- Water Resource Specialists

Does "green" sound interesting? Get the *Handbook* and read more about these exciting and interesting opportunities.

TOP INDUSTRIES AND COMPANIES

The workplace is vast, and it takes a considerable amount of time to determine where to begin looking for a new job. First, learn the industry that best suits your interests and aptitude and then look for companies within that industry. As you begin your exploration, consider the following criteria: industry importance to the US economy as a whole; the social value of its products and services; the projected industry rate of growth as measured by Standard & Poor's, a financial services research company; the job opportunities the particular industry provides now.

Here are some industries I consider a cut above the rest based on the criteria listed above, on personal experience working in the staffing business, on research, and on anecdotal information from a variety of sources:

- Education, especially the online sector and study abroad sector
- Energy, particularly solar and nuclear
- Healthcare/Pharmaceuticals, especially remote technology for diagnostic procedures, DNA testing and prognosis, and cancer treatments
- Insurance, new policies to cover cybercrime
- Security, protection against personal, corporate, and government hacking

- Technology, especially artificial intelligence (AI) and robotics
- Transportation, self-driving automobiles and trucks

All are growth industries, and, taken as a group, they employ tens of millions of workers. These seven industries offer endless job opportunities for all let-go workers who are moving forward in their careers and considering alternate industries for employment. Here is a brief review of each industry to set you moving in the right direction. Do remember that many of the job skills and leadership skills you acquired in your previous position are transferable to a job in a new industry.

THE EDUCATION INDUSTRY

The broadly defined education industry consists of for-profit schools like DeVry Institute, Highlights for Children, McGraw-Hill Education, Pearson, Scholastic, and the University of Phoenix. There are nonprofits, too, like Educational Testing Service (ETS), Measured Progress, and The College Board.

These companies are scattered throughout the United States and offer jobs spanning the entire range of specialties like sales, marketing, finance, editorial, product development, information technology, and human resources. Workers in the education industry find much job satisfaction because the products are instructional materials and services for K-12, higher education, and adult education, which benefit individuals and the country as a whole. Some companies in this industry are:

- **Educational Testing Service (ETS),** www.ets.org
- **Highlights for Children,** www.highlights.com
- **McGraw-Hill Education,** www.mcgrawhill.com
- **Measured Progress,** www.measuredprogress.org
- **Pearson,** www.pearson.com
- **Scholastic,** www.scholastic.com

THE ENERGY INDUSTRY

The energy industry is massive and includes petroleum companies, natural gas companies, LPG companies, nuclear energy companies, solar energy companies, and many others. This industry employs millions of workers in technical jobs that require very specific STEM (science, technology, engineering, and mathematics) skills and nontechnical jobs requiring sales, marketing, and finance skills. This industry is noted for paying above-average wages and offering attractive benefits. Here are a several large companies to explore for job opportunities across the country:

- **ExxonMobil,** www.exxonmobile.com
- **Chevron,** www.chevron.com
- **Southwestern Energy,** www.southwesternenergy.com
- **ConocoPhillips,** www.conocophillips.com

THE PETROLEUM INDUSTRY AND WOMEN

According to a recent Bureau of Labor Statistics (BLS) report, 46 percent of the new jobs in the petroleum business have gone to women. No, that is not a mistake. Check this out at www.bls.gov. Once again, the numbers tell it all. Regardless of your gender, religion, race, or ethnicity, go for any job in an industry that interests you. Work stereotypes are falling fast, and the playing field is quite level. Don't fall for the hype. Always look at the numbers before drawing any conclusions.

THE HEALTHCARE AND PHARMACEUTICAL INDUSTRIES

These two industries include pharmaceutical companies that produce prescription drugs and over-the-counter medications, medical device manufacturers, hospitals, and physical therapy treatment centers, just to name a few. These are robust industries that will see exponential growth as millions of baby boomers reach their senior years and require more frequent health services. Here are some of the more robust companies in this industry:

- **Cleveland Clinic,** www.my.clevelandclinic.org
- **Johnson & Johnson,** www.jnj.com
- **Medtronic,** www.medtronic.com
- **Pfizer,** www.pfizer.com

The list of companies could go on for several pages, attesting to their vigor. In fact, *Fortune* magazine's list of the top one hundred companies to work for includes nineteen healthcare/pharmaceutical companies. In addition, *Fortune*'s list of the ten best companies for women included the following seven healthcare companies. Go to their websites for more information:

Work in the healthcare industry consists not only of medical professional jobs like physician, nurse, certified nurse midwife, and physical therapist, but also nonclinical jobs in sales, marketing, information technology, finance, and human resources. One does not need professional experience in clinical healthcare to work in this booming industry.

THE INSURANCE INDUSTRY

Some consider this industry boring and concerned only with making money at the expense of policyholders. Who wants to do something as unexciting as working with policies for life insurance, auto insurance, homeowners insurance, short- and long-term disability insurance, flood insurance, and retirement instruments like annuities? Insurance is just an invention by greedy corporate executives to make money, right? Well, think again.

THANKS, BEN!

The insurance industry in the United States was founded by none other than Benjamin Franklin. He taught us that insurance is an instrument to minimize risk and deal with unforeseen occurrences, like a fire, that might consume your home and all of its contents. In so doing, Ben gave birth to an industry where it is almost impossible to fail, one that employs some of the most brilliant mathematical minds on Earth. These mathematical geniuses are the actuaries. They deal with massive amounts of data to determine risk levels and then price insurance policies accordingly.

Insurance products have become a necessity to live as a responsible, self-sufficient human being. Insurance policies provide monetary benefits to policyholders who suffer misfortunes, whether it is an illness that costs thousands of dollars to treat or an accident that causes temporary or permanent disability resulting in loss of wages, which in turn can cause inestimable hardship. Insurance provides numerous and varied job opportunities in sales, marketing, technology, finance, human resources, underwriting, and highly technical jobs, as well. Here are some of the best in the industry based on general reputation for integrity, financial strength, longevity, and community outreach:

- *MassMutual,* www.massmutual.com
- *Northwestern Mutual,* www.northwesternmutual.com
- *State Farm,* www.statefarm.com
- *USAA,* www.usaa.com
- *Unum,* www.unum.com

THE SECURITY INDUSTRY

The security industry has been growing exponentially because of cybercrime against government agencies and private companies. Hacking of both American government and corporate websites by criminals from foreign countries seems to make the news every day. Companies in the security industry undertake a wide variety of initiatives, however: preventing cheating on exams; securing private property; protecting financial information; protecting confidential data, both private and governmental; and reducing the threat of terror attacks. There are many companies in the security industry, and each limits its activities to one or two specialties. Here are two examples:

- *Caveon,* www.caveon.com. This company focuses on preventing cheating on tests and test scores in K-12 schools and colleges.

- *Raytheon,* www.raytheon.com. This American icon located in the Boston area is a leader in cybersecurity for both industry and government.

THE TECHNOLOGY INDUSTRY

Technology moves at the speed of light, and there are always companies coming and going in the technology business. Working for a technology start-up can be exciting but carries substantial risk. A safer bet is to look at established technology-driven companies. Here are some of the best:

- *Salesforce.com,* www.salesforce.com
- *Amazon,* www.amazon.com
- *Adobe,* www.adobe.com
- *Nvidia,* www.nvidia.com
- *Facebook,* www.facebook.com

THE TRANSPORTATION INDUSTRY

This industry includes companies that produce automobiles, airplanes, boats, trains, railroads, trucks, and bicycles and companies that offer support items like tires, batteries, rails, seats, and windows. Many interesting companies fit into this category and many are household words. One thing is certain in this world in addition to death and taxes: there will always be a need to move people and goods from one place to another. Here is a sampling of prominent and respected transportation companies:

- *Boeing,* www.boeing.com
- *Hertz,* www.hertz.com

- *Lockheed Martin,* www
  .lockheedmartin.com
- *Southwest Airlines,* www.southwest
  .com
- *Tesla*, www.tesla.com
- *Toyota,* www.toyota.com
- *Union Pacific Railroad,* www
  .unionpacific.com

Do not overlook this booming industry. It offers jobs throughout the country, good jobs with security, attractive wages, and excellent benefits.

TOP-RANKED LARGE COMPANIES: ENTERTAINMENT, FINANCE, FOOD, RENTAL, TECHNOLOGY

The usual route that many let-go workers follow is to look on the job boards and scour social media for leads to job opportunities with *any* company that may be hiring.

There is a better way to find good potential employers. Search for companies that have been in business for many years and that have been profitable. Target companies whose products and services are in constant demand throughout the business cycle, and that have a good reputation with their workers for fair play. Why spend your time throwing darts at the entire board of American companies?

To start you headed in the right direction, here is a list of prominent companies in various industries. It is not by any means a complete list, but it will give you an idea of important characteristics and criteria for assessing employers. Note that this list includes companies that produce tangible products and companies that provide services.

- *The Blackstone Group,* www
  .blackstone.com. This is one of the world's leading investment and financial advisory firms. It is headquartered in New York City, with eight regional offices spread throughout the country and offices abroad, as well. Blackstone services include management of corporate private equity funds, real estate opportunity funds, hedge funds, mezzanine funds, senior debt vehicles, proprietary hedge funds, and closed-end mutual funds. The company has a solid reputation for treating its employees and customers fairly. In addition, it contributes millions of dollars to community charitable organizations.
- *Coca-Cola,* www.coke.com. This one-hundred-plus-old company has provided jobs for millions of people not only in the United States, but also throughout the world. Coke treats its workers well and is in reorganization mode. Many of Coke's workers are nearing retirement age, and midcareer workers are taking over. They have new ideas, use technology effectively, and are positioning Coke to reach new levels of performance and revenue.

- *Costco,* www.costco.com. Costco employs 174,000 workers, most working behind the scenes in real estate, finance, marketing, technology, supply chain management, purchasing, construction, online retail sales, and human resources. Working at Costco is not only about stocking shelves and working the cash register. Management jobs are plentiful, from local store managers to IT directors at the corporate and regional levels. But there is more to the Costco story. Among big box retailers, Costco ranks number one in wages paid to store employees, $21 per hour. Costco sells more wine than any other company in the world, and that's not all. Costco sells more than 140 million rotisserie chickens and 150 million hot dogs each year. Hungry for a good job, a hot dog, a rotisserie chicken, and a nice bottle of wine from the Loire Valley in France? Work at Costco. As Costco grows and opens more stores, it will need more midcareer workers at the store and corporate levels to manage an expanding workforce.
- *Disney,* www.disney.com. This iconic company is part of the entertainment industry and provides job opportunities throughout the world. Check out the website to review a variety of openings spanning everything from sales to human resources. Disney has a reputation for being an employee-friendly company and for supporting community programs.
- *Dow Chemical,* www.dow.com. Dow products are used in almost every facet of our lives. The company has grown exponentially worldwide and has won many "best employer" awards in countries around the world. Many consider Dow one of America's best employers because of its reputation for creating a diverse workforce where everyone is welcome. Dow employs over 55,000 workers and has sales revenues of approximately $60 billion. Dow is merging with DuPont.
- *General Electric*, www.generalelectric .com. GE, founded in 1892, has its fingers in many manufacturing pots and is undergoing a massive reorganization with a new CEO. GE is a multinational conglomerate, which means that it manufactures and produces a multitude of products that are sold in many countries. Many GE products, such as power plants and engines, are used by the US military. The company has an excellent record for philanthropy and community outreach and for promoting from within. The company is quickly carving out a niche in technology while maintaining its manufacturing profile.

- **General Mills,** www.generalmills.com. "Wheaties. Breakfast of Champions." General Mills has been serving up this breakfast cereal in its iconic orange box, which highlights professional and college athletes, for the past eighty years. The company is doing a lot right like producing foods that customers enjoy and find nutritious. General Mills employs forty-one thousand workers and generates $18 billion in annual sales. It has created a diverse workforce, pays its employees well, is active in community outreach, and usually promotes management-level workers from within.

- **Home Depot,** www.homedepot.com. Where else can you find houseplants, light bulbs, home appliances like dishwashers, and sheets of plywood for home construction under the same roof? This is a very profitable company with locations across the US and abroad. The company employs 365,000 workers and has annual revenues exceeding $100 billion. As the real estate market grows, so does Home Depot. Whenever someone buys a house, they always need fix-up products, and the most convenient place to find those products at fair prices is this company. Its stock price has grown substantially, reflecting shareholder confidence that this company is headed in the right direction.

- **IHG,** www.IHG.com. The InterContinental Hotels Group includes famous names like Holiday Inn, Holiday Inn Express, InterContinental Hotels, Crown Plaza, and others. On their career page, you will find hundreds of jobs listed by job title and location, both domestic and international. IHG has hotels in eighteen countries and counting and has increased its number of hotels in the United States. Each new facility creates more jobs and greater rewards for its shareholders. They are in acquisition mode, which means they are growing and hiring new management-level employees.

- **Johnson Controls,** www.johnsoncontrols.com. Johnson Controls is the world's leading provider of control mechanisms for the building and automotive industries. Annual revenues exceed $42 billion. Your automobile could not run without their products. Johnson is a technical organization and has a constant need for employees having a STEM background. As building and transportation initiatives, like driverless cars, increase, so will jobs for midcareer workers.

- **Lowe's,** www.lowes.com. A WWII veteran, Carl Buchan, founded this major home supply company, which has a reputation for treating its employees like family. In addition, Lowe's is customer-focused and community-conscious. As with all large retailers, most of the jobs at Lowes are located off the floor.

- *McDonald's,* www.mcdonalds.com. This company is expanding its fast-food menu constantly and is located in almost every country on the planet. It has been in business for over sixty years and employs approximately two million workers in one hundred countries. Annual revenues are approximately $30 billion. McDonald's is noted for supporting community outreach activities, especially those related to children.

- *Qualcomm,* www.qualcomm .com. This company is a global semiconductor designer and a manufacturer and marketer of digital wireless telecommunications products. It is one of the best in the business and has been around since 1985, a long time in the technology business. Qualcomm is based in San Diego and employs thirty thousand workers. The demand for all types of semiconductors is growing exponentially, and Qualcomm is considered by industry analysts to be well positioned to meet that need. In addition, the company has a reputation for community service in California and provides special employment opportunities for military veterans.

- *Salesforce.com,* www.CRM.com. This is the preeminent cloud-computing company headed by a highly respected CEO, Mark Benioff. Recently, the company created a nonprofit division targeting the higher-education market. The stock price has been increasing steadily because company revenues have been increasing and investors consider Salesforce.com to be the best of breed. The company has an excellent track record of service to the community and contributes to worthy causes. Recently, it has formed strategic relationships with Amazon and IBM. More jobs will follow.

- *Starbucks,* www.starbucks.com. A few years ago, people asked, "What can a coffee house do for America? What's all the fuss about another coffee joint?" Well, for starters, a good cup of joe in the morning is the traditional way that most Americans begin their day. It is part of our culture. A cup of morning coffee is just as much a part of our culture as is the demitasse cup of super strong espresso that the Italians drink before going to work. However, there is more to this story than drinking coffee.

Starbucks has provided both part-time and full-time jobs for millions of Americans from coast to coast, and it treats its workers fairly. Many workers who start as baristas (don't you love the job title?) move up to executive-level management positions. In addition, the former CEO, Howard Schultz, has made a concerted effort to bring jobs back to America by using only American manufacturers to provide essential items such as paper coffee cups, which are manufactured in Ohio. In 2015, Starbucks initiated an online college scholarship program for all employees.

Starbucks has a bright future, and we recommend that you check out the website for job opportunities. You will see jobs in supply-chain operations, finance, global development, information technology, retail sales, coffee roasting operations, and many others.

- *Texas Instruments*, www.ti.com. TI is seventy years old. It is not a Johnny-come-lately to the technology world, and it produces more than calculators. TI produces technology products like RFID barcodes and sophisticated semiconductors, those little beasts that make your digital toys run. TI has a presence in thirty-five countries and employs thirty-five thousand workers. Annual revenues top $14 billion. The company is based in Dallas, Texas, and has offices scattered throughout the United States and abroad.

TI has a reputation for treating its workers like family despite its size, which explains why people work there for many years. TI has one of the best mentoring programs in the business, and one of its most attractive benefits is a profit-sharing program that has made many workers very wealthy.

- *Tiffany & Co.,* www.tiffany.com. This American icon of upscale jewelry and fine home furnishings has been in business since 1837. Do you want to work in a pleasant environment surrounded by beautiful objects of art for the home and personal adornment? Do you get high looking into a flawless two-carat diamond? If you answer "yes" or even "maybe," the next step is to review the career pages on the Tiffany website.

- *United Rentals,* www.unitedrentals .com. This is one of the largest tool and equipment rental companies in the world and offers many interesting opportunities for midcareer workers. As our economy continues to grow, so does the demand for construction equipment. United Rentals offers generous employee benefits and will continue to grow as our country embarks on a new round of infrastructure rebuilding.

- *Verizon,* www.verizon.net. The country's largest wireless carrier offers employment opportunities in all states and is at the forefront of all forms of digital communication. The array of jobs with this communication giant is impressive. It is very employee-friendly and enjoys a reputation for promoting from within.
- *Whole Foods,* www.wholefoods.com. This company deserves an A+ for leading America toward better eating habits by selling organic foods that are free from chemicals and pollutants, which are harmful to our health. In addition, the CEO is committed to working with the community to provide assistance to those who need a basic item for survival—food. Based in Austin, Texas, Whole Foods is one of the most socially responsible companies in the world. The company employs approximately sixty thousand workers, and annual revenue tops $12 billion. *Fortune* magazine ranks Whole Foods in the top one hundred best companies for workers. Whole Foods has an excellent benefits program for its employees and offers a career path for workers seeking long-term employment. Whole Foods has been purchased by Amazon.

These are just a few of the large companies that hire millions of workers each year. When you explore any company, focus first on the company's financial strength and its projected growth rate by industry analysts. If you like what you see, explore the career pages and apply for a position that matches your profile. Remember to send your résumé and career profile to the human resources director or department hiring manager by name. Never send career information to "Employment Manager" or "Position #257." *The job-hunting process includes building a relationship with a named person who is in a position of authority to hire job candidates such as you.*

SMALL BUSINESSES ARE BIG EMPLOYERS

The Bureau of Labor Statistics defines small businesses as those companies employing fewer than five hundred workers. There are 28 million small businesses in America, and they employ over 50 percent of all workers. Approximately 543,000 small businesses are started each year. A small business can be anything from a corner deli employing three or four workers to a niche technology firm with several hundred workers.

Working for a small business, as opposed to a large company like one of those listed above, offers both considerable advantages and considerable challenges. Many small businesses have greater sensitivity to disruptions in the economic climate. They are subject to going out of business at the first hiccup in the economy because they depend on month-to-month revenue to stay alive. (Large companies usually have cash reserves to carry them through lean times, or they have readily available sources to borrow money.)

Generally, working for a small business carries more risk for workers than working for a large corporation. Small business owners usually do not have the resources to provide salaries and benefits offered by large firms, even for their managerial-level employees. Some small businesses do not offer retirement plans, such as a 401K or IRA, and their benefits packages may offer only legally required medical and hospital insurance. Compensation is usually less in a small business than it is in a large corporation.

On the plus side of the equation, small businesses can be more flexible in providing personal time off and more relaxed work rules. Usually the culture is friendlier and employers are more flexible on job requirements. Previous work experience and formal education requirements are not as rigid as they are in a large company.

Owners of small businesses usually carry out the hiring process personally, while large companies hire recruiters to conduct candidate searches or post their openings on numerous job boards. The hiring process in a small business is abbreviated. Frequently, a job candidate receives an offer after the first personal interview. The hiring process with a large company can be onerous and take sixty to ninety days, or more, beginning to end. The reason is that more company personnel are involved in the decision-making process, and they have more candidates in the vetting process for a particular position. In a small business, the hiring manager could be your potential boss or the president of the company.

SOURCES FOR EVALUATING COMPANIES

Midcareer workers in transition should devote time and attention to a complete and impartial evaluation of any potential employer. In addition to hearsay, trusted networking sources, and social media chatter, there are sources that provide objective reports on any company you are considering for employment. Here are two reliable Internet resources for locating information about companies that interest you. All of them provide financial information, company product information, and industry standing.

1. *Investopedia,* www.investopedia.com
2. *Hoover's,* www.hoovers.com

NOTE ON LEADERS AND FOLLOWERS

Regardless of the employer and its size, all workers fall into two categories, leaders and followers. Where you want to go is a matter of choice. One is not better than the other.

The media is filled with hype about becoming a leader and how one should acquire leadership skills. Little is ever said about followers, but one cannot exist without the other.

Leaders seem to get our attention, but they would not be successful if they did not have skilled followers. It is nothing less than a symbiotic relationship. For example, a vice president for sales will be successful only if the followers, the territory sales representatives, bring in the orders.

However, all leaders must be good followers, as well. For example, a marketing director is a leader who not only has direct reports to manage, but also is a follower of the boss, the vice president for marketing or the president. Regardless of your rank as leader, you will always be a concurrent follower, unless you are the sole owner of the company.

SKILLS REQUIRED FOR GOOD LEADERS AND FOLLOWERS

Midcareer workers who aspire to higher levels of management must acquire certain skills and personal qualities to inspire, mentor, and motivate their followers to attain goals. Some of these required skills are clear and concise written and verbal communication, delegating authority, planning, prioritizing, vision, honesty, commitment, adaptability, and relationship building.

A dictionary definition of a follower reads, "One who accepts the teachings of another." Midcareer workers who would rather take the path of follower must possess job skills and social skills, too. Some of these are loyalty, knowledge of the company products and services, passion for completing the mission, adherence to the rules and regulations laid down by the leader (i.e., the boss), intelligence to learn the details of the mission, patience, and honesty.

MOVING FORWARD

The usual path midcareer workers take is to find employment with another company in the same industry. However, they have the option of changing industries, or doing something else like saying good-bye to a large company or small business employer and starting one's own business, an attractive option for many laid-off workers. I will lead you through the process in the next chapter.

CHAPTER TAKEAWAYS

- All companies and small businesses are part of a larger entity called an industry.
- The hiring process for a large company is more detailed and lengthier than it is for a small business.
- A record of community outreach is one important factor in evaluating a company.
- Companies with a long record of profitable operations are usually good employers.
- Being a good follower is just as important as being a good leader.

PRINT AND DIGITAL RESOURCES

Adair, Troy, PhD. *Corporate Finances Demystified*. McGraw-Hill, 2011.

Cramer, Jim. *Jim Cramer's Real Money*. Simon & Schuster, 2009.

"Customized Industry Reports." Profound. www.marketresearch.com. This site provides company research reports and industry analyses.

Dun & Bradstreet. www.dnb.com.

Fortune magazine. *Fortune* is published monthly, print or digital, at a reasonable cost to subscribers.

Hoover's. www.hoovers.com.

SmartBrief on Leadership. www.smart-brief.com/industry/business/leadership. This site provides articles on leadership and business generally authored by its own writers and outside sources, as well.

US Department of Labor. *The Occupational Outlook Handbook.* JIST Publishing, 2016–2017.

CHAPTER 17

STARTING YOUR OWN BUSINESS OR BUYING A FRANCHISE

For most workers seeking a new beginning in midcareer, the thought of starting a business is intriguing, but how do you toss the first pitch in this ball game? Street talk tells only the stories of entrepreneurs who dropped out of college, locked themselves in a garage for a couple of years, and then emerged with a business called Apple Computer or Microsoft or Virgin Air. Continue listening to the street, and you hear that it can happen only if you are rich, famous, or have significant family connections.

Reality is much different. Any midcareer worker with intelligence, energy, and passion can start their own business by following a few simple rules and listening to successful entrepreneurs like Elon Musk, founder and CEO of SpaceX and cofounder of Tesla Motors; Richard Branson, founder of Virgin Air; Chris Weiss, founder and owner of RaffertyWeiss Media; and Ruth Fertel, founder of Ruth's Chris Steak House chain.

As you begin exploring this initiative, make your first stop the US Small Business Administration (SBA), www.SBA.gov. The SBA provides information in nontechnical language about how to start and operate your business and make money in the process.

WHO STARTS A NEW BUSINESS?

Join the thousands who have started their own businesses instead of working for someone else. The fact that you have a wide array of skills learned in your previous jobs, a college degree, or both, does not mean that you are destined to work for a big corporation or a small business. Working for a company, particularly a large one, where the ground rules can be oppressive, may not be your idea of a good time. The alternative is to start your own business.

What must you do before hanging out a sign with your name on it? Isn't it true that most business owners have money in the family and are mostly upper class? To clear up those misconceptions, here is the profile of people who start their own businesses according to an article that appeared in the *Wall Street Journal:*

WHO STARTS A NEW BUSINESS?

Fewer than 1 percent of people who start a business come from extremely rich or extremely poor backgrounds. 71.5 percent come from a middle-class background. 70 percent used their own savings as the source to fund their own businesses.

So much for the stereotypes of business owners. I like numbers. They usually set the record straight.

PORTRAITS OF SUCCESSFUL BUSINESS OWNERS

Who are some of these successful entrepreneurs? Are there any good examples of workers who decided to make it on their own instead of casting their lot with a company? The answer is a resounding "yes." Here is an inspirational story written by a midcareer worker who left corporate work and did it his own way.

CAPTAIN KIEL KING OF NEW YORK (US ARMY RET.)

First, I am medically retired as an Army Captain. Upon returning to the United States from Germany, I spoke with the Lucas Group, an executive recruiting firm, which provided job leads, including one at Coca-Cola. My bachelor's degree is in chemistry & life sciences from West Point, but it did not come into play while taking my interview with the Coca-Cola Bottling Company. I was hired after the first interview. I started with Coca-Cola as a production manager a month after leaving the military. But, after one year, I found that I was working in a field that I did not enjoy. I believe I was hired due to my leadership experience in the Army and my education at West Point. After a bit of soul-searching, I decided it was important to continue my education in an area that I truly loved and went back to school to complete a graduate degree in physical rehabilitation sciences. I have since started my own company called Kings of Fitness, where the mission is to educate, motivate, and inspire individuals to live a healthy and physically active lifestyle. While I was in the Army, helping people was extremely important to me, and now that I am medically retired, helping people is still the most important thing that gives me true job satisfaction. I did not have that with Coca-Cola.

Here is what we can learn from Captain King:

- Education must continue at all stages in one's career.
- There are sources of help available to entrepreneurs.
- Start a business that grabs your interest and provides meaning for your life.
- Define the mission.
- Plan your work. Work your plan.

HOW TO GET STARTED

The rules of business entrepreneurship apply equally to everyone. There are not two sets of rules. Consider what Richard Branson said in his first blog entry for LinkedIn, posted in 2012: "As LinkedIn is a business that started in a living room, much like Virgin which began in a basement, I thought my first blog on the site should be about how to simply start a successful business." Here are Branson's five top tips:

1. Listen more than you talk.
2. Keep it simple.
3. Take pride in your work.
4. Have fun, success will follow.
5. Rip it up and start again.

These are the first steps that Richard Branson took when founding one of the most successful businesses on the planet. Branson always has good ideas for entrepreneurs and has authored twelve books about starting businesses and operating them profitably. I've listed two of them in the resources at the end of this chapter.

Go to LinkedIn periodically and read Branson's blogs. You will receive advice from one of the world's most successful business owners at a terrific price—*free*. We can learn much from him. He's been there, done that without a college degree, without family money, while working from a basement office. He planned his work and worked his plan. Success followed.

MORE FAMOUS ENTREPRENEURS

If you explore how other entrepreneurs founded their businesses, their stories will be similar to Branson's. For example, in 2005, Arianna Huffington founded the Huffington Post, which has become an American media icon. She sold the Post to AOL for $315 million but still plays an active role as editor. Her net worth is estimated to be $50 million.

Steve Jobs and Steve Wozniak both dropped out of college after their first year and founded Apple Computer . . . working out of a garage. Then we have Larry Ellison, founder and CEO of Oracle, who bypassed college altogether and founded one of the world's largest software companies. His net worth is close to $50 billion. What does he do with his money? Several years ago, he purchased the entire island of Lanai in the Hawaiian Islands. Yes, the entire island, not just a couple of acres. He still has plenty of money left over, much of which he donates to charitable causes.

And let's not forget Mark Zuckerberg, founder and CEO of Facebook, another person with big dreams and little appetite for continuing his education at Harvard. He dropped out of college and founded Facebook. Mark is in midcareer, and his start-up, Facebook, is a publicly held company with more than two billion users. Mark's net worth is over $50 *billion*. He and his wife contribute hundreds of millions of dollars to charitable causes.

I WANT TO DO IT MY WAY

These successful businesses all began as someone's dream, which was refined into a viable business while working from a garage or basement. (I'm not sure why garages and basements are so attractive for entrepreneurs. That's just the way it is.) Captain Kiel King, Bill Gates, Steve Jobs, Steve Wozniak, Larry Ellison, and Mark Zuckerberg could do it, and so can you. The business you start does not have to be another Microsoft in order to be successful. There are thousands of small businesses founded, owned, and operated successfully by someone who had the courage to say, "I want to do it my way." Here is another story of such an individual.

COLONEL HARLAND SANDERS

Harland Sanders was born in 1890 and spent the first forty years of his life working in a variety of jobs. As a child, he learned to cook family-style meals from his mother while working on a farm. In 1906, he enlisted in the Army and was honorably discharged after serving his country. He had no clear career path and bounced from job to job working primarily for railroads. At nights, he worked on a law degree by mail correspondence from La Salle Extension University, a forerunner of today's online universities. After practicing law for a brief time, he accepted an offer from the Shell Oil Company to operate a gas station in Corbin, Kentucky. A true multitasker, Harland began cooking and selling meals from his own house adjacent to the gas station. One of his specialties was chicken, not fried or baked, but cooked in a new device called a pressure cooker. Word spread that Sanders's chicken was the best you could buy, and he gave up the gas station business and opened restaurants that featured his specialty, chicken. At about the same time, the governor of Kentucky commissioned Harland as a Kentucky Colonel, an honorary title. In 1940, Harland created and promoted his "secret recipe" for his now-famous chicken, attracting rave notices from food critics who spread the word nationwide. In 1952, he franchised his first restaurant and named it Kentucky Fried Chicken. The rest of this story is history.

Harland Sanders's story proves that successful entrepreneurs do not have to be technology gurus like Gates or Zuckerberg. Any smart midcareer worker using their intelligence, energy, and passion can do the same. If the thought of founding a company that has your name on it sounds exciting, go for it! There are many books and websites offering ideas about how to get started, and there are many support groups ready to help entrepreneurs accomplish their goals.

STARTING YOUR OWN BUSINESS AS A SOLE PROPRIETOR

Can you really start your own business, as did Sanders, Zuckerberg, and Gates? How long does it take before you can make serious money to become self-sufficient? What kinds of businesses are there?

Many entrepreneurs have founded successful small businesses. Where are they? Take a walk down Main Street, USA, and talk with the owner of a storefront business, and you will get the answer. For now, look at several small businesses that were started by people who had a dream and ambition.

GARY FROM PHILADELPHIA

I was looking for someone to wash the windows at our home in suburban Philadelphia. Fortunately, we found Gary through a referral from a neighbor. The job took Gary about six hours, and we paid him $400, which translates into $66 per hour. We have employed Gary for the past seven years. He begins work at the appointed hour, supplies all window-cleaning products, and maintains the high quality of work. Recently, Gary added another service to his business—residential exterior power washing—which is a perfect complement to the window-washing business.

I can hear the snickering now. Window washing with a college degree? You have to be kidding! Well, what if I told you that Gary's business generates a revenue stream comparable to that of a corporate manager and that he works only ten months of the year? (Gary works only ten months because inclement weather in January and February prevents him from working outside.) Now what do you think about the residential window-washing business? Compare that to a corporate job. An average midcareer corporate job will bring in about $135,000 per year. You will get three weeks' vacation, report to work each day at a specific time, and will work in a corporate people kennel, also called a cubicle. You will be on call 24/7 and have little time to call your own. Gary, on the other hand, makes an annual six-figure income, works on his own terms, and reports to a boss named . . . Gary.

So what is Gary's background? What kind of education do you need to start your own business? Here's the rest of the story. Gary graduated from Temple University in Philadelphia with a bachelor's degree in business administration and began working in the corporate world. One of his employers was General Electric, where he held a managerial position. He was not happy and decided to make it on his own. He researched several business possibilities and found there was no competition in the residential window-washing business. He started his own window-washing business with a modest investment and a few years later had several people working for him.

Gary's story is about how to make a living on your own terms. Owning and operating your own business is one of the most satisfying things you can do. Your business will provide a good income, the option to work on your own terms, and time to give back to the community by participating in your choice of outreach programs. The term "work" does not always mean putting in time with a Fortune 500 company. Gary's work is not window washing. *His work is running a service business that he calls his own.*

CONSULTING BUSINESSES

Frequently, laid-off workers start their own businesses as consultants working in a variety of roles in a particular industry. They undertake specifically defined assignments for a certain period of time. After completing an assignment, they move on to another. It is a quick and inexpensive way to put the past behind and continue generating income. If your past career focused on marketing in the publishing business, make that the focus of your consulting business and seek assignments from your contacts in the industry. Some workers make consulting a full-time occupation instead of returning to a managerial-level corporate job.

Another reason why some let-go midcareer workers hang out their own shingles as consultants is to remain business-active while seeking new full-time opportunities. In addition to providing much-needed income, consulting provides opportunities to build new business relationships. Newly minted consultants usually do this by attending conferences at major convention centers where they frequently find new business clients.

Starting a consulting business is not complicated, but it takes courage. Here is a list of guidelines to begin your own consulting business:

- Decide what kinds of assignments you can complete successfully. For example, if you have experience managing a sales team, seek assignments from companies in your industry who might need part-time sales help to introduce a new product to a specific group of potential customers.
- Name your company. It need not be fancy. "James Henry, Marketing Consultant" works well.
- Set up an e-mail address, a Twitter account, and a Facebook account reflecting your new consulting business.
- Construct a website. You can do this on your own or have an online source construct it for you. However, if you are just biding your time while seeking another full-time corporate job, you can skip this step in the process.
- Purchase business cards. It sounds elementary, but you will need something for identification when you are seeking customers and building your network at conferences.
- Contact your former employer(s) to solicit business as an independent consultant. Frequently, workers who have been laid off because of budget

cuts find part-time assignments from their former employers.

- Attend conferences in your industry at local convention centers and visit each exhibit booth to solicit business.

STARTING A BUSINESS WITH A PARTNER

Another way to start your own business is with a partner who has interests and values similar to yours. Selecting the *right* partner is an important first step and requires a complete examination of that person's skills, energy, intelligence, passion for self-employment, ethics, values, and interest in the ideas you have for starting a business. Researching your potential partner is critical. If you select just a good friend instead of a *good business friend* who is compatible with you in every way, your business could turn into a nightmare. Many entrepreneurs have failed because they selected the wrong partner.

Here is a good example of a successful partnership, in the words of a successful businessman, Chris:

CHRIS FROM SILVER SPRING, MARYLAND

I worked as a video producer at a large telecommunications corporation for approximately five years. I stayed there longer than I wanted to as I waited first for stock options to increase in value. When that didn't happen, I waited to see if I could obtain a buyout package. That didn't happen either, but I decided to leave because the company was in trouble. It was just a matter of time before I could be let go.

I talked to a freelance producer, Patrick Rafferty, whom I had met when he worked at the same company but on a contract basis. We seemed like a good fit. We got along well personally, and we both had a similar amount of experience in the profession. What sold us on each other was that while we had some overlap in terms of our strengths, in other areas my strengths complemented his weaknesses, and vice versa. To test our compatibility as business partners, we decided to start working together on projects as independent entities.

Our first year as a company was lean, even though we had a number of contacts around town. We each took in about $30,000 gross that first year, which would not have been sustainable for either of us for much longer. However, business picked up in the second year, and our revenues have increased substantially every year after that. In January 2017, we began our sixteenth year working together as a partnership in the video production business. Our company is RaffertyWeiss Media.

The video production business is not for the faint of heart. It requires exceptional written and verbal communication skills, bottom-line business skills, creativity, imagination, and technical expertise. While Chris possessed all of those qualities, the time requirements for operating a successful media business as a sole proprietor are significant. When Chris found a partner with similar values and skills, he founded RaffertyWeiss Media.

STARTING YOUR OWN BUSINESS WITH A FRANCHISE

Another way to start your own business is to purchase a franchise. Franchises focus primarily on products and services related to the big three survival industries: food, shelter, and clothing. Some popular franchise businesses involve fast food restaurants, retail clothing and accessories, home and commercial cleaning services, residential real estate, and personal grooming.

Of course, the first franchise names that come to mind are McDonald's, Burger King, Starbucks, Five Guys, Dairy Queen, Chipotle, KFC, and ServPro Cleaning Services, all of which are very profitable businesses. In addition, there are hundreds of worthy franchise operations that cost less money to enter and generate substantial income.

HOW A FRANCHISE WORKS

There are two entities involved in the franchise operation. First is the *franchisor*, the company that owns the brand name, like McDonald's. The other part is the *franchisee*, the person who buys the product name and sells the franchisor's products at an individual store or online. The franchisor provides the location, training, marketing, sales support, advertising, and other requirements needed to operate a business. The company charges the individual store operator a franchise fee to begin the business and takes a percentage of the business revenue.

Purchasing a franchise can cost serious money. For example, McDonald's requires a minimum of $250,000 in cash to be considered for a franchise. You cannot borrow this amount; it must be $250,000 that is unencumbered, and that is just the beginning. Before you are finished, it will cost anywhere from $600,000 to $1.5 million to purchase a McDonald's franchise. However, other interesting franchise opportunities are available for as little as $10,000.

The following list of popular and successful franchises and their *approximate* buy-in cost, furnished by Franchise Business Review in 2017, will give you an idea of what you can expect to spend to purchase a franchise:

1. Visiting Angels: $77,000
2. MaidPro: $59,000
3. Pinot's Palette: $76,000
4. CertaPro Painters: $135,000
5. Wild Birds Unlimited: $150,000

Do remember that stated costs associated with purchasing a franchise are estimates. Final cost depends on a number of variables, including location.

FRANCHISE RESOURCES FOR MIDCAREER WORKERS

Here are popular online resources to learn about starting your own business with a franchise. These sources describe the business, furnish franchise costs, provide contact information, and list locations where franchise sites are available. In addition, most provide detailed financial information so that you can determine the company's strengths and weaknesses.

- *Business Franchise Review,* www .franchisebusinessreview.com
- *Entrepreneur,* www.entrepreneur.com. This source is available in magazine format, too. Recent issues contained interesting articles about former corporate workers who started their own businesses with a franchise.
- *Franchise Direct,* www .franchisedirect.com
- *Franchise Opportunities,* www .franchiseopportunities.com
- *Top 100 Franchises,* www .top100franchises.net

FRANCHISE BUSINESSES

Here is a list of franchise businesses to investigate. You may not have heard about all of them, but they are successful and have been in business for decades. Note that many focus on services for the home and commercial building industry, a.k.a. the shelter industry.

1. Pillar to Post Inspection Services
2. Jan-Pro Cleaning
3. Aire Serv HVAC
4. Mr. Appliance Corporation
5. WIN Home Inspection
6. Mr. Electric

7. Jani-King
8. Amerispec Home Inspection Services
9. Matco Tools
10. Anytime Fitness

WHAT KIND OF BUSINESS CAN I START?

The list of business ventures is endless, but a good place to start is with a business whose products and services are in constant demand, and in which you have an interest. Food. Shelter. Clothing. Transportation. Technology. Insurance. Education. Healthcare. These are necessities for all regardless of age, gender, geography, race, or religion. Apply the same rules that you did for seeking work in the corporate environment: learn your field of interest, determine your aptitude, define your work experiences, and then translate all into a business venture.

BUSINESSES ON MAIN STREET, USA

The next time you leave the house, look at the businesses on either side of Main Street. A majority of them will be stores focusing on food, shelter, clothing, and related products. The point is this: if you want to strike out on your own as an entrepreneur rather than work for someone else, just do it. Play to your passion. Do something that turns you on every day, as Branson said.

BUSINESSES THAT DO NOT REQUIRE A STOREFRONT

There are many ways to start your own business that do not require a storefront. The least expensive way to start working on your own is to become an independent sales representative. Independent sales reps usually carry products related to one specific industry. Take cutlery for example. Sales reps working in this narrow market niche might carry products for three or more different manufacturers, both domestic and foreign, and sell them to restaurants both large and small, or to wholesalers that distribute and sell not only knives, but also related products such as metal cooking pots and pans. For example, take Mickey, an independent sales representative in New Jersey who sells only cutlery to restaurants in the Mid-Atlantic region. He's been doing that for more than twenty years and has an income exceeding that of a corporate vice president. His marketing slogan? "My products are a cut above the rest."

FIVE GUIDELINES FOR STARTING YOUR OWN BUSINESS

1. Produce and sell the number one life-sustaining product, food, as Colonel Harland Sanders did.

2. Provide services for homes and businesses, as Chris and Gary did.

3. Sell products of any kind as an independent sales representative, as Mickey did.

4. Go to school to earn certification in a field of interest, as Captain King did.

5. Follow your passion, as Richard Branson did.

OKAY. WHERE'S THE MONEY?

All entrepreneurs ask, "Where do I find the money to start a business?" It is a valid question. You can start some businesses with little money in your bank account; others require substantial amounts of money. How much money you will need depends on what you intend to do. Let's get practical and explore how you can find the financial resources to start your business:

1. *Your own personal savings.* Some businesses do not cost much to begin operating. If you have only $1,000 saved, it could be enough to get you started. Remember Gary from Philadelphia? How much could it have cost to buy supplies to start a window-washing business?

2. *Family money.* Many entrepreneurs borrow start-up money from parents and other family members. Tapping into family money involves trust and confidence. If you are exercising this option, prepare a detailed business plan and present it to your family member just as you would present it to a loan officer at a bank. There is one hard-and-fast rule about asking family members for money: vow to repay every cent of the loan. You are not a charity case, and family members have their own lives to lead. Present a written statement for family members stating when you will begin repaying

the loan and how much each payment will be.

3. *Banks.* Local banks make money by lending money to entrepreneurs. You must create a detailed business plan to attract a banker's attention. There are online sources that give advice about preparing a credible business plan. Approach the most local of banks in your area, an independent bank, not a branch of Wells Fargo or some other multinational banking company. The process is to learn the name of the loan officer and make an appointment for a personal interview to present your business plan, your résumé, and your career profile. This is a no-nonsense deal, so dress accordingly. Remember that bankers make every effort to minimize risk.

4. *Angel funding sources.* These are individuals or small organizations that provide seed money to entrepreneurs. You can find these sources online, by networking through social media like LinkedIn, or through loan officers at a local bank.

5. *Loans from government organizations.* A variety of government sources provide loans for entrepreneurs. Learn where they are by reviewing the US Small Business Administration website, www.sba.gov.

6. *Venture capital funding.* Large companies that specialize in funding start-up businesses are known as venture capital firms. They generate revenue by lending money to start-up firms that have little downside risk. Usually, they seek businesses that are already generating revenue and that require upwards of one million dollars to expand operations.

MOVING FORWARD

Owning a business requires your undivided attention and much time. However, if you like what you are doing, the time factor becomes insignificant. This oft-repeated advice rings true: *Do what you love, and you will never work a day in your life.* If the risk of starting a business is not your idea of an interesting career path, consider something with more stability, like working in a local, state, or federal government job. In the next chapter, I'll walk you through the process.

CHAPTER TAKEAWAYS

- Plan your work. Work your plan. This is a critical first step when starting your own business.
- Follow your passion when selecting the kind of business you would like to start.
- Select a business that provides basic goods and services for consumers.
- You alone can make a difference by applying your intelligence and energy to an idea about which you are passionate.

PRINT AND DIGITAL RESOURCES

Aluet, Bill. *Disciplined Entrepreneurship: 24 Steps to a Successful Start-up*. Wiley, 2013.

Branson, Richard. *Like a Virgin: Secrets They Won't Teach You at Business School*. Virgin Books, 2012.

Branson, Richard. *Losing My Virginity*. Virgin Books, 2013.

Fishman, Stephen. *Working for Yourself: Law & Taxes for Independent Contractors, Freelancers & Consultants*. NOLO, 2011.

International Franchise Expo. www .internationalfranchiseexpo.com. This annual trade show for franchise companies is held each year in New York City and attracts five hundred franchise companies. The franchisor's representatives will give you a detailed description of their businesses and disclose how much money you will need to buy in.

Schiff, Lewis. *Business Brilliant: Surprising Lessons from the Greatest Self-Made Business Icons*. Harper Business, 2013.

Shirk, Martha, and Anna Wadia. *Kitchen Table Entrepreneurs: How Eleven Women Escaped Poverty and Became Their Own Bosses*. Basic Books, 2009.

Tracy, Brian. *GOALS: How to Get Everything You Want, Faster Than You Thought Possible*. Berrett-Koehler, 2010.

CHAPTER 18

LOCAL, STATE, AND FEDERAL GOVERNMENT JOBS

The American workplace is divided into the public sector and the private sector. The public sector consists of all elected and appointed government jobs at the federal, state, and local levels. The public sector employs workers in jobs as diverse as president of the United States, state senator, governor, city building commissioner, and administrative assistant for the mayor of Waukesha, Wisconsin.

There are approximately 22 million local, state, and federal government jobs according to the Bureau of Labor Statistics. Yes, you read that correctly—*twenty-two million*. Of that number, the federal government alone employs 2.8 million workers. State governments employ 5.1 million. And local governments employ 14.1 million.

LOCAL GOVERNMENT JOBS

Jobs in towns, cities, and counties are just around the corner from every midcareer worker looking for new opportunities. For those who have decided to pursue a career in government or politics, the local level is a good place to start. Here, at the grassroots level, you will learn how government works and the role you can play in it. Former Massachusetts congressman Tip O'Neill offered this sage advice for those seeking a career in politics: "All politics is local." All successful politicians must know how it works on their own turf, at the local level.

How do you get started? Begin by reviewing your local government website, where you will find a list of both full-time salaried jobs and part-time hourly-pay jobs.

Specific instructions govern application for all government jobs, one of which is applying online. If you see something appealing, complete the application, submit it, and go to the next step, which is making a personal visit to the city offices and asking to see the town manager or mayor personally. If that person is not available, ask to see the administrative assistant. *Do not sit at home and wait for an answer to your online application.*

PROACTIVE JOB HUNTING FOR LOCAL GOVERNMENT JOBS

If you do not see a job posting for local government jobs, put on your business attire and with your résumé in hand make a personal visit to the government office and tell the receptionist you are there to see the mayor, or the highest-ranking official for that government entity, about job opportunities. Tell the gatekeeper (the receptionist or administrative assistant) you are there to see the mayor. If you cannot arrange a personal visit with the mayor, or another high-level official, ask the receptionist to give your résumé to the mayor or the mayor's administrative assistant. Remember to request a personal interview. Receptionists and administrative assistants have more power than you might suspect in the hiring process. You always want them on your side. Several days later, follow up by calling the mayor or the admin to make sure they have reviewed your résumé.

Sometimes government jobs, at any level, are awarded to those who know a prominent government official or businessperson. If you have family members or friends who work in government, use that person as the referral agent. Networking is often a key factor in obtaining a government job.

STATE GOVERNMENT JOBS

Follow the same process to explore jobs at the state level—start by looking up your state government website online. You will find many different departments and a listing of jobs at different locations throughout the state. Follow the instructions for applying online and then visit the office personally, repeating the procedure you used at the local level.

You cannot circumvent the application rules for government jobs because legislation governs the employment process. Always try to use a referral source if you have one.

FEDERAL GOVERNMENT JOBS

The federal government is the country's largest employer and offers a variety of interesting jobs spanning every possible occupation. It employs 2.8 million workers, according to statistics released by the US Office of Personnel Management and the Bureau of Labor Statistics. (Walmart is the second largest employer with 2.3 million workers.)

A common misconception is that federal government jobs are located primarily in Washington, DC. Once again, the BLS statistics set us straight. Eighty-seven percent of federal government jobs are located outside of Washington. There are federal government jobs in every state and in many foreign countries, as well.

The processes for finding work with the federal government are sometimes complex and even contradictory. In fact, all federal government departments require that résumés be structured as directed on the job description. Go to the BLS website and read the article titled "How to Get a Job in the Federal Government" by Olivia Crosby. The information and instructions in this article will demystify the federal government employment process, save you time, and possibly lead to the Promised Land of employment.

Note that the federal government does not post its jobs on Internet job boards or advertise them in nongovernment media, and it does not use recruiters. These jobs are posted only on the websites of a federal government department and on the official federal government website, USA Jobs, referenced below.

Government jobs such as senator, representative, or president are not permanent positions. They come and go with periodic elections. However, other jobs exist regardless of the political party in power. They are called civil service jobs, and they keep the wheels of government turning regardless of the party in power. These jobs offer attractive salaries and excellent benefits and are comparable to private sector jobs. For example, a federal government department, such as the Department of Agriculture, hires workers at every level to operate its budget, prepare online and print ads, and conduct informational workshops for agribusinesses, farmers, and the general public. If you are coming from a marketing job in the private sector, your management skills will qualify you for a marketing job in this, or any other, federal government department. The same applies for midcareer workers who have corporate experience in finance. Their skills are transferable and will qualify them for work in places like the Office of Management and Budget, an important department in the executive branch. Expertise you acquired in the private sector will always find a home at one of the many departments operating the federal government.

To learn which positions are available, go to the website of the department that interests you. For example, if you are interested in education-related jobs, go to the website of the US Department of Education, www.ed.gov, and click on "Jobs." When I last checked, I found a position for a lead human resources specialist based in Washington, DC. The salary range was $108,000–$141,000.

Government is something that touches every citizen, and your participation in the process is a significant responsibility. Government jobs, political or civil service, in a country with a population nearing 330 million offer the opportunity to do something meaningful and long-lasting. Yes, one person can make a difference. It is not all partisan politics.

HOW A POLITICIAN CAN MAKE A DIFFERENCE

Elected or appointed political jobs offer opportunities for everyone regardless of education or work history. The most important qualification is passion for completing a mission in your area of interest. Here's an example of how one person followed her passion for improving quality of life for women and children across America as an elected politician. This Colorado representative applied her intelligence, energy, and passion to get the job done. When you read her story, note well what she did for all American workers.

CONGRESSWOMAN PATRICIA "PAT" SCHROEDER

Mrs. Schroeder was a mother of two young children when she decided to make a difference and run for political office in Colorado. She had no family history in politics, no one to pave the way for her through political connections, and no family money to pay for her election campaign. After a hard-fought campaign, she was elected to the United States House of Representatives and went on to serve twelve consecutive two-year terms. Few elected politicians serve for twenty-four years at the federal level.

During her tenure in the House, she became the Dean of Congressional Women; cochaired the Congressional Caucus on Women's Issues for ten years; served on the House Judiciary Committee and the Post Office and Civil Service Committee; and was the first woman to serve on the House Armed Services Committee. As chair of the House Select Committee on Children, Youth and Families from 1991 to 1993, Mrs. Schroeder guided the Family and Medical Leave Act and the National Institutes of Health Revitalization Act to enactment in 1993, a fitting legislative achievement for her lifetime of work on behalf of women's and family issues. In addition, she was active on many military issues, expediting the National Security Committee's vote to allow women to fly combat missions in 1991.

Another accomplishment was her program to improve the situation of families through passage of the Family Medical Leave Act in 1985. The importance of this Act cannot be understated. The US Department of Labor describes it like this: "The FMLA entitles eligible employees of covered employers to take unpaid, job-protected leave for specified family and medical reasons with continuation of group health insurance coverage under the same terms and conditions as if the employee had not taken leave. Eligible employees are entitled to twelve workweeks of leave in a 12-month period."

When you are in need and the FMLA comes to your support, think of Congresswoman Schroeder. Her story proves that one person can make a difference. If she did it, so can any midcareer worker who chooses to become an elected politician.

RESOURCES FOR EXPLORING FEDERAL GOVERNMENT JOBS

There are many sources of information and support for midcareer workers seeking employment with the federal government. Before you begin your exploration, carefully review all of the sources listed below.

- *USA Jobs,* www.usajobs.gov. This site boasts being the federal government's official job site. It provides general information about working in a federal government job and specific advice about how to begin your search. In addition, this site provides location-specific federal government jobs postings. When I entered my zip code, I found postings for the following jobs right in my backyard:

- Communications Program Specialist, base annual salary: $125,000.
- Public Health Veterinarian, base annual salary range: $57,000–90,000.
- Flight Operations Specialist, base annual salary range: $49,000–64,000.
- Supervisory Supply Technician, base annual salary: $54,000–70,000.

- ***US Office of Personnel Management,*** www.opm.gov. Think of this as the human resources department for the federal government. It manages all hiring procedures including recruiting, training, and benefits. In addition, it conducts background checks on all job candidates.
- ***The Book of US Government Jobs.*** This book, authored by Dennis Damp, is in its 11th edition, which tells you what a valuable resource it is. Over 450,000 copies have been sold. It is available from Amazon, Barnes & Noble, independent bookstores, and the publisher Bookhaven Press. It has won numerous awards and is the best on the market for understanding how the federal government employment process works. The rules and regulations for government employment can be onerous. This book will help you through the process and save you time.
- ***Federal Government Jobs,*** www.federaljobs.net. The author of the above-listed book, Dennis Damp, a former federal government employee, operates what is considered the most useful website for current information about federal government jobs. It includes instructions for applying to federal government jobs, government job listings, blogs written by staffing experts, résumé-writing instructions, and references to additional resources. Make this your first stop for learning about federal government jobs.

MOVING FORWARD

Midcareer workers seeking a new career path frequently overlook government jobs. Do not make that mistake. Jobs at all government levels offer rewarding careers that pay well, provide attractive benefits, provide work satisfaction, and offer attractive pension plans.

Finding work with a large company, a small business, a government agency, or starting your own business requires much time and effort. It is a labor-intensive process, and there are times when one needs to call upon outside resources for guidance and support. Where does one find such resources? In the next part, I'll tell you how to access career care providers to lend a hand when you have run out of ideas and are looking for help . . . and a friend.

CHAPTER TAKEAWAYS

- Government jobs pay well and provide attractive benefits.
- Most government jobs are *not* political.
- Applying for government jobs can be challenging. Allow extra time to learn the process.
- Government jobs are not posted on Internet job boards or with recruiters.

- Eighty-five percent of federal government jobs are outside of Washington, DC.
- Elected political jobs offer the opportunity to make a significant difference.
- Using a referral can be an important factor in winning government jobs.
- Prepare a special résumé for government jobs following online specifications.

PRINT AND DIGITAL RESOURCES

Damp, Dennis. *Federal Government Jobs.* www.federaljobs.net.

Damp, Dennis. *The Book of U.S. Government Jobs.* Bookhaven Press, 2011.

PART IV

Reaching Out to Career Care Providers

Don't walk behind me. I may not lead.

Don't walk in front of me. I may not follow.

Just walk beside me and be my friend.

—Anonymous,

sometimes attributed to Albert Camus

CHAPTER 19

CONSULTING WITH CAREER COACHES, CAREER COUNSELORS, AND OUTPLACEMENT SERVICES

There are times when midcareer workers find themselves walking in a dark cloud of anxiety or even depression after being fired or laid off. They look for slivers of daylight but find nothing but more darkness. The universe seems unresponsive. They do not want much, maybe just someone who says, "I understand where you are. Just take my hand and I'll help you out of this mess." That person may be a career coach, career counselor, or an outplacement service, all career care providers.

Reaching out to a career care provider takes courage, understanding, and a good deal of common sense. Where do you find them? What do their services cost? What are their qualifications? And what do these outplacement services really do? All are valid questions. Let's deal with career coaches and counselors first.

CAREER COACHES AND CAREER COUNSELORS

Go online and enter "career coach and career counselor," and you will find an array of hits naming specific individuals, with or without titles. Some are named Joe Smith, Life Coach, or Mary Jones, Executive Career Counselor, or Robert Brown, PhD. Who are the successful ones? Who are the pretenders? Let's look for answers to help you see daylight, to find a break in the dark cloud.

Career coaches are providers who are solution-oriented. They focus on helping clients define career objectives, like finding an industry that includes nonprofit companies where passion for the mission is as important as the bottom line. They exude a spirit of optimism, educate you about the job market, and show you how to navigate your way through the world of work. Most will help you craft a résumé and provide you with job-hunting rubrics. Some are former human resources directors or executive recruiters. Almost all have experience working in the corporate world.

Career counselors perform many of the same services as career coaches but extend their efforts to uncovering any emotional, behavioral, or psychological barriers that might impede your search for the meaning of work and a new career. Some are certified psychologists or former human resources directors or both. Many hold a master's degree in counseling and are certified by the National Board of Certified Counselors. They can help you work through complex issues, like why it is that you always have problems with authority figures like your former boss.

All career coaches and career counselors charge a fee for their services, which are delivered by phone, Skype, e-mail, or in face-to-face meetings.

FEES FOR SERVICES

The fees can range from $75 to $500 for a forty-five- or sixty-minute session. Some career coaches and counselors offer package deals that contain a certain number of sessions spread out over a certain amount of time. Others offer their services on an as-needed basis. Personal sessions will cost more than phone sessions. Specialized sessions will cost more than general sessions. For example, some providers work only with executive-level clients, like former presidents, CIOs, CFOs, or CEOs, whose career searches target positions of like kind. Fees for such clients will be considerably higher.

Few coaches and counselors will advertise their fees online, which means that everything is negotiable. Do not hesitate to negotiate a mutually acceptable fee with a provider. Do not be intimidated by a fancy shingle like "Dr. Aldus Geronimo, Certified Career Counselor." Everyone is open to negotiating fees . . . even PhDs.

Career counseling services provided by a certified psychologist or psychiatrist may be covered by your medical insurance. Check with your career care provider and insurance company.

ASSESSING PROVIDER CREDENTIALS

The background and experience of coaches and counselors vary widely. Some have no formal training, while others have had training at bricks-and-mortar institutions. Many have completed online certification programs. The most reputable coaches and counselors have written certifications for successfully completing coaching and counseling programs. Here are some of the more reputable training organizations for career coaches and counselors. All award written certifications for successful completion of training courses. Use the information provided by these resources to assess the credentials of career coaches and counselors.

- **International Coach Federation (ICF),** www.coachfederation.org. This is a highly regarded coaching organization that provides online certification courses for coaches. Access this site for information about the coaching business generally and about suggestions for finding the right coach or counselor who will suit your needs.
- **National Career Development Association,** www.NCDA.org. This respected organization dates back to 1913 and provides not only credentialed programs for coaches, but also assistance for those seeking help in a particular location. For example, go to the website and enter your home zip code in the box beneath the section titled "Need Career Help?" and you will get the names and contact information for coaches and counselors within a fifty-mile radius of your home. Those who successfully complete the NCDA career coaching program receive the Global Career Development Facilitator (GCDF) certificate. When you are interviewing prospective coaches, always ask if they have this certification.
- **Professional Association of Résumé Writers and Career Coaches (PARW C/C),** www.parw.com. This organization provides intensive career coaching training and awards those who successfully complete the course with the Certified Professional Career Coach (CPCC) credential. In addition, PARW C/C offers credentials to coaches who complete training for interviewing techniques and for résumé writing, and it offers help for those starting their own businesses.
- **The Academies,** www.theacademies .com. The founder and CEO of this organization is Susan Whitcomb, an author and expert trainer for career coaches. Her work is frequently quoted in the *New York Times* and the *Wall Street Journal*. Coaches who are trained at the Academies are well versed in all facets of career building. Earmark coaches with the Academies certifications.
- **AARP,** www.aarp.org. This organization is no longer focused exclusively on retired workers. For a low membership fee of $16 per year, workers age fifty and over can access their many benefits. One of them is career counseling for unemployed workers or for workers making a career change.

HOW TO SELECT A CAREER COACH/ COUNSELOR

Select a career coach using the same common-sense rules that you'd apply in making any serious business decision:

1. Make a plan that defines your needs and expectations from a coach or counselor.

2. Contact your network for referrals to professionals specializing in your field of interest and expertise.

3. Go online to find providers in your local area.

4. Interview each person on your list, personally or by phone.

5. Learn the coach's fee structure and how payments are structured.

6. Ask for referrals to their previous or present clients.

7. Ask for a written statement describing their experience in coaching including how many assignments they have completed.

8. Learn their education background, including career coaching certification.

9. Learn if they provide a trial counseling session.

10. Review the extent of their business experience.

COACH SELECTION RESOURCES

There are online resources that provide information about career coaching generally and about criteria for selecting the right person. Here are three reliable sources:

- **International Coach Federation (ICF),** www.coachfederation.org, is the premier global organization for training life and career coaches. Founded in 1995, the ICF provides professional development and support for its members, in addition to training new coaches seeking certification. The ICF publishes an online magazine titled *Coaching World*. IFC recommends that you ask these questions when interviewing a prospective coach:
  - What is your coaching experience (number of individuals coached, years of experience, types of coaching situations, etc.)?
  - What is your coach-specific training (enrolled in an ICF-accredited training program, other coach-specific training, etc.)?
  - What is your coaching specialty or areas in which you most often work?
  - What types of businesses do you work with most often? And at what levels (executives, upper management, middle management, etc.)?
  - What is your philosophy about coaching?
  - What types of assessments are you certified to deliver?
  - What are some of your coaching success stories (specific examples of individuals who have succeeded as a result of coaching)?
  - Are you a member of ICF? Do you hold an ICF credential?

- **NOOMII, *The Professional Coach Directory,*** www.NOOMII.com. This online service recommends coaches based on your stated goals. NOOMII offers an interesting approach to recommendations for coaches. After completing a questionnaire, you are given a number of certified coaches whose expertise is aligned with your profile and goals. We suggest that you review their services. We like the cost: free.

- **Kathy Caprino, *Women's Career Coach and Leadership Trainer,*** http://kathycaprino.com. Kathy is one of the most celebrated career coaches in the world. She was laid off in mid-career and after much soul searching started her own business focusing on career training and coaching. She offers a free subscription to her weekly newsletter and valuable rubrics for moving forward in your career. Be sure to read her article "The Top Five Regrets of Midlife Professionals." She believes they are:

  - I wish I hadn't listened to other people about what I should study and pursue.
  - I wish I hadn't worked so hard and missed out on so much.
  - I wish I hadn't let my fears stop me from making change.
  - I wish I had learned how to address toxic situations and people.
  - I wish I hadn't let myself become so trapped around money.

Career coaches and counselors are typically caring individuals who are passionate about lending support and direction to laid-off or fired workers. Many have had that experience themselves and understand your predicament. When it seems that you are nearing the end of your own self-help resources, reaching out to a coach or counselor is a wise decision.

WORKING WITH AN OUTPLACEMENT SERVICE

Outplacement is not a mom-and-pop business; rather, it is a large industry with national or multinational companies in its fold. Employers frequently provide bricks-and-mortar or virtual outplacement services for midlevel and above workers they let go. This service is expensive and costs the employer upwards of $5,000 per each let-go employee. For high-level executives, outplacement services could cost the employer as much as $25,000 per executive. If your employer did not include outplacement in your severance package, you can purchase it as an individual.

The traditional outplacement service consists of group sessions in an office setting. Weekly or semimonthly group sessions held at an office location and spearheaded by an experienced leader/teacher offer much-needed support for laid-off or fired workers. A spirit of mutual support and assistance are invaluable aids to the let-go person still working through the grieving period or in job-hunting mode. It is reassuring to know that you are not alone in this battle. I myself can attest to the effectiveness of this model, having attended group outplacement on-location in Philadelphia after having been laid off from a technology consulting firm that was purchased by a competitor. For example, when I reported to the group leader, he took me into his office for a private counseling session. That was followed by a half-day group meeting with other laid-off workers where we exchanged experiences and offered each other support and direction. Six weekly meetings followed. Our leader provided excellent rubrics for crafting a résumé and tips for interviewing. We devoted part of our weekly meetings to reviewing a wide array of companies in the area who were potential employers. Also, we had access to computers and could immediately go to the Internet to access potential employers using the rules we had just learned in class. Most helpful in my experience was the group interaction. I learned that I was not the only one in a tough spot. The entire experience hastened my trip through the grieving process. Try to find an outplacement service that still offers that kind of personal service.

Today, some outplacement services are rendered online, by e-mail, phone, Skype, or a combination of these options. Individual attention is what the current model advertises. Services included in most packages are general career counseling, résumé preparation, interviewing techniques, industry and company evaluations, cover- and follow-up letter writing, and referrals to recruiters or human resources directors. Most outplacement companies advertise one-on-one sessions focused on the items you select.

Outplacement services, particularly in a bricks-and-mortar environment, will be highly beneficial for the newly laid-off worker seeking support, understanding, and direction for moving forward. Finding the service right for you is key. Seek a service that is close to home, provides personal meetings and class meetings, and has a verifiable record of success.

OUTPLACEMENT RESOURCES

To find an outplacement provider, use the same techniques suggested for finding a career coach. When you go online, make sure to localize your search. If you live in New York, try to find a service in the NY Metro area, not in San Diego. Here are several references to get you started:

- *Reaction Search International,* www .reactionsearch.com. This service ranks outplacement firms located in a specified geographical location, a valuable feature because working with a company close to home renders effective outcomes.
- *Quest Outplacement,* www .questoutplacement.com. Quest offers a variety of one-on-one outplacement packages to individual let-go workers. The cost varies between $850 and $2,950, depending on the length of

time and the support items offered. Their support is through phone and online tools. They do not provide an office location.

- **Lee Hecht Harrison,** www.lhh.com. LHH is a multinational recruiting and outplacement firm with three hundred offices scattered throughout the United States and abroad. Home offices are in Woodcliff Lake, New Jersey. The company has been in business for fifty years and has a sterling reputation for quality service.

Always review the reputation of any outplacement firm using the following two sources, which provide references, recommendations, and evaluations that will help you make the right decision:

1. *Glassdoor,* www.glassdoor.com
2. *Outplacing.com,* www.outplacing.com

MOVING FORWARD

Employing a career coach/counselor or an outplacement firm is a serious business decision. Finding the right provider, one with whom you connect personally and professionally, is key to a successful outcome. However, help does not stop here. There are additional services providers that tackle the career rebuilding process from a different perspective. These are faith-based organizations, which are located in every community. To learn more about these additional resources, proceed to the next chapter.

CHAPTER TAKEAWAYS

- Selecting a career care provider is a business decision.
- Always check and verify the credentials of a career care provider.
- Local providers offer the most effective services.
- Craft a plan defining your needs and goals before employing any services.
- Working with a career coach or outplacement firm will keep you focused on your objectives and provide direction to find your way out of the dark cloud of unemployment.

PRINT AND DIGITAL RESOURCES

"8 Tips for Hiring and Using a Career Coach." *Forbes,* September 8, 2014. www.forbes.com /sites/nextavenue/2014/09/08/8-tips-for-hiring -and-using-a-career-coach. Go online and enter "Forbes career coaching" for more information.

Glassdoor. www.glassdoor.com. This site provides free reviews for everything job-related, including coaching and outplacement services.

Monster. www.monster.com. Review the article titled "7 Tips for Working with a Career Counselor."

Psychology Today. www.psychologytoday .com. This resource is available as a print or online magazine. It offers a special section titled "Work."

Yates, Julia. *The Career Coaching Handbook.* Routledge, 2014.

CHAPTER 20
TAPPING INTO FAITH-BASED RESOURCES

Being fired or laid off in midcareer can be one's worst nightmare. Political correctness refers to being let go as a challenge, but a fired or laid-off worker realistically calls it a problem, a *huge problem*, one that needs multiple resources to resolve. When the paycheck stops and you have bills to pay, like a home mortgage or apartment rent, property taxes, car payments, utility bills, insurance premiums, childcare, school or college tuition for the kids, and the unforeseen megabill for replacement of a heating system that quits in the middle of the winter, you have more than a "challenge." You have a very serious problem.

Added to the monetary problem is the angst that accompanies being fired or laid off and the tension generated in the job-hunting process. What's left is a worker who needs a comforting hand and down-to-earth friendship in order to move forward and out of the cloud of uncertainty. Finding your way to a new career that offers a paycheck to keep the wolf from the door, plus job satisfaction, plus a sense of purpose, is a multifaceted problem requiring help from multiple sources. Career coaches,

counselors, and outplacement services can help fix the multiple problems, but there are other resources, as well.

FINDING YOUR WAY OUT OF THE CLOUD

So where does one find support, the kind of support that not only offers practical solutions, but also addresses the various stages of the grieving process? Many work through it on their own. Others reach out to friends and family. And some workers, who can't find their way out of the cloud on their own or with help from friends, turn to faith-based resources such as:

1. Career workshops offered by a local church or place of worship of any denomination.
2. Discussion groups led by a staff member of the theology department of a college or university.
3. Counseling sessions with members of the clergy.

Each option has merit. Knowing which to use will save time and result in a better outcome. Here's a succinct review of each.

LOCAL CHURCH COUNSELING SERVICES

Places of worship are noted for providing courses of every kind after Saturday or Sunday services and throughout the week. One does not have to be a member of a particular church to attend, but using the services of your own faith can be reassuring. All are welcome at all churches, at any time.

To learn what is being offered at a local church, simply Google its name and look at the website. For example, I entered "Old St. Patrick's Church in Chicago." What I found was an impressive list of services provided by the church staff, including personal counseling from a parish member whose credentials include an MBA from Northwestern and a master's degree in counseling.

Workers living in medium and large cities throughout the country will find a host of career-related services provided by Jewish career services. For example, in Louisville, Kentucky, you will find a very active center, The Jewish Family and Career Services (JFCS). Its services include career counseling, job-hunting advice, and leads for jobs in the local area and nationwide, as well.

COLLEGE AND UNIVERSITY SPIRITUAL RESOURCES

Some colleges and universities throughout the country have departments of divinity whose reach goes beyond academics. Staff members not only work with students in a traditional academic environment, but also reach out to the community. Outreach includes workshops on traditional theological topics and secular issues such as career planning and counseling for workers seeking support while unemployed.

Everyone who lives within reach of a college or university will find career-related initiatives that come in different flavors. Some are informal discussion groups; others are formal classes held on a regular schedule. For example, one such group is the Princeton Faith and Work Initiative. It meets monthly on a preannounced Saturday morning at Nassau Presbyterian Church, located on the Princeton, New Jersey, campus of Princeton University. It is led by Dr. David Miller, who earned his PhD in social ethics from Yale University after working in the private sector for sixteen years in business and finance with multinational companies in the UK and the US. The group describes its mission as follows:

PRINCETON UNIVERSITY FAITH AND WORK INITIATIVE MISSION

The purpose of the Princeton Faith and Work Initiative is to generate intellectual frameworks and practical resources for the issues and opportunities surrounding faith and work. The initiative investigates the ways in which the resources of various religious traditions and spiritual identities shape and inform engagement with diverse workplace issues as ethics, values, vocation, meaning, purpose, and how people live out their faith in an increasingly pluralistic world. The initiative explores pressing marketplace topics including ethics, global competition and its ramifications, wealth creation and poverty, diversity and inclusion, conflicting stakeholder interests, and social responsibility.

The group accomplishes its mission through a mixture of teaching, lectures, conferences, discussion groups, and research. Attendees include workers of all rank from companies representing multiple industries.

This is just one example of a spiritual resource from a college that sheds light on the relationship between work and faith and offers support for workers seeking a new beginning in the workplace. Check online for a college or university near you that offers career-related discussion groups or workshops.

COUNSELING FROM A CLERGY MEMBER

Advice and guidance are always available from clergy members of your local place of worship. Some clerics will hold one-on-one sessions for general counseling regarding the problems related to your unemployment status. Others will lead group discussions on career-related topics. These are caring, compassionate, and resourceful women and men whose mission is helping people connect faith, work, and family on life's journey.

Some clergy members have broad and deep experience in the secular workplace acquired before they entered the ministry. Many have had teaching and counseling experience. Their networks include hiring managers from companies representing diverse industries. All are sympathetic listeners who offer not only sound advice, but also the hand of friendship to those in need.

MOVING FORWARD

When all else seems to have failed, laid-off workers have another option, seeking help from the God of their faith. The next chapter will shed light on how one can move beyond the temporal for help in the job-hunting process.

CHAPTER TAKEAWAYS

- Spiritual resources offer support, counseling, and friendship.
- If your church has several clergy members, try to connect with those who have had secular workplace experience.
- Some churches offer support from its members who have professional counseling training.

PRINT AND DIGITAL RESOURCES

Christian Counselor Directory. www.christiancounselordirectory.com. Go to this online service to find faith-related services from certified counselors. It provides the names and profiles of counselors throughout the country by zip code.

Christian Jobs. www.christianjobs.org. This is the leading Christian job site connecting Christian-friendly employers and job seekers.

It provides résumé help and career coaching, as well.

Jewish Family and Career Services. www .jfcslouisville.org. This is a very active career center in Louisville, Kentucky. Go online to find similar Jewish centers in your own location.

CHAPTER 21

MOVING BEYOND THE TEMPORAL

Throughout my career in the staffing business, I have witnessed events that have no logical explanation. After applying the rules for solving problems and coming up dry, I believe there must be *something else* working behind the scene that goes beyond the temporal into a realm that includes the supernatural, like a God, a Force, or the Universe.

When seeking help, it is customary to address the care providers, coaches, counselors, ministers, priests, and rabbis by name. But how do you address a deity? What is his or her name? Followers of different faiths call their Gods by different names. The Christians have multiple names for their God depending upon the particular denomination; *Jesus, Father, Savior, Holy One* are customary. The Jews call their god *Adonai*, which translated means "my Lord." The Muslims refer to their god as *Allah*. The Hindus have multiple gods called by different names like *Krishna, Vishnu,* and *Shiva*. Some believe there is one universal God called the Force. But for our purposes, let's call that Supreme Being God.

Petitioning God when in need is instinctive when all else seems to have failed. You need not be a follower of any particular faith to ask God for help through a tough time, like being fired or laid off. It makes no difference what your religious faith might be. God is God. The name makes no difference.

THERE ARE NO ATHEISTS IN FOXHOLES

So what does all of this have to do with job hunting? You may have heard the proverb "There are no atheists in foxholes." The origin of this proverb is attributed to a World War II correspondent, Ernie Pyle, who reported what was happening on the front line of battle, a very unfriendly place.

For those not familiar with war jargon, here is what it means. When soldiers are on the battlefield and see bombs dropping and bullets flying, and witness their buddies to the left and right being blown to smithereens, these soldiers instinctively call on God to save their lives. Their prayers to God are ones of supplication: "God, please spare my life!"

Job hunting is much like fighting in the trenches, as you may have experienced. Following that traumatic experience, being let go from your job in the middle of a career that you thought was forever, life has not been easy, especially the job-hunting part. You never realized how difficult it is, how competitive it is, how frightening it is when you have bills to pay and nothing seems to be working in your favor. Interviews go wrong, your network seems to have taken an extended vacation, and hiring managers are saying you are overqualified or they can't afford to pay you market price for your experience and expertise. If you have been fighting on the battlefield of the workplace for six months or more with no success, you will get the analogy. Job hunting is not easy. It is not for the timid. It is not for the faint of heart. The competition is fierce. You never know when and where the next defeat will occur.

The proverb "There are no atheists in foxholes" could easily read, "There are no atheists among job hunters fighting in the workplace for a few bucks to buy food, shelter, and clothing."

GOD AT WORK

My experience as an executive recruiter is replete with examples that point to a Force working with midcareer workers who have made every conceivable effort on their own and with help from career counselors to find solutions to their unemployment challenges.

I have named that force working in the background the *Job God*. Here are just a few examples of what I have witnessed:

Sally was a San Francisco resident seeking a step up from her job as a vice president of marketing for a major education publisher. I was conducting a number of searches for which she was eminently well qualified. Sally did not wish to move from San Francisco but was open to relocation for the "right" job. She interviewed for the presidency of a company in Portland, Maine, but it did not work out for a number of reasons. Her next stop was in New York City, where she interviewed for a senior vice presidency with one the country's largest publishers. She liked them and they liked her, but they could not get together on compensation. Her next interview was in Chicago, but the company demands proved impossible for her to meet. Sally, dejected by her job-hunting experiences, returned to San Francisco and tried to determine what happened. Then, unexpectedly, she received a call from the human resources director with a well-known company who invited her to interview for a VP position as head of the newly formed education division. Sally interviewed for the job and got it. Big salary. No relocation. Terrific benefits package. There was no logical reason why this happened. There were candidates who were better qualified for this job, but Sally got it. Why?

And then there was Dick, who lived in San Antonio. He was hired for a marketing position, even though he was the least qualified of five finalists for a position titled "Director of Marketing." There was no logical reason why Dick got that job.

And then we have Jane. Five respectable companies rejected her candidacy claiming she was overqualified. Jane was at the point of depression. Nothing was working for her no matter how hard she tried. Then suddenly she received a job offer from an esteemed employer right in her hometown, one who just a few weeks ago told us, "Sorry, there is nothing available here for Jane."

What was it that led these three job candidates to the Promised Land of employment?

Serendipity? Timing? Fate? These true stories about how Sally, Dick, and Jane found employment working against all the odds went beyond my comprehension. Lacking any evidence for a logical explanation, we hypothesized that it could be something beyond the temporal, something working behind the scene.

SEARCHING FOR TEMPORAL ANSWERS

Others searching for answers might come to different conclusions. If Malcolm Gladwell, author of the bestselling book *Outliers*, had put Sally, Dick, and Jane to the test, he may have found an answer. Gladwell's theory is that if you look hard enough, you will always find an answer to the question "Why did this person succeed?" He even goes so far as to say it could have been the influence of grandparents, or even *great*-grandparents, the culture in which the person lived, date of birth, and a host of other variables. However, none of our three candidates met Gladwell's prime requirement for success: ten thousand hours of experience in a particular field of endeavor, whether it be music, as with the Beatles; or computer technology, as with Bill Gates; or science, as with Albert Einstein.

What accounted for the success of our three candidates? When I found no plausible answers, I hypothesized that it was the *Job God* at work, that Force who controls heaven and Earth, the Supreme Being who in some mysterious way is looking out for all of us. Some might say, "Oh my Lord, this is nuts, plain nuts, to posit that God has any interest in how we find work to provide food, shelter, and clothing for our existence here on Earth." Well, everyone has a theory about why things happen as they do, and our theory seems to be as plausible as Gladwell's.

CONNECTING

How do you reach out to your God? What do you say? How do you petition God for a favor such as success in finding a job? You might recall prayers learned in childhood religious training: you memorized them and recited them back to your parents or teacher. They meant little because they did not come from you. Even today, prayers we hear during religious services may sound contrived and hold little meaning. A meaningful prayer must come from you, from your inner core.

So how do you begin the prayer journey? By hastily fabricating one on your smartphone or iPad? By writing it on a sheet of paper in flowery prose? Anything will work, but we suggest composing your prayer in the vernacular of your faith. It does not have to be eloquent or put in writing. Make it conversational. Ask God's help in the same way you would ask one of your friends for a favor. For example, immediately after the attacks on the World Trade Towers on 9/11, two Air Force fighter jets hurriedly took off from their base in Arizona and headed toward New York City and New Jersey to intercept any other attacks. The importance of getting there quickly was more important than fully arming the planes, so they took off semiprepared. It was a dangerous mission. In a CNN interview with the pilots after the mission was completed, one of them told the interviewer they realized the extreme danger heading into combat without being fully armed, and as they were flying toward the action, they prayed the pilot's prayer, "God, don't let me screw this up." A prayer does not have to be eloquent. If you need examples, we offer these resources:

- Tevye's Sabbath Prayer from the play *Fiddler on the Roof*
- The Lord's Prayer, available online or from the Bible
- Sample Prayers. Thoughts about God. www.thoughts-about-god.com /reflecting/sample-prayers.htm

A SAMPLE PRAYER

If you don't have the time or inclination to access these resources, and if you have not reached out to God since childhood and have no idea about how to begin, try something like this when you need a hand going through one of the steps in the job-hunting process, like the exercise that strikes fear into the hearts of most job seekers, *the interview*:

A PRAYER TO THE JOB GOD

God of all, I'm coming to ask your help. This may not be eloquent, but this is just between You and me, so who cares how it sounds. I'm opening the door to my life and asking you to come in and lend a hand. I need Your help securing employment. I've tried my best, but nothing seems to be working out. I have an interview scheduled with a hiring manager and would appreciate Your support. I'll meet this challenge with a positive attitude and use my intelligence, energy, and passion to get the job done. The bottom line is this, God. When I go in for the interview, I ask that You take my hand and be with me during the entire process. I am sure that with Your help, this will have a favorable outcome. Thanks in advance, God. Amen.

CHAPTER TAKEAWAYS . . . FROM MOTHER TERESA

- Life is an opportunity, benefit from it.
- Life is beauty, admire it.
- Life is a dream, realize it.

PRINT AND DIGITAL RESOURCES

Kushner, Harold S. *When Bad Things Happen to Good People*. Anchor Books, 2004.

Lamott, Anne. *Help, Thanks, Wow!* Riverhead Publishing, 2012.

Payne, Stephen. *The Joy of Work: How to Stay Calm, Confident & Connected in a Chaotic World*. Balboa Press, 2012.

Osteen, Joel. *I Declare: 31 Promises to Speak Over Your Life*. Faith Works, 2013.

The Prayer Coach. "How to Pray." www.prayercoachingprinciples.wordpress.com/how-to-pray.htm.

Warren, Rick. *What Am I Here For?* Zondervan, 2012.

APPENDIX A
MAJOR CONVENTION CENTERS

Every city and state has convention centers that host trade shows and conferences, which are the best locations to find hiring managers and job opportunities. Managers and directors from sales, marketing, product development, technology, advertising, human resources, event planning, and finance work in the trade show exhibit booths.

What do you do at a trade show? Stop at a booth, introduce yourself, and ask for help securing employment. Does it get any easier than that? Potential employers are not hiding under rocks; rather, they hang out at convention centers, the names and locations of which are just a couple of clicks away.

Go online and contact the convention centers on the list below. Each center will provide the dates and names of the trade shows for the entire year and, in many instances, will provide links to the companies attending. In addition, you will find the price of admission and other pertinent information that will make your visit there more profitable.

MAJOR US CONVENTION CENTERS BY STATE

Alabama
Birmingham-Jefferson Civic Center
www.bjcc.org
2100 Richard Arrington Jr. Blvd. N
Birmingham, AL 35203
(205) 458-8400

Alaska
Anchorage Convention Centers
www.anchorageconventioncenters.com
555 West Fifth Ave.
Anchorage, AK 99501

Juneau Centennial Hall Convention Center
www.juneau.org/centennial
101 Egan Dr.
Juneau, AK 99801
(907) 586-5283

Arizona

Phoenix Convention Center
www.phoenixconventioncenter.com
111 N 3rd St.
Phoenix, AZ 85004-2231
(602) 262-6225

Tucson Convention Center
www.tcc.tucsonaz.gov
260 S. Church St.
Tucson, AZ 85701
(520) 791-4101

Arkansas

Statehouse Convention Center
www.littlerockmeetings.com
#1 Statehouse Plaza
Little Rock, AR 72201
(501) 376-4781
(800) 844-4781

California

Long Beach Convention and Entertainment Center
www.longbeachcc.com
300 Ocean Blvd.
Long Beach, CA 90802
(562) 436-3636

Los Angeles Convention Center
www.lacclink.com
685 South Figueroa St.
Los Angeles, CA 90017
(213) 689-8822

San Diego Convention Center
www.visitsandiego.com
111 West Harbor Dr.
San Diego, CA 92101
(619) 525-5214

Moscone Center
www.moscone.com
747 Howard St.
San Francisco, CA 94103
(415) 974-4000

Colorado

Colorado Convention Center
www.denverconvention.com
700 14th St.
Denver, CO 80202
(303) 228-8000

Connecticut

XL Center (formerly the Hartford Civic Center)
www.xlcenter.com
One Civic Center Plaza
Hartford, CT 06103
(860) 249-6333

Delaware

Delaware does not have a major convention center. Check the convention centers in Baltimore, MD; Philadelphia, PA; Atlantic City, NJ; and Washington, DC.

District of Columbia
Washington Convention Center
www.dcconvention.com
801 Mount Vernon Place, NW
Washington, DC 20001
(202) 249-3000

Florida
Fort Lauderdale/Broward Co. Convention
Center
www.ftlauderdalecc.com
1950 Eisenhower Blvd.
Fort Lauderdale, FL 33316
(305) 765-5900

Miami Beach Convention Center
www.miamibeachconvention.com
1901 Convention Center Dr.
Miami Beach, FL 33139
(305) 673-7311

Orange County Convention Center
www.occc.net
9800 International Dr.
Orlando, FL 32819
(407) 345-9800

Tampa Convention Center
www.tampaconventioncenter.com
333 S. Franklin St.
Tampa, FL 33602
(813) 274-8511

Georgia
Georgia World Congress Center
www.gwcc.com
285 Andrew Young International Blvd. NW
Atlanta, GA 30313
(404) 223-4200

Hawaii
Hawaii Convention Center
www.hawaiiconvention.com
1801 Kalakaua Ave.
Honolulu, HI 96815
(808) 943-3500

Idaho
Boise Center
www.boisecenter.com
850 West Front St.
Boise, ID 83702
(208) 336-8900

Illinois
McCormick Place
www.mccormickplace.com
2301 S. Lake Shore Dr.
Chicago, IL 60616
(312) 791-7000

Navy Pier
www.navypier.com
600 East Grand Ave.
Chicago, IL 60611
(312) 595-PIER

Indiana
Indiana Convention Center
www.icclos.com
100 South Capital Ave.
Indianapolis, IN 46225
(317) 262-3400

Iowa
Iowa Events Center
www.iowaeventscenter.com
730 Third St.
Des Moines, IA 50309
(515) 564-8000

Kansas
Overland Park Convention Center
www.opconventioncenter.com
600 College Blvd.
Overland Park, KS 66211
913-439-5382

Kentucky
Kentucky International Convention Center
www.kyconvention.org
221 Fourth St.
Louisville, KY 40202
(502) 595-4381

Louisiana
Ernest N. Morial Convention Center
www.mccno.com
900 Convention Center Blvd.
New Orleans, LA 70130
(504) 582-3023

Maine
Cumberland Convention Center
www.theciviccenter.com
One Civic Center Sq.
Portland, ME 04101
(207) 775-3481

Maryland
Baltimore Convention Center
www.bccenter.org
1 West Pratt St.
Baltimore, MD 21201
(410) 649-7000

Massachusetts
Boston Convention and Exhibition Center
www.bostonconventioncenter.com
415 Summer St.
Boston, MA
(617) 867-8286

John B. Hynes Convention Center
www.massconvention.com
900 Boylston St.
Boston, MA 02115
(617) 867-8286

Michigan
Cobo Conference/Exhibition Center
www.cobocenter.com
One Washington Blvd.
Detroit, MI 48226
(313) 877-8777

Minnesota
Mayo Civic Center
www.mayociviccenter.com
30 Civic Center Dr. SE
Rochester, MN 55904
(507) 281-6184

Duluth Entertainment Convention Center
www.decc.org
350 Harbor Dr.
Duluth, MN 55802
(218) 722-5573

Minneapolis Convention Center
www.minneapolisconventioncenter.com
1301 Second Ave. S
Minneapolis, MN 55403
(612) 335-6000

Mississippi
Mississippi Coast Convention Center
www.mscoastconventioncenter.com
2350 Beach Blvd.
Biloxi, MS 39531
(228) 594-3700

Missouri
Kansas City Convention

www.kcconvention.com
Convention & Entertainment Centers
301 West 13th St.
Suite 100
Kansas City, MO 64105
(816) 513-5071

America's Center
www.explorestlouis.com
701 Convention Plaza
St. Louis, MO 63105
(800) 325-7962

Montana
Butte Silver Bow Civic Center
www.butteciviccenter.com
1340 Harrison Ave.
Butte, MT 59701
(406) 497-6400

Mansfield Convention Center
www.greatfalls.net/mansfieldcenter.com
4 Park Dr.
Great Falls, MT 59401
(406) 455-8510

Helena Civic Center
www.helenaciviccenter.com
340 Neill Ave
Helena, MT 59601
(406) 461-8785

Nebraska
CenturyLink Center
www.centurylinkcenteromaha.com

455 N. 10th St.
Omaha, NE 68102
(402) 341-1500

Nevada
Las Vegas Convention and Visitors Authority
www.lvcva.com
3150 Paradise Rd.
Las Vegas, NV 89109
(702) 386-7100

New Hampshire
Check the convention centers in Maine and
Massachusetts.

New Jersey
Atlantic City Convention Center
www.accenter.com
2301 Boardwalk
Atlantic City, NJ 08401
(800) 214-0663

Meadowlands Exposition Center
www.mecexpo.com
355 Plaza Dr.
Secaucus, NJ 07094
201-330-1172

Edison Convention Center
www.njexpocenter.com/eb&cc
97 Sunfield Ave.
Edison, NJ 08837
(732) 661-1205

Garden State Convention & Exhibit Center

www.gsec.com
50 Atrium Dr.
Somerset, NJ 08873
(732) 417-1400
Wildwoods Convention Center
www.wildwoodsnj.com/cc
4501 Boardwalk
Wildwood, NJ
(609) 729-9000

New Mexico
Albuquerque Convention Center
www.albuquerquecc.com
Second & Tijeras NW
Albuquerque, NM 87102
(505) 842-9918

New York
Buffalo Niagara Convention Center
www.buffaloconvention.com
Convention Center Plaza
Buffalo, NY 14202
(716) 855-5555

Jacob K. Javits Convention Center
www.javitscenter.com
655 West 34th St.
New York, NY 10001
(212) 216-2000

North Carolina
Charlotte Convention Center
www.charlotteconventionctr.com
100 Paul Buck Blvd.
Charlotte, NC 28217

(704) 339-6000

Metrolina Expo Center
www.metrolinatradeshowexpo.com
7100 Statesville Rd.
Charlotte, NC 28221
(704) 596-4650

North Dakota
Check the convention centers in Minnesota and South Dakota.

Ohio
Duke Energy Convention Center
www.duke-energycenter.com
525 Elm St.
Cincinnati, OH 45202
(513) 419-7300

Cleveland Convention Center
www.clevcc.com
500 Lakeside Ave.
Cleveland, OH 44114
(216) 928-1600

I-X Center
www.ixcenter.com
6200 Riverside Dr.
Cleveland, OH 44135
(216) 676-6000

Dayton Convention Center
www.daytonconventioncenter.com
22 E. Fifth St.
Dayton, OH 45402

(937) 333-4700

Seagate Convention Centre
www.toledo-seagate.com
401 Jefferson Ave.
Toledo, OH 43604
(419) 321-5007

Oklahoma
Cox Convention Center
www.coxconventioncenter.com
1 Myriad Gardens
Oklahoma City, OK 73102-9219
(405) 602-8500

Cox Business Center
www.coxcentertulsa.com
100 Civic Center
Tulsa, OK 74103
(918) 894-4350

Oregon
Oregon Convention Center
www.oregoncc.com
777 N Martin Luther King Blvd.
Portland, OR 97232
(503) 235-7575

Pennsylvania
Pennsylvania Convention Center
www.paconvention.com
1101 Arch St.
Philadelphia, PA 19107
(215) 418-4700

Lawrence Convention Center
www.pittsburghcc.com
1000 Ft. Duquesne Blvd.
Pittsburgh, PA 15222
(412) 565-6000

Rhode Island
Rhode Island Convention Center
www.riconvention.com
One Sabin St.
Providence, RI 02903-1814
(401) 458-6000

South Carolina
Charleston Convention Center
www.charlestonconventioncenter.com
5001 Coliseum Dr. North
Charleston, SC 29418
(843) 529-5050

Palmetto International Exposition Center
www.palmettoexpo.com
One Exposition Ave.
Greenville, SC 29607
(864) 233-2562

South Dakota
Sioux Empire Fairgrounds
www.souixempirefair.org
Sioux Empire Fair Office
4000 W 12th St.
Sioux Falls, SD 57107
(605) 367-7178

Tennessee
Nashville Convention Center
www.nashvilleconventionctr.com
601 Commerce St.
Nashville, TN 37203
(615) 742-2002

Texas
Austin Convention Center
www.austinconventioncenter.com
500 E. First St.
Austin, TX 78701
(512) 404-4000

Kay Baily Hutchinson Convention Center
www.dallasconventioncenter.com
650 S. Griffin St.
Dallas, TX 75202
(214) 939-2750

George R. Brown Convention Center
www.houstonconventioncenter.com
1001 Avenida de las Americas
Houston, TX 77010
(713) 853-8090

Henry B. Gonzalez Convention Center
www.sahbgcc.com
200 E. Market St.
San Antonio, TX 78205
(877) 504-8895

Waco Convention Center
www.wacocc.com
100 Washington Ave.
Waco, TX 76702
(254) 750-5810

Utah
Salt Palace Convention Center
www.saltpalace.com
100 SW Temple
Salt Lake City, UT 84101
(801) 534-4777

Dixie Convention Center
www.dixiecenter.com
1835 Convention Center Dr.
St. George, UT 84790
(435) 628-7003

Vermont
Check the convention centers in Massachusetts and New York.

Virginia
The Greater Richmond Convention Center
www.richmondcenter.com
403 N. Third St.
Richmond, VA 23219
(804) 783-7300

The Virginia Beach Convention Center
www.vbcvb.com
1000 19th St.
Virginia Beach, VA 23451
(757) 385-2000

Washington
Meydenbauer Center
www.meydenbauer.com
11100 NE Sixth St.
Bellevue, WA 98004
(425) 637-1020

Washington State Convention & Trade Center
www.wscc.com
800 Convention Place
Seattle, WA 98101-2350
(206) 694-5000

Spokane Center
www.spokanecenter.com
334 W. Spokane Falls Blvd.
Spokane, WA 99201
(509) 353-6500

West Virginia
Charleston Civic Center
www.charlestonciviccenter.com
200 Civic Center Dr.
Charleston, WV 25301
(304) 345-1500

Wisconsin

Wisconsin Center

www.wisconsincenter.org

Wisconsin Center District

400 W. Wisconsin Ave.

Milwaukee, WI 53203

(414) 908-6000

Wyoming

Casper Events Center

www.caspereventscenter.com

One Events Dr.

Caspar, WY 82601

307-235-8441

APPENDIX B
CONVENTION CENTER AND TRADE SHOW SPOTLIGHT

A number of state convention centers and trade shows deserve special attention because of their strategic locations and the important conferences they attract. Having attended hundreds of trade shows across the country, I know the top sites and trade shows and would like to share some of them with you. Here are my recommendations:

CALIFORNIA

The Moscone Center

www.moscone.com. Located in the heart of San Francisco, the Moscone Center hosts some of our largest conventions. In recent years, it attracted the National Auto Dealers Association, the Molecular Medicine Convention, and a number of "Green" conferences dealing with environmental products and services.

FLORIDA

Miami Beach Convention Center

www.miamibeachconvention.com. The Americas' largest jewelry show meets here each year. It is sponsored by the Jewelers International Showcase (JIS) and features three shows annually that attract thousands of exhibitors and thousands of attendees. A recent show had approximately 1,200 exhibit booths. The JIS trade shows attract companies and attendees from 50 countries in the Caribbean, Latin America, and North America. If you like gold, silver, diamonds, rubies, and pearls, this is the place to go to find a job in the jewelry industry.

The Orange County Convention Center

www.occc.net. Located in Orlando, this is one of busiest convention centers in the world, hosting national and international conferences. There are two separate facilities a block apart, and each can accommodate tens of thousands of visitors at one time. The convention halls are massive, so be prepared to do a lot of walking. Some conventions to attend here are the Orlando Home Show, the Florida Educational Technology Conference, and the Golf Industry Show. The Golf Show attracts 500 companies, which means there are 500 potential employers all gathered under one roof. Attendance usually runs over 50,000. Do you like the sporting industry? Attend the Golf Show.

The Tampa Convention Center

www.tampaconventioncenter.com. This is one of the premier conference centers in the Southeast. It accommodates medium-sized conferences that attract hundreds of companies exhibiting their products and services. Its location is on the waterfront in downtown Tampa.

GEORGIA

The Atlanta Convention Center

www.atlconventioncenter.com. This large conference facility (more than 800,000 square feet) attracts many national and international trade shows each year. For example, the International Society for Technology in Education (ISTE) recently held a convention here that attracted 15,000 attendees. This conference hosted 500 exhibiting companies that produce educational technology products for K-12 and higher education. More than 4,500 company representatives worked the booths.

HAWAII

The Hawaii Convention Center

www.meethawaii.com. This one-million-square-foot convention center is just down the street from famed Waikiki beach and is one of the best of its kind in the world. It holds many large and small conferences around the calendar, many of them with exhibitors staffed by key employees, like hiring managers. Check out the careers, listed under "jobs," on their website.

Ready for some sun, surf, and a luau on weekends after convention hours? That's working in Hawaii. Does it get any better than that?

ILLINOIS

McCormick Place

www.McCormickplace.com. This facility, located on the shore of Lake Michigan in Chicago, is Illinois's largest convention facility. Go there now on your smartphone, iPad, tablet, or laptop. Click on "full calendar" and then go to the "monthly calendar." This convention center is one of the most popular in the country because of its central location. Some of the shows it hosts annually are the Progressive Insurance Boat Show, the International Home and Housewares Show, and the National Restaurant Show.

Go to the website and click on the show title, and it will take you to that particular website. You will find all the information you need including the names and addresses of hundreds of companies that will be exhibiting.

INDIANA

The Indianapolis Convention Center

www.icclos.com. This popular conference center hosts many national and regional conferences representing all industries. Its central location and reasonable attendance fees make it a popular location. One of the most important regional conferences held here is the Indiana Bankers Association. I checked out a recent conference, and it listed all of the attending banks, many of which were national financial institutions. And *it listed the names of the attendees from each bank*. Pay dirt!

IOWA
Iowa Events Center
www.iowaeventscenter.com. The Iowa-Nebraska Equipment Dealers Association hosts the Iowa Power Farming trade show here each year. The convention brings together under one roof manufacturers and dealers of farming equipment, all of which are potential job targets. If you are interested in agribusiness, where better to find a job than in Iowa, at the Iowa Events Center in Des Moines?

When I reviewed the Iowa Events Center website, I found an interesting array of job opportunities in marketing, sales, events management, and food and beverage operations.

NEW YORK
The Javits Convention Center
www.javitscenter.com. This is one of the best-known convention centers in the world and attracts an impressive array of important conventions. Companies that exhibit here always send their executives and hiring managers, making the Javits one of the best venues for job hunting.

One of the most interesting and important annual conventions held at the Javits each October is Photo Plus Expo. It attracts approximately 300 companies that exhibit their latest products and services for the photography and imaging industry. Hundreds of hiring managers staff the various exhibit booths. Attending this conference is not only a good job-hunting experience, but also an interesting learning experience.

WASHINGTON, DC
The Washington Convention Center
www.dcconvention.com. Our nation's capital has one of the most frequently used convention centers for regional and national trade shows and exhibits. Check the website frequently because conventions in Washington draw a large number of both vendors and attendees. Hiring managers and top-level executives of major companies attend DC conventions.

In addition, many large DC hotels, such as Marriott, Holiday Inn, and Hilton, host trade shows, and I suggest checking their websites for conference information. If you cannot find it online, call the hotel and ask to speak with the conference manager.

BEST TRADE SHOWS FOR JOB HUNTING BY INDUSTRY
The following list of annual trade shows by industry could be your ticket to finding a new career path after being fired or laid off. Click on the show nearest to your location or the show focusing on an area of interest, like photography, housing, food, shelter, travel, or educational technology and publishing. The organizations listed below hold conferences in different locations each year.

To get you started, I'm focusing on only seven industries: Education, Insurance, Healthcare, Transportation; and the *Big Three*, Food, Shelter, and Clothing.

EDUCATION

The Education Industry is truly worker-friendly. Many work in this industry because they find a sense of mission, job satisfaction, and attractive compensation. At all of these exhibits, you will meet hiring managers working for companies like College Board, Educational Testing Service (ETS), Scholastic, McGraw-Hill, Texas Instruments, and Pearson. Here are some of the best:

American Association of School Administrators (AASA)

www.aasa.org. Hundreds of companies exhibit here to display their products to school superintendents and other high-level school administrators. The companies attending this convention are publishers and producers of instructional materials, school supply companies, bus companies, insurance companies, security companies, and more.

American Booksellers Association (ABA)

www.bookweb.com. The ABA holds an annual conference and several regional conferences where you can see many companies in the print and digital publishing industry. The 2016 show was held in Chicago and the 2017 annual convention (BookExpo) at the Javits Center in New York. This is the largest publishing conference in the United States.

Association of Educational Publishers www.aepweb.org.

This organization sponsors an annual conference in June each year in Washington, DC. Attendees include high-level educational technology and publishing company executives, all of whom are hiring authorities. In 2013, this organization merged with the Association of American Publishers (AAP), www.publishers.org.

American Library Association (ALA)

www.ALA.org. This conference focuses on books and digital products related to public and school libraries and online education. It is a fascinating show with hundreds of exhibitors from the education, publishing, and online learning industries. When you are on this website, click on "Education and Careers" for job opportunities with the organization.

American Society for Training and Development (ASTD)

www.astd.org. This nonprofit organization focuses on training and professional development for educators and government workers. It holds an annual conference in a major city, plus four regional conferences throughout the country. A recent conference met in Dallas and attracted approximately 9,000 attendees from 80 different countries. More than 300 companies exhibited their products and services. The fee for entrance to the exhibits? Free! Track the annual and regional conferences because this is where you will meet many employers in the flesh, each one being the source for employment.

Association for Supervision and Curriculum Development (ASCD)
www.ascd.org. Members of ASCD are involved with curriculum matters at K-12 schools. Thousands of these administrators, called curriculum coordinators or assistant superintendents for instruction, attend this show.

International Literacy Association (ILA)
www.literacyworldwide.org. This organization is for teachers and administrators who teach reading and literacy to K-12 students. When you access this site, click on "career center," where you will find ten or more pages of open positions for entry-level and experienced workers. If you have any experience in education, and are interested in literacy education, this is the conference to attend to explore job opportunities.

International Society for Technology in Education (ISTE)
www.iste.org. This show focuses on products and services related to educational technology and meets each June at a different location. If you are interested in an industry that makes a difference for kids, this one is for you. Do not miss it, because here you will find hundreds of exhibitors under one roof. Each is a potential employer.

In addition, there are a number of curriculum-related education conferences held annually in different locations. They are:

National Association of Biology Teachers (NABT)
www.nabt.org

National Council for the Social Studies (NCSS)
www.ncss.org

National Council for Teachers of English (NCTE)
www.ncte.org

National Council of Teachers of Mathematics (NCTM)
www.nctm.org

National Science Teachers Association (NSTA)
www.nsta.org

Software and Information Industry Association (SIIA)
www.siia.org

Texas Computer Education Association (TCEA)
www.tcea.org

INTERNATIONAL EDUCATION BOOK FAIRS

There are several international publishing conventions each year, and if you are in the area, plan to attend. Companies from America and other countries host exhibits staffed by workers who will tell you about job opportunities *and* provide the names and contact information for hiring managers. Foreign companies may be looking for workers to represent their interests in America, and you might be the one for such a job. Here are some of the best international trade fairs in the education and communications industries.

Beijing International Book Fair (BIBF) www .combinedbook.com. If you find yourself in China during the month of August, visit this fascinating conference to meet more than 500 exhibitors from around the world, with an emphasis on Asian companies. This is a long way to go to meet American companies, but you will find many of them exhibiting alongside their foreign counterparts. Beijing is the host city for this annual conference.

Bologna Children's Book Fair www.bolo -gnachildrensbookfair.com. This interesting book fair focuses on products related to K-12 education. Hundreds of companies publishing books and digital products exhibit here. Bologna, Italy, is the host city for this annual conference. Check it out if you happen to be in Italy in spring.

Frankfurt Book Fair www.buchmesse.de /en/company. This convention attracts 7,000 exhibitors from around the world and is the mother of all international book fairs. It meets in Frankfurt, Germany, every October. Can you imagine 7,000 potential employers under one roof?

The London Book Fair (LBF) www.london -bookfair.co.uk. This major bookseller event meets in London each spring. It attracts close to 1,000 exhibitors ranging from retail booksellers to educational publishers and communications companies in general.

INSURANCE
Like it or not, you need insurance. Many insurance companies have been in business continuously for more than a hundred years and are attractive places for long-term employment. The industry hosts many conventions throughout the calendar year in many different cities. Here is one on the largest conferences in the industry:

The National Association of Mutual Insurance Companies (NAMIC) www.namic.org. This is one of the largest insurance professional organizations in the business, and it hosts an annual convention at a different location each year. Recent conferences were held at the Gaylord National Resort and Conference Center in National Harbor, Maryland, and at the San Diego Convention center. It is hard to beat the insurance industry for long-term employment. The best place for information about insurance trade shows is the *Insurance Journal*. Visit the website at www.insurancejournal.com.

HEALTHCARE
Under the broadly defined label of "healthcare," there are numerous subgroups: pharmaceuticals, physicians, radiologists, certified nurse midwives, medical equipment producers, physical therapists, medicinal packaging, and the like. There

is no large catch-all healthcare convention, but there are many small conventions serving segments of the healthcare industry. Many of these conventions are local or regional in scope. Here are some of the larger national conventions sponsored by professional healthcare organizations:

- **Nurse Practioners in Women's Healthcare, NPWH,** www.npwh.org
- **Federation of International Medical Equipment Suppliers,** www.fimeshow.com
- **Radiographical Society of North America,** www.rsna.org
- **Healthcare Information and Management Systems Society,** www.himss.org
- **American Society of Clinical Oncology,** www.asco.org
- **International Society for Pharmaceutical Engineering (ISPE)** sponsors the annual Pharma Expo conference. www.pharmaexpo.com
- **American College of Nurse-Midwives,** www.acnm.org
- **American Physical Therapy Association,** www.apta.org

The largest in this group is Pharma Expo, www.pharmaexpo.com, a convention devoted to packaging medicines and medical equipment. A recent convention was held in Denver in conjunction with PACK EXPO, the national convention for the general packaging industry. Approximately 1,800 exhibitors and over 30,000 industry workers attended this convention.

TRANSPORTATION

In addition to food, shelter, and clothing, transportation is one of the basics for modern living. The transportation industry conducts hundreds of conventions each year in locations throughout the country, and it would be impossible to list all of them. Google "auto shows," add the largest city close to home, and you will find all the information you need. Here is an example of a major transportation show to get you started:

Food

This huge industry includes everything imaginable including fast foods, beverages, restaurants, online grocery shopping, and hospitality. There are many local, regional, and national conventions catering to the food industry. Check out those listed below:

The International Restaurant and Food Service Show

www.internationalrestaurantny.com. Meet 500 exhibiting companies and 16,000 workers in this interesting venue at the Javits Center in New York. The convention is the best in this market niche.

National Restaurant Association

www.show.restaurant.org. How can you beat a convention with 2,000 exhibitors (all potential employers) and 45,000 attendees? If your interest is the restaurant niche, plan to attend this conference, which meets at McCormick Place in Chicago each year. For general information about this part of the food industry, contact the National Restaurant Association, www.restaurant.org.

New York International Auto Show

www.autoshowny.com. This conference is one of the largest auto shows in the country and hosts hundreds of companies, which exhibit on the floor of the Javits Center. Attend this conference, and you will find potential job opportunities in the automobile industry. Guaranteed.

Specialty Food Association

www.specialtyfood.com. This show attracts over 1,200 exhibitors and tens of thousands of attendees. Its location changes each year.

CLOTHING

This industry includes a number of specialties, like children's clothing, sportswear, women's fashion apparel, textile manufacturing, footwear, and exercise gear, just to name a few. As a result, there are no national conventions catering to the clothing industry as a whole. The best way to find trade shows in a specialty of the clothing industry is to conduct an online search for your area of interest.

One of the best and largest shows for women's accessories is held at the Javits Center in New York each January and is known as Apparel Sourcing USA. Check it out at www.10times.com/apparelsourcing.

SHELTER

You might recall that one of the three necessities for survival is shelter. Therefore, it is not surprising there are many home and commercial building shows throughout the United States that attract thousands of companies exhibiting their products. Each one is a potential employer. Where do you find them? At conference centers throughout the country. For example, do you live in or near the Chicago area? There are several home shows in different area locations hosting many hundreds of exhibitors. Go to www.chicagohomeshow.net to find out more.

There are so many home shows that it would take many pages to list all of them here. An easy route to find these conferences is to Google "home trade shows" in your local area. Sometimes these shows combine home building and improvement companies with garden and horticulture organizations. As an example of what you will find, I'll highlight just two:

National Association of Home Builders (NAHB)

www.hahb.com. The annual convention is called the NAHB International Builders Show. At this show, you will find approximately 1,000 exhibiting companies, all potential employers. If the shelter part of survival intrigues you, attend this show and other home shows that take place in major cities. In addition to providing an opportunity to meet hiring managers, or workers who can lead you to them, this show will provide an education about how the shelter industry works in the US. Attend this show or other regional home shows, and your knowledge of the housing industry will increase exponentially.

Philadelphia Home Show

www.phillyhomeshow.com. This conference takes place in Philly each February and hosts hundreds of exhibitors. Most are local companies, but some are national, too. While you are there, remember to have one of those famous Philadelphia cheesesteak sandwiches. Also, visit the Philadelphia Art Museum where you can have your picture taken beside the famous bronze of Rocky. And remember to save a day to visit Independence Hall and the Liberty Bell.

One of the most important takeaways in this book it to build conference attendance into your work plan. A trade show at a major convention center is a unique opportunity to meet hiring managers, in the flesh, to build a relationship that will ultimately lead to a job.

ALSO BY JOHN HENRY WEISS

Operation Job Search: A Guide for Military Veterans Transitioning to Civilian Careers

Welcome to the Real World: A Complete Guide to Job Hunting for the Recent College Grad

You may leave comments for the author at Weiss4Jobs@aol.com.

ACKNOWLEDGMENTS

My thanks to the many workers who contributed to *Moving Forward*. They reviewed the manuscript, in whole or in part, and offered encouragement and valuable advice for making improvements.

Laura Bair. Digital designer and wedding consultant.

Marilyn Baker. Certified nurse midwife and staff midwife with Robert Wood Johnson Hospital Hamilton . . . and my wife.

Vicki Smith Bigham. Pre-K–adult education teacher, administrator, trainer, and industry consultant.

Lisa Bingen. Director of marketing, Heinemann Publishing Company.

Diana Cano. Executive director of Enterprise Technology Strategy, Innovation and Architecture, based in Princeton, NJ.

Eric Gootkind. Certified senior professional in human resources (SPHR); director of employment and employee relations, Measured Progress, Inc.

Olga Greco and Caroline Russomanno. Editors, Skyhorse Publishing Inc., who were responsible for making this book a reality. Thank you, Olga and Caroline!

Tina Hamilton. Educational technology consultant and contractor.

John C. Meeker, PhD. Author, encore career coach, executive recruiter, teacher.

Ed Meell. Founder of MMS Education, former editorial director for McGraw-Hill films, US Army Veteran.

Alice Miller. Station manager/program director, WWFM, The Classical Network.

Joanne Silvestri. Education account director, Salesforce.com.

Vincent Vezza. Author, senior vice president, teacher.

Chris Weiss. Video producer, founder, and partner, RaffertyWeiss Media.